MEMORY AND MIGRATION
Multidisciplinary Approaches to Memory Studies

Memory and Migration

Multidisciplinary Approaches to Memory Studies

EDITED BY JULIA CREET
AND ANDREAS KITZMANN

UNIVERSITY OF TORONTO PRESS
Toronto Buffalo London

ISBN 978-1-4426-4129-7

Library and Archives Canada Cataloguing in Publication

Memory and migration: multidisciplinary approaches to memory studies /
edited by Julia Creet and Andreas Kitzmann.

Includes bibliographical references and index.
ISBN 978-1-4426-4129-7

1. Memory – Social aspects. 2. Collective memory. 3. Recollection
(Psychology) 4. Emigration and immigration – Psychological aspects.
5. Immigrants – Psychology. I. Creet, Julia, 1958 – II. Kitzmann, Andreas

BF378.S65M44 2011   153.1'2   C2010-907158-1

University of Toronto Press acknowledges the financial assistance to
its publishing program of the Canada Council for the Arts and Ontario
Arts Council.

  Canada Council   Conseil des Arts
         for the Arts   du Canada

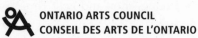 ONTARIO ARTS COUNCIL
         CONSEIL DES ARTS DE L'ONTARIO

This book has been published with the help of a grant from the Canadian
Federation for the Humanities and Social Sciences, through the Aid to
Scholarly Publications Programme, using funds provided by the Social
Sciences and Humanities Research Council of Canada.

University of Toronto Press acknowledges the financial support of the
Government of Canada through the Canada Book Fund for its publishing
activities.

Contents

Acknowledgments

The editors would like to thank our two assistant editors, Jordana Greenblatt and Faye Guenther, for their invaluable contributions at several stages of the preparation of this volume. At York University, the support of York International, the former Faculty of Arts, and the former Atkinson Faculty of Liberal and Professional Studies was essential to the staging of the Memory and Migration Workshop, held in September 2006, which became the impetus for this collection of essays.

We would also like to thank the external reviewers for their thoughtful responses to the manuscript. Their astute readings and suggestions for revisions prevented some embarrassing omissions and sharpened the focus of the collection overall. As well, our editors at University of Toronto Press, Siobhan McMenemy, Ryan Van Huijstee, Frances Mundy, and Ken Lewis, shepherded us through the publication process with personal and professional care, for which we are deeply appreciative.

Finally, we would like to thank the contributors to this collection, who tolerated numerous edits and participated enthusiastically in our ongoing conversation.

Notes on Contributors

Amira Bojadzija-Dan received her PhD from the Graduate Program in Social and Political Thought at York University in 2010 with a doctoral dissertation titled 'Sense Memory in the Holocaust Survival Literature.' Her interests span twentieth-century French philosophy, notably Deleuze and Merleau-Ponty.

Nergis Canefe is an associate professor of political science at York University, and resident faculty at Centre for Refugee Studies. She has taught at the London School of Economics, and Bilgi and Bogazici Universities in Turkey. Her areas of interest are nationalism, minority rights in war-torn societies, diaspora politics, critical citizenship studies, memories of exile and trauma, and crimes against humanity. She is the author of *Citizenship, Identity and Belonging: Limits of Turkish Nationalism* (2006) (in Turkish) and co-editor with Mehmet Ugur of *Turkey and the European Integration* (2004). Other publications have appeared in such journals as *Citizenship Studies, Nations and Nationalism, Balkanologie, Turkish Studies,* and *Rethinking History*.

Julia Creet is an associate professor in the Department of English at York University, where she specializes in memory studies, literary non-fiction, and sexuality studies. She received her PhD from the History of Consciousness Program at the University of California, Santa Cruz, and produces work that is broadly interdisciplinary, across genres. She has directed a documentary, *MUM*, about the memoirs of a Holocaust survivor who tried to forget, and is completing a book of literary nonfiction based on the same story. She has published numerous essays on identity, memory, and testimony in various academic and literary journals, including *Journal of Aesthetics and Culture, differences, Applied Semiotics, Paradoxa, English Studies in Canada, Resources for Feminist Research, Toronto Life, West Coast Line,* and *Exile.* Several of her essays have been translated into Hungarian and Polish, and others published in edited collections in Sweden and the Netherlands.

Marlene Goldman is an associate professor at the University of Toronto, where she teaches Canadian literature. She is the author of *Paths of Desire* (1997) and *Rewriting Apocalypse in Canadian Fiction* (2005). Her most recently completed book is titled *DisPossession: Haunting in Canadian Fiction,* about the motif of haunting in contemporary Canadian fiction. She has also co-edited three special issues of the *University of Toronto Quarterly* on 'Ethics and Canadian Literature,' 'Haunting in Canadian Culture,' and 'Models of Mind and Consciousness,' and published numerous scholarly articles on such Canadian writers as Dionne Brand, Timothy Findley, Thomas King, Joy Kogawa, Daphne Marlatt, Alice Munro, Michael Ondaatje, Jane Urquhart, and Aritha van Herk.

Laurenn Guyot received her PhD in political science and teaches at the University of Law and Political Sciences in Rennes 1, France. She specializes in conflict studies, immigration, and collective memory. Among her publications are 'EU Membership and the Geopolitical Constraints of the Kurdish Issue,' in M. Downes and R. Keane, eds, *Political Science Forum: Perspectives on Central and Eastern Europe* (2002) and 'Kurdish Asylum Rights in France,' in E. Doru and K. Khayati, eds, *Kurdish Integration in Europe* (2002), which was financed by the EU Commission, Rome, Italy.

Andreas Kitzmann is an associate professor in the Department of Humanities at York University. He received his PhD in comparative literature from McGill University and has written widely on the impact of communications technology on the construction and practice of identity, electronic communities, and the influence of new media on narrative conventions. His publications include *Saved from Oblivion: The Place of Media, from Diaries to Web Cams* (Peter Lang, 2004), *Hypertext: The Straight Story* (Peter Lang, 2006), and, as co-editor, *Memory Work* (Peter Lang, 2005).

Mona Lindqvist is a clinical psychologist and psychotherapist working at the Centre for Traumatic Stress in Karlstad, Sweden. She holds a certificate as a specialist in clinical psychology and has worked with refugees in Finland, Norway, and Sweden. Since 2009 she has also been a PhD candidate in sociology, working on a dissertation about refugee women and the social construction of mental health.

Chowra Makaremi is a PhD candidate in anthropology at Université de Montréal. She has led field research and worked as legal assistant in alien detention centres at the borders in France. Her recent publications include, as co-editor, *Alien Exclusion: Between Circulation and Confinement*, a special issue of *Cultures et Conflits* 71.3 (2008), and *Enfermés dehors: Enquêtes sur le confinement des étrangers* (le Croquant, 2009); and, as author, 'Zone of "No-Right" in Democracy: Emotions and the Law,' in M. Pandolfi and V. Crapanzano, eds, *The Passions: At the Heart of Politics*, special issue of *Anthropologie et Société* 32.3 (2008), and 'Governing Borders in France: From Extraterritorial to Humanitarian Confinement,' in A. Pratt and L. Sossin, eds, *Dilemmas of Discretion*, special issue of *Canadian Journal of Law and Society* 25.1 (2010).

Tomasz Mazur received his PhD from the Institute of Philosophy of Warsaw University, where he has lectured since 2001 in the philosophy of religion. His main academic fields of interest are axiology, logics, didactics, and stoicism in a modern context. He has published two books: *Redemption through Philosophy: An Interpretation of Henryk Elzenberg's Writings* (2003) and *Socrates' Capricious Gods: Human Being and the Realm of Values in Western Philosophy* (2008). He has also written a play, *Return of the Stoics*, and is the founder and head of the (non-academic) Centre for Stoic Practice.

Luiza Nader is an assistant professor at the Institute of Art History, University of Warsaw. Her interests are concentrated on avant-garde and neo-avant-garde art (with special focus on Central European art), memory, trauma, and the relations between history writing and the experience of psychoanalysis. Most recently, her work has involved the study of artistic production in Central Europe after 1945 viewed from the perspective of the theory of affects. She is the author of *Conceptual Art in Poland* (Warsaw, 2009), and has published texts, reviews, and translations on European and American art in catalogues (*Grupa Zamek, Lublin, 1956–1960: Experience of Structures*, Muzeum Sztuki Łódź, 2002), periodicals (*Artium Quaestiones, Ikonotheka, Obieg, springerin*), and anthologies (*Memory/Haunting/Discourse, Art after Conceptual Art*).

Srdja Pavlovic teaches at the Department of History and Classics, University of Alberta. He specializes in the modern political and cultural history of the South Slavs, with emphasis on nationalism and identity construction in the Balkans. His current research focuses on the reconciliation efforts and problems of the post-conflict resolution in the former Yugoslavia. Dr Pavlovic's most recent publication is *Balkan Anschluss: The Annexation of Montenegro and the Creation of the Common South Slavic State* (Purdue University Press, 2008). While coordinating the Balkan Monthly Interdisciplinary Series at the University of Alberta and co-editing *Spaces of Identity* (York University) and *Kultura Polisa* (University of Novi Sad), Dr Pavlovic is currently editing a volume entitled *Transcending Fratricide: Political Myths, Reconciliations, and the Future in the Former Yugoslavia* (forthcoming from McGill-Queen's University Press).

Zofia Rosińska is a full professor at the University of Warsaw Institute of Philosophy. She is the chair of the Department of the Philosophy of Culture. Broadly, her interests lie between psychology and philosophy. She has published and co-authored seven books in Polish: A History of Psychology; Jung; Freud; Leopold Blaustein and the Idea of the Reception of Media; What Is Philosophy of Culture? Memory in Twentieth-Century Philosophy; and Freud and Modernity. She has published over one hundred articles. Her current area of study focuses on the interface between psychoanalysis and phenomenology.

Yvonne Singer is an associate professor at York University in visual art and a practising artist with an active international and national exhibition record. Her installation works employ multimedia techniques, often with cryptic texts to articulate cultural issues of disjuncture and perception. She is particularly interested in the intersection of public and private histories. Singer was born in Budapest, Hungary, and received an MFA Honours from York University, Toronto, and a BA in English literature from McGill University in Montreal. Singer is the former graduate program director in visual art at York and has served on several gallery, magazine, and art council boards. Currently she is a member of Loop Gallery in Toronto. Her recent exhibitions include: *Signs of Life: An Intimate Portrait of Someone I Don't Know*, Loop Gallery, Toronto; *Salut des Femmes*, McCord Museum, Montreal; *The Veiled Room*, ACC Gallery, Weimar, Germany; *The Ironic Turn*, touring exhibition in Germany, France, and Canada. A comprehensive survey of her work can be viewed on the ccca.ca database.

John Sundholm is senior lecturer in film studies at Karlstad University, Sweden, reader in cultural analysis at Åbo Akademi University, Finland, and member of the examination board for the PhD program in fine arts at the Academy of Fine Arts in Helsinki, Finland. Recent books: *Gunvor Nelson and the Avant-garde* (2003, editor); *Memory Work* (2005, co-editor); *Collective Traumas* (2007, co-editor); *From Early Animation to Video Art: A History of Swedish Experimental Film* (2010, co-author). He is currently working with memory studies and minor cinemas, the latter a research project funded by the Swedish Research Council (2010–12). He has published widely on experimental film and cultural theory in such journals as *European Journal of Cultural Studies, Canadian Journal of Film Studies, Framework, New Cinemas, Polygraph, Review of Communication,* and *Studies in European Cinema.* He has been a member of the research group on memory studies at Karlstad University since 2002.

Veronika Zangl completed her doctorate in German literature from the University of Vienna in 2004. Since 2006, she has lectured at the Department of Theatre, Film and Media Studies and at the Department of German Studies at the University of Vienna. Current research interests include Holocaust studies, gender studies, and cultural and educational policy discourses in Austria after 1945. Recent publications include *Poetik nach dem Holocaust: Erinnerungen – Tatsachen – Geschichten* (2009); *Körperkonstruktionen und Geschlechtermetaphern: Zum Zusammenhang von Rhetorik und Embodiment* (co-editor with Marlen Bidwell-Steiner, 2009); '"Ich empfinde diese Massnahme persönlich als ungerecht": Heinz Kindermanns Entlastungsstrategien 1945–1954,' in Birgit Peter and Martina Payr, eds, *Wissenschaft nach der Mode? Die Gründung des Zentralinstituts für Theaterwissenschaft an der Universität Wien 1943* (2008).

MEMORY AND MIGRATION
Multidisciplinary Approaches to Memory Studies

Introduction: The Migration of Memory and Memories of Migration

JULIA CREET

Memory, in all its forms, physical, psychological, cultural, and familial, plays a crucial role within the contexts of migration, immigration, re-settlement, and diasporas, for memory provides continuity to the dis-locations of individual and social identity, particularly in a country like Canada, a nation in large part formed by migration and the memory of migrants. And yet contemporary theories of memory have mostly considered memory *in situ*, and place itself as a stable, unchanging environment. The link between memory and place has historically attended the study of memory in every sense: in its contents (our at-tachment to memories of home); in its practices (place as an aid to rote memorization); in its externalizations (monuments and museums); in its linguistic expressions ('I can't quite place you'); and in its psycho-logical and physiological theorizations (the conscious and unconscious brain as the loci of memory, firing across well- or little-used synaptic gaps). As Natalie Zemon Davis and Randolph Stern put it, 'Proust's *petite Madeleine*, Maurice Halbwachs's seminal work on the "social frames" of collective memory, and even cognitive studies and biologic-al research on the "location" of memory in the brain are all reminders that memory seeks its local habitations.'[1] The contributors to *Memory and Migration* explore this crucial observation about the locations of memory in relation to a pressing contemporary question: How do we understand memory that has migrated or has been exiled from its local habitations? It would be a simpler question if mobility and distance were not generally understood to produce 'artificial' memory, or some-thing akin to history. A very brief survey of the terrain of memory stud-ies will illustrate an established conundrum with respect to the fixity of place in memory, intensified in an age of mass migrations.

Recent scholars of memory credit Frances Yates with reviving the study of the 'where' of memory as she reintroduced readers of her now-classic 1966 study *The Art of Memory* to the classical oratory aid of associating an idea to be remembered with a part of a real or imagined building or architecture. The idea as image is mapped onto a *locus*, a place that acts as a wax tablet on which to imprint the idea; good *loci* can be wiped clean and used again. *Loci* are tools of 'artificial memory,' as Yates framed it, distinct from spontaneous memory, a division that began with the Greeks and one that has resonated in memory studies since, generally phrased as the dichotomous, though related, processes of spontaneous recollection versus the effort of recall, evocation versus search, affection versus representation (pathos versus icon).[2] Places as aids to artificial memory might be real or imagined, have a strong emotional resonance for the individual, or be 'corporeal similtudes,' highly symbolic places that became repositories of collective memory, as were spatial renditions of Heaven and Hell for the artificial memory of the Middle Ages or the theatre for the Renaissance.

One of the most influential modern advocates of the divide between 'true' and 'artificial' memory tied explicitly to place is Pierre Nora. Quite opposite to Yates, from whom he borrows, nonetheless, the language of 'memory places,'[3] Nora insists that place is the most natural of all locations of memory, only to be made artificial in our efforts to remember it. In his theoretical introduction to his seven-volume collaborative work on the national memory of France, *Les Lieux de mémoire*, Pierre Nora insists on a geographic concretization of the real/artificial division. We create, Nora laments, memory places or sites of memory (*lieux de mémoire*) 'where memory crystallizes and secretes itself' because we no longer have 'real environments of memory,' stable, geographic, generational environments in which memory flows unremarked and unresponsive to the demands of history.[4] Nora observes that memory has become an object of study precisely because we have moved on and have therefore created fixed monuments to remind us of what was once there. Real memory can only occur in environments of continuity and stability; any necessary effort to remember produces history, which always responds to the political and institutional framing of the past. '*Lieux de mémoire* originate with the sense that there is no spontaneous memory, that we must deliberately create archives, maintain anniversaries, organize celebrations, pronounce eulogies, and notarize bills because such activities no longer occur naturally.'[5] 'With the appearance of the trace, of mediation, of distance, we are not in the realm of true memory but of history.'[6] According to Nora, unsullied 'real memory' exists only *in situ*, and place is a stable, unchanging environment.

To agree to Nora's line of argument, which has set the tone for much of the debate about history and memory for the last two decades or so, is to concede that time is the only movement which memory tolerates. Nora's polemic is a jab against 'self-consciousness' and the archive, against reconstructed genealogy and the fixing of official memory (history) in the light of lost communities and unspoken traditions.[7] In particular, his exhortation to examine the political, national, and historiographic narratives of commemorative sites has been enormously important and influential.[8] His claim, however, that falsity – or artificiality – attends to modern memory because of the loss of natural environments of memory is inadequate to the study of memory in a world of migration if the implication is that migrations of one kind or another can only produce history: once one leaves a territory of origin, memory is lost entirely. If we cede this Manichean divide between the fixity of history produced by distance and self-awareness and fluidity of memory tied to place and blissful ignorance, then we are completely constrained in our studies by the notion of a place of origin, and a continuing dichotomy between real and artificial memory, or memory and history in which place is by turns naturalized and imaginary.[9]

Nora's casting of sites of memory as learned history (or artificial memory) stimulated by place (or symbols of time and place, including calendars and national flags) obviously has a long history in the study of mnemonics. But, what if one assumes, in contrast to Nora, that memory is not a product of stability, but quite the opposite, that it is always attended by migrations? What, then, do we make of his categorical statement that 'memory attaches itself to sites, whereas history attaches itself to events'? This may well be an accurate assertion if we think of memory as a kind of parasitic or nomadic function, so that memories may move on with individuals or communities, while others may indeed continue to cling to a place until they eventually shrivel away and drop off. But only in a nation with a long history that resists the integration of new populations could this fusion of the fluidity of memory with the stability of place be a truism, as Tony Judt pointed out in his review of the English edition of Nora's *Realms of Memory:*

France is not only the oldest national state in Europe, with an unbroken history of central government, language, and public administration dating back at least to the twelfth century; it was also, of all the countries of Western Europe, the one which had changed the least until very recently. The landscape of France, the rural community and its way of life, the occupations and routines of daily existence in provincial towns and villages had been less disrupted by industry, modern communications, or social and demographic change than was the case in Britain, Germany, Belgium, Italy, or any other comparable Western state.[10]

In contrast, a large portion of the world's population has moved from nations with long memories to states with short histories (and sometimes exactly because of the fixity of particular memories associated with place). Does this mean that, in addition to exile, expulsion, emigration, economic or otherwise, the migrant has also been expelled from the land of memory itself, relegating place only to the devices of artificial memory? Does memory only adhere to the point of origin? Should we not, given our mobility, begin to ask different questions of memory, ones that do not attend only to the content of memory, but to the travels that have invoked it? Perhaps stability does continue to play a role in the creation of memory, or, at least, the illusion or pretence of stability, but how do we understand this fixity if movement or migration is a constant?

What if, instead, we studied the quality of movement that shapes memory, rather like Freud's dream mechanisms, which, he argued, were where one could find the meaning of a dream rather than in its content, latent or otherwise? This does not mean that the content becomes secondary, but, rather, that the content is not sacred, but manifest, not measured by distance from point of origin, but by the passage itself. If we separate the idea of origin from the authenticity of memory, we can show that the manner in which memory travels is a quality of memory itself, not a flaw, not a lessening, not a shift in category, but constitutional, of memory, a constant constantly on the move, archiving itself rhizomatically. All investigations of memory involve a necessary study of fixity, but at its most present rather than its most anterior. Memory is where we have arrived rather than where we have left. What's forgotten is not an absence, but a movement of disintegration that produces an object of origin. In other words, memory is produced over time and under erasure.

Possibly, migration is the condition of memory, psychically and physically the only measurable thing, since the point of origin is lost entirely, and, though entirely real in its effects, of little matter to the mechanisms of memory. That said, without question, the idea of place still often constitutes an important anchor for memory as a remembered or fabricated origin or an origin made 'real' by matters of faith and custom. As Paul Ricoeur argues in his monumental *Memory, History, Forgetting*, inhabiting physical places is crucial to the phenomenology and recovery of memory:

> The transition from corporeal memory to the memory of places is assured by acts as important as orienting oneself, moving from place to place, and above all inhabiting. It is on the surface of this habitable earth that we remember having travelled and visited memorable sites. In this way, the 'things' remembered are intrinsically associated with places. And it is not by chance that we say of what has occurred that it took place. Is it indeed at this primordial level that the phenomenon of 'memory places' is constituted, before they become a reference for historical knowledge ... These places 'remain' as inscriptions, monuments, potentially as documents, whereas memories transmitted only along the oral path fly away as do the words themselves.[11]

However, Ricoeur, in a dialectic that characterizes his engagement with the aporia, the impasses, of memory (invoking yet another spatial metaphor), then argues strenuously that place is not a stable geographic place, but, rather, relational, an instance of the deictic: '"here" and "now" occupy the same rank, alongside "me," "you," "he," "she," among the other deictic forms that punctuate our language.' 'Here,' 'there,' 'then,' and 'now' are the deictics of geographic and temporal relativity. [12] This presents an insoluble contradiction for memory studies in that places may be at once 'sites,' in Nora's sense of the word, geographic or symbolic constancies onto which memory has been secreted, but also inherently relational, given that the body constitutes the 'primordial place, the here in relation to which all other places are there.'[13]

For Maurice Halbwachs, against the grain of the subjective emphasis, to some extent, of Henri Bergson, Ricoeur, and Nora, the spatial deictic consolidates in collective memory. Halbwachs, a key thinker for many contributors to this volume, insists on social context and structure as the determinants of individual and collective memory. Only in dreams are we ever alone, he argues, and here our memory is completely chaotic: we need others to remember. [14] Individual memory is a product of collective memory rather than the other way around, and place, particularly linked to the idea of truth, is as much an effect of collective memory as collective memory is produced by place. While the *ars memoria* deploys *loci*/images in an imagined topography, in Halbwachs's concept of collective memory we find an overlapping of *loci* and topography, since it is (imagined) memory that gives a meaning to location and vice versa. In his chapter entitled 'The Legendary Topography of the Gospels in the Holy Land,' Halbwachs uses the fervour of religious faith to argue that the memory of a place becomes significant, becomes a place at all, because it helps believers to remember that something happened there. 'A group in a sense takes with it the form of the places where it has lived. When it returns after a long absence (like the Jews and the Judeo-Christians after the reconstruction of Jerusalem), even if the appearance of these places has changed, it seeks them and finds, at least in part, the material frame of which it has preserved the imprint.'[15] Topography is a stabilizing factor for Halbwachs, but contrary to the *ars memoria*, topography is not imagined but 'real,' a public-social concept rather than a practice of rhetoric, and one with often deadly consequences in embattled regions steeped in religious memory. However, Ricoeur, holding the fort for phenomenology against the resurgence of Halbwachs's recent popularity, argues:

> It remains to be explained how the sentiment of unity of self derives from this collective thought. It occurs through the intermediary of consciousness we have at every instant of belonging at the same time to different milieus; but this consciousness exists only in the present. The only concession that the author [Halbwachs] makes is providing every consciousness with the power to place itself within the viewpoint of the group, and, in addition, to move from one group to another.[16]

A short-lived concession, according to Ricoeur, since the forces of social habituation in Halbwachs's model act on individuals unbeknownst to them.[17]

So, to make a quick and reductive summary, following Yates, for most of Western thought, place is one of the most evocative and powerful imaginary aids for the artifices of memory: *locus*. For Nora, *loci* and topography, as the study of place, aggregate in a manner typical of a post-war generation who became self-conscious about personal memory, often fixed in a particular location, a 'site,' that was already artificial. For Ricoeur, place is deictic and always relational with respect to the phenomena of memory, and for Halbwachs, place as social environment is the precondition of memory itself. What is clear is that location and local habitations matter for memory, particularly with respect to individual and collective identity, but that there is little agreement about how place matters. Again, this debate would be less of an issue if the question of false consciousness, or at least the charge of history, didn't adhere to most discussions of the dislocations of memory.

In this volume, we argue that migration rather than location is the condition of memory. Between times, places, generations, and media, from individuals to communities and vice versa, movement is what produces memory – and our anxieties about pinning it to place. Certainly, scholars of memory have thought about how memories shift over time and distance, usually coupled with adjectives about unreliability and fading, falsity and fantasy. Yet, they assume an origin moment for memory, that its formation is synchronic with event or person, its motion away from the point of origin, in eccentric circles, erratic or otherwise. Movement always attends memory, yet we tend to take stasis as its measure. What would it mean to take the quality of memory's migration rather than the distance from its forever-lost point of origin as our object of study? And what can we learn by tracing its anxious fixity in the constant flow? In this collection, we investigate movement as the condition of memory, and our desire for its fixity, or at least the fixity of its geographic and temporal origins. This fundamental paradox between location and migration governs most of our thinking about memory.

We might also observe that every epoch evokes a model of memory that best suits its time, that memory as a concept reflects the time and place from which it emerges and that profound shifts in concepts of memory are often a product of collective traumas born of particular places.[18] Our theme of memory and migration encompasses, then, both the migration of memory as a phenomenological concept and the memories of migration as socio-political phenomenon, staging a confrontation between them in the hopes of suggesting different configurations of *locus*/topography. How do we remember mobile habitations and local dislocations? How does place still function as mnemonic device and how, particularly, in the context of migration?

Many of the contributors to this volume belong to an established network of multidisciplinary scholars interested in all facets of memory studies, in particular, what we call 'cultural memory,' focused to a large extent on the emergent model of memory from post-war Europe. The theoretical domain of contemporary cultural memory has been dominated by European studies, where memory studies have been central to discussions of nation formation and reform since the Second World War, and even more intensely so in post-1989 Eastern Europe, a time and context that produced, as Conny Mithander and John Sundholm call it, 'the memory turn' of both monument and intellect, framed by the memory of the Second World War.[19] The traumas of the Second World War, in particular, the themes of testimony, absence, and the transmission of loss in the body of literature and theory generated by the Holocaust and its physical and cultural geographies, and its diasporas, undergird the turn to memory in the late twentieth century.[20] Emerging from these theoretic and socio-geographic and cultural contexts, contributors across disciplines as various as refugee studies and fine arts were asked to address the migrations of memory and memories of migration, an exercise that demanded an engagement with both the historical shifts in theories of memory and its contemporary geographic (dis)locations. Consistent themes began to emerge: value, melancholy, the absence of origins, the inability to return, and the suspension of memory itself as an effect of migration. If value is a measure of what causes us to fix a particular memory in place (a return of *loci*), melancholy is what continues to draw us back to it. If leaving is the only option, where one leaves becomes a nostalgic past. If memory is elicited in the name of a national or nationalistic discourse, it reconfigures the nation that wants it. If memories of trauma drive a migrant from one place to another, forgetting may be an essential phase of testimony. The overarching conclusion of this collection is that place matters with respect to memory, not because it is a stable location from which one departs, or because one never has to think about it or use artificial architectures, but because displacement is more likely to produce immobile memories and radical forgetting.[21] Which is not to say that memory *in situ* is pure or that displacement produces false memories, but that migration has an effect on how and what we remember and that displacement intensifies our investments in memory, illuminating the *topos* of memory itself. Memory is always migrating, generating its own topological demands, never more so than now.

Section One: The Melancholy of No Return

We begin our collection with the impossibility of return, a general condition of memory amplified by physical dislocation. If individual and collective identity are rooted so firmly in place, then what of those large populations of the world that are on the move? Does migration then restructure the concept of self and other? Of home and away? Does place remain in place if one leaves or is forced to leave? Or, does place change even if one stays put? The essays in this section examine these questions with the multiple perspectives of philosophy, autobiography, literary criticism, and an anthropological field study.

Our collection is framed by an essay by Zofia Rosińska from the Institute of Philosophy, Warsaw University, a philosopher who has written extensively on the phenomenology of time in memory. Here, she takes up the experience of displacement as another dimension of the phenomenology of memory. Distinguishing emigration from other kinds of human movements, such as tourism or nomadism, Rosińska's evocative chapter, 'Emigratory Experience: The Melancholy of No Return,' analyses emigratory experience for its traits typical of melancholy: the sense of estrangement, of sadness, of loss, and want of meaning in life, and, most significantly, a loss of identity. 'Memory plays a triple role: it is identity-forming by maintaining the original identifications; it is therapeutic because it helps bear the hardships of transplantation onto a foreign culture; and it is also community-forming, by creating a bond among those recollecting together.' But, 'the experiences of all the other elements of emigration are intensified by the final shared characteristic: an inability to return.' We are Walter Benjamin, committing suicide at an impassable border, rather than Odysseus returning home triumphant. 'Emigration' as a category of experience does not figure in psychological or philosophical dictionaries, she points out, and yet, in the modern condition of living in an environment of change, the transcendental element comes to the fore. Emigration, Rosińska argues, is the necessary condition of modern subjectivity. Estrangement and alienation, emigratory melancholies, are also reactions to sociopolitical transformations and to progress, which stage a confrontation with the other, or more precisely with one's self *through* the other. Emigratory memory, even *in situ*, may be the model for a new global subjectivity, in which place itself is mobile.

Drawing on his experiences of exile from Yugoslavia and his eventual arrival in Canada, Srdja Pavlovic in his lyric 'Memory for Breakfast' articulates Rosińska's melancholy of the émigré, writing in a '"dead language," a language spoken by only one person, a language frozen in some linguistic past.' He describes it as an exercise in 'mnemohistory,' a 'product of a loneliness that is accustomed to being public.' Here Charles Taylor's argument about the nature of modern identity – that we struggle to maintain the *capacity for authenticity* – is writ large in the processes of remembering and displacement. Pavlovic struggles with the truth of an old saying of the immigrants from eastern Europe: 'Once you cross the Ocean, you'll always be on the wrong side of it.' And yet, a stable topography does not mean the stability of an unchanging place. 'If anything,' Pavolvic says,

> history teaches us that naming space does not always guarantee the eternal existence of people and our memories of them, let alone provide safe harbours for our fragile identities … [A]ppropriating space by naming it according to tribal, ethnic, national, or religious criteria produces a short lasting effect at best. Kolozsvar used to be Klausenberg, but now it is called Cluj Napoca. The town once known as Hermannstadt is now softly referred to by Romanians as Sibiu. What the Szeklers call Szekelyudvahely is to Romanians Odorheiu Sigishoara. What was once Roman Apulum becomes first Karlsburg and then Gulafehervar.

Nonetheless, endless naming and renaming becomes an anchor of belonging and home for immigrants inside the imaginary landscape of Canadian multiculturalism.

For migrants who do manage to return from emigration or expulsion, the place to which they return can often be irrevocably different, if only because they have been so altered by their experiences of exile. In 'Remigration and Lost Time: Resuming Life after the Holocaust,' Veronika Zangl shows how survivors who returned to the cities, towns, and countries from which they had been deported were better off without memories. While survivors of the Nazi concentration camps shared an intensely collective memory, particularly embodied in environment and sensation, they returned to an apparently familiar social world, sometimes horrifyingly unchanged. Memories that didn't succeed in lending meaning to life 'afterwards' became, in Charlotte Delbo's words, 'useless knowledge.' Interviewed in 1950, a returnee describes her return to Amsterdam. 'I felt strange. I walked through streets, which were deserted; I walked through the Jewish quarter. Empty spaces where once stood houses, houses from which everything had disappeared; dismal houses with broken windows. They stared at me and I ran away.'[22] Simliarly, Gilberte, having lost her sister in the camps, returns to their house: 'Where could I run, fade away so as not to be captured by the past, or go knocking against the walls, things, memories? At the same time, everything was unreal, as though deprived of consistency.'[23] Drawing on works by Jean Améry and Delbo, and on early testimonies from Holocaust survivors collected by the Netherlands Institute for War Documentation, Zangl's essay examines the dynamics of remigration. Returning survivors found themselves unable to return in all but an administrative fashion, severing their memories from their environment. In Zangl's essay, we see the dislocation of memory from space, the break of *locus* and topography, where the location hasn't changed but bears no resemblance to its memory.

The last essay in this section explores the most melancholy place of all: nowhere. In 'The Waiting Zone,' Chowra Makaremi, an anthropologist working in the detention centre at Roissy Airport in France, describes what happens when testimony fails absolutely in the face of the law, and how the law, in this case immigration law, strips those refugees subjected to it of the ability to narrate their migrations of place and identity. Based on the story of Ghislaine K., one of the twenty thousand undocumented aliens who are held each year in the detention centre of Roissy Airport, Makaremi offers a poignant insight into the narrative demands placed on asylum seekers. During her detention, Ghislaine is invited to 'tell her story' in four interviews of ten to fifteen minutes each, a personal narrative by which the administration determines the 'good faith' of the asylum seeker. Makaremi examines the conditions and the contexts that make Ghislaine unable to produce a coherent or credible account of herself or her migrations, an inability that leads to her deportation three days after her arrival. For refugees, credible narrative memory is the key to refuge and migration, yet must be produced under conditions of 'mis/trust' embedded in the national and political framework of controlling borders and mobility. France emerges as a place whose memory is very much controlled by protecting its borders from those who have no credible means of entering it. Migration and national identity are thus negotiated in tandem, Makaremi argues, 'where the "hosting" national community is being redefined – literally, through a process of filtering and exclusion of those who do not belong, and figuratively, through the affirmation of the rationality and the moral values on which national identity stands, such as democratic assistance or protection of the welfare system against abuses and "fakes."' The undocumented alien who cannot offer coherent memory is deprived even of membership in the 'community of nations,' in Hannah Arendt's terms. In the end, Ghislaine's fate is documented by two letters, 'BE,' which stand for *Bien Embarquée*, meaning 'well-taken on board' – returned by the state to her place of 'origin.'

Section Two: Collective Memory Ghettos

If, as Veronika Zangl argues in the introduction to her essay, the concept of memory itself shifts in times of crisis, the following papers all trace the extent to which memory resolidifies in response to collective traumas, particularly from afar. What becomes clear in the grouping of these studies is that collective memory is rarely singular, is often contested, and is the most easily configured, abused, and manipulated form of memory. At the same time, strategies of 'shared memory,' as Avishai Margalit calls it in *The Ethics of Memory*, can promote an ethics of caring among communities of memory. The collective enterprise of memory-making is not necessarily inclusive and is, generally, political in the broadest sense of the word. Moreover, that community of memory has everything to do with which events and places will be remembered, and, in dialectic fashion in turn, how that community will be constituted. A general observation drawn from these studies seems true: that displacement makes the working-through of traumatic times and events much more difficult. Distance makes it hard to move on.

Andreas Kitzmann's chapter, 'Frames of Memory: WWII German Expellees in Canada,' is based on a series of personal interviews with ethnic Germans expelled from Europe at the end of the Second World War who immigrated to Canada in the late 1940s and early 1950s. It considers the complexities of remembering and representing the *Vertreibung*, 'the Expulsion': fifteen million *Volksdeutsche* were forced to flee their homes in eastern and southeastern Europe. But though well documented, the topic of the *Vertreibung* is not well represented in most normative accounts of the Second World War and, as such, has been generally excluded from public discourse. This is especially the case in Germany, where the topic has been politically uncomfortable for decades. Kitzmann's essay draws attention to the complex relationships among memory, testimony, and the fixity that documented history is said to provide, bringing us back to the question of value, following from the 'negative symbiosis,' as Saul Friedlander puts it, between Jewish and German memory. Do we value the memory of losers, or is the memory of victimization a privilege of the victor? How can a population deal with the experience of expulsion when a discourse of shame precludes any discussion? As Ursula K., one of Kitzmann's interviewees puts it, 'When we talk about the war, we have to be careful ... How long does this go on? We pay and we pay ...' Ursula's point 'leads to a kind of paradox on her part,' says Kitzmann. 'On the one side, she emphasizes that the history of the war and the Holocaust "needs to be told," yet, on the other, she struggles with the continued representation of Germans as Nazis and the collective guilt that still persists within the German psyche and nationhood (both within and outside of Germany).' Even though it was a consequence of law there was no justice in the expulsion. Testimony, here drawing on Giorgio Agamben, is one of the few forms of discourse that can counter the false closure of law.

John Sundholm, in film studies at the University of Karlstad, Sweden, tracks in his essay, 'The Cultural Trauma Process, or the Ethics and Mobility of Memory,' how the memory of war by those who were on 'the wrong side' is worked through *in situ*. Sundholm's study covers similar thematic ground – the memories of being wrong – but finds it normalized and perhaps even ethically deployed. Sundholm follows the narrative of 'The Unknown Soldier,' first published as a novel in 1954, which soon became a foundational story for Finnish collective memory of the Second World War. The rapid film adaptation of the story, one of the most successful films in Finnish history, fused the novel and the film into a new story creating a socio-historical imaginary, a survival story for a nation on the wrong side of the war. Sundholm argues that 'The Unknown Soldier' is a collective creation constituting an ethics of memory that enabled a linking together of all those who lived through the events of 1939–44 without judging who did what to whom or classifying people into heroes, friends, foes, traitors, or victims. Working through this example of 'cultural trauma,' a term borrowed from sociologist Jeffrey Alexander, Sundholm shows his case study of Finnish war memory to be a phenomenon of migration insofar that is it the effect of something that is absent. Controversially, Sundholm argues that

> ... in this framework, the relation between event (origin) and its meaning (trauma) is foremost considered to be a question of social value rather than of epistemology. In a sense, it is consequential, when we talk about a phenomenon that is constructed by human beings in the present, that the question of a presumed origin becomes of minor importance because it is, after all, the present that triggers the situation and thus launches the

meaning. Therefore, memories actualized in the present are migrating symptoms that have to be considered and understood in the now in which they appear.

By insisting on the possibility and necessity of building a community of caring based on value in the present, in Margalit's sense, without disavowing that collective forces shape individual memory, Sundholm threads a way through what seems to be the impasse between Ricoeur and Halbwachs with respect to the presentness of the past.

In her contribution, 'Locked in a Memory Ghetto: A Case Study of a Kurdish Community in France,' Laurenn Guyot, a political scientist at the University of Rennes I in France, argues that memory – especially war memory – is not handled with the same intensity within the context of immigration, that immigration places a new set of demands on the collective formation of memories of war. Guyot examines the evolution of memory within the Kurdish community currently living in France and finds them trapped in a kind of 'memory ghetto,' organized around a myth of return and a frozen conception of their region of origin. Unable to grieve their territory of origin or the war, more concerned with protecting the memory than integrating into the host country, afraid that immigration will mean a loss of traditional values and prevent their return, Kurds living in France have not successfully confronted the past, freezing their memory at the moment of departure. 'Every reference to the difficulty of war and the harshness of exile strengthens feelings of belonging to the group. As a consequence, attempting to come to terms with the past could be pernicious.' Instead of coping with the changes imposed by life in France, they imprison themselves in the past, whereas the Kurds living in Turkey are adapting to the present. Moreover, Kurds in France show a new dimension to Benedict Anderson's 'long-distance nationalism' in their efforts to preserve an identity threatened in the country of origin by playing a significant political role in their countries of origin from afar.

In 'Home in Exile: Politics of Refugeehood in the Canadian Muslim Diaspora,' the final essay under the theme of collective memory, Nergis Canefe, a political scientist who works in the Centre for Refugee Studies at York University, profiles two public figures in the Muslim-Canadian community, Tarek Fatah and Haideh Moghissi, who arrived in Canada as refugees and have become deeply embroiled in debates within their community over the memory of home in exile. Preserving identities imported from afar can take on a deadly dimension in a host country if a diasporic community has stakes in maintaining its public cohesion in the face of local discrimination. While memories of home are a form of hope for many refugees, 'exile leads to a particular and highly political genre of remembrance of personal, communal, and national histories,' writes Canefe. She charts the dangerous tensions in the diaspora between refugees and migrants arriving from the same country of origin or the same geographical region who have very different memories of home and very political stakes in representing a non-critical image of home, particularly in a post-9/11 world. While Fatah and Moghissi share a memory of forced migration, their public statements sometimes run 'unequivocally against collective memories of migrants from the very countries from which they were exiled.' Returning to Nora's historical scholarship and to the field of memory studies, in general, Canefe asks why it is that 'the issue of remembrance in the diaspora or its relation to migration remains understudied'? Her answer is one that this volume has tried to address, to some extent, in that 'remembrance in the diaspora is a fragmented form of commemoration that cannot be contained within the traditional, nation-state format of memory studies.'

Section Three: The Smell of Flowers and Rotting Potatoes

The contributors in this section shift their analyses from nation and citizenship to the embodiment of memory and migration and the migration of memory through embodiment. Here the linkages between trauma and memory that have formed so much of our understanding of twentieth-century memory, including Freud's concepts of symptom and hysteria, are revisited in the contexts of displacement, refuge, and 'remigration' in bodies that carry with them from place to place memory as sensation, sometimes articulated, but often not, expressed rather as aporia, gaps and intensities in physical presence, broadly understood as 'sense memory.'

Mona Lindqvist, a clinical psychotherapist who works at the Centre for Traumatic Stress, in Karlstad, Sweden, presents a case study from her clinical practice, 'The Flower Girl: A Case Study in Sense Memory.' 'Natasha,' a twenty-six-year-old female refugee from Uzbekistan, is suffering physical symptoms with no physiological source. The difficulty of working with Natasha is one that underlies the history of clinical practice: 'how to transform a vague reminiscence impressed by one or several sense modalities, into words and a comprehensible narrative about the person, the patient, and the past,' compounded in this case by displacement. Suppressed memories or psychogenic loss of memories are quite frequent among traumatized refugees, and the senses, in this case the powerfully memorial sense of smell, play an important role in carrying reminiscences from one part of the world to another and from the past into the present. Natasha's memory of being brutally raped sometime before she migrated to Sweden is finally triggered by the scent of a few flowers that happened to be in Lindqvist's office. Here Proust's *petite Madeleine* is turned into something immeasurably darker, though the ties between smell, our 'oldest' sense, and place prove to be some of the most durable. Scent memory, however, has little language, as Linqvist points out: 'We are able to name forms and colours we have seen, to describe tunes and sounds that we have heard, and to explain how things feel soft or hard. But odours are considerably more difficult; try, for example, to describe how an orange smells.' Nonetheless, scent is the key to Natasha's necessary reconstruction of a rape that she must first come to understand as an event (you remember Nora's claim that events are the purvey of history) before she can reintegrate it into memory. Lindqvist's moving case history shows how 'sense memory' is crucial to reconstructing the life histories of migratory human beings.

In 'Reading Sensation: Memory and Movement in Charlotte Delbo's *Auschwitz and After*,' Amira Bojadzija-Dan, a doctoral graduate in social and political thought at York University, takes up this idea of 'sense memory' as a communicative act in her reading of Delbo's strikingly fragmented memoir of survival. Taking the idea of indeterminacy as a cue, Bojadzija-Dan considers the possibility of thinking of sense memory in terms of its movement, 'a stream of affect' that takes us into a place of visceral collective memory in a way that monuments cannot. In *None of Us Will Return* Delbo describes this relationship in terms of a carnal bond, in which each individual body represents a blood vessel within 'a single circulatory system.' Rather than treat the memory of survivors as individually fractured, as so much of the work in Holocaust memory assumes, traumatic memory is an entirely social phenomenon, rendered meaningful, not by the accuracy of the memories of the survivor or the authority of her narrating voice, but through circulation and movement inside the circulatory system of a collective memory. Delbo writes of a night in Auschwitz: 'This shadowy cavern breathes and puffs, stirred in every one of its innermost recesses by a thousand pain-filled nightmares and fitful sleep.' Imprinted on the senses, memories return physically, as Delbo's friend Mado describes: 'One day I feel I'm walking by the kitchens: it's because I left a potato rotting at the bottom of my vegetable basket. At once everything surfaces again: the mud, the snow, the blows of the truncheons . . .' Sense memory is 'already "common,"' says Bojadzija-Dan: 'common to two moments and two places.' Sense memory can be staged as Christian Boltanski does in *Réserve, Canada*, an installation of a warehouse in Auschwitz in which the Nazis stored the belongings of the deported in an unaired room filled with old clothes, piled up to the ceiling, smelling of must. Migratory and flowing, sense memory, even as it is invoked in art and literature has the power to engender caring, suggesting a somatic ethics of the collective body.

Through a reading of Margaret Atwood's historical novel *Alias Grace*, Marlene Goldman, a professor of English at the University of Toronto, shows how fiction has played a crucial role in shaping our understanding of normal and pathological memory and, in this case, illuminating the relationships among memory, madness, and migration. The central figure of *Alias Grace*, Grace Marks, was an impoverished Irish immigrant who, with the help of a fellow servant, James McDermott, murdered both her well-to-do Tory employer, Thomas Kinnear, and his pregnant housekeeper and mistress, Nancy Montgomery. Grace's incarceration was part of a pattern in the mid-1800s when Irish women, particularly those who worked as servants, were arrested and convicted of crimes or committed to insane asylums in numbers far greater than all other ethnic groups combined. In Goldman's reading, *Alias Grace* 'explicitly probes the racialized links between memory, madness, and migration, and highlights how these links were disseminated in narrative form.' Grace's mother dies on the passage and continues to haunt her daughter in the form of enraged spirit, who Grace imagines is 'trapped in the bottom of the ship because we could not open a window, and angry ... caught in there for ever and ever, down below in the hold like a moth in a bottle, sailing back and forth across the hideous dark ocean.' This ghostly voice, a 'prisoner of the passage,' to borrow Michel Foucault's words, plays a role in fracturing Grace's psyche, battered by earlier trauma and the narrative gaps that come with immigration. Grace's 'wandering story' bears a strong resemblance to Chowra Makaremi's study of Ghislaine and Mona Lindqvist's case history of 'Natasha,' all three of which enunciate, though none in straightforward fashion, how necessary narrative is in order to come to terms with the memories of physical disorientation.

Section Four: Architectures of Memory

In this last section, we return to manipulations and stability of the *ars memoria*, in which space or architectural detail is a mnemonic device, with the idea that, conversely, we also structure space according to mnemonic value. We end with the question of value, since value is the handmaiden of preservation. Moving memory from 'room to room' is Tomasz Mazur's metaphor for the practice of memory as an exercise in values, good and bad, in which we reapportion content, primarily through, according to Plato, the art of telling stories. What begins as a metaphor turns to architectural and inhabited space through the installation art of Krzysztof Wodiczko and Yvonne Singer, whose artistic practices externalize the manner in which space itself is shaped by public and private memory and those excluded from it. At the end of this section, and of the collection, we turn, appropriately enough, to forgetting as a reason for and a consequence of migration. As Mazur will show in Plato's thought, and as Ricoeur will argue at the very end of *Memory, History, Forgetting*, ordinary forgetting, or forgetting enabled by wine, is an essential attribute of the human psyche. Forgetting in the context of migration or expulsion, however, is rarely ordinary, and the reconstruction of 'post-memory,' memory a generation displaced, in Marianne Hirsch's formulation, is itself often spatial, most obviously in the values of recollection, selection, and preservation in archives, a place where memory and migration reach a temporary stasis.

In the first essay of this section, 'Value of Memory – Memory of Value: A Mnemonic Interpretation of Socrates' Ethical Intellectualism,' Tomasz Mazur, from the Institute of Philosophy, Warsaw University, explores Western models of memory by investigating three basic Platonic metaphors: memory as wax tablet, as aviary, and as a garment we wear. For modern readers of Plato, knowledge lies somewhere between an ideal unchanging world of truth and a constant flux of immediate experiences. Mazur asks, 'What is the value of memory?' and finds that to practise memory is to reorder the proportions of its content, moving it from 'room to room,' embedding value and knowledge in the process. What's striking about Mazur's contribution, for the purposes of this collection, is that the wax tablet and the aviary exemplify the relationship between fixity and motion. The wax tablet, as Ricoeur points out, begins its life as a metaphor of an innate physical imprint that metamorphizes through the *ars memoria* to a place that is primarily imaginary and practised as an aid to remembering.[24] For Mazur, however, following Plato, remembering is not solely an intellectual exercise in the sense of possessing memory. One must also 'have' or 'wear' memory as a form of ethical action. Moreover, it is through the repeated, but always amended, telling of stories that we modify memory as a means to developing values.

Luiza Nader, an art historian at Warsaw University, moves us from the metaphor of 'wearing memory' as a value to the costumes and instruments by which Polish artist Krzysztof Wodiczko spatially externalizes the undervalued memories of migrants. Nader begins her essay, 'Migratory Subjects: Memory Work in Krzysztof Wodiczko's Projections and Instruments,' with a discussion of Georges Bataille's famous hatred for architecture, understood as a sort of mirror stage of identity. Wodiczko's projections and instruments (*Alien Staff*, *Mouthpiece*, *Dis-Armor*) act against this architectural body by introducing biographical memory into the urban spaces around the world – in these examples, Tijuana, Boston, New York, and Paris – in which the immigrant is evicted from social and political life, a screen for otherness, understood both as uncanny and foreign, never 'at home,' either literally or metaphorically. Wearing Wodiczko's instruments or projected larger-than-life onto architectural structures, his immigrant subjects become spectacles of the repressions and foreclosures in urban space, the memory transmitted by architecture, and the homelessness of a migrant's mnemonic experience. As he observes, 'There is nothing more disruptive and astonishing in a monument than a sign of life.'

In 'The Veiled Room,' Yvonne Singer talks about three of her installations that deal specifically with the memories of a migrant family: *In Memoriam: Forgetting and Remembering Fragments of History*; *The Veiled Room*; and *Signs of Life: An Intimate Portrait of Someone I Don't Know*. Her artistic practice over the last fifteen years has investigated the work of inheritance and the burden of history, probing the relationships that exist between the intimate and the public, between moments of personal significance and events of global resonance. These three exhibits, spanning 1993 to 2008, explore the figures and loci of her Christian childhood in a (Jewish) Hungarian family who migrated to Montreal. Singer uses the frame of the family photo album and the archive as architectures of memory in three dimensions. Drawing on Marianne Hirsch's generative idea of 'post-memory,' Singer uses the space of the gallery to install memories that she never had, but lived with nonetheless. The installations are conceived as a stage but offer the viewer an immersive experience, working with the premise that memory is an accumulation of sensory experiences that remain in permanent fluctuation.

The volume concludes with 'The Archive as Temporary Abode,' which explores the often paradoxical terrain of the archive and its relationship to personal and 'official' narratives and to memory and history. Personal testimony in the archive is, according to Paul Ricoeur, the threshold document between memory and the writing of history. Within an archive, documents may well serve to keep memories in motion; at the same time, the archive can also be the place where memories become frozen and inert. Yet, without archived testimony, memory will sooner or later expire. Both states are states of stasis; in other words, within or without the archive, stasis is the end of memory and movement its condition. Archives required the motion of bodies sifting through their contents and moving them about, literally unsettling the dust that tends to collect. Assumed to be the most stable of locations, archives are, in the end, surprisingly mobile.

In order to illustrate this idea, I use my mother's papers as a case study to show how my deposition decisions will change the course of her memory. Her papers follow the path of a Canadian immigrant who wanted to leave her past behind; yet one option is to return parts of them to Hungary, the nation that betrayed her, and another, to donate them to a Jewish archive, an identity she disavowed. In the context of our theme of memory and migration, some very specific questions arise about the relationship of fixity and motion for the immigrant archive: Should the records of the immigrant be remigrated to his or her country of origin; or, be forever housed wherever she or he last arrived? Is the testimony of the life lived in several languages best kept together as a documentary by-product of the totality of a life, or split according to the ideal of access? In other words, which is more important to the memory of an immigrant and her nations: what she left behind or where she came to rest? These are not only personal questions, but ones that have also dominated the debate about how to embrace multi-ethnic collections as part of the nation-building exercise of Archives Canada.

NOTES

1 Natalie Zemon Davis and Randolph Stern, 'Introduction,' *Representations* 26 (1989): 2–3. This issue of *Representations* published Pierre Nora's influential

essay 'Between Memory and History: *Les Lieux de mémoire*,' the theoretical
introduction to his seven-volume collaborative work on the national
memory of France, *Les Lieux de mémoire*.

2 See Frances Yates, *The Art of Memory* (Chicago: University of Chicago Press,
   1966).

3 Pierre Nora, 'Between Memory and History: *Les Lieux de mémoire*,' *Representations* 26 (1989): 7–25. See note 25.

4 Ibid., 7

5 Ibid., 12.

6 Ibid., 8.

7 Ibid., 7.

8 See, for example, James Young, *At Memory's Edge: After-images of the
   Holocaust in Contemporary Art and Architecture* (New Haven: Yale University
   Press, 2000), and *The Texture of Memory* (New Haven: Yale University Press,
   1993); Marita Sturken, *Tangled Memories: The Vietnam War, the AIDS Epidem-
   ic, and the Politics of Remembering* (Berkeley: University of California Press,
   1997); Andreas Huyssen, *Twilight Memories: Marking Time in a Culture of
   Amnesia* (New York: Routledge, 1995); Jeffrey Olick, *States of Memory:
   Continuities, Conflicts, and Transformations in National Retrospection* (Durham,
   NC.: Duke University Press, 2003); and Jay Winter, *Sites of Memory, Sites
   of Mourning: The Great War in European Cultural History* (Cambridge:
   Cambridge University Press, 1995), to name only a few.

9 Here we take for granted and eschew, to some extent, an extensive debate
   about the memory/history divide. Dominick LaCapra's engagement with
   this debate and the 'turn to memory' (see Simon Schama, *Landscape and
   Memory* [New York: Knopf, 1995]) in *History and Memory after Auschwitz*
   (Ithaca, NY: Cornell University Press, 1998) provides an excellent summary
   of the issues, also played out in the pages of the journal *Memory and History*,
   with its editors and such key contributors as Saul Friedlander, Dan Diner,
   Galie Ne'eman, Omer Bartov, David Lowenthal, and James E. Young
   participating in the genesis of memory studies as a field. The idea that
   memory is the 'raw material' of objective history, as Jacques Le Goff put it
   in his preface to the 1992 edition of his collection of essays *History and
   Memory* (New York: Columbia University Press, 1992), has slowly been
   replaced by a more nuanced understanding of the imbrications of memory
   and history and the transformational processes between one and the other.
   A particularly helpful way out of this irresolvable debate is to follow Paul
   Ricoeur's distinctions of scale: '… historians can work according to
   hierarchized scales, something which memory cannot do. In contradistinction with memory, history can manipulate the choice of duration, as it

were.' Microhistory, or 'case studies,' can provide memorial testimony on a small scale, often orally, which produces an indeterminate read, often based on 'situations of uncertainty within which individuals ... attempt to orient themselves.' History, in retrospect, can be more deterministic, but Ricoeur lauds the 'new capacity that the historian as acquired: to learn to move between scales' ('Memory, History, Forgiveness: A Dialogue between Paul Ricoeur and Sorin Antohi,' *Janus Head* 8, no.1 (2005): 12–14).

10 Tony Judt, 'A la Recherche du Temps Perdu,' review article of *Realms of Memory: The Construction of the French Past*, edited by Pierre Nora, English-language edition edited by Lawrence D. Kritzman, translated by Arthur Goldhammer (Volume I: *Conflicts and Divisions*; Volume II: *Traditions*; Volume III: *Symbols* [New York: Columbia University Press, 1996]), in *New York Review of Books* 45 no. 19 (1998), n.pag., http://www.nybooks.com/articles/650.

11 Paul Ricoeur, *Memory, History, Forgetting*, trans. Kathleen Blamey and David Pellauer (Chicago: University of Chicago Press, 2004), 40.

12 Ibid., 43.

13 Ibid.

14 Maurice Halbwachs, *On Collective Memory*, trans. Lewis A. Coser (Chicago: University of Chicago Press, 1992), 39.

15 Ibid., 203.

16 Ricoeur, *Memory*, 123.

17 In this respect, Halbwachs's idea of collective memory is a precursor to the work of Louis Althusser, who argues that subjectivity itself is 'always already' a product of 'interpellation' into 'ideological state apparati,' many of them located in the same places which Halbwachs identifies as the primary locations of collective memory: the family home, the school, the church, and social class. See Louis Althusser, *Lenin and Philosophy and Other Essays*, trans. Ben Brewster (New York: Monthly Review Press, 1972).

18 Thanks to Veronika Zangl for pointing out to me how Halbwachs contributed to the reformulation of the tradition of *topos*.

19 See their introduction to *Memory Work: The Theory and Practice of Memory*, ed. Andreas Kitzmann, Conny Mithander, and John Sundholm (Brussels: Peter Lang, 2005), in which the editors argue that 'the memory turn' that has dominated thinking across the humanities and the social sciences in the 1990s is very similar to 'the linguistic turn' of the 1960s followed by the postmodern 'cultural turn' of the 1980s. Examples of recent key texts in this 'memory turn' are Tony Judt, *Postwar: A History of Europe since 1945* (New York: Penguin, 2005); Alfred-Maurice de Zayas, *A Terrible Revenge: The Ethnic Cleansing of East European Germans* (New York: Palgrave-Macmillan,

2006); Benjamin Lieberman, *Terrible Fate: Ethnic Cleansing in the Making of Modern Europe* (Chicago: Ivan R. Dee Publisher, 2006); Jan-Werner Muller, *Memory and Power in Post-War Europe: Studies in the Presence of the Past* (Cambridge: Cambridge University Press, 2002); Tvestzan Todorov, *Hope and Memory. Lessons from the Twentieth Century*, trans. David Bellos (Princeton: Princeton University Press, 2003); and Daniel Levy and Natan Sznaider's crucial argument about 'cosmopolitan memory' in *The Holocaust and Memory in the Global Age* (Philadelphia: Temple University Press, 2006).

20 See the groundbreaking work on testimony and the transmission of memory in monographs and collections by Cathy Caruth, Shoshana Felman and Dori Laub, Lawrence Langer, Marianne Hirsch, and Geoffrey Hartman, much of it based on Jewish survivors who immigrated to the Unites States, a population whose memory was extensively documented by the testimonial projects of Fortunoff and Speilberg's video archives. Daniel and Jonathan Boyarin have made exceptional contributions to the field of Jewish diasporic memory, particularly in the United States, grounding work to which our current project owes some debt. One might also point to the vast opus of memoirs and literary works that have formed the primary sources for much of the memory turn. I mention here the names of only a few: W.G. Sebald, Elie Wiesel, Primo Levi, David Grossman, Art Spiegelman, Imre Kertesz, Charlotte Delbo.

21 Our discussion references, if not directly, key links between melancholy and displacement – often in the context of minority populations – that has echoed through the places where psychoanalysis meets diaspora studies. Anne Anlin Cheng's 'Melancholy of Race,' in the *Kenyon Review* (Winter 1997), precipitated an idea that racial otherness and the processes of assimilation by the other or incorporation of the other into a dominant culture might be theorized along the lines of the melancholic loss of self and incorporation of the other, a kind of Möbius strip of inclusion and exclusion that reflects the state of irresolvable racial differences in America. Similarly, Julia Kristeva in *Contre la dépression nationale: entretien avec Philippe Petit* (Paris: Texuel, 1998) and *Étrangers à nous-mêmes* (Paris: Fayard, 1988) diagnosed a French malaise, a national melancholy stuck on the loss of a unified nation, one unable to incorporate the faces of immigration. Bringing Kristeva and Cheng together, in what is the closest articulation to the phenomenon we describe here, is Sam Haigh's essay 'Migration and Melancholia: From Kristeva's "Dépression Nationale" to Pineau's "Maladie de L'Exil,"' in *French Studies* (2006). Haigh asks what happens to the foreigner herself as the excluded other of a nation, and traces in Gisèle Pineau's *L'Exil selon Julia* (Paris: Stock 1996) the

melancholic loss of 'Julia,' brought to France against her will. 'From the start,' writes Haigh, 'she experiences her exile as "le manqué de pays" – as a lack, a loss, a wound, and as the prospect of returning to Guadeloupe gradually fades, she sinks into full-blown depression, becomes physically ill, and refuses to leave her bed, suffering from what her family names "[l]a maladie de l'exil" (*L'Exil*, 129)' (242). This is a manifestation, clearly, as Zofia Rosińska will put it, of the 'melancholy of no return.' We would also be remiss not to note David L. Eng and David Kazanjian's edited collection *Loss: The Politics of Mourning* (Berkeley: University of California Press, 2003), which takes melancholia to be a productive, continuous engagement with loss and its remains, an engagement which 'generates sites for memory and history' (4).

22 Jacques Presser, *Ondergang: De vervolging en verdelging van het Nederlandse Jodendom, 1940–1945* ('s-Gravenhage: Staatsuitgeverij, 1965), 501. [Het was mij vreemd te moede. Ik liep door straten, die uitgestorven waren; ik liep door de Jodenhoek. Lege ruimten waar eens huizen hadden gestaan, huizen waaruit alles verdwenen was; grauwe huizen met stukkende ruiten. Zij gaapten mij aan en ik vluchtte weg.]

23 Delbo, *Auschwitz and After*, 252.

24 Ricoeur, *Memory*, 62–3.

SECTION ONE

The Melancholy of No Return

1 Emigratory Experience: The Melancholy of No Return

ZOFIA ROSIŃSKA

The Emigrants

Wide-eyed, down the busy Broadway,
my little hand in your strong hand,
we took our first steps into the New World.

My son, you said,
this world is a raw jungle.
Against its claws
you have but bare hands
clenched into a fist.

Be stronger than the strong.
There is no help for you here when you fall.

Work, son, work until you can no more.
For when they come to judge you,
that will be all they concede your own.

So you spoke as we walked down Broadway,
my little hand in your strong hand,
and never once did we look back
on the vast calm ocean that swelled behind.

– Łukasz Zieliński, 2007[1]

Encyclopedias define emigration as a social phenomenon of the translocation of people from their native country to another, either permanently or for an extended period of time, for economic or political reasons. Sociologists categorize emigration depending on its ends and its causes under headings such as voluntary, forcible, permanent, temporary, political, and economical. The entry 'emigration' does not figure in psychological or philosophical dictionaries. And yet, besides its sociological significance, the phenomenon of emigration has a psychological and philosophical dimension as well, and that dimension will be the main focus of this essay.

Not every translocation of people constitutes emigration, and not all emigration can be reduced to translocation. We often speak of 'internal emigration,' which does not involve any physical displacement. In Polish, the term 'internal emigration' is commonly used to refer to the forms of passive resistance against an oppressive regime that consist of boycotting political institutions and non-involvement in official civic activities, resulting in alienation from one's environment that is much akin to actual 'external' emigration. By contrast, we do not refer to nomadic tribes as emigrants even though they change territories. Likewise, we distinguish emigration from tourism, flaneurism, or pilgrimages. Intuitively, we sense the difference between these terms, but it is not easy to formulate a clear-cut criterion that would permit their differentiation. Perhaps the question of motives behind the translocation could shed light on this criterion. It seems, for instance, that curiosity and boredom – common motivations for tourism or flaneurism – are rarely a cause of emigration, even the voluntary kind.[2] A tourist or a flaneur seeks sensory gratification. A tourist pays for the appearance and gets the appearance in return. A pilgrim seeks spiritual growth and renewal. But they all merely pass through the visited lands, without getting involved in, or integrating into, the local communities. Their knowledge of the world is expanded, but that knowledge is of a superficial kind. They may return to their homes with new subjects of conversation, but they are rarely substantively changed. Even the pilgrims, though they may grow spiritually, are unlikely to have their world view altered in any significant measure.

The emigrant, on the other hand, struggles for survival amidst new customs, new people, new language. He does integrate into the foreign community. He joins in its daily lives, partakes of its victories and concerns, and his mental horizons expand by new vantage points. Even if he succeeds professionally and establishes himself in the new world, or perhaps especially then, his awareness and consciousness will have been irrevocably altered. In the age of technological globalization, the paradigmatic form of emigrant experience is being transformed into a weaker form, typical of other less traumatic types of migration. I argue this by constructing a model of emigrant experience and then pointing to those elements of it that are subject to transformation due to technological innovations, resulting in new types of experience.

Three concepts – identity, memory, and melancholy – form the structural bases of the emigratory experience. Each one delineates a distinct thematic and problematic area. They are joined in the emigratory experience.

1. Identity

When we speak of personal identity, we have in mind not just its end form but also the process of its development. The process that leads to emigration commonly involves the experience of helplessness, dissatisfaction, and rebellion. It seems that a necessary condition for complete emigratory experience is the loss of the object of identification, which could be the physical habitat including geographical setting and owned property, lifestyle, value system, language, faith, or ideals. We must keep in mind, however, that the object of identification is not an actual physical object but rather a bundle of varied experiences and impressions. It is the smells, the views, the sounds, the intonations, warmth and cold, desires, hopes, disappointments, and, finally, safety: home in the broad sense of the word.

A nomad does not become an emigrant by moving his camp to another location, but he would by changing his group or his lifestyle. It is the *group* and the *lifestyle* that fix his identity and not a particular geographical region or physical setting. Nomadic tribes, therefore, although they relocate physically and change their surroundings, do not change that which they identify with most: their group and their customs. They do not change their identity.

From a sociological point of view, the exodus of the Israelites from Egypt or Odysseus's travels might be considered emigration. In either case, however, the element of the loss of the object of identification or personal identity is absent. The sense of melancholy is missing as well, blocked by the power of identity-forming memory. Yahweh commands the Israelites to remember the *events* that took place, the *miracles* he performed, and the *moral code* regulating personal conduct. Odysseus remembers and longs for his *Ithaca*. Calypso offers him immortality so that he will forget Ithaca; he does not. He remembers and is remembered. The guarantee of the Israelites' identity is *God*, and for Odysseus it is *Ithaca*.

The guarantee of identity for Eva Hoffman – a young Polish-Jewish emigrant from Poland – is the *language*: 'Our Polish names did not refer to us, they were as surely us as our eyes or hands. The new appellations, which we ourselves can't pronounce are not us. They are identification tags, disembodied signs pointing to objects that happen to be my sister and myself.'[3] In the process of acculturation, however, her mastering of the English language is accompanied by the sense of loss of her original self-identification. For a long time, she experiences a double identity. The existence of two selves within her bothers her long after she moves to America. It is well expressed by the following recollection:

> Should you marry him? The question comes in English.
> Yes –
> Should you marry him? The question echoes in Polish.
> No –
> But I love him; I'm in love with him.
> Really? Really? Do you love him as you understand love?[4]

Despite very different family experiences – 'The kind of Russian family to which I belong … had … a traditional leaning toward the comfortable products of Anglo-Saxon civilization'[5] – Vladimir Nabokov also perceives a similar loss of language: 'My private tragedy, which cannot, indeed should not be anybody's concern, is that I had to abandon my natural language, my natural idiom, my untrammeled, rich, and infinitely docile Russian tongue for a second-rate brand of English.'[6]

Emigration in cultures that have not developed *principium individuationis*, translated as 'the sense of individual identity,' is never voluntary. It is always a punishment. The *kris* – the council and highest court of the Gypsy communities – considers exclusion from the community as the highest form of punishment. The Inuit communities are similar in this respect. In anthropological descriptions, an Inuit is invariably described as a model of strength and toughness, a man who can cut off his frostbitten fingers without as much as a groan, yet cannot handle one thing

– being alone. Anthropology is full of similar descriptions. Here we see most clearly how intimately intertwined together the fate of the individual and the life of the group can be; how deeply rooted in a human being is the sense of belonging to a group.

In Euro-American culture, the relation between the group and the individual is no longer perceived as an obvious subjugation of the individual to the group. We observe here not just the need and longing for the sense of belonging, but also the inability to satisfy the group and the conflicted desire to be free of it. The experience of these ambivalences and anxieties is painful. Socrates emphasizes that he would choose death rather than an existence away from Athens. Walter Benjamin would like to belong but cannot.[7] Witold Gombrowicz would like to liberate himself from these group ties and from his sense of belonging. He writes of his desire: 'To relax our subjugation to Poland, to tear ourselves away just a bit. To reveal and legalize this other pole of sensing that commands the individual to defend himself against his people as against any tyranny of the collective … being Polish, to be simultaneously someone ampler and grander than a Pole.'[8] The fact that he wants to be free of this attachment does not mean that it is a stranger to him. On the contrary, he feels it very powerfully. Let us also quote Julian Tuwim's 'Polish Flowers,' which is recognized as the most 'emigrant' of all Polish poetry. Tuwim, like Gombrowicz, an emigrant in South America, but in Rio de Janeiro rather than in Buenos Aires, writes: 'As with that drawer, so it is with the homeland. You won't throw anything away. Something forbids you to clear out the attic of attachments and discard the "unnecessary" and the "unused."'[9]

The sense of personal identity is not always as unconflicted and unshakeable as it is in the characters of Odysseus, the Israelites, and Socrates, or in the poetry of Tuwim. Especially when dealing with the process of formation of personal identity, there arise states of rebellion, discord, and resignation. Their focus may be social norms and traditions, political and social repression, or the inability to realize one's potential and ideals or to express one's values and beliefs. Rebellion and rejection of the status quo do not always result in the change of external reality. Often we are impotent or helpless to do so. We may decide to leave the country, group, or language with which we identify ourselves, in the hope that elsewhere it will be easier for us to realize our needs and desires that we consider as more important to our sense of identity than what we are leaving behind. Often, we are compelled to do this by political repression. But can we give up these aspects of identity entirely?

Can we forget? And if Freud was right, and what once enters the psyche stays there forever, then our earliest identifications – tastes, smells, intonations of the voice, etc. – although repressed or forgotten, will resurface in the guise of unspecified longings, in the desire to return. This desire, it might be added, is impossible to satisfy; nothing remains the same, including ourselves.

Rebellion and rejection of the status quo may concern our relations not only with the external world but also with ourselves. Lack of self-acceptance and a desire to be someone else often motivates us to change our present attachments. It compels us to endless soul-searching. This desire opens up a region of difficult experiences that are frequently, though not exclusively, connected with emigration. Sandor Marai describes this beautifully and insightfully: 'The desire to be someone else: stronger desire cannot inflame the human heart ... because we always love *otherness*, we seek it at each crossroads in life.'[10]

One characteristic of emigration in the strong sense of the word is the inability to return. This inability to return – whether for political or economic reasons – intensifies the desire to return and the sense of longing for home. It recalls remembered contents, often even creates them. Thus are born the illusions that satisfy our desires. This particular characteristic can be observed in the experiences of Polish emigration during the period of Romanticism, spurred by the disappearance of the homeland due to foreign power partitions. Similar to the case of the Israelites, here we are dealing with a flight from enslavement; except, in a partitioned Poland, there is no Promised Land or return to Ithaca. Inconsolable laments, the feeling of solitude and isolation, and of simply being 'not there,' are the expressions of a melancholy state of mind, but also an accusation of fate. Memory aids in holding on to identity, but most of all it has a therapeutic effect, soothing the suffering caused by this sense of loss. Memory calls back an image of the lost reality, which, however, as Julia Creet points out, need not be representative of the actual origin point for that memory.[11] This is perhaps what Plato alludes to in the dialogue 'Ion,' where he writes that 'the god draws the human mind in any direction he wishes, hanging a chain of force from one to the other.'[12]

A perfect example of the image of the lost reality is the epic poem 'Pan Tadeusz.' Adam Mickiewicz, its author, found himself alongside other Polish poets in Paris as a political émigré:

For us unbidden guests in every clime
From the beginning to the end of time

There is but one place in this planet whole
Where happiness may be for every Pole
The land of childhood! [13]

The memories described in 'Pan Tadeusz' provided a distraction from the hostile reality and transported the listeners into an uplifting and beautiful vision of the past. They brought back the lost world but also created a community for those who had to leave their homeland and suffered on account of this loss. Mickiewicz read his poems at meetings with friends. They made comments, added their own memories, corrected one another – in other words, they co-created the past. He describes this process in the poem: 'And in those days my friends would oft afford / Help for my song, and threw me word on word.' [14]

As a result of this collective remembrance, Mickiewicz reflects: 'I live thereby in Lithuania, in the woods, in the taverns, with the Polish noblemen, with the Jews. If not for the poetry, I would run away from Paris.'[15] He was also conscious of the fact that he was preserving and recording in human memory a world that was already passing. Was he recording a true image? In the opinion of Czesław Miłosz, 'Pan Tadeusz' is a metaphysical work. Its subject is the order of existence, as an image of pure being. Sunrises and sunsets, and ordinary activities like making coffee and picking mushrooms, are just the surface, which hides underneath it a great acceptance of the world that animates and upholds the descriptions.[16] One might ask how is it possible that in the state of embitterment, resentfulness, and solitude there appears a poem that is the extreme opposite of melancholy, as an epitome of order and groundedness. Let us remember that one of the qualities of the state of melancholy is self-revelation externally enacted. Grievances and complaints are accusations, and these must be publicly exposed. Thus, we can describe the writing of the poem in terms of the power of the desire: the talent that creates the illusion of the poem satisfies the desire in a psychoanalytical sense. The aesthetics of melancholy, then, turn into the harmony of fulfilment, a utopia. According to Kenneth R. MacKenzie, the English translator of 'Pan Tadeusz,' it is not a poem in praise of Poland, but a poem about the love of country. 'It matters not that the lineaments of the beloved are not those of our own … it is a corner of that heavenly country to which all men belong.'[17]

If the emigratory experience is of the melancholy kind born out of an unsettled sense of identity, the creative process with the aid of memory conjures up images with which it constructs a vision of the world permitting emotional equilibrium.

2. Melancholy

Analysis of the emigratory experience shows that, at least in part, it contains traits typical of melancholy: the sense of estrangement, sadness, and loss, and the want of meaning in life. As I discussed earlier, melancholy demands expression and understanding, through words, pictures, and music, but also in illness, mystical experience, and philosophy. It wants to be understood. But although efforts at understanding melancholy have been undertaken ever since Ancient Greece, and although they still continue to reveal its new qualities, no one can claim to have understood it fully. Melancholy does not take kindly to the doctors who would like to shut it inside the body and call it depression. But what is it, then? Freud likens it to mourning, though he explains there are differences as well as similarities between these two forms of emotion: 'Mourning is regularly the reaction to the loss of a loved person, or to the loss of some abstraction which has taken the place of one, such as one's country, liberty, an ideal, and so on. In some people the same influences produce melancholia instead of mourning.'[18] In melancholy, however, 'there is a loss of a more ideal kind,' writes Freud in his essay 'Mourning and Melancholy.'

'It never occurs to us to regard it [mourning] as pathological condition, and to refer it to medical treatment ... Profound mourning, the reaction to the loss of someone who is loved, contains the same painful frame of mind [as melancholy], the same loss of interest in the outside world ... the same loss of capacity to adopt any new object of love ... and the same turning away from any activity that is not connected with thoughts of him ... It is really only because we know so well how to explain it that this attitude does not seem to us pathological.'[19] Freud continues: 'In melancholy one cannot see clearly what it is that has been lost ... he knows whom he has lost but not what he has lost in him.'[20] This underlines what was already mentioned earlier: namely, that the object of identification is not a specific real thing, but rather a whole medley of vague impressions.

'Melancholy is in some way related to an object-loss which is withdrawn from consciousness, in contradistinction to mourning in which there is nothing about the loss that is unconscious.'[21] 'The melancholic displays something else besides which is lacking in mourning – an extraordinary diminution in his self-regard, an impoverishment of his ego on a grand scale ... In mourning it is the world which has become poor and empty; in melancholia it is the ego itself.' In Freud's opinion, melancholy is the disease of the conscience: 'We see how in him one part of the ego sets itself over against the other, judges it critically and as it were, takes it as its object. What we are here becoming acquainted with is the agency commonly called "conscience" ... it is one of the major institutions of the ego ... it can become diseased on its own account. In the clinical picture of melancholy, dissatisfaction with the ego on moral grounds is the most outstanding feature.'[22]

I will not here analyse Freud's conception in any detail. I just want to underscore two observations he makes: first, the 'breaking' of the ego and the permanent self-analysis and self-evaluation that this breaking entails; secondly, the inability to ever know precisely what it is that we lost together with the lost object. This is the reason why, as John Sundholm puts it, the emigratory experience is always traumatic.[23]

To the characterization of the melancholic state, one often adds also the sensation of not being here. Jerzy Pluta writes: 'For only I know that I was born in the wrong century, in the wrong country, in the wrong family, and on the wrong planet.'[24] Emil Cioran also emphasizes the aesthetic tinge to melancholy. He describes it as peacefulness, lack of tension, and dreaminess.[25]

Let us recall here that it was the Italian Renaissance that began the process of the enobling and elevation of melancholy. From a despised ailment, it grew to be a prerogative for genius. Ficino contributed significantly to this process, but he was much aided by Aristotle's formulation: 'Why is it that all those who have become eminent in philosophy or politics or poetry or the arts are clearly of an atrabilious temperament, and some of them to such an extent as to be affected by diseases caused by black bile?'[26] *Furor melancholicus* becomes equivalent to *furor divinus*.

Is aestheticism always present in melancholy? Let's recall again Benjamin and his desire to belong. His friend Theodor Adorno wrote of Benjamin: 'He knew that it is impossible to adapt, yet he never gave up that wish. In all the households he called on the one thing he could accomplish without fail was to make all the residents feel more like household members.'[27]

3. Memory

The concept that connects emigration, melancholy, and memory is the notion of loss. The experience of loss is a common element in all three phenomena. Its presence in melancholy and in emigration is non-controversial. Not so, perhaps, in memory. Must one lose in order to remember? Aristotle writes that memory refers to the past, but already Saint Augustine does not limit the concept of memory only to the past but also enlarges it to include present experience and the future. He links it with personal identity, and to describe it he employs, among others, the metaphor of the stomach: he likens memory to the belly of the mind. He says: 'The memory doubtless is, so to say, the belly of the mind: and joy and sadness are like sweet and bitter food, which when they are committed to the memory are, so to say, passed into the belly where they can be stored but no longer tasted.'[28] Clearly, he notices a 'loss of taste' or distortion of recollected emotions. This is borne out by another quotation from the *Confessions*:

> This same memory also contains the feelings of mind; not in the manner in which the mind itself experienced them, but very differently accord-ing to the power peculiar to the memory. For without being joyous now, I can remember that I once was joyous, and without being sad, I can re-call my past sadness. I can remember past fears without fear, and former desires without desire. Again the contrary happens. Sometimes when I am joyous I remember my past sadness, and when I am sad I remember past joy.[29]

Remembering, then, does not presume loss, and although it typically refers to the past, the past need not be perceived as a loss.

How to comprehend memory so that it contains the experience of loss? How to comprehend it in order to understand how it plays the role of an art form with respect to the feeling of loss? First of all, mem-ory would need to be construed as mnemonic experience,[30] and a tem-poral construct. This construct would contain in itself elements such as committing to memory or forgetting, but also the processes of remem-bering, recollecting, repetition, and narration. Mnemonic time would not be linear, but rather a circular mixing and overlapping of the past, the present, and the future. As noted already by Saint Augustine and developed by Freud and Heidegger, memory is not capable of storing and preserving the past intact and unchanging. A recollected memory is never the same but rather changes its meaning depending on the horizon of other experiences that surround it.

To sum up our discussion, we can say that although the emigratory experience has an idiographical aspect that is lived through and experienced individually and therefore depends on individual desires and needs as well as on social, economic, and historical conditions, it also always exhibits several common qualities. First, it always challenges the existent identity or the ongoing identity-forming process. Original identifications or sense of personal identity are a condition *sine qua non* for the emigratory experience. Second, it is always accompanied by a sense of loss and the following melancholy. I don't mean here the loss of material objects, but rather the feeling of want or lack of something intangible and ideal. Material loss may, of course, have sentimental value attached, but it is always the loss of an object in terms of its emotional meaning that is the subject of melancholic longings. Third, the emigratory experience is strongly influenced by memory, and recollection, in particular. Memory plays a triple role: it is identity-forming by maintaining the original identifications; it is therapeutic because it helps bear the hardships of transplantation into a foreign culture; and it is also community-forming, by creating a bond among those recollecting together. Fourth, the experiences of all the other elements of emigration are intensified by the final shared characteristic: an inability to return.

These four common qualities, when occurring together, become the formative and defining characteristics of emigratory experience. They have a paradigmatic character. But they may, and often do, occur independently, and combine with other experiences. They may take on various forms and different degrees of intensity in each individual instance of emigratory experience.

Analysis of particular elements of the emigratory experience has revealed to us its transcendental character. It has shown that the emigratory experience constitutes a condition of possibility for experiencing the identity of one's own subjectivity. Without the challenge of emigration, a deeper, expanded sense of personal identity might never arise.

In the times of technological globalization, emigration within the developed world has acquired a new face. Its fourth element, the inability to return, comes into play only in rare cases: thus the intensity of perception of the other elements of the emigratory experience. The 'other pole of sensing,' whose strengthening Gombrowicz craves, also is more potent, and the unsatisfied desire to belong to a group no longer threatened with death. Thus, emigration rarely appears in its strongest form or paradigmatic character. It becomes *mi*gration. However, the longing for memory's points of origin, for 'home,' still remains.

In the modern experience of emigration as migration, it is the transcendental element that comes to the fore as the condition of the ability to experience the identity of one's subjectivity. The 'other pole of sensing' reveals in experience its dark side. Subjectivity as the obvious source of certainty and autonomy begins to be disputed. We experience anxiety, uncertainty, and discomfort. The feeling of not being here and the sense of loss become acute. Emigration permits the confrontation with the other or, more precisely, with one's self *through* the other. We experience dependence on what it is we strive to liberate ourselves from, such as false, casual identity. At the same time, as a result of breaking with these dependencies, we experience alienation, emptiness, lack of meaning, and solitude. We feel a want. Of course, not every lost element is identity-forming to the same extent. Some losses are more easily acceptable than others.

One could say that life is a permanent emigration, involving the passage from one stage or region to another and the next. It is not always voluntary; nor is it always accompanied by rebellion and rejection, and followed by punishment. However, it always involves the possibility of reflection on the identity of one's subjectivity. Let's point out that the experience of certain elements of the emigratory structure, such as estrangement and alienation, is related to socio-political transformations and to progress as it is broadly understood. The advance of civilization changes interpersonal relations. One need not seek out exceptional examples; everyday life will suffice. Sociopolitical transformations, even if they improve the common lot, often engender the feeling of loss. This experience is described by young Polish writers who are also emigrants. Janusz Lewoń writes that after the move, 'nothing was like it used to be, the shards of the shattered world have not re-collected themselves. In the condominium apartment there was a bathroom and hot water and gas in a bottle; but there was no longer the post office … And the post office ceased to exist as our world and our kingdom.'[31] So why didn't the broken shards 're-collect themselves'?

They do so for Odysseus. He knows where he is going. He remains himself. The sense of identity of his subjectivity remains intact. Why is it that Odysseus, despite such long seafaring peregrinations and a myriad adventures, does not doubt the identity of his subjectivity, yet we, today, doubt it? Don't we trust Odysseus? Is it that we no longer identify with him, but rather with the experience of Walter Benjamin, his homeless wanderings, his exile rather than travel?

Characterizing the emigratory experience, I barely touched on the issue of acculturation: the acceptance of the foreign culture and being accepted by it. The process of entering another culture, of discovering and assimilating its codes, traditions, and customs, let alone learning the foreign tongue, has not yet been fully explored and described. How long it lasts, which factors facilitate it and which make it more difficult, what is the internal experience of dual identity, and finally, what are its psychological consequences – all this requires philosophical reflection. It seems that accepting and being accepted may be another step in the process of personal identity formation. If we don't want to be stuck in the sensation of 'not here,' and 'not in this time,' in the feeling of dichotomy and longing, then new identifications are necessary. Does this necessitate giving up the old ones and severing all ties with the past? Along with the weakening of the emigratory experience, and its becoming more like other weaker forms of migration, it no longer produces a sense of schizophrenia and severed ties; instead, it is enough to transform them.

NOTES

1 Łukasz Zieliński, 'The Emigrants,' 2007.
2 See the contributions of Srdja Pavlovic, Laurenn Guyot, and Andreas Kitzmann to this volume.
3 Eva Hoffman, *Lost in Translation: A Life in a New Language* (Harmondsworth: Penguin Books, 1989), 105.
4 Ibid., 199.
5 Vladamir Nabokov, *Strong Opinions* (London: Weidenfeld and Nicolson, 1973), 79.
6 Ibid., 15.
7 See Edmond Jabès, *The Book of Dialogue*, trans. Rosemarie Waldrop (Middleton: Wesleyan University Press, 1987), 55.
8 Witold Gombrowicz, *Trans-Atlantyk* (Kraków: Wydawnictwo Literackie, 1988), 55.
9 Julian Tuwim, *Kwiaty polskie* (Warszawa: Czytelnik, 2003), 65.
10 Sandor Marai, *Zar* (Warszawa: Czytelnik, 2006), 88–9.
11 See Julia Creet's Introduction to this volume, p. 6.

12 Plato, 'Ion,' vers 536, in D.A. Russell and M. Winterbottom, eds, *Classical Literary Criticism* (Oxford: Oxford University Press,1989), 7.

13 Adam Mickiewicz, *Pan Tadeusz*, trans. Kenneth R. MacKenzie (New York: Hippocrene Books, 1992).

14 Alina Witkowska, *'Pan Tadeusz' Adama Mickiewicza* (Warszawa: IBL, 1999), 11.

15 Ibid., p.10.

16 Czesław Miłosz, *Ziemia Urlo* (Warszawa: PIW, 1982), 133. See also Czesław Miłosz, *Native Realm: A Search for Self-Definition*, trans. Catherine S. Leach (Harmondsworth: Penguin Books, 1988).

17 Kenneth R. MacKenzie, 'Introduction,' in Mickiewicz, *Pan Tadeusz*, 5

18 Sigmund Freud, 'Mourning and Melancholia' (1917), in vol. 14 of *The Standard Edition of the Complete Psychological Works of Sigmund Freud* (London: Hogarth Press, 1917), 243. For a reading of melancholia and the loss of country or the ideal of nation, see Sam Haigh,'Migration and Melancholia: From Kristeva's "Dépression Nationale" to Pineau's "Maladie de L'Exil,"' *French Studies* 60, no. 2 (2006): 232–50.

19 Freud, 'Mourning and Melancholia,' 243.

20 Ibid.

21 Ibid., 245.

22 Ibid., 248.

23 See John Sundholm, 'The Cultural Trauma Process, or the Ethics and Mobility of Memory' in this collection.

24 Jerzy Pluta, *Melancholica Polonaise* (Bydgoszcz: no publisher, 1987), 3.

25 Emil Cioran, *Na szczytach rozpaczy*, trans. I. Kania (Kraków: Oficyna Literacka, 1992).

26 Aristotle, *Problemata* xxx.1 953a 10–14, in *The Complete Works of Aristotle*, vol. II, ed. Jonathan Barnes (Princeton: Princeton University Press,1984).

27 Gary Smith, ed., *On Walter Benjamin: Critical Essays and Recollections* (Cambridge, MA: MIT Press, 1988), 19.

28 *Augustine's Confessions*, trans. Albert C. Outler, Book 10.14.21 (http://www .ccel.org/ccel/augustine/confessions/html).

29 Ibid.

30 See Edward S. Casey, *Remembering: A Phenomenological Study* (Bloomington: Indiana University Press, 2000).

31 Janusz Lewoń, 'Sniking for Grunwald,' *Migotania, przejaśnienia* 10 (2006): 12.

2 Memory for Breakfast

SRDJA PAVLOVIC

These notes are an exercise in mnemohistory, and the product of a loneliness that is accustomed to being public. This is a story of sediment, a
remnant of the years in exile retold as a story of dislocated identity that
undertakes Icarian flights in all directions. My speech leaves its cask
alienated and personal at the same time. It is the voice of longing for a
once known and now lost presence, whose broken pieces still float
through my veins, shaped by the journey I had to undertake, inescap-
ably connected to all the pleasures as well as the discomforts associated
with movement across space and time, and through a multitude of
languages. Migration is a condition of memory, indeed.[1] Movement
(voluntary or not) creates a story that gives shape to memory. Along the
way, the fragile balance between remembrance and forgetting is struck.

Living outside of my native cultural and social framework is a dichotomy between the sweetness of the sound of 'I,' which is born within, and its external echo. To borrow Charles Taylor's argument about
the nature of modern identity: we struggle to maintain the *capacity for
authenticity* – that is, the *ability* to find a *way of being* which is somehow
true to oneself.[2] We struggle with selective remembering and displacement, and with identities in flux. That is the story about an orchard and
an apple tree, and the obligatory presence of a serpent, and a story
about a field from the Old Testament where Cain's psalm rules.

As Jan Assmann points out, the *truth* of a given memory lies not so
much in its *factuality* as in its *actuality*.[3] This never-ending actuality of
exile fascinates me. Those of us displaced indeed live in a moment that
lasts a lifetime. It is the moment of departure which becomes the *plexus
solaris* of our daily existence. Departure is not only the physical act of
separation from loved ones, but it also freezes time for both myself and

those who stayed behind. I carried away memories of those dear to me and memories about my life at home. Those will remain with me forever, timeless and unchanged. Similarly, those who stayed behind remember me just the way I was on the day the train pulled out of the Podgorica train station.

In the early days of my exile, memories of home were drowned in bitterness caused by war. Every time I tried to speak or write about the former Yugoslavia, I was overwhelmed by hopelessness. Back then the former Yugoslavia was the land of nationalism and hatred, a land of the Devil, of despair, of heart ailments, of hereditary high blood pressure, of hard-heartedness, of wasted bones, of apathy. It was the land of daily violence and nightly murders, of police informers, and 'knights' who carry the icon and the axe into heathen darkness. It was the land criss-crossed by borders and a land of death. Because I spoke publicly and wrote against the war and nationalism, I was branded a traitor. In my police file there was a note of instruction to the officers, dated 15 October 1991, stating that I was armed and dangerous, and that I should be approached 'with extreme prejudice.'[4]

Yugoslavia dissolved, my English improved, and it was time to replace broken dreams with the refuge of distant places. I will never forget the fateful day I stepped onto the tarmac of Heathrow Airport, severing my umbilical cord with the only home I knew. By early July 1992, I was living in London, sipping espresso in a cafe on the Chiswick High Road, and trying to decide what to do with my life.

In time, the bitterness subsided and was replaced by longing, and an effort to remember as much as possible. I now know that I am fighting a losing battle. After fifteen years of living in England and Canada, fragments are all that I remember about the place of my birth. Every sentence awakens memories of my youth and brings back faces of my parents. I see my father smiling. Ghosts of his white shirts on the wind suddenly appear through the washing lines, and I can hear his voice that still says whenever I visit him: *I hope you've had your coffee, we've just had ours.* Again, I can smell the colours of my homeland. On some days, that is the smell of a defeat.

Since then, I wake up every morning into a language that is not mine, and try to make the best of it for the day. Living in-between languages means that the master of the extravagance of words and verbal acrobatics slowly loses those faculties. I am, nevertheless, still hoping that living within the strange echoes of the foreign language might help me learn more and appreciate its beauty. On the other hand, I am becoming obsessed with my native tongue and suffer from the nostalgia for the homeland of my own words. I am aware that sooner or later I will write in a 'dead language,' a language spoken by only one person, a language frozen in some linguistic past. Following Derrida, everything I do only reinforces the omnipresence of my monolingualism.[5] Such disorder of identity is the result of exile. Often, I console myself by thinking of Henry Miller's advice to writers: live abroad and soon you will sense a new flow of energy that highlights the only language you are capable of expressing yourself in. So, every day I try to recapture from outside what I possess from the inside, possess so completely that I do not even know about it. I become alienated and detribalized. My intelligence becomes that of a clever immigrant, who belongs only by clever adaptation and not by instinct. I never quite fit anywhere. To paraphrase Salman Rushdie's *Shame*: it is like standing naked in the street, shivering and envying others their brocades of belonging and identity.[6]

For years I thought that the physical and spiritual connection to the land of our ancestors, that *sacro egoismo della patria* (sacred egoism of the motherland) is what gives us strength. Today, the notion of *homeland* reminds me of a tree and its roots, and of the story about Anteus. It seems that such a concept is a rather conservative myth constructed in a way that keeps us immobile because each crossing of a border (boundary) is an act of bravery and disobedience. Crossing the border and boundary presupposes flexibility and inevitably brings about a change in one's perspective. After so many years of living outside of my native cultural, social, and political frameworks, I think of my own past traditions and culture in a more critical fashion. The old idyllic reflection in a Balkan mirror has slowly faded away and turned into a gray spot, like an old burn mark that still hurts but heals in time. To me, the Balkans resembles a torso eroded by history and the self-deception of its peoples that is finally washed onto the beach. You see, I cannot stop thinking about it! No matter how hard I try to change, that coded message of belonging will always stay a part of me. Some things will never happen and my heart is breaking loose. I will continue to be one of the many people who eat memory for breakfast and seek an escape route from that deep and dark well of the past.

My exile was provoked by political repression. I assume this is true for many other exiles, regardless of geography and time frame. Andreas Kitzmann's contribution to this volume, on the survivors of the post–Second World War expulsion of ethnic Germans from much of eastern and central Europe (*Vertreibung*), clearly shows the dominance of *realpolitik* over the concerns for human dignity. It is true that to the victors go the spoils, but, as Kitzmann has illustrated, the victors of the Second World War were seldom concerned with protecting the innocent. I do believe that exile is either the result of force being exerted upon an individual (or a group), or the consequence of an unbearable choice. People rarely leave their country of origin because they dislike the climate. When forced to choose between political servitude, being sent to the front line, or being imprisoned for refusing to do so, exile appears to be the best available option. Others opted differently. For many of my fellow countrymen, being absorbed into the nation with a war cry was a nice way of forgetting one's own weakness and forcing others to forget it. It is obvious that from the outset of the nationalistic fever in the former Yugoslavia, there was uncertainty, ignorance, and greed. Alongside this was fear, and the need to define and contain it. The Tribe became Power. When you say 'Power,' you must also say 'Party Religion.' For, like a Religion, the Party needs to have priests to protect its 'purity' – a notion founded on misrepresentation and often on lies. By the time this lie is exposed, the Tribe has become a closed fist, according to the principle *Abiit ad Plures* (to join the majority; to die).

I never was, nor will I ever be, willing to kill or to die for someone else's dream or nightmare. I prefer to be wretched on my own than to borrow from the nation by being absorbed in it. The echo of the ideological slogans that have mobilized many of my fellow countrymen never moved me. I always felt indifferent towards all those neatly dressed factory workers and those sharp-looking defenders of the faith who marched down the avenues waving huge red flags. It is not so wonderful, as many think, to join them with great fanfare. I am more of a poetic disposition, dreaming about the Great Wall of China and giving myself away to the sound of Deep Purple, Ian Gillan's tones, and to all those beautiful girls 'under the raincoats in the park on hot days.'[7] It runs in the family, I guess. I was aware that going into exile meant the exchange of one form of living death for another, but I had to leave.

Some years ago, when I was a new émigré in Canada, I learned an old saying of the immigrants from eastern Europe. In their phases of resignation, they would murmur: 'Once you cross the Ocean, you'll always be on the wrong side of it.' I believe that such nostalgic lamenting is neither specific to any region or people, nor an exclusive product of modernity. The feeling of loss that resonates from it has been pronounced throughout the centuries, in many languages and over many continents. What is shared to this day is the *intimacy of exile* because everyone who is displaced ponders the same questions. A specific language of loss and a memory of people and things left behind, as well as a particular geography of displacement, only reinforce the shared experience. Mimicking the statement by Amira Bojadzija-Dan: the remembered and the forgotten are in constant communication with each other, and that buzzing of a beehive of memory gives meaning to life outside of the protective cocoon of a romanticized *Heimat*.[8]

Back then I failed to grasp the full meaning of this lament. I moved from England without knowing much about Canada. I was told that people here are calm and friendly, that they drive carefully and obey the traffic signals. And most important of all, no one asks where you come from. Only your speech betrays your origins. Now, fifteen years and two countries later, I do understand. It is all about learning: learning how to bear the fact that you left your homeland; learning how to forget and forgive; learning about a different cultural code, different logic, and a new way of life; learning how to be flexible.

Each step I take, and each time I move, this new Canadian space demands that I conceptualize myself in relation to it. One could not exist without locating and simultaneously subjectifying and positioning oneself. For me, this is a daily struggle. I have to rename the place/space in order to name myself. I, thus, am a Montenegrin-Canadian, trying to hold on to both ends of the hyphen.[9] That is my existential condition. Indeed, a hyphen is a description with historical connotations, personal meanings, and cultural resonance drawn from our conscious environment but reflective of our subconscious selves. Each *French-Canadian, Serbian-Canadian, Irish-Canadian, Japanese-Canadian*, etc., has its own story of spirits, demons, tribal fires, and ancestors, which, through enfiguration, are molded into history. While naming this new space, I am appropriating a story and locating myself within a history, thus claiming ownership of all three: space, story, and history. I do believe, however, that this is much more than a simple appropriation by a newcomer who longs for a safe port of call. This space, story, and history I now own, appear to me new and unique. What gives them meaning is, to borrow Julia Creet's term, the movement of memory,[10] which is my own experience of exile and my own journey of self-discovery. It is therefore a process of creating the new and unique space, story, and history that are mine. Because of what is remembered, these signifiers of identity often resemble the matrix of lost homeland and recuperated memories. Because of what is forgotten along the way, those memories are also impregnated with new meanings.

I want to believe that through naming I am free to choose – but am I really? – to be the same as others in this new multicultural space or to be different. I want to believe that I do have a choice. The question is: how am I to use such a choice? Through what language should I express it? Should my choice be an expression of my memories about the past and my sense of belonging to the 'old country'? Should I approach this new (Canadian) space/place/territory/landscape in a different way, as an experience of a first kiss: new, unique, and detached from the past? Should I resort to my mother's tongue in naming my Canada, or should I use Latin to tell the story, and name the space *insula nova undecisimo die Junius nubibus revelata* (the new cloud-covered island discovered on June eleventh …)?

I live within the pieces of my native sound-castle, with a few memorabilia that are bound to wash away in time. I take refuge on this *insula nova* – in a home away from home, distanced from my own people and deprived of my own language. Of course, one could argue that my language remains with me wherever I go. Even Derrida said that monolingualism is our natural condition! Moreover, following Jacques Lacan's observation that 'no language can speak the truth about truth,' it would be naïve of me to believe that naming space, and appropriating it by imposing my memories of my ancestors, could endow me with anything but a temporary and unstable sense of ownership. If anything, history teaches us that naming space does not always guarantee the eternal existence of people and our memories of them, let alone provide safe harbours for our fragile identities. The different names that were given in different times to spaces, cities, and towns in central Europe and the Balkans remind us that appropriating space by naming it according to tribal, ethnic, national, or religious criteria produces a short lasting effect at best. Kolozsvar used to be Klausenberg, but now it is called Cluj Napoca. The town once known as Hermannstadt is now softly referred to by Romanians as Sibiu. What the Szeklers call Szekelyudvahely is to Romanians Odorheiu Sigishoara. What was once Roman Apulum becomes first Karlsburg and then Gulafehervar.[11] But what to do when the language we are born into becomes a tool of memory and not of everyday life? What to do when it becomes a linguistic burden, only useful as a reminder that 'true' life is (was) somewhere else? It is like carrying the bones of ancestors with me in a bag: they are white with silence. They do not talk back.

Frightened by the power of silence and the vastness of the Canadian space, I am trying to fill it up with names and voices from my past, and anchor myself within it, as if subconsciously trying to define my own thoughts and ideas about myself. Like an ant, I am rushing to reach the top of a shaky pyramid of grass and dirt with the hope that my effort to thicken its walls with the substance of memory will provide security and stability for my uncertain identities. While struggling to define my-self by the shape, size, height, and thickness of those walls, I am feeding a Janus-faced beast called commonality (tribal, ethnic, national, supra-national). At least for a short period of time, I become space and space becomes me, but all I am doing is endlessly naming and renaming my-self and anchoring my notion of belonging and home, deep inside an imaginary landscape of multiculturalism.

Like all emigrants, I also dream of remedying my longing for home by re-creating a collage of past lives in a space I remember as once being 'inhabited' by those lives, and now vacant. Such re-creation usually has no real bearing on my past life but is constructed out of hopes, imagin-ary relationships with space and its silence, and possesses many ele-ments of a fantasy. It resembles what Socrates called a divine madness.[12] Like Callimachus, the famous third-century BCE cataloguer of the an-cient Alexandrian library and the author of *Pinakes*, I am also nostalgic, since nostalgia is a longing for an ideal presence that is no longer and might never have been.[13] Such sentiments are expressions not only of loss but also of displacement. Moreover, it is a love affair with one's memory of past lives and a fantasy that is frozen in time. Our relation-ship to space/place is inherently personal. It is the art of naming – a subtle but nonetheless everlasting struggle between spaces and identi-ties, between our immediate environment and us – that defines this relationship. It is all about persistent appropriation coupled with our un-willingness to admit, or our inability to grasp, human ephemerality and the fact that we are only the percentage of the reckoning.[14]

This relationship consists of two major building blocks that differ somewhat from one another at the start of a journey. The difference could be defined as that of the difference in meaning between *my beloved landscape* and the *landscape of my beloved*. The former signifies notions of space in terms of geography (territory), which is being imagined (recognized) as mine alone and has symbolic and strategic value. This is a tale about a tree, its roots, and its branches. It is also a dream of the colours of (*my*) paradise; imagining a beautiful and ex-quisite female who shall, at the end, fall prey to one of the warring par-ties. The latter meaning is the projection of the idea (ideal) of home, belonging, and softness of women's skin, wrapped in a warm blanket of the memory of 'good old days.' In other words, it is a portrait of an imaginary geography of the soul and an effort to change the nature of time and materialize it, so that we could revisit the past much in the same manner we are able to walk through the old neighbuorhood once again.[15]

In the end, the differences evaporate and the two notions merge. I find myself stranded an ocean away from my Ithaca; away from *my beloved island* on which *my beloved* shall forever remain unreachable. Thus, the island becomes a symbol and a substitute for both a longing for space and for the intimacy of social poetics of a collective. Forever out of reach, the island is *my beloved landscape* and the *landscape of my beloved*. My relationship with it is a romance with all the twists and turns of a Hollywood blockbuster: love, affection, sensuality, betrayal, anger, revenge, regrets, blood, and tears. It is a tale of picking up scattered remnants of my former self and putting back together the puzzle of identity in a slightly different way. It is simultaneously an archaeology of belonging and the re-composition of being: the traces of past lives that are hastily glued together in order to fit as best as they could within the new imagined homeland.

NOTES

1 See Julia Creet's Introduction to this volume, pp. 6, 9–10.
2 See Charles Taylor, *Sources of the Self: The Making of the Modern Identity* (Cambridge: Harvard University Press, 1989). See also Amy Gutmann, ed., *Multiculturalism: Examining the Politics of Recognition* (Princeton: Princeton University Press, 1994).
3 Jan Assmann, *Moses the Egyptian: The Memory of Egypt in Western Monotheism* (Cambridge: Harvard University Press, 1997).
4 In November 2005 the Montenegrin Parliament passed a law that declassified a number of documents, allowing the public access to previously secret police files. Thanks to that law, I have learned about my file and the aforementioned note.
5 Jacques Derrida, *Monolingualism of the Other or the Prosthesis of Origin*, trans. Patrick Mensah (Stanford: Stanford University Press, 1998), 5.
6 Salman Rushdie, *Shame* (London: J. Cape, 1983).
7 Michael Ondaatje, 'Burning Hills,' in *The Cinnamon Peeler: Selected Poems* (London: Picador, 1989), 48.
8 See Amira Bojadzija-Dan's contribution to this volume, p. 204.

9 I have adopted Michel de Certeau's distinction between 'place' (point on a map, and the geographical location) and 'space' (inhabited, existential, or lived-in space). See Michel de Certeau, *The Practice of Everyday Life*, vol. 1 (Berkeley: University of California Press, 1984), 117.

10 Creet, Introduction, p. 9.

11 See Ken Smith's 'Hungarian Quartet,' in *Shed: Selected Poems* (London: Bloodaxe Books, 2002), 264–6. See also Srdja Pavlovic, 'My Beloved Landscape: Naming the Self in the Balkans,' in *Floodgates: Technologies, Cultural (Ex)Change and the Persistence of Place*, ed. Susan Ingram, Markus Reisenleitner, and Cornelia Szabó-Knotik (Vienna: Peter Lang, 2006), 123–32.

12 See Tomasz Mazur's contribution to this volume, p. 237.

13 Callimachus on nostalgia: 'I wept as I remembered how often you and I had tired the sun with talking and sent him down the sky' (Joseph Epstein, *Friendship* [New York: Mariner Books, 2007], 231). See also Svetlana Boym, Introduction, in *The Future of Nostalgia* (New York: Basic Books, 2001), xiv–xvi.

14 Modern-day alpinists often refer to climbing high mountain peaks as 'bagging the peak.' The doctor-recommended physical exercise for overcoming natural barriers in order to maintain a healthy lifestyle is therefore motivated by a thrill of conquering, and such effort is awarded not only with medals, a leaner body, and a desirable shape, but it is also followed by an overwhelming sense of the satisfaction of appropriation.

15 Srdja Pavlovic, *Iza Ogledala: Eseji o Identittetu i Politici Pripadnosti* (Podgorica: CID, 2001), 27.

3 Remigration and Lost Time: Resuming Life after the Holocaust

VERONIKA ZANGL

In looking over the various concepts of memory, it becomes apparent that these concepts often emerge as symptoms of a deep socio-political crisis. This is true for some of the most famous founding legends of memory, for instance, the discovery of the book Deuteronomy, as described in the Old Testament, or the story of the orator Simonides, as told by Cicero. Both legends tell the story of a catastrophe against the background of either a deep rupture of identity (Deuteronomy) or the violation of identity (Simonides). But ruptures not only shape concepts of memory. They also seem to bring about philosophical, aesthetical, or sociological explorations of memory. In this context, it is of interest that several contributions to the present volume refer to concepts of memory that evolved in a time of crisis. Tomasz Mazur, for instance, reflects on the concept of memory as framed by Socrates, a contemporary of the Peloponnesian War.[1] Zofia Rosińska refers in her article to Saint Augustine and his opus magnum *Confessions*, which does not primarily deal with Saint Augustine's personal crisis, but echoes first and foremost the crisis of the Roman Empire turning to Christianity.[2] John Sundholm mentions Maurice Halbwachs, who developed his concept of collective memory during the early 1920s, a time of far-reaching social and political change.[3] Taking these precedents into account, it is striking that the concept of memory only became a methodological or theoretical issue again in the 1970s. After 1945, a date that marks the end of a radical disruption of civilization, memory has been condensed in two seemingly simple phrases: 'Never forget!' and 'Remember!' After more than two decades of memory studies, these two commandments can be interpreted as early and consequent representations of Walter Benjamin's concept of shock in the moment of insight.[4] However, during the last sixty years these representations turned into icons of an impossible memory.

In this chapter, I will discuss the impact of the Holocaust on current concepts of memory. In her Introduction to this volume, Julia Creet states that 'movement is what produces memory.'[5] Starting from this notion, I would like to define movement and motion as categories that not only produce memory as an anthropological phenomenon but also shape the concept of memory, that is, the way we think about memory. I am interested in the question of why – besides its challenging and productive implications – migration has become a decisive condition of memory at the beginning of the twenty-first century. In several chapters of this volume, including the contributions by Chowra Makaremi and Zofia Rosińska, a static concept of memory is explicitly and critically linked with the concepts of the nation state and identity.[6] On the other hand, Zofia Rosińska questions not only the concept of memory but also the concept of migration in an increasingly globalized world. Yet, whenever memory is linked to migration as a social phenomenon, it becomes fragmented, ghettoized, neurotic and hysterical, no matter if it is about Turkish emigrants in France (Laurenn Guyot), German expellees in Canada (Andreas Kitzmann), a Rwandan asylum-seeker at the border detention centre of Roissy Airport in France (Chowra Makaremi), or a refugee from Uzbekistan in Sweden (Mona Lindqvist). Migration as a social phenomenon seems to freeze the motion of memory in a certain time and place, while the texts about these migrated memories reverberate like 'the long roll of thunder that follows' the lightning flashes of knowledge, as Walter Benjamin puts it in *The Arcades Project*.[7] This description applies especially to the contribution by Srdja Pavlovic, where emigration is worked through as social and aesthetic phenomenon[8] or, to quote Jill Bennett, 'is not so much *speaking of* but *speaking out of* a particular memory or experience.'[9] Migration in Pavlovic's text turns out to be an experience of enduring shock that struggles to become memory. Measuring the content of memory by the passage that memory takes, as Julia Creet argues in the Introduction, reveals the quality of memory as highly problematic, fractured, and precariously related to the world or reality. In this sense, memories of migration reflect perfectly the postmodern understanding of subjectivity and identity. By following John Sundholm's suggestion to 'downplay the epistemological problem of memory' and instead 'study effects of an absent event,'[10] I will read the concept of traumatic memory as effect of an absent event. Yet, in conjunction with the experience of the concentration and annihilation camps used under the rule of National Socialism, it is precisely the absent event that resists shifting or moving memory. My argument is that one of the manifestations of troubled memories is the 'loss of memory.'

Because I focus my analysis on the remigration of survivors of the Holocaust to their native country, it is first of all important to clarify whether the term 'remigration' is appropriate. After all, Marita Krauss explicitly states in her study on remigration to Germany after 1945: 'The return of Jews from concentration camps will not be discussed, since it would go beyond the scope of the issue of remigration.'[11] Yet, even though it would be downright unacceptable to equate the perse-cution and deportation of Jews during National Socialism with any form of emigration, I consider it reasonable to look at the return of sur-vivors in terms of the premises of remigration or repatriation. Firstly, this view implies the recognition of the remigrant as citizen, and there-fore the (primarily administrative) act of remigration or repatriation can be interpreted as one step in the recovery of individuation. That this administrative act more often than not has been experienced as re-enacted humiliation does not contradict the basic principle. It only shows the obstacles of a clinically administered nation state. Secondly, by focusing on what happened upon re-entry into an apparently famil-iar social world – which occasionally turns into the horror of a seem-ingly unchanged world – it is possible to shed light on the interaction between individual and collective or cultural memory. Finally, based on my analysis of works by Jean Améry[12] and Charlotte Delbo,[13] and by referring to sources of Jacques Presser's historical work *The Destruction of the Dutch Jews*,[14] I will discuss the question of why memory did not succeed in lending meaning to life 'afterwards.'

Amira Bojadzija-Dan analyses the narratives of sense memory in Charlotte Delbo's trilogy, *Auschwitz and After*, by focusing on the com-municative power of affects:

> Given that the art and literature cannot transmit meaning directly to the reader, or 'traumatize' by the way of representation, it is necessary that we examine the capacity of the literary text to communicate affect contained in the narratives of sense memory, which can be engaged with based on one's lived experience.[15]

The first two volumes of Charlotte Delbo's trilogy, which literally work through the experience of Auschwitz-Birkenau, are indeed constructed as narratives of sense memory. Yet, the third volume of her trilogy, entitled *The Measure of Our Days*, is based on interviews with survivors of the deportation train of 24 January 1943 from Romainville to Auschwitz-Birkenau, whom Delbo had contacted about twenty years after their liberation. In these conversations, sense memory is regularly a topic but hardly ever narrativized. A mainly reflective discourse encircles sense memory but at the same time is often poignantly vigilant not to give it a voice. Charlotte Delbo's conversation with Françoise, one of the former deportees, starts with the following statement: 'To start life over again, what an expression … If there is a thing you can't do over again, a thing you can't start over again, it is your life. You could erase and begin anew … Erase and cover with writing the words that were there before … It doesn't seem possible.'[16] Many Holocaust survivors counter this often uttered advice with the assertion that it is impossible to start life over again.

Imre Kertész not only refuses the advice to start life over again but unmasks this impossibility as a problem of language. 'The few who dared their existence in order to bear witness to the Holocaust knew exactly that the continuity of their life was shattered, that it was impossible for them to continue their life, if I may say so, in a way required by society, to articulate their experience in a pre-Auschwitz language.'[17] Kertész's answer to the experience of the Holocaust is the construction of an atonal language that does not even echo tonality. Kertész's atonal language does not mark a movement of memory or the displacement of memory, but repeats the 'unimagined reality'[18] of the Holocaust as a performative act. In a way, Françoise's question to those who apparently did succeed in continuing their life mirrors Kertész's concept of atonality: 'How did they do it, those who did it? Graft a new heart upon a bloodless one … Where do you find the blood you need to have that patched heart beat again?'[19] Even though Françoise uses strong body metaphors in order to express the impossibility not only of starting life over again but also of continuing life in a meaningful way, these metaphors contain no transmittable affect. First and foremost they express the fact of being trapped in memory. Françoise's description of trying to 'erase and cover with writing the words that were there before,' at first view, seems to directly relate only to the experience of the Holocaust, but as I will show later, it often includes the past before the Holocaust. In order to further analyse the possibility or impossibility of beginning life anew, I will first of all focus on the point of return.

1. Return

Jean Améry did not remigrate to Austria, his native country, after his liberation from Auschwitz, but instead to Belgium, the country he fled to in 1939. He starts his essay 'How Much Home Does a Person Need?' with this plain statement: 'Anyone who is familiar with exile has gained many an insight into life but has discovered that it holds even more questions. Among the answers there is the realization, which at first seems trivial, that there is no return, because the re-entrance into a place is never also a recovery of the lost time.'[20] Yet, not only is the space-time question opposed to the possibility of regaining Proust's lost time, it is first and foremost Améry's 'search of the time that was impossible to lose.'[21] Charlotte Delbo's conception of 'deep memory' and Améry's notion of 'time that was impossible to lose' break up concepts of memory based on rectilinear movements between past and future. In the same way, they disrupt the definition of memory as bridging the gap between the individual and the collective. Lawrence L. Langer, whose concept of 'deep memory' is based on Charlotte Delbo's reflections in her book *Days and Memory*, stresses the untenability of chronological time and elaborates the different qualities and characteristics of common memory and deep memory. In his essay 'Memory's Time,' he categorically states: '... there was an Auschwitz, and there was an afterward, and unless you understand that the two terms do not represent a chronology, you cannot begin to enter the abyss of the place we call Auschwitz.'[22]

Although 'time that was impossible to lose' determines practically all testimonies of Holocaust survivors, distinct differences from 'lost time' are recognizable, which show that although it is not possible to regain time, one might at least be able to reconstruct it. In short, the difference between 'time that was impossible to lose' and 'lost time' can be characterized by the difference between either staying captivated in an impossible memory or the ability to shift or even displace memory. With regard to 'time lost,' it is of importance to distinguish different preconditions of the return, such as the country that one returns to and the reasons for deportation. With a single exception, Charlotte Delbo's interlocutors are all former political prisoners. Even though the idea of return implies time and again a strong longing for a familiar social surrounding, these accounts repeatedly express the horror of an unchanged world, as for example in the case of Jacques:

Coming out of the station, I recognized one or two employees ... They were still here? That seemed strange indeed. It's difficult to express what I felt. I had hoped to find things and people as they'd been before my departure, and yet I was surprised because everything was the same. Surprised and off balance. It was strange to be the only one to have changed.[23]

The horror expressed in Jacques's account rests on the discrepancy between 'Inside' and 'Outside.' In a sense, this discrepancy refers to the fact that Jacques's experience has not yet turned into memory, has not yet moved from the individual to the community. In contrast, the unchanged outer world in the account by Gilberte, another survivor whom Delbo spoke to, becomes unbearable because it has lost its framework of reference due to the death of her sister, Dédée, in Auschwitz:

At home, everything was as I remembered it. Dédée's things here and there, her room, were all the same. Gradually, as the fog began to lift, objects reacquired their contours, usage, the traces of their past. Everything became sharp, threatening ... Where could I run, fade away so as not to be captured by the past, or go knocking against the walls, things, memories? At the same time, everything was unreal, as though deprived of consistency.[24]

In a way, Gilberte's account confirms Julia Creet's statement that 'memory is where we have arrived rather than where we have left,'[25] because it expresses the clash of an unchanged past, on the one hand, and the impossibility to experience time, on the other, divided by an unbearable loss. However, neither of their memories relates to experience as a category of life, or to reality understood as a socio-political category – with the effect that, as Gilberte observes, 'everything was unreal, as though deprived of consistency.' Therefore, it is possible to formulate the hypothesis that the motion of memory achieves an essential function in the process of relating meaning to private life and the reality normally associated with the public sphere.

While political prisoners still could expect an unchanged (or restored) world, because micro-structures and macro-structures of the community had not been completely destroyed, Jewish deportees expected to find themselves in a changed world. Jacques Presser states in his historical study *The Destruction of the Dutch Jews* (1965): 'Naturally, Jews realized that they would be returning to a changed Netherlands, but they could not foresee how different it would be. If they expected the world in general to show sorrow for the millions of innocent victims, to open its arms to the few Jewish survivors, they were soon to be cruelly disappointed.'[26] In the chapter 'Return,' he quotes a

Dutch Jewish woman who gave her account to the Netherlands Institute for War Documentation in 1950: 'The Netherlands, my native country, the country that I have loved so much. How did it oppress me to have to return there. How did I have to live on? My family destroyed, I myself a wreck, my family for the biggest part massacred. I didn't know.'[27] Subsequently, she expresses her impressions of Amsterdam after her return: 'I felt strange. I walked through streets, which were deserted; I walked through the Jewish quarter. Empty spaces where once stood houses, houses from which everything had disappeared; dismal houses with broken windows. They stared at me and I ran away.'[28]

In his epilogue to *The Destruction of the Dutch Jews*, Presser points out that there have been not only reservations but also open hostility towards Jewish repatriates and their legal claims in the Netherlands. Numerous articles, published as early as 1945, attest to the fact that the situation was not at all better in Germany. Eugen Kogon, who survived Buchenwald and in 1946 published his fundamental study *Der SS-Staat*, stated in April of that year:

> The shock-policy [of the Allied forces] has not inspired the power of German conscience, but the power of defence against the accusation of being jointly responsible for the infamous actions of the National Socialist without exception. The result is a fiasco ... Thus, it had come about, that I could meet people who cold-bloodedly uttered, it probably would have been better if all 'Kazettler' had perished. And that no reasonable man in Germany stays without spontaneous defensive reaction anymore – against us [the former prisoners of concentration camps], as soon as he hears the infamous sound 'KZ' ... Accounts from concentration camps elicit usually at most astonishment or a disbelieving shake of the head; they barely become a language of reason let alone the matter of disturbing sensation.[29]

Given such a hostile atmosphere towards remigration, Jean Améry's hypothetically formulated premise for a return to Germany seems downright utopian: 'The only therapy could have been history in practice. I mean the German revolution and with it the homeland's strongly expressed desire for our return. But the revolution did not take place, and our return was nothing but an embarrassment for our homeland, when finally the National Socialist power was crushed from without.'[30] Therefore, Améry's plain, and at the same time sober, answer to the question 'How Much Home Does a Person Need?' reads: 'It is not good, to have no home.'[31]

I would like to highlight two aspects of the concept of return: on the one hand, it is a question of the preconditions of social and political frameworks; on the other hand, testimonial accounts render this return to be, what Gilberte identifies as time and again, something 'unreal' or 'deprived of consistency.' I will further discuss this aspect along with the key terms 'imagination' and 'memory.'

2. Imagination

As I analyse in my study *Poetik nach dem Holocaust* (Poetics after the Holocaust), the radical undermining of the power of imagination occurs at central moments within the process of disintegration of the individual in concentration and annihilation camps.[32] Delbo elucidates the consequences of the destruction of the imaginative power in the second volume of her trilogy, *Useless Knowledge*:

> You may say that one can take away everything from a human being except the faculty of thinking and imagining. You have no idea … Imagination is the first luxury of a body receiving sufficient nourishment, enjoying a margin of free time, possessing the rudiments from which dreams are fashioned. People did not dream in Auschwitz, they were in a state of delirium.[33]

Hannah Arendt characterizes the power of imagination as a fundamental moment in the ability to create reality and, in a broader sense, as a precondition for the ability to relate to the world or public sphere. The unreal and, at the same time, radically real Reality of concentration and annihilation camps is ultimately due to the obliteration of the power of imagination by way of permanent terror and torture. Jean Améry states in his essay 'At the Mind's Limits':

> We emerged from the camp stripped, robbed, emptied out, disoriented – and it was a long time before we were able even to learn the ordinary language of freedom. Still today, incidentally, we speak it with discomfort and without real trust in its validity … For we brought with us the certainty that remains ever unshakable, that for the greatest part the intellect is a *ludus* and that we are nothing more – or, better said, before we entered the camp we were nothing more – than *homines ludentes*. With that we lost a good deal of arrogance, of metaphysical conceit, but also quite a bit of our naïve joy in the intellect and what we falsely imagined was the sense of life.[34]

In order to further analyse the discomfort that Améry is talking about, it is important to examine the relationship between the power of imagination and reality. In *Useless Knowledge*, Delbo describes the conditions of Raisko, a camp where the circumstances were better than in Birkenau: 'And suddenly, in the small camp, we were coming back to life, and everything was coming back to us.'[35] Yet, 'coming back to life' obviously does not include 'coming back to reality,' since for weeks and months after her liberation it is impossible for Delbo to perceive reality as true or at least as truthful:

> Everything was false, faces and books, everything showed me its falseness and I was in despair at having lost the faculty of dreaming, of harboring illusions; I was no longer open to imagination, or explanations. This is the part of me that died in Auschwitz. This is what turned me into a ghost ... How can one continue living in a world stripped of mystery?[36]

But, like Améry, Delbo reacquires the ordinary language of freedom – a language that does not in the first instance correspond to concepts of world or reality but rather to tangible everyday acts: 'With the utmost difficulty, the ultimate effort of my memory – but why speak of memory since I had none left? – an effort I cannot name, I tried to recall the gestures you must make in order to assume once again the shape of a living being in life. Walk, speak, answer questions, state where you want to go, go there. I had forgotten all this.'[37]

Consequently, what is the difference between 'coming back to life' and 'coming back to reality'? In this respect, I would like to consider Améry's notion of disorientation as a crucial term that is distinguished – and here, I argue with Hannah Arendt – by the superimposition of reality and truth. The 'time that cannot be lost' that characterizes the experience of the Holocaust is on a broad scale based on the impossibility of transcending the unreal reality by means of the power of imagination. But Delbo mentions that it was occasionally – depending on the circumstances – possible to 'come back to life.' At such times, in the midst of this unreality and inhumanity, a deeply human atmosphere emerged that Hannah Arendt analyses as a characteristic of pariah people. This kind of humanity, as elaborated by Arendt in her essay 'On Humanity in Dark Times,'[38] 'is the great privilege of pariah peoples; it is the advantage that the pariahs of this world always and in all circumstances can have over others. The privilege is dearly bought; it is often accompanied by so radical a loss of the world, so fearful an atrophy of all the organs with which we respond to it.'[39] This kind of humanity – 'a joy in the simple fact of being alive'[40] – finds an expression in Delbo's interview with Gilberte, who recapitulates about the time in the camps: 'As soon as I found myself among you, I was comforted, reassured, warmed. I remember it as one of the most powerfully joyful moments of my life ... I had dreamt of freedom throughout deportation. Was this freedom, this intolerable solitude, this room, this fatigue?'[41] The problem resulting from this radical experience is that it acquires the signification of an absolute truth and that it subsequently is superimposed on the perception of reality. Yet Arendt notes: 'The humanity of the insulted and injured has never yet survived the hour of liberation by so much as a minute. This does not mean that it is insignificant, for in fact it makes insult and injury endurable; but it does mean that in political terms it is absolutely irrelevant.'[42] But the ordinary language of freedom, at least as Améry conceptualizes it, not only implies 'taking up life,' but also 'coming back to reality.' Of course, it would be an inadequate shift of cause to explain the discomfort Améry is talking about – and he definitely also refers to reality and the public sphere – solely by the superimposition of truth and reality concerning Holocaust survivors. Améry diagnoses, not without good reason, the need for therapy with respect to the historical process. Nor does Arendt use the term 'disorientation' with regard to the individual. Instead she analyses 'disorientation' as a fundamental socio-political consequence of National Socialist policies. In her essay 'The Aftermath of Nazi Rule,' Arendt sheds light on the fact that the Nazis not only falsified reality – in that case, it would still have been possible to distinguish truth from lies. Arendt argues that the devastating consequences of National Socialist policies are, on the contrary, due to 'their consistent denial of the importance of facts in general: all facts can be changed and all lies can be made true.'[43] In this sense, disorientation with respect to the public sphere can be attributed to the inability to distinguish between truth and lies. Even though Kogon acknowledges that the Germans were perfectly able to recognize Nazi propaganda as lies, he attributes the repudiating response of many Germans to the Allied education program to their turning-away from Goebbels's propaganda machinery.[44] But then 'turning-away' does not imply an inability to differentiate between truth and lies, but rather indifference regarding truth and lies. It is precisely this indifference that Arendt recognized when she visited Germany in 1950:

And the indifference with which they walk through the rubble has its exact counterpart in the absence of mourning for the dead, or in the apathy with which they react, or, rather, fail to react, to the fate of the refugees in their midst. This general lack of emotion, at any rate this apparent heartlessness, sometimes covered over with cheap sentimentality, is only the most conspicuous outward symptom of a deep-rooted, stubborn, and at times vicious refusal to face and come to terms with what really happened.[45]

Germans' disorientation and indifference seem to be the core obstacles to setting memory in motion, whereas survivors of concentration and annihilation camps stay trapped in their memories by way of superimposing truth and a radically real reality. If the reality of concentration and annihilation camps is equated with absolute truth, it is impossible to negotiate or transcend any kind of reality under the premise of truth or truthfulness after the Holocaust. Both phenomena – disorientation and being trapped in memory – are due to either the lack of power of imagination or the radical undermining of the imagination.

3. Memory

If the motion or migration of memory achieves an essential function in the process of relating meaning to life or reality, it might be of interest to ask what Jean Améry precisely means by coming out of the camp, 'stripped, robbed, emptied out' – after all, he signifies the loss with something of 'what we falsely imagined was the sense of life.'[46] To be sure, Améry refers in his statement to the intellect and to metaphysics, but intellect and metaphysics nevertheless can provide a framework for memory. I would like to draw attention to the fact that Jean Améry's statement relates to the time before the Holocaust. But losing the framework of memory, or as Améry formulates it, 'our naïve joy in the intellect,' not only implies the impossibility of shifting the pre-war-memory to the present, but it also means there is no framework in the present that could function as a carrier of memory. Moreover, it is relevant that besides the framework of memory, the faculty of memory itself seems to have been at stake after the experience of the Holocaust. Jacques Presser quotes in his historical study *The Destruction of the Dutch Jews* a Jewish woman who, on her way back to the Netherlands in 1945, writes: 'The past is burned away and thoughts of the future fulfill us with anxiety and fear. We shall never really "return," never shall we be part of the "others" again.'[47] Similarly, Charlotte Delbo's friend Mado sums up the effects on memory, first by expressing an important function of memory that is repeatedly mentioned in accounts of Holocaust survivors:

Over there we had our entire past, all our memories, even memories from long ago passed on by our parents. We armed ourselves with this past for protection, erecting it between horror and us in order to stay whole, keep our true selves, our being. We kept on dipping into our past, our child-hood, into whatever formed our personality, our character, tastes, ideas, so we might recognize ourselves, preserve something of what we were, not letting this situation dent us, annihilate us ... Each one of us recounted her life thousands and thousands of times, resurrecting her childhood, the time of freedom and happiness, just to make sure all this had existed, and that the teller was both subject and object. Our past was our lifeline and reassurance. But since I came back, everything I was before, all my memories from that earlier time, have dissolved, come undone. It is as though my past had been used up over there. Nothing remains of what was before ... Today, my memories, my past are over there. When I project my thoughts backward they never overstep these bounds.[48]

In the course of this detailed self-analysis by Mado, the experience in the various concentration and annihilation camps becomes an absolute point of reference after the liberation. Nevertheless, I would like to raise the question of whether 'burned away,' 'emptied out,' and 'used up' can only be resolved on an individual level. Why does the past lose its validity at the turning points of liberation and return? And why does the loss of memory become evident at these points?

Even though 'the loss of memory' is definitely linked to the experi-ence of the Holocaust in the accounts mentioned above, it is still im-portant that a great many traditions and concepts within the public sphere had already been in a state of erosion before the Second World War. As Hannah Arendt expressed it in her acceptance speech to the Free City of Hamburg when she was given the Lessing Prize, the 'pil-lars of the best-known truths'[49] had already been shaken in Lessing's time. In this case, 'memory' plays a central role for it illuminates col-lective frameworks that still might be valid enough to continue. There-fore, after the war it was not possible to simply continue traditions or concepts of the public sphere. Even if this was attempted, as it was in Germany or Austria, it left an escapist and ghostly atmosphere.[50] There-fore, the question that should be asked is which social and political frameworks were available after the Second World War, or rather which frameworks of reference emerged after the war to inscribe the experi-ence of the Holocaust? Thus, the point is not to 'erase and cover with writing the words that were there before,' but rather to 'write new words,' or to write, like Imre Kertész, in a different, atonal language. That does not mean there have not been any endeavours to face 'what really happened,' as Arendt demands in her essay 'The Aftermath of Nazi Rule.'[51] Theodor W. Adorno, Max Horkheimer, Karl Jaspers, and Günther Anders each devoted their work to the task of finding an appropriate way to deal with the Holocaust. But at least during the first years after the war, hardly anyone put these questions to the survivors – and I am referring to Homer's Odyssey: 'Who are you, what have you suffered, why are you crying?' Instead there were feverish, but nonetheless valuable, endeavours to administrate and document the immense movements of refugees all over Europe. Of course, these activities did not always meet the expectations of survivors. A notable example can be found in Jacques Presser's epilogue to *The Destruction of the Dutch Jews*, where he quotes a survivor-witness as follows: 'The years after 1945 really finished me ... Above all, there was the trouble with the authorities. Where I would have expected sympathy, I met the curt, non-committal, forbidding amorphous mass that goes by the name of officialdom. I can only say that these years were a real nightmare.'[52]

Interestingly enough, the somewhat ironic notion at the end of this statement is omitted in the American translation. The witness actually remarks: 'I can only say that these years were a real nightmare, but without adventure.'[53] Even if there are probably not many Holocaust survivors who would like to characterize their suffering as an adventure, I would like to draw attention to the fact that by leaving this unusual remark out, one also omits the possibility of 'arriving' or of the 'emerging of something new' – connotations that are clearly inscribed by the English term 'adventure.' At this point, I would like to pick up the vital advice of Julia Creet to consider the idea of the palimpsest,[54] because it allows for the reformulation of Françoise's phrase 'erase and cover with writing the words that were there before' into 'recreate those words which have been erased.' The metaphor of the palimpsest provides a material framework for the search for different layers of words and memory of 'new' text written on an old one. This metaphor also gives space to different languages or shifts of memories, that is, the concept of intervention that Adorno elaborated, or the concept of an atonal language that Kertész conceptualized. However, in using this metaphor, one also has to take the risk that the letters may prove to be a *mene tekel*, as Imre Kertész descibes: 'I am the black page in the book of triumphs on which the script does not come through, not Jew, but all-embracing human denial, the *mene tekel* on the wall of total oppression.'[55] However, my analysis aims to elucidate that it takes more than an individual or even a prophet to decipher these words and to live with their consequences, in order to shift memory.

NOTES

1 See Tomasz Mazur's contribution to this volume.
2 See Zofia Rosińska's contribution to this volume.
3 See John Sundholm's contribution to this volume.
4 Walter Benjamin, *The Arcades Project*, ed. Roy Tiedemann, trans. Howard Eiland and Kevin McLaughlin (Cambridge: Harvard University Press, 1997), 457.
5 See Julia Creet's Introduction to this volume, p. 9.
6 See Chowra Makaremi's contribution to this volume.
7 Benjamin, *Arcades Project*, 457.
8 See Srdja Pavlovic's contribution to this volume.
9 Jill Bennett, 'The Aesthetics of Sense-Memory: Theorising Trauma through the Visual Arts,' in *Trauma und Erinnerung / Trauma and Memory: Cross-Cultural Perspectives*, ed. Franz Kaltenbeck and Peter Weibel (Wien: Passagen, 2000), 87. See also Amira Bojadzija-Dan's contribution to this volume.
10 Sundholm, p. 129.
11 Marita Kraus, *Heimkehr in ein fremdes Land: Geschichte der Remigration nach 1945* (München: Beck, 2001), 127. [Die Rückkehr von Juden aus den Konzentrationslagern soll hier nicht thematisiert werden, da sie den Rahmen des Remigrationsthemas sprengen würde.]
12 Jean Améry, *At the Mind's Limits: Contemplations by a Survivor on Auschwitz and Its Realities* (Bloomington and Indianapolis: Indiana University Press, 1980).
13 Charlotte Delbo, *Auschwitz and After*, trans. Rosette C. Lamont (Vol. 1, *None of Us Will Return*; Vol. 2, *Useless Knowledge*; Vol. 3, *The Measure of Our Days*) (New Haven: Yale University Press, 1995).
14 Jacques Presser, *The Destruction of the Dutch Jews*, trans. Arnold Pomeroms (New York: E.P. Dutton & Co., 1969).
15 Bojadzija-Dan, p. 197.
16 Delbo, *Auschwitz and After*, 348.
17 Imre Kertész, 'Die exilierte Sprache,' in *Die exilierte Sprached: Essays und Reden* (Frankfurt am Main: Suhrkamp, 2003), 212. [Die wenigen, die ihre Existenz daransetzten, Zeugnis vom Holocaust zu geben, wußten genau,

daß die Kontinuität ihres Lebens zerbrochen war, daß es für sie unmöglich war, ihr Leben, wenn ich so sagen darf, in der für sie gesellschaftlich gebotenen Weise fortzusetzen, ihre Erfahrungen in der Vor-Auschwitz-Sprache zu formulieren.]
18 See Lionel Richard, 'Auschwitz und kein Ende,'in *Kunst und Literatur nach Auschwitz*, ed. Manuel Köppen (Berlin: Erich Schmidt, 1993), 27.
19 Delbo, *Auschwitz and After*, 348.
20 Améry, *At the Mind's Limits*, 42.
21 Ibid., xiii.
22 Lawrence L. Langer, 'Memory's Time: Chronology and Duration in Holocaust Testimonies,' in *Admitting the Holocaust: Collected Essays* (New York: Oxford University Press 1995), 18; see also Lawrence L. Langer, *Holocaust Testimonies: The Ruins of Memory* (New Haven: Yale University Press, 1991).
23 Delbo, *Auschwitz and After*, 318. See also Saul Friedländer, 'Trauma and Transference,' in *Memory, History, and the Extermination of the Jews of Europe* (Bloomington and Indianapolis: Indiana University Press, 1993), 117–37.
24 Delbo, *Auschwitz and After*, 252.
25 Creet, Introduction, p. 6.
26 Presser, *Destruction of the Dutch Jews*, 544.
27 The Dutch version of Presser's study contains a chapter, 'Return,' which interestingly enough is not part of the American translation. Therefore, I quote from the Dutch version, *Ondergang: De vervolging en verdelging van het Nederlandse Jodendom, 1940–1945* ('s-Gravenhage: Staatsuitgeverij, 1965), 501. [Nederland, mijn geboorteland, het land, waar ik zoveel van gehouden heb. Hoe benauwde het mij om daar terug the keren. Hoe moest ik verder leven? Mijn gezin verwoest, ik zelf nog een wrak, mijn familie voor een groot deel uitgemoord. Ik wist het niet.]
28 Ibid., 501. [Het was mij vreemd te moede. Ik liep door straten, die uitgestorven waren; ik liep door de Jodenhoek. Lege ruimten waar eens huizen hadden gestaan, huizen waaruit alles verdwenen was; grauwe huizen met stukkende ruiten. Zij gaapten mij aan en ik vluchtte weg.]
29 Eugen Kogon, 'Gericht und Gewissen,' *Frankfurter Hefte: Zeitschrift für Kultur und Politik* 1, no. 1 (April 1946): 28–31. [Die Schock-Politik hat nicht die Kräfte des deutschen Gewissens geweckt, sondern die Kräfte der Abwehr gegen die Beschuldigung, für die nationalsozialistischen Schandtaten in Bausch und Bogen mitverantwortlich zu sein. Das Ergebnis ist ein Fiasko … So ist es also gekommen, daß ich Leuten begegnen konnte, die kaltblütig meinten, es wäre wohl besser gewesen, wenn alle, Kazettler' zugrundegegangen wären. Und daß kein vernünftiger Mensch mehr in

Deutschland ohne spontane Abwehrreaktion – gegen uns bleibt, wenn er
den berüchtigten Klang KZ hört … Berichte aus den Konzentrationslagern
erwecken in der Regel höchstens Staunen oder ungläubiges Kopfschütteln;
sie werden kaum zu einer Sprache des Verstandes, geschweige denn zum
Gegenstand aufwühlenden Empfindens.]

30 Améry, *At the Mind's Limits*, 51.

31 Ibid., 101.

32 See Veronika Zangl, *Poetik nach dem Holocaust. Erinnerungen – Tatsachen
    – Geschichten* (München: Fink, 2009).

33 Delbo, *Auschwitz and After*, 168.

34 Améry, *At the Mind's Limits*, 20.

35 Delbo, *Auschwitz and After*, 168.

36 Ibid., 239.

37 Ibid., 236.

38 Hannah Arendt, *Men in Dark Times* (London: J. Cape, 1970), 3–31.

39 Ibid., 13.

40 Ibid.

41 Delbo, *Auschwitz and After*, 243.

42 Arendt, *Men in Dark Times*, 16.

43 Hannah Arendt, *Essays in Understanding, 1930–1954: Formation, Exile, and
    Totalitarianism* (New York: Schocken Books, 1994), 252.

44 See Kogon, 'Gericht und Gewissen,' 29.

45 Hannah Arendt, *Essays in Understanding*, 249.

46 Améry, *At the Mind's Limits*, 20.

47 Presser, *Ondergang*, 500. [Het verleden is weggebrand en de gedachten aan
    de toekomst vervullen ons met zorg en angst. Nooit zullen wij werkelijk
    'terugkeren,' nooit zullen wij weer behoren bij de 'anderen.']

48 Delbo, *Auschwitz and After*, 258.

49 Arendt, *Men in Dark Times*, 10.

50 See Arendt, *Essays in Understanding*, 249.

51 Ibid., 249.

52 Presser, *Destruction of the Dutch Jews*, 541.

53 Presser, *Ondergang*, 512. [Ik kan u zeggen, dat deze jaren voor mij een
    verschrikking waren, maar zonder avontuur.]

54 Julia Creet, personal communication.

55 Imre Kertész, *Galeerentagebuch* (Galley Boat-Log) (Reinbek: Rowohlt, 1993),
    55 (my translation; the page number refers to the German edition).

4 The Waiting Zone

CHOWRA MAKAREMI

A sentence uttered makes a world appear
Where all things happen as it says they do;
We doubt the speaker, not the words we hear;
Words have no words for words that are not true.
                              – W.H. Auden, 'Words'[1]

Ghislaine K. is one of the twenty thousand undocumented aliens who are held each year in the detention centre of Roissy Airport in France, in what is called the 'waiting zone' or 'Zapi 3.' She has been put in room number 56, at the end of the corridor. She will be deported back to Congo-Brazzaville – from whence she came – three days after her arrival.

1. Giving an Account of Oneself

I met Ghislaine K. while I was doing a field study in the waiting zone while working as a legal assistant. In May 2004 she was 'controlled' upon her arrival at Roissy Airport and considered 'non-admitted' to French territory. She passed through the border control with family reunification documents forged by smugglers, who had also provided her with a fake passport and a plane ticket. Checking her family re-unification documents, guards in the border control division contacted the man in France who, according to Ghislaine, was her father. The man denied any family link. It then became clear that she had taken advantage of the family reunification process[2] to enter French territory illegally. Ghislaine was interviewed for a long time in the police offices located in the airport terminal. As do many detainees, she kept a vivid memory of this first interview in the police office. She described the initial stage of her trajectory in the waiting zone as a time of anxiety and great humiliation, remembering the annoyed and violent behaviour of the border control agents who rushed her, their irritation when they accused her of being a liar, and how they laughed at her and fiercely accused her of 'taking them for fools.' Ghislaine was then transferred to a cell where eight other people were already being held. She waited there in a room of four square metres, with no window or ventilation, cement walls, and a cement floor on which she and her fellow detainees sat. Those who were not deported within the first six hours following their detainment were transferred to the detention centre located two kilometres away from the airport, a facility with direct access to the runways. The centre is a modern rectangular two-storey building that looks like other buildings in the industrial area, except for the fact that it has a barbed-wire fence, wire-netting four metres high, and surveillance cameras. It can hold 160 people. Inside, the concrete walls are painted in white, yellow, and orange. There are two TV rooms, a garden with a view of the runway, games for the children, and a cafeteria.

As she was being transferred within the waiting zone, Ghislaine met with an officer from the Interior Ministry who asked her to explain her fraud. After this meeting, a request for asylum was registered. Later, Ghislaine was called over the intercom – which regulates detainee life in the centre – and asked to go down to the interview rooms with her police papers. Ghislaine became frightened and locked herself in her room. After several calls, police officers came up to look for her and finally brought her down. However, Ghislaine did not know that the interview she was having was about her asylum application. During the interview, she refused to speak. Although the officer in charge of examining asylum requests invited her several times to 'tell him the truth,' Ghislaine kept on telling the family reunification story her smugglers had taught her. A few hours later, she was notified that her request for asylum was considered 'manifestly unfounded' and had been refused, and that her expulsion was scheduled for the next flight to Congo-Brazzaville. The missed connections between the detainee and the authorities in charge of her asylum request play out an untold narrative which reveals the real issue surrounding the request:

GHISLAINE: I come from far away (*silence*). I come from far away (*silence*).
   I come from far away …
MAKAREMI: The officer did not want to hear you?

G: Yes. I told him, 'Okay, I will tell you everything,' but he threw me out. He said, 'Now it's enough, you are lying anyway, you take us for fools.' They did not want to hear my voice anymore.

M: What did you want to tell them?

G: Well, it's very difficult. At home we were a lot of girls, it was very difficult. My father, he took a new wife, and my stepmother did not want to see us anymore. We couldn't study anymore. I got married young; and I followed my husband to Rwanda.

M: To Rwanda?

G: Yes, my husband was from Rwanda. We went and settled in his village there. I didn't see my father anymore, he didn't even want to talk to us anymore. He died, but I only found out later. Well, one day they came to the village and everyone told you: you must leave now. You knew that they took the people and killed everybody, everybody. I was at home and I left immediately. My husband, I don't know where he was, they killed him, but I managed to leave. Well, we walked a lot. I was with neighbours, and we left, we walked and walked. We had to jump over the dead, so we put on bandanas, you know, pieces of tissue in the nose because of the smell of cadavers. I went back home.

M: To Brazzaville?

G: No, not to Brazzaville, I had no one left there anymore. I was alone, my husband wasn't there anymore, nor my son.

M: You have a son?

G: Yes.

M: And where is he now?

G: I don't know … he's fourteen. When they came to the village, my son, he was playing with his friends, and then I don't know.

M: You don't know what happened to him?

G: No, when they arrived I left immediately, everybody told you to leave. My son was in the village with his friends, he was outside, I don't know what happened to him, I left confused … I left for the Congo, but there again there was a war you know. With hope, I had the Lord. The Lord is good, He sees everything … I pray to the Lord, and for them, the police, I pray for the Lord too. I stood in a church at home, I slept in the church, I cleaned the church and they gave me money. You know, … I have God. And when they [the officers in Zapi] treat me as if I was nothing … they don't know my value but God knows my value.

At this point our interview was interrupted by a judicial assistant from the Anafé, the Migrants' Rights Defence NGO working in the waiting zone. The judicial assistant volunteer had worked before for the International Penal Court in Rwanda and had spent several months in the country. She told me Ghislaine was Rwandan. I asked Ghislaine and she admitted the fact: she was a Tutsi from Congo, of Rwandan citizenship. She had not wanted to reveal her true citizenship because the smugglers had advised her to keep her identity hidden. Moreover, after her past experiences in the Congo, Ghislaine was convinced that if she was known as a Rwandan, she would immediately become undesirable to the French authorities. While she knew that refugees from Rwanda and Tutsi minorities suffer from segregation in the Congo, she was unaware that the French administration employs an affirmative action policy in favour of asylum seekers from Rwanda. However, Ghislaine's narrative did not reach those in charge of administrating her claim.[3] She was deported back within the following days.

In the waiting zone, the personal narrative of Ghislaine K. – somehow dislocating the linear coherence of her autobiography – and the story that it tells are disconnected from her administrative file, which looks like a typical case of an illegal migrant abusing the family reunification system through smuggling networks. How has this situation been produced? What do these significant discrepancies teach us about the apparatus of border detention? The experiences of Ghislaine K., like those of many other asylum seekers facing deportation, invite us to consider issues of memory and migration within the national and political framework of controlling borders and mobility, which has been the dominant migration policy in Western democracies in the last thirty years. The present chapter will explore how memory is embedded in the power relations that shape migration control, relations built from issues of narration, 'mis/trust,' and identification.

2. Migration, Narration, Control

The waiting zone is an extra-territorial zone of detention, where undocumented aliens are held from a few hours to several weeks while they await decisions on their entry to a given territory or recognition of their refugee status. In response to security concerns – and the tension between the movement of human capital and the will of Western welfare states to control migration at their borders – new control devices have emerged in the European Union in the last twenty years.[4] The camp of 'Zapi 3,' in which I conducted field research in 2004, 2005, and 2007, is the heart of a system of alien deportation at the border, based on a persistent consensus in matters of immigration in the global North that is best summed up by the famous French expression: 'We cannot welcome all the misery of the world.'[5] The waiting zone is part of a wider policy across the EU, which consists, on the one hand, of ever-stricter control of illegal flows of migration deployed as an electoral matrix of migration policies, and, on the other hand, a shift from reception to control structures, from control to detention – and to a denial of basic rights where the real 'borders' of our democracies are being drawn.[6] The waiting zones are the result of legal evolutions in modern rules of law, technical adjustment in the disciplinary management of alien populations, and evolutions in the political speech about migration, which is now commonly referred to in terms of a control of 'stocks and flows.'[7]

In France, the Interior Ministry applies the sovereign prerogative of the state over its borders, and complies with EU migration policies through a set of material facilities, administrative procedures, and legal provisions that organize a system of deportation in real-time at the country's borders. However, this deportation policy is restricted by international law and the general presumption to a right of asylum, to which the French state is obligated as contractor of the Geneva Convention (1951). Undocumented aliens registered as asylum seekers at the borders cannot be deported back before their claim is reviewed. In this context, the asylum procedure is a key issue in border detention, as the site where the power of the state has a grasp over refugees who still remain 'outside' – within an exceptional space beyond the normal national legal and administrative frameworks – by making them enter specific administrative classifications and identification processes. At the heart of this decisive moment lie refugees' personal narratives, while their oral audition for state agents is the actual basis of the procedure.[8] The conditions of the possibility of migration are thus being negotiated in this space of power and language where the 'hosting' national community is being redefined – literally, through a process of filtering and exclusion of those who do not belong, and figuratively, through the affirmation of the rationality and the moral values on which national identity stands, such as democratic assistance or protection of the welfare system against abuses and 'fakes.' For those experiencing this exclusionary relationship at the border, issues of control and resistance adhere to the critical work of 'giving an account of oneself,'[9] of putting one's memory into words. However, this narration is itself determined by a refugee's immediate situation and the administrative context of the border detention procedure. Here, the issue of memory is double-sided. On the one hand stand the narrations drawn from – or not, as a result of mistrust – the personal memory of the migrant: the structure and formulation of these narratives anchor their cultural, social, and psychic condition, including their experiences of border detention. On the other hand, these narrations of memories evoked by border discourses have to confront, fit, avoid, and decode a national memory belonging to the 'hosting' country, which is at play in practices and power relations that institute the administrative world of border control and 'production of indifference' towards those subjected to it.[10]

3. Mis/trust

To understand the mechanism of the denial of personal narrative, we first have to place it in context: the administration of asylum in border detention. At the border, the encounter between the rationality of control bureaucracies and the migrant's world relies on the notion of trust, or rather mistrust. Valentine Daniel and John Knudsen have opened a critical path to an anthropological outlook on (forced)-migration by putting in perspective the existential experience of disruption that operates within the techniques of movement control and restrictive policies of asylum in the West.[11] This anthropological outlook synthesizes the experience of refugee-ness as a 'process of the breakdown of trust' in which 'the refugee mistrusts and is mistrusted.'[12] This sense of mis/trust is the one that appears spontaneously in Ghislaine's narration about her detention. The power relation between state agents and migrants, within the process of refugee determination, is based on an exercise of mutual mis/trust about the identity of the detainees, their stories, and their origins. However, Daniel and Knudsen use the word in a given meaning, opening the double-sided experience of disruption and of control to another level of understanding: 'By trust we do not intend a largely conscious state of awareness, something akin to belief, but rather its opposite ... what Martin Heidegger called "being-in-the-world."'[13] It is the breakdown of this familiar way of *being-in-the-world* that Ghislaine experiences in the waiting zone, when she locks herself in her room in fear of being tortured after she is called for her asylum interview – not knowing that it is her only chance of negotiating a way out of the zone.

The trajectory of detainees at the border is, most of the time, beyond their understanding, stuck as they are between the urgency of administrative decisions and the indefinite time of the waiting. The first denial which Ghislaine experienced is the denial of information. Lack of information is what creates the atmosphere of psychological insecurity in this centre, where the windows have no handles. The practice of detention institutes the border control through physical isolation of the person, which is characterized by difficulty in communicating with the outside world, and intensified by the absence of information within the centre. When information is actually provided, it is in a language that detainees do not speak. Detainees do not know what their judicial status is, nor their rights and their fate. Often, they are driven to the court without being notified of the high stakes of their audience; what the appointed lawyer says in their defence is not translated to them. In the waiting zone, they have no clue of where they are being transferred under escort (up to several times a day), and thus live in the constant fear of being driven to the plane and expelled by force. These factors of insecurity and worry make the relationships between detainees and state agents difficult. This is mainly the framework in which the chaotic trajectory of Ghislaine, who came with falsified family reunification documents and was finally registered as an asylum seeker, took place.

Such a degree of incomprehension and ignorance about the French political and administrative systems can create deep psychic distress for the refugees. This is somehow acknowledged by the anti-suicide measures in the facilities: no plastic bags for garbage, no plastic knives or forks, no razors (the Red Cross humanitarian mission is in charge of shaving the detainees). The security measures are the same as in jails, and the prison environment manifests in the specific relations to time and space.

The exile experiences transit and detention at the same time, trapped in time they do not control between long periods of empty waiting, which form the everyday life of border detention, and the urgency of hearings and proceedings that set the rhythms for their administrative lives. The decision to authorize or refuse asylum seekers entry to the country is rendered by an officer from the French Office for the Protection of Refugees and Stateless People (OFPRA),[14] after a hearing for the asylum seeker. The hearing takes place in a closed room, face-to-face between the state agent and the detainee. One of the consequences of this practice is that the state proceeds directly, without mediation, in a condensed time and space. Ghislaine's reaction of fear and resistance towards this bureaucratic system reveals the force of an encounter that, in such proximity, is almost a direct physical confrontation between the state – its essential territorial sovereignty affronted – and the alien who is considered responsible for this infraction. A characteristic of the asylum process at the border is the time pressure that relates to the urgency of real-time management of human flows. Observation shows that asylum seekers who arrived at the airport at 10:00 a.m. were transferred to the holding centre by 2:00 p.m., had a hearing with the OFPRA officer by 4:30 p.m., were notified of refusal on the following day – and finally deported back by the evening. Time and urgency superimpose themselves on a fragmented space, where proximity is intensified at all levels. As Denis Salas – a magistrate working in the court division in charge of undocumented aliens – highlights, the hearings with the civil liberties magistrate in charge of watching and extending the administrative detention after seventy-two hours, take place in haste and material proximity, which results in suppressing the symbolic power of justice.[15] The same contiguity applies to administrative hearings, in the offices of the police, the Interior Ministry, as well as the OFPRA, which are entirely compartmentalized areas in the holding centre. The fragmented space suppresses distance. But the devices of space and time also enclose the administration of asylum: on the one hand, it crushes subjective elements, such as the individual narrative, which is supposed to be the very basis for the judgment; on the other hand, it muzzles the proceedings' dysfunctions that could surface in an integrated process.

Migrants at the border are in a moment of exile, which is 'a vacuum form of existence,'[16] with no references, no criteria of definition, nor models of identification: they exist without having any official existence. Border detention is a space of suspicion about one's name and identity, where the alien is no longer himself, identical and identifiable. Ghislaine, who came to France with a fake passport, exists in the waiting zone under a fake name and a fake nationality. This is why the administrative lists of detainees in the holding centre lack clear personal names, and registered her as: 'Ms. K ... alias W ... or X1.' Then, the question is: How is one's identity transformed at the instant when one becomes X1, a 'human being in general ... and different in general, representing nothing but his own absolutely unique individuality which, deprived of expression within an action upon a common world, looses all significance'?[17]

In terms of administrative practice, as well as subjective experience, this 'vacuum form of existence' involves issues of anonymity and identity. Or rather, it mixes the multiple losses of identification that

configure the aporias of border detention: the inability for the administration to identify the detainee and the inability for the detainee to
identify the world he is dwelling in. Mis/trust becomes a complex and
double-sided process in this situation, which brings about a 'crisis of
the presence,'[18] where notions such as the familiar, the identical, the
identifiable lose meaning, opening the path to radical political forms
of life. In his ethnographic study of ritual dances in southern Italy,
Ernesto de Martino documents a psychic and cultural process of blurring of the self under socio-political situations of domination in which
he refers to the danger of 'not being there anymore' versus the evidence of being there as a presence identical to oneself.[19] What de
Martino identifies as a 'crisis of the presence,' which offers clues for
exploring further the process of a 'radical disjunction between ... familiar *way-of-being* in the world and a new reality of the socio-political
circumstances,'[20] also acquires a second meaning in border detention.
It introduces us to the desubjectifying practice of deportation – another crisis of the presence – in which unwanted asylum seekers are
transported as a pack, with their hands and feet bound together and
their mouths taped shut. This violence, which is the horizon of border
detention, is a decisive form of mistrust: the last step in 'radical disjunction.' It is a lack of trust that expels the detainee from the space of
language and negotiation, entailing the process that changes him into
a body, without legal or political status, that must be taken care of and
eventually deported. G: '... he threw me out. He said, "Now it's
enough, you are lying anyway, you take us for fools." They did not
want to hear my voice anymore.'

4. Subjects at the Margins

Facing several interviews, either Ghislaine maintained her version of
family reunification, which was revealed to be fake upon first check,
or she kept quiet. However, she also asked twice to be heard, showing
the desire to 'tell everything' about her situation, in vain. First, at the
very end of her interview with the Interior Ministry agent, she changed
her mind and told the officer that she was ready to tell him 'all the
truth.' But her hearing was over and her interlocutor asked her to
leave the office. After she received her notification of refusal, once
again, Ghislaine asked to be heard, as she was now willing to deliver
the true version of her story; this request was left unanswered.
Ghislaine had the strong feeling that narrative mediation had been

denied her. She felt that her story remained confiscated. While the migrant is reduced to a silenced body, however, her personal narrative emerges – finally. In a game of resistance and power, the alternative practice of narration – coming too late – embeds the reifying horizon of administrative control within original practices of 'subjectivation.'[21] Using the notion of subjectivation to understand Ghislaine's confiscated narrative identifies relations and techniques of domination that have a structuring effect. However, these relations and techniques cannot be understood in terms of an 'alienation,' insofar as a subjectivity is redefined – foremost by the subject itself – in the very moment of subordination. Individuals form themselves as moral and political subjects within the relation that subjects them to an exercise of a power. The moment of bureaucratic categorization and administrative moral judgment is also the moment of resistance and individual affirmation through the drawing of one's singular – although reactive – moral cosmology, bound in one's long-standing itinerary. Although Ghislaine would not put it in these words, asylum appears intuitively as a key element of her wandering. It is an extension of another 'asylum,' that of the church, a traditional space of 'asylum' in the history of the West that has long been one for her in the Congo:

> I left for the Congo, but there again there was a war you know. With hope, I had the Lord. The Lord is good, He sees everything ... I pray to the Lord, and for them, the police, I pray for the Lord too. I stood in a church at home, I slept in the church, I cleaned the church and they gave me money. You know, ... I have God. And when they [the officers in Zapi] treat me as if I was nothing ... they don't know my value but God knows my value.

The exile answers to police mistrust by reminding us of her flight and refuge in a church. This narration takes place at a moment when she is confronted by administrative definitions and classification of asylum, which she discovered for the first time at the French border since she was ignorant about the 'right of asylum.' During her detention, like the other detainees, she kept her police papers and her refusal notification with her all the time. However, it is significant to notice how little she understood the issues at stake in her asylum request and the meaning of its refusal. Indeed, Ghislaine first told me she had not claimed asylum, nor had she been interviewed for this purpose. When I explained to her what an asylum interview looked like, she recognized that she had gone through a similar process indeed, but she did not know who was interviewing her, or the purpose of the interview. Gathering her memories of flight in a narration that revives the historic and cultural roots of asylum in the West, Ghislaine's narration frames her own definition of refuge as an assimilation of, and a reaction to, the process of refugee determination through which she experienced the administrative exclusionary violence. Her experience of mis/trust and state control is thus an experience of subjectivation: an 'operation by which individuals and communities constitute themselves as subjects, at the margins of constituted knowledges and established powers, even if it means giving place to new knowledges and powers.'[22] Through mobility and its control, populations on the move are engaged in disjuncture and recompositions of the definition of the self in its social, political, and moral dimensions.

5. Linearity and Violence

Thus, what is at stake is a moral redefinition of subjects, initiated by different elements such as self-narration, the status of the lie, standards of truthfulness of a story,[23] the disqualification of the detainee by the police officers who blame her for an abuse of the system, and the way she recaptures dignity in response by referring to transcendent values to counter the moral accusation of 'abuse.' The issue of moral definition is not a side effect of administrative categorizations; rather, I argue that it takes a great part in the very practice of categorization. The relation of the nation to the stranger, in the context of the idea of hospitality, is a key element in the moral qualification of detainees. This process of moral qualification participates in shaping the power relations at play in detention.

The interviews that mark out the asylum process in detention are all based on specific administrative rationalizations, which participate in this dehumanizing situation of confusion. Reasons for refusing asylum claims include the argument of a 'manifestly unfounded' (*manifestement infondé*) request, the denunciation of 'stereotyped narratives,' and of inaccuracies 'capable of throwing doubt' (*de nature à jeter le doute*) on the authenticity of the claim. Such arguments are built on two fictions: first, the good faith of the OFPRA officer, who works under the pressure of restrictive rates of admission;[24] and, second, the ability of the asylum seeker to recapture an autobiographical linearity and to relate, in a perfectly coherent way, a relevant version of his or her life story in a short amount of time – an average of ten to twenty minutes. Ghislaine's trajectory in the waiting zone is regulated by succeeding interviews, which are characterized by a proliferation of interlocutors, brevity, and the repetition of misunderstandings between administrative officers and the detainee. During her detention, Ghislaine has, in total, four interviews of ten to fifteen minutes each; she is invited several times to 'tell her story.' The personal narrative is the basis on which the administration examines asylum demands. Indeed, the narrative – in its coherence and its credibility – is what determines the 'good faith' of the asylum seeker. The autobiographical narrative also establishes whether the personal case of the asylum seeker fits into the receiving country's asylum criteria, set up after the Geneva Convention on Refugees of 1951. These criteria, in the case of France but also all western countries in general, are evolving towards an ever more restrictive interpretation of the Geneva Convention. Moreover, norms of narration do not accept temporal voids: the 'truthfulness' of the claim requires all events to be in a line, strictly following each other from the threat, to the flight, to the arrival. In contrast, Ghislaine's story seriously challenges these standards of linearity. What did she do between the early years of 2000 to 2005 when our meeting took place? Why would the French state offer her asylum for a danger she suffered several years ago – as numerous decisions of refusal argue? Ghislaine, after she learned that one of her cousins was living in France, planned to join her, and spent the last eight years earning and borrowing the money to pay the smugglers. In fact, intolerance to suspensions in the trajectory of the autobiographical narrative ironically overlooks a critical reality of migration: exiles have to find ways of getting out and reaching well-protected, safer countries – mobility is expensive. In contrast, narrative standards of bureaucracy dismiss the unequal conditions of mobility in favour of more control. The asylum seeker is required to tell in a linear form the reason why her life has taken the path it has, to report the succession of her flights in the right order and to explain the reasons for them, to distinguish different types of violence she lived through – the one during the genocide and the one that burst out later in Congo, each of which would subsequently be classified as either fitting the French interpretation of the Convention or not.

Facing her interlocutor's demands for narration, not only does Ghislaine keep quiet, but also, when she finally does tell her 'story,' it is marked by suspensions and digressions. She described again her husband's death and her escape from Rwanda in detail. She remained vague and became confused when she talked about the civil war in Congo from 1998 to 2000. In contrast, she came back several times to the massacres in Rwanda, yet showed difficulty in seizing a linearity in her autobiography of the past ten years, from her escape to the Congo to her arrival in France. As I suggested earlier, this non-linear narrative is a subjective reappropriation of the experience of forced migration and its control. It recaptures a voice that '*they* did not want to hear anymore' and opposes both her exclusion from the space of language, and the submission of her language (her narrative) to the linearity that is forced on asylum seekers. In this context, Judith Butler offers precious insight on the specific, 'ethical' violence implied in a process of refugee determination based on coherent narration, and helps us reread the confiscated narrative of the detainee: if 'we (violently) require that another do a certain violence to herself, and do it in front of us by offering a narrative account or issuing a confession, then, conversely, if we permit, sustain, and accommodate the interruption, a certain practice of non-violence will follow.'[25]

At the margins of bureaucratic hearings, moments of self-narration play an important rule in the social life of the border camp. They carry on another function of the camp that opposes bureaucratic purposes: a process of re-socialization after the journey. This alternative, non-linear narration plays on a *minor modus*, opening spaces of intimacy within the housing facilities where the administration of the detainee population performs a confiscation of intimacy. While the main Red Cross office stands as the key centre of everyday life in the camp, Red Cross workers report that a small office at the end of the corridor – the 'second office' – is in fact more important. Personal stories and confidences are told there, announced by the ritual question 'Can I see you in the second office?'[26] These narrations between detainees or with non-bureaucratic actors allow refugees to tell their stories in ways that can freely diverge from the standards of linearity and truthfulness set by the refugee determination procedure. Narrators take the liberty to detail some facts extensively and to silence others. They can insist retrospectively on certain important elements of their personal autobiography, which have been key elements in constructing the trajectory that brought them to the border, even if the link does not clearly appear to the auditor:

M: What did you want to tell them?

G: Well, it's very difficult. At home we were a lot of girls, it was very difficult. My father, he took a new wife, and my stepmother did not want to see us anymore. We couldn't study anymore. I got married young; and I followed my husband to Rwanda.

I remember an Eritrean asylum seeker, who had escaped the army that had abducted her, sitting on her bed in the waiting zone, describing in detail for a long time the summer afternoon when she went to the train station and waited anxiously for her two brothers who were engaged in the war at the Ethiopian border, ten years before she herself was abducted. She told how for hours she went from groups of officers to boards with lists of names, until she eventually found out that her brothers had been killed, and fainted. Resistance is performed through techniques of an autobiographical re-conquest: telling the personal story that lies beyond the one taught by the smugglers – the one linked with a name that then is kept silent. In these moments that interrupt imposed linearity, the narrator looks back on his journey and possibly gathers information: she inserts the conditions and effects of her detention within her narration. Her actual experience at the border is being embedded in the trajectory of her exile. The narration reintegrates a crucial issue dismissed by asylum administration: the way border control emerges within a larger migratory trajectory and the way it will influence it – particularly through the impact of deportation. Emerging and confiscated narrations at the borders inform the ways that migrants detained at the border experience subjectivation and – temporarily – occupy a *place* again, be they assigned to it or claiming it, be they confronting it or resigned to it, be they wanting to go around it or to avoid it.

6. Memory and the State

Migration entails the loss of the social frame in which migrants were born and in which they have set up their own place in the world – the space where they once existed. However, what makes the case of these undocumented aliens singular is not the loss of their place in the world, but rather their difficulty in finding any other place. Deprived of citizenship, the undocumented alien is put aside from the human community, insofar as it is understood by a 'community of nations.' Hannah Arendt relates the aporetical refugee system to the system formed by a community of nation states, such that whoever is excluded from one of the political communities is excluded from the entire family of communities.[27] According to the law, the detainee who leaves her country to come to France with a fake passport, and who is refused entry to the territory, can leave for any other destination of her choice where she would be legally admitted; however, without a passport, she will be received nowhere. Suddenly, there is no place on earth where the detainee can go. It is not a matter of available space (that there is not enough room for him on Earth), but a matter of political organization.

Despite being tied to a nation state–centred conception, Arendt's analysis reveals an essential issue: the question of citizenship and its relationship with the 'boundary.' For Arendt, there is no useful distinction to be made between refugees and people who decide not to benefit from the protection of their state: refugees are considered as *de jure* stateless, whereas the others are *de facto* stateless. While state sovereignty thwarts the full realization of the rights of man (or *because* it does), such rights cannot be protected without the sovereign state. Arendt's analysis shows, through historical cases, the tension between the *idea* of the universal and its application, which depends, in practice, on state traditions and contexts. Theoretical notions of right of asylum and humanitarian assistance are embedded in actual national practices and administrative rationalities, which reflect and give a form to a state memory. Ghislaine's trajectory shows an ambivalent process of judgment and compassion: while, on the one hand, her 'voice' is not heard and she is mocked and eventually deported back, on the other hand, the initial officer was compassionate in a manner that is exceptional in the context of the practices I observed in the waiting zone during three years of field study. In border detention, police more often than not fail to register asylum claims so as to deport the migrants immediately – which is one of the main violations of basic rights denounced by external observers.[28] It has to be noted, however, that the officer acted in favour of Ghislaine after this first interview, insofar as he registered an asylum request even though she had not explicitly asked for it – an exception in administrative practices. Bad will and bad faith of state officers are often denounced when external observers refer to unacceptable situations of border detention and indignant treatment in the waiting zones. However, an examination of the concrete functioning of the border and the way it shapes subjective experience shows that such abuses by the state officers are not the key elements responsible for this reality, which appear instead to be a series of misunderstandings and lost occasions. Rather, what the functioning of the border control points to is an apparatus that socially produces exclusion and the inhumane practices of deportation. I argue that these administrative encounters are shaped by memory in three ways.

First, interactions between bureaucrats and their 'clients' presuppose that the client masters specific rationalities and convincing ways of being that in fact draw lines of national exclusion and make them effective.[29] At the border, administrative responses to asylum claims – based on argumentative and rhetorical tools integrated by the bureaucracy to demonstrate that the demands are ill-founded – show how the disjunction between these national terms of reference and the claimants' moral and rational systems produce exclusion. The resulting mistrust is intimately bound to national memories on both sides. For the migrants, the encounter with the administration (and the more powerful and specific administration of the police) is determined by national culture and practices, and former experiences of administrative interactions. Ghislaine's mistrust emerges from a memory of fear. Ghislaine was heard, however, several times by different officers; in her twisted trajectory, she is the one responsible for making her case nearly inaudible to the officers working in the administration of the waiting zone. As she confessed to me, she was afraid of being tortured once it became obvious that she had lied to the police. This is why she did not show up when she was notified to, and why she refused to reveal her true citizenship and to tell her personal story when she was urged to. Had Ghislaine been more informed about where she was and about what asylum meant, she would have also known that this kind of interview can in no way turn into torture. Ironically enough, her failure to address her narration to the administration in charge of asylum appears as the more 'tangent' demonstration that she needed asylum. That cultural and moral disjunctures between the detainee and the administration eventually led to the confiscation of Ghislaine's narrative, calls into question bureaucratic indifference as a means of management and control.

Second, the administrative world in charge of managing detainees is less a system of its own than it is a mirror of national myths and shared moral values forged in the public sphere. Offering complementary, although challenging, insights into the works of the Frankfurt School about the epistemic ground of administrative rationality,[30] and the work of Hannah Arendt on the 'banality of evil,'[31] Michael Herzfeld argues that the process of administrative classification is an application of the nationalistic logic 'of distinguishing between insiders and outsiders, and of representing these distinctions as given in nature – as matter of essence rather than of cultural or historical contingencies.'[32] Post–Second World War theories on bureaucracy tended to identify it as a somehow auto-referential machinery capable of applying, through specific hierarchies and rationalities, any national policy – including the mass killing of millions of Jews. However, Herzfeld goes further in his empirical investigation and analysis, arguing that the classificatory impulse on which administrative rationality stands is very much tied to national conjuncture since it is produced by a national memory of the inside and the outside. This national memory shapes the 'social production of (administrative) indifference,' which is so striking in Ghislaine's experience with French administration; 'the power to refuse hospitality is the basis on which indifference is built: it is a denial of common substance.'[33] In this regard, it is significant to note that, since the mandate of President Nicolas Sarkozy, bureaucracies of the Interior Ministry and Foreign Affairs have been reorganized and merged in a new Ministry of 'Immigration, Integration and *National Identity*.'[34]

Third, the process of claiming and attributing asylum is embedded in a postcolonial memory of national histories and relations of power. In the novel *Transit*, by Djiboutian writer Abdourahman A. Waberi, the central protagonist, 'Harbi,' who is an asylum seeker waiting at Charles de Gaulle Airport, goes on a long and bitter soliloquy:

> I can't wait to find some kind of peace of mind and body again. To control my brain where morbid and incongruous ideas run wild, smother this little giggling voice. Stick back together the pieces of my dislocated being. In a word, get used to my new identity. A memory firmly rooted in the nest of my mind is coming back to me. I must have been four years old, maybe five and I can see again very clearly the frightened look on the child's face. One day, in the company of my aunt, we passed on an avenue in our neighborhood some soldiers on patrol. Just like a chrysalis about to blossom, the question came all by itself:
> – Who are these people?
> – They're the French, our colonizers.
> – And why are they here?
> – Because they are stronger than us.[35]

Significantly, the memory of the colonized past binds to the present situation of confinement and asylum claim in the protagonist's free association of thought. Why is it 'coming back' in transit at the border? Waberi's literary fiction evokes how a memory of colonial domination, and its actualization in the global world, shape practices of (forced) migration and asylum. This is made clear through the administrative practice of giving more credit to certain asylum claims according to the country of origins. The French state has long applied, and still applies, an affirmative action policy towards asylum seekers from Rwanda. This policy is not without links to the ambiguous role of France in the Rwandan genocide and the catastrophic French intervention during these events.[36] Being aware, as an actor in the waiting zone, of these informal rules in the administration of asylum, I came to understand Ghislaine's history in border detention in terms of mis/trust, and to measure how disjuncture is reorganized as a mean of management and control when I realized she did everything to hide her Rwandan nationality to the administration. She was not aware that being known as a Rwandan would not expose her to persecution, as it would in the Congo, but would rather help her to benefit from less restrictive criteria in regards to her asylum claim.

Another example of how national political consideration is connected to both a postcolonial memory and actual power relations, while also shaping asylum devices, came in the winter 2004–5 when hundreds of asylum seekers from Ivory Coast were quickly refused entry and sent back into their country. Ivory Coast had been engulfed in violence in what was the beginning of a civil war. When French troops tried unsuccessfully to intervene, they were exposed to military attacks and denunciations of 'postcolonial domination,' and finally withdrew. On Christmas Eve, 2004, an Ivorian asylum seeker facing deportation cut his throat with a bottle of aftershave. A few days later, a Congolese refugee who had been living in a refugee camp in Ivory Coast, which he had left after the camp was attacked and the people massacred, was deported back by force. For a few months, I received his e-mails: he was terrified; he was hiding and asking for help.

7. Conclusion

This chapter has argued that the core issues of border detention practices are not the 'dysfunctions' and other unfortunate mistakes inherent to devices of control, but instead their very functional characteristics. The waiting zone is a greased machine that plays a game of denial, mapping the borders of democracy. The story of Ghislaine K. offers insight into the power practices at stake in the administration of detainees, and the treatment of asylum demands as involving a process of denial of the asylum seeker's narrative – her memory of lifelong migrations and flight. Humiliated, confused, fiercely accused of taking the police for fools, the detainee also experienced efforts to recapture her autobiographical integrity within an administrative trajectory made of disruption and silence in a waiting zone. What her confiscated personal narrative relates is a search for asylum, which is denied her.

Mechanisms of the seizure of individual narratives are entailed by a conjunction of different factors. These heterogeneous elements all stem from the perception by the French authorities of the migratory 'problem,' and the administration of asylum that results from such a perception, in terms of disciplinary management of flows and the fight against perceived abuses of the welfare system. Migration and its control install asylum seekers in processes of subjectivation that are articulated around issues of mis/trust. The narration of exile is the basis on which asylum procedures are administrated. Yet, this narration is opposed by bureaucratic rationalities that are anchored in national logics and memory, and by a demand for linearity as the support of truthfulness and ethical judgment, which result in the suspension of confiscated and alternative narrations – the confused work of a 'living' memory, 'something we might tentatively call the truth of the person, a truth that, to a certain degree … might well become more clear in moments of interruption, stoppage, open-endedness – in enigmatic articulations that cannot be translated into narrative form.'[37] However, in defining 'living' memory, Judith Butler makes clear that her purpose is not to celebrate 'a certain notion of incoherence, but only to point out that our "incoherence" establishes the way in which we are constituted in relationality: implicated, beholden, derived, sustained by a social world that is beyond us and before us.'[38] The violence of border detention is in the collapsing and the illegibility of this social world. 'Mistrust' doubly binds migrants to the violence of an 'address' which constitutes them as subjects of control, and to the assignation into silence where the 'incoherence' of singular narratives becomes trapped within the evolution from relationality to the exercise of a force.

Ghislaine K. was deported back, supposedly to Congo. I know this because of two letters in front of her name on the police list, 'BE,' which stand for *Bien Embarquée*, meaning 'well-taken on board.' I do not know what became of her, as is the case for many other well-boarded asylum seekers. For them, border detention and deportation will be a memory in a long-lasting journey, of which we, on this side of the fence, know so little.

NOTES

1 W.H. Auden, *Collected Poems* (New York: Faber and Faber, 1976), 473.
2 The 'family reunification' is the process by which family members of a migrant can legally come and reside in the same state. In EU member states, the conditions under which migrants are 'authorized to bring their spouse, under-age children, and the children of their spouse' are rigorously restricted and can be submitted to 'contracts' of cultural integration, age restrictions, and DNA tests to prove family links, as is the case in France (*Loi du 20 novembre 2007 relative à la maîtrise de l'immigration, à l'intégration et à l'asile*). For further developments, see Chowra Makaremi, 'On the Spirit of Laws: Some Reflections Concerning the "DNA Law" in France,' *Eurostudia* 3, no.2 (Dec. 2007), http://id.erudit.org/iderudit/017839ar (accessed 25 August 25 2008).
3 I addressed a letter to the office in charge of asylum, explaining Ghislaine's story and asking for another asylum audition for her. This request was left unanswered, as is usually the case in the waiting zone.
4 Ryszard Cholewinski, 'No Right of Entry: The Legal Regime on Crossing the EU Border,' in *In Search of Europe's Borders: Immigration and Asylum Law and Policy in Europe*, Vol. 5, ed. E. Guild, K. Groenendijk, and P. Minderhoud (The Hague / London / New York: Kluwer Law International, 2003), 105–30; Chowra Makaremi, 'Alien Confinement in Europe: Violence and the Law: The Case of Roissy-Charles de Gaulle Airport in France,' in *The Camp: Narratives of Internment and Exclusion*, ed. Colman Hogan and M. Marín Dòmine (Newcastle: Cambridge Scholars Publishing, 2007), 39–54.
5 Jacques Rancière, *Aux bords du politique* (Paris: Gallimard, 1998).
6 Étienne Balibar, *Nous, citoyens d'Europe? Les frontières, l'Etat, le peuple* (Paris: La Decouverte, 2001), 191 et seq.
7 Didier Bigo, 'Detention of Foreigner, States of Exception, and the Social Practices of Control of the Banopticon,' in *Borderscapes: Hidden Geographies and Politics at Territory's Edge*, ed. Prem Kumar Rajaram and Carl Grundy-Warr (Minneapolis: University of Minnesota Press, 2007), 3–35.
8 Unlike the asylum procedure that takes place on French territory, at the borders there is no option of using an asylum form or written demands; the whole process is oral and takes place in an extremely short period of time. The audition can last from ten minutes to two hours, and the answer is usually given one to three days after the claim has been registered. Asylum seekers applying from within French territory have one month to complete their written demand, which is then followed by an oral interview.

9 Judith Butler, *Giving an Account of Oneself* (New York: Fordham University Press, 2005).
10 Michael Herzfeld, *The Social Production of Indifference: Exploring the Symbolic Roots of Western Bureaucracy* (Chicago and London: University of Chicago Press, 1992).
11 E. Valentine Daniel and John Knudsen, eds, *Mistrusting Refugees* (Berkeley: University of California Press, 1995).
12 Ibid., 1.
13 Ibid.
14 Office Nationale de Protection des Réfugiés et Apatrides. Officially, OFPRA officers give a consultative notice to the Interior Ministry, which is in charge of the final decision. In practice, OFPRA's decisions are systematically applied.
15 Denis Salas, '" Incriminés, discriminés ...": immigration illégale et pratiques judiciaires en France,' *Hommes et Migrations*, no.1241 (Jan.-Feb. 2003): 78–88.
16 See Smaïn Laacher, *Après Sangatte, ... nouvelles immigrations, nouveaux enjeux* (Paris: La Dispute, 2002).
17 Hannah Arendt, *The Origins of Totalitarianism* (New York: Harcourt Brace Jovanovich, 1973), 302 (emphasis added).
18 Ernesto de Martino, *Le Monde Magique, Oeuvres, I* (Paris: Editions Synthelabo, Les Empêcheurs de penser en rond, 1999), 151.
19 Ibid., 95.
20 Daniel and Knudsen, eds, *Mistrusting Refugees*, 1.
21 Michel Foucault, *Histoire de la sexualité II: l'usage des plaisirs* (Paris: Gallimard, 1984); and 'Le sujet et le pouvoir,' in *Dits et Ecrits*, Vol II, 1976–88 (Paris: Quarto Gallimard, 2001), 1041–61.
22 Gilles Deleuze, *Pourparlers* (Paris: Editions de Minuit, 1992), 206 (author's translation).
23 Bernard Williams, *Truth and Truthfulness: An Essay in Genealogy* (Princeton: Princeton University Press, 2006).
24 Three per cent of asylum claims at the border were accepted in 2003. The rate has risen to about 10 per cent since 2004. The admission of asylum seekers at the border had shifted towards a restrictive tendency in recent years, before the National Office for the Protection of Refugees and Stateless People decided in 2004 to harmonize its admission decisions at the borders with the rates of refugee acceptance by the territory, which vary from 12 to 20 per cent.
25 Butler, *Giving an Account of Oneself*, 64.
26 Chowra Makaremi, interview with a Red Cross worker, 7 July 2005.

27 Arendt, *Origins of Totalitarianism*, 297.

28 Association Nationale d'Assistance aux Frontières pour les Etrangers (Anafé), 'Une France inaccessible: rapport de visites en aérogares, zone d'attente de Roissy-Charles de Gaulle' (Report of an observation campaign in terminals, waiting zone of Charles de Gaulle Airport), December 2007, http://www.anafe.org/publi2007.php (accessed on 10 August 2008).

29 Herzfeld, *Social Production of Indifference*. 158.

30 Theodor Adorno and Max Horkheimer, *Dialectic of Enlightenment* (London: Verso, 1979).

31 Hannah Arendt, *Eichmann in Jerusalem: A Report on the Banality of Evil* (New York: Viking, 1963).

32 Herzfeld, *Social Production of Indifference*, 174.

33 Ibid., 177.

34 'C'est parce que la France a une identité propre dont elle peut être fière qu'elle a les moyens d'intégrer des immigrés qui respectent nos valeurs et qu'elle peut organiser de façon sereine l'immigration. Telle est l'ambition de ce nouveau ministère: lutter contre l'immigration irrégulière, organiser l'immigration légale en favorisant le développement des pays d'origine afin de réussir l'intégration et de conforter l'identité de notre Nation' ['It is because France has its own identity of which it can be proud that it has the means to integrate the immigrants who respect our values and that it can organize immigration in a serene way. This is the ambition of this new Ministry: fighting against illegal immigration, organizing legal immigration by promoting development in the countries of origin in order to manage integration and to reinforce the identity of our nation' (author's translation)] (from 'Missions and Function,' Ministry of Immigration, Integration, National Identity and Joint Development, official website, http://www.immigration.gouv.fr/ [accessed 10 August 2008]).

35 Abdourahman Waberi, *Transit* (Paris: Gallimard, 2003), 16.

36 Gérard Prunier, *The Rwanda Crisis: History of a Genocide* (New York: Columbia University Press, 1995).

37 Butler, *Giving an Account of Oneself*, 64.

38 Ibid., 65.

SECTION TWO

Collective Memory Ghettos

5 Frames of Memory: WWII German Expellees in Canada

ANDREAS KITZMANN

Part One: Difficulties

This has been a difficult chapter to write. The reasons for this difficulty are, however, cagey and of the sort that resist being grounded within a stable context of definition. It has been difficult to write because on the surface it should not appear to be difficult at all. This chapter deals with first-hand accounts of an historical occurrence, in this case the experiences of the *Volksdeutsche* (ethnic Germans) who were forced to flee their homes in eastern and southeastern Europe at the end of the Second World War. Consequently, the writing of such a chapter would appear to be mainly the result of comparing such accounts to historical facts and certainties, which in turn would presumably allow one to get closer to the very truth of the matter at hand. All that needs to be done, then, is to carefully establish and articulate the historical context, identify the major issues and highlights, and then slot in the interview material as appropriate. A simple task of checks and balances, compare and contrast, verify or disqualify.

But one can never go by appearances alone, and the presumed simplicity of this project is chimerical at best. I am dealing with memories, which, as we are asserting in this volume, are constantly in motion and thus never absolutely locatable with respect to their proximity to the unassailable truth. Yet, at the same time, memories are 'true' in the sense of being linked to very real material circumstances and experiences. As a result of such a dilemma, I initially found myself staring at my interview transcripts and a small mountain of books, wondering what to do next, writing countless introductions to an essay that craftily refuses to begin.

Another reason behind the difficulty of writing this chapter has to do with the nature of the material itself – which is to say, the discomfort and emotional upset created by engaging with individuals who have suffered traumas far beyond my own life experience. Adding to the emotional weight of the interviews is the fact that my mother and her immediate family were among the estimated fifteen million people who were forced to flee their homes as the war ground towards its bloody conclusion. So, mixed in with the traumatic details from the recollections of strangers are self-created images of my mother, grand-parents, aunts, and uncles also enduring great hardships, injustices, and humiliation.[1]

Taken together, such academic and personal emotional difficulties are strangely instructive, insomuch as they draw our attention to the complex relationships among memory, testimony, and the fixity that documented history is said to provide. With respect to the latter, the details of the Expulsion of ethnic Germans after the Second World War are detailed in a number of sources, including two books by Alfred de Zayas, *A Terrible Revenge* and *Nemesis at Potsdam*, and thus will not be repeated here at length.[2] Briefly stated however, the Expulsion can be broadly understood as the mass deportation of ethnic Germans from present-day Poland, the Czech Republic, Slovakia, Hungary, Yugoslavia, the German province of Eastern Prussia, and several other Eastern European countries. There were two major forces behind the Expulsion. The first was that of the advancing Soviet Army, which swept over the Eastern Front in 1945. The Russian soldiers, many of whom had images in their mind of the destruction of their own homeland by the German military, ruthlessly attacked and persecuted any Germans they encountered. In much of the historical documentation and in my own interviews, accounts of brutality, rape, murder, and robbery are common, as are recollections of rampant drunkenness and lack of discipline on the part of the Soviet military. As a result, many ethnic Germans fled their homes in fear of Russian reprisals. The second major impetus behind the Expulsion was the Potsdam Conference, held in the city of Cecilienhof in Potsdam, Germany, from 17 July to 2 August 1945. Attended by the major players of the Allied Powers – Joseph Stalin, Winston Churchill (later Clement Attlee), and Harry S. Truman – the conference resulted in the reconfiguration of German borders and a plan to forcibly expel all Germans who remained in countries located outside of redefined borders of the German state. The rationale behind the Expulsion was complex and intertwined with the specific political machinations of the various nations involved in the process. Arguably, however, it was the Soviet Union's insistence on forcing the German population out of Eastern Europe that drove the process – an insistence partly fuelled by a desire for reparation and partly as a means to extend Soviet influence in the post-war world. While the other Allies were critical of such a large-scale resettlement, they eventually ceded to Soviet demands and justified the Expulsion as a necessary means to securing lasting peace and stability in all of Europe.[3] The process was articulated in Section XII of the proceedings, titled 'Orderly Transfer of German Populations':

> The Three Governments, having considered the question in all its aspects, recognize that the transfer to Germany of German populations, or elements thereof, remaining in Poland, Czechoslovakia and Hungary, will have to be undertaken. They agree that any transfers that take place should be effected in an orderly and humane manner.[4]

By many accounts, the 'population transfer' was anything but orderly and humane. Rather, it was traumatic and often brutal, considering the estimated fifteen million Germans affected by the transfer, an act that had profound and lasting consequences, not only for individuals and communities, but arguably on the very nature of European post-war identity – an identity that is largely formed around the collective experience of uprooting and ethnic cleansing. As Éva Kovács notes, '… discourse on flight and expulsion produced the deepest cleavage between Western and Eastern approaches to the politics of history. As sad as it is, the memory of the expulsion, together with the memory of Communism, overshadows the memory of the Shoah in Eastern Europe.'[5]

Yet despite the fact that the Expulsion is well enough documented by historians, it is not well represented in most normative accounts of the Second World War and, as such, has been generally excluded from public discourse.[6] This is especially the case in Germany, where the topic of the *Vertreibung* has been politically uncomfortable for decades, and the recent actions of Erika Steinbach, the current president of the Bund der Vertriebenen or BdV (The League of German Expellees) have raised the discomfort to new levels. Much of the current debate around Steinbach revolves around her ambition to create a permanent centre for documenting the plight of the expellees after the war. As a step towards establishing this centre, a recent exhibition in Berlin entitled 'Paths Unchosen,' organized by the Centre against Expulsions, was criticized by many, especially the Polish government, as a form of historical revisionism.[7] Jaroslaw Kaczynski, president of Poland, condemned the exhibition and Steinbach's ambitions, in general, as an 'attempt to relativize the history of World War II. It's important to remember who the murderers were and who the victims were.'[8] The BdV has been controversial since its inception in 1953, partly due to issues of land claims by former expellees and partly due to its effects on the political relationships between Germany and Central and Eastern European countries, significantly Poland.[9]

While such contexts are certainly relevant to this present study, my main concern is with former expellees in the Canadian context, who are generally removed from the highly politicized debates within Germany as well as Central and Eastern Europe. This is not to imply, however, that German-Canadians are ignorant of these debates, nor that the efforts of the likes of Steinbach and the BdV are completely absent from the North American discursive landscape. Indeed, the German World Alliance (GWA), an American-based organization, created in 2002 to pursue its stated goal of 'guarding human rights of persons of German cultural, linguistic or ethnic heritage worldwide,' cites the BdV as one of its member organizations and has issued favourable press releases of Steinbach's activities.[10] The GWA has close contacts with many regional German organizations in North America, including the German Canadian Congress (GCC), which is described as an 'umbrella association for German clubs, churches, companies and private persons,' established to 'give German-Canadians a united voice towards government, media and the public at large.'[11] Like the GWA, the GCC also employs the language of human rights to legitimate its activities, stating that their main goals include taking 'a firm stand against unfair stereotyping and untrue accusations against Canadians of German heritage,' and to protect 'the rights of every individual person within the laws of Canada and the Human Rights Declaration of the United Nations.' It is under this discursive umbrella of human rights that the GCC has served as a forum to highlight and debate issues around the bombing raids on Dresden, the deportation of suspected Canadian-German war criminals, notably Helmut Oberlander,[12] and the *Vertreibung*. Its former vice-president Paul Tuerr has been particularly vocal about the lack of public discourse on German suffering during the war and has voiced his concern for what he terms 'German bashing' in the press and in academia.[13] However, the GCC is far from a radical political organization, and the bulk of its activities revolve around promoting German culture in Canada, such as the popular Oktoberfest in Kitchener, musical events, and seasonal activities such as the Christkindlmarkt during Christmas. In this respect, the GCC is similar to the many other cultural organizations that exist within Canada's officially mandated multiculturalism, which, in the language of the Canadian Multiculturalism Act, aim at recognizing 'the importance of preserving and enhancing the multicultural heritage of Canadians.'[14]

Part Two: History, Testimony, and the Flow of Memory

Paul Ricoeur insists that everything starts from testimony, claiming that 'we have nothing better than testimony, in the final analysis, to assure ourselves that something did happen in the past, which someone attests to having witnessed in person, and that the principal, at times our only, recourse, when we lack other types of documentation, remains the confrontation among testimonies.'[15] The image of testimonies engaged in a confrontation with one another is an especially arresting one in this case and is perhaps yet another source of my stubborn writer's block. At the core of the confrontation is, of course, the matter of Germany's crimes against humanity during the period of National Socialism and the ongoing issues and concomitant discourses around accountability, responsibility, and guilt. Such issues and discourses make the articulation of specifically German suffering problematic, insomuch as it counters the normative representation of Germans as the perpetrators of evil by representing them as victims.

Yet, as Saul Friedlander observes, the relationship between perpetrators and victims is complex and perhaps better understood as a kind of 'negative symbiosis' between Jews and Germans:

> On a symbolic level ... one may speak of a Jewish memory of Auschwitz and of a German one. Although the incompatibility between these two memories may be growing, they are helplessly interwoven in what has been called a 'negative symbiosis'... Any re-elaboration of one memory directly impinges on the other; any neutralization casts an overall shadow of oblivion. Neither Jews nor Germans can relate to their own memory without relating to the other's as well.[16]

This 'helpless interweaving,' if it can be phrased as such, was made strikingly clear in the course of my own investigations. During a phone call to set up an interview, I was asked by one individual what my 'agenda' was. I did not exactly know how to respond given that in my perhaps naïve self-designation as the objective, impartial collector of data, I never considered the idea that my project could be conceived as one driven by an agenda, whether explicit or hidden. But, of course, as I quickly discovered, this is resolutely not the case. Why bring up the issue of how ordinary Germans were mistreated during and after the war if not to correct a gap in the historical narrative and, in even more confrontational terms, to extend the list of victims beyond those normally associated with the Second World War? Or, as one of my respondents repeatedly attempted to convince me, to help initiate steps towards addressing the injustices enacted against the *Volksdeutsche*, which in some cases should include the redrawing of borders that now define contemporary Germany. Or, as is more common and benign, to promote the idea that the hardships endured by the fifteen million expellees should serve as a kind of universal marker of inhumanity and injustice, and thus be used to shout the message 'never again' to present and future generations?

What such 'agendas' make clear is the extent to which testimonies are caught within a form of perpetual motion in which they are carried aloft by an array of equally shifting historical and ideological projects and ambitions. Michel de Certeau, as cited by Ricoeur, notes how materials, in this case testimonies, are placed within archives and thus 'situated in a chain of verifying operations, whose provisory end is the establishment of documentary proof.'[17] This idea of 'placement' is particularly relevant – how my testimonies, once contained within an archive (if only of my own making), are redistributed into places that allow, discourage, or forbid specific discourses and interpretive assemblages.

Ricoeur comments further that testimony written or spoken 'in pain' also 'raises a question, to the point of soliciting a veritable crisis concerning testimony,' that effectively separates this form of documentary proof from the general process of historiography.[18] Why is this the case? 'Because it poses a problem of reception that being placed in an archive does not answer and for which it even seems inappropriate, even provisionally incongruous. This has to do with such literally extraordinary limit experiences – which make for a difficult pathway in encountering the ordinary, limited capacities for reception of auditors educated on the basis of a shared comprehension.'[19]

The Holocaust serves as one of the definitive markers of such limit experiences that are far in excess of normative frames of reference. As a number of thinkers explore, with Primo Levi and Hanna Arendt being amongst the most well known, the acts of recollecting and speaking of these limit experiences pose a particular challenge given that the witness lacks any form of distance from the events, which, according to Primo Levi, introduces the additional barrier of shame.[20]

In the case of the expelled *Volksdeutshe* there is the added barrier of collective guilt, which has dominated much of the political and cultural discourses of post-war Germany via the project of *Vergangenheitsbewaltigung* – 'of effectively working through, coming to terms with the immediate past.'[21] To a significant degree, Germans who immigrated to North America have not been part of such discourses. According to Alexander Freund, this has compelled them to confront the past in a manner that is significantly different from Germans living in Germany. The first difference between Germans' *Vergagenheitsbewaltigung* in Germany and in North America is an issue of power relations. In Germany, Germans were insiders; they belonged to the nation and defined themselves in opposition to the Other, 'the foreigners.' In North America, however, they were (at least at first) outsiders and themselves defined as Other.[22]

In North America, as Freund notes, Germans were directly confronted by the historical realities of the Second World War and the Holocaust in a manner that made it 'rather difficult – although not impossible – to demand to be seen as a victim or to ignore the discourse.'[23] Such a denial (or at least a suppression) of victimhood has been a source of frustration amongst some of the individuals I have interviewed. For many, the historical account of the Second World War cannot be complete unless the *Vertreibung* is made a part of the public discourse. Indeed, what some of the former expellees want is mainly to be written back into history and its offshoots in popular culture (such as films, historical novels, etc.).

That said, the social and cultural dynamics of collective guilt within Germany after the Second World War are of an intensity and longevity not experienced in North America. Consequently, while Germans in Germany may indeed be 'insiders' as Freund suggests, they are concomitantly compelled to confront issues of accountability, responsibility, and moral culpability in a way that is integrated deeply into the formation and evolution of their identity as Germans. By contrast, Germans in Canada or the United States have the choice of forging a new identity around their adopted nations. They can choose, as many have, to downplay their German roots and assimilate as seamlessly as possible into the mainstream of society, while at the same time celebrating and practising relatively apolitical aspects of German identity and culture (such as music, food, folklore, customs, etc.) without the burden present in Germany itself of nationalist discourses and identity formations. As Laurenn Guyot notes in her discussion of Kurds living in France, such persistent and overt integration on the part of immigrants is not uncommon, and is often motivated by a general desire to diminish a shared negative past and the shame and stereotypes associated with a particular group identity.[24]

Such dynamics complicate the discursive and material formations of history. As a way through such complications, it is worth considering Reinhart Koselleck's theory of the concept of history, which can be briefly summarized via four major assertions:

> [First,] historical process is marked by a distinctive kind of temporality different from that found in nature. Second, historical reality is social reality, an internally differentiated structure of functional relationships in which the rights and interests of one group collide with those of other groups and lead to the kinds of conflicts in which defeat is experienced as an ethical failure requiring reflection on what went wrong to determine the historical significance of the conflict itself ... Thirdly, a critical historical consciousness is born of an awareness of a gap between historical events and the language used to represent them – both by the agents involved in these events and by historians retrospectively trying to reconstruct them.[25]

What is informative about the theory for the purposes of this chapter is the understanding that historical knowledge 'knows itself to be always provisional and open to revision,' which is not to say that it disintegrates into a kind of formless relativism. Rather, Koselleck's 'concept of history' provides a means to navigate through the various 'falsifications of history,' in a manner that provides a stable base from which to assess and augment that space of experience in which individuals 'build a notion of humanity that is both always changing and ever more becoming itself.'[26]

Gil Eyal's term 'will to memory' nicely encapsulates the use of memory for historical practice and resonates with the assertions developed by Koselleck:

> Memory might well be somewhat imprecise and indeterminate, but it is only when we expect it to answer some pressing need that we begin to problematize it as such, or to become concerned with its quality and

quantity. And it is not enough to say that memory is expected to reflect accurately the collective or individual past, because this merely begs the question: why do we need an accurate representation of the past to begin with? How accurate should it be? For what purpose?[27]

How then to proceed? In addition to working through some of these theoretical concepts and issues, I feel compelled to also include at least some of the personal accounts rendered by my interviews. Yet towards what ends and for what purposes? And how might – or should – these testimonies be subjected to a temporary period of fixity? Srdja Pavlovic's essay in this same volume provides one response to such questions. He cites Jan Assmann as pointing out that 'the *truth* of a given memory lies not so much in its *factuality* as in its *actuality*.'[28] Likewise, the truth of the memories about to be unfolded here has little to do with fact and certainty or even with providing a context from which to pursue the artifice of justice – a topic I will turn to at the conclusion of this essay. In other words, content is not king here, but rather the movement engendered by the constant rearticulation and repositioning of this content, which in itself is by no means stable or fixed.

As a stop-gap measure, I will proceed as follows: I shall create a number of frames, and within those frames, I will situate a number of testimonies that will, in turn, be employed as vehicles to question and probe the frame in which they have been placed. To the inevitable and repeated question about what my objectives are in proceeding this way, I offer this reply: to affirm that the act of accumulating testimony can and must be understood in terms of potential and material (mis)uses and affects. This 'act' is not without its responsibilities, and, as such, those who materialize the memories of the past must not do so lightly. By deliberately identifying and foregrounding potential frames, I hope to achieve what metaphorically may be conceived as a form of stop-motion photography. The memories that I have transcribed here from a series of videotaped interviews have only an illusory and contrived form of fixity. They are frozen moments that by definition are no longer part of the flux of living memory. However, as Julia Creet reminds us in the Introduction to this volume, this does not mean that these memories are secondary or so labile that they cease to be meaningful.[29] It is, rather, that they in themselves are not sacred, not beyond reproach, not permanently engraved on a static place of memory, as Pierre Nora would insist. They exist in flux and in motion, and it is in this constant state of movement that their very real value and energy lies. The best that we can do is to momentarily capture these memories before releasing them again into the maelstrom from which they came.

Part Three: Frames of Memory

Frame One: Losers and Winners

Wars have losers and winners, and, as such, much of the discourse around the historical circumstances and effects of the Second World War (or any war, for that matter) stems from this basic opposition. In this case, Germany was both clearly the aggressor and the loser – a designation that has made it difficult, until relatively recently, to speak of ordinary Germans as victims. In his commentary on German post-war literature, Peter Schneider notes that 'only in the past three years or so have German writers and historians begun to tackle a topic previously taboo: the sufferings of the German civilian population in the last years of World War II.'[30] The reasons behind such silence have to do with the apparently self-evident conception that 'the critical authors of postwar Germany considered it a moral and aesthetic impossibility to describe the Germans, the nation responsible for the world war, as being the victims of that war.'[31] Such a sentiment has been addressed in various ways throughout the course of my interviews with survivors of the Expulsion. 'I know it's hard,' states Ursula K., 'and I always say we lost the war and we have no right to complain but there were so many people in Germany … it was not their fault.'[32] A similar sense of unacknowledged loss, helplessness, and the absence of guilt on the part of 'ordinary Germans' is expressed by Haidi S., who, as a young woman of sixteen, was sent to a labour camp in Siberia for five years: 'When you lost the war, you have no rights. That was the idea. We were all victims and nobody talked about it. And that was it. But when you really think it over, us ordinary people, what did we do? What could we do? We did not really have any choice. If you did not obey, you know what happened.'[33] This notion that 'ordinary Germans' – a designation not without its own issues – were either ignorant or forced into their compliance with the Nazi regime is a deeply complex and troubling issue and not one that I want to tackle here.[34] For the purposes of this chapter, what I would like to draw attention to is the manner in which expellees, who were in a large part *Volksdeutsche* and not *Reichsdeutsche*, positioned themselves within the victim/perpetrator divide.[35] In the course of my interviews, the moral culpability and the consequences it wrought upon the German nation were acknowledged as being a direct result of the actions and politics of the Nazi regime. Such an acknowledgment on the part of those whom I had the chance to interview did not necessarily diminish the expellees' sense of anger or injustice with respect to their individual experiences, which ranged from forced migration to torture and death. They had clearly been wronged, but such a wrong was tempered by the overall context of the greater evils committed by Nazi Germany. In one such instance, Heinz M. recalls during his retelling of his experiences in a town just east of Warsaw an incident when he was attacked by survivors just released from a concentration camp: 'Some people from a concentration camp were let out ... and I was beaten up ... I was not really mad at them. I understood that this was a natural reaction to what they had suffered.'[36] Similarly, Ron S. comments that the Expulsion was Germany's fault 'because they [the Germans] listened to Hitler.'[37] Against such sentiments are recollections of kindness and highly ethical behaviour on the part of many expellees towards others. Hubert L. recalls his family's treatment of the Polish workers who were assigned to work at the family farm by the German state. He directly attributes his family's having survived the war to their fair and kind treatment of the workers: 'We were somehow lucky. Maybe it was something else. Maybe because my people were good to people. They treated their Polish workers like human beings.'[38] In speaking about his father, Hubert notes that 'my dad was a humanitarian. You treat people nicely in this world and it pays you back.' In his case, the 'payback' was a relatively 'light' expulsion in the sense that there was no loss of life nor acts of brutality experienced within the immediate family. This is not to say, of course, that Hubert and his family did not suffer greatly. He continues by adding that 'to me, we did bad. We paid early for it. But you cannot only blame the war on the Germans. World War II started with World War I. The Treaty of Versailles was not good for Germany. If there had been a half decent treaty, things would have been different ... [but] we paid for it [the war]. We paid big time. Thousands and thousands of Germans died and no one counts them.'

Frame Two: Let the Past Rest

For Germans the question of how to address the past is persistent and troubling. Within Germany itself, the political and cultural conditions prompted by the *Aufarbeitung* (coming to terms with the past) – or *Vergangenheitsbewaltigung* (mastering or overcoming the past) – have occupied centre stage since the 1960s. Among the early proponents to actually formalize a political stance or agenda to 'come to terms with the past' are Adorno and Horkheimer and their work on what they term 'the authoritarian personality.'[39] A much more specific course of action, however, was detailed in Adorno's 1959 essay 'What Does Coming to Terms with the Past Mean?' Central to his argument is establishing a difference between a genuine working through of the past in the spirit of 'critical self-reflection,' as opposed to simply 'turning the page' on the past in order to erase it from memory. In the former case, Adorno advocated a form of 'subjective enlightenment' that was 'essentially that sort of turn toward the subject: reinforcement of a person's self-consciousness and, with that, of a sense of self.'[40]

In his critique of the *Aufarbeitung* and, in particular, the normative political discourses and practices in Germany around the subjects of public and private memory, Alf Ludtke argues that the bulk of commemorative practices, again both public and individual, are largely limited to formalized public gestures and speeches by representatives of the state and society. Among the immediate results of this 'view from above' is a kind of moral passivity on the part of individual Germans, which causes them to leave matters of accountability and the acknowledgment of guilt to the public, as opposed to the personal, realm. Moreover, according to Ludtke, the victims of Nazism tend to remain abstracted in the sense of being represented anonymously (i.e., among the six million) rather than as discrete and identifiable individuals. This is made particularly concrete in the many memorials erected around Germany for the 'fallen comrades of 1939–45':

> On the memorial in Gottingen as well as on many similar memorials, inscriptions refer to general and anonymous 'relationships to violence' (*Gewaltverhaltnisse*). Thus, respect should be paid to all victims of all 'relationships of violence.' No specific perpetrators are named or referred to. No individuals or groups, not to mention 'criminal organizations' (such as the SS and Waffen-SS), figure in these inscriptions. Keeping 'it' at a distance; this was and still is the implicit as well as the explicit message. Even more, aspects of shared complicity by hundreds and thousands of people have remained out of sight at these sites of commemoration.[41]

Notable and disturbing here is the tendency to keep 'it' at a distance, which applies not only to the victims of the Nazi regime but also to the individuals who helped make the regime possible in the first place.

'The interpretation of fascism as "catastrophe" did not offer a different perspective. Again, adherents held that only a small group of "criminals" had actively organized the system and the politics of terror and mass murder as well as the war efforts and war activities.'[42] As a result, Germans are able 'rigidly to demarcate "us" from "them": victims from perpetrators. Who, except for Hitler and a half-dozen others, was, then, considered a perpetrator? This effort to liberate oneself from any questioning cut across lines of class and cultural or political milieu.'[43]

In the case of the expelled *Volksdeutsche*, the *Aufarbeitung* is an especially difficult terrain, given a number of factors. First, as already mentioned, are the differences between Germans in Germany and those outside the country, with respect to their experience of normative public discourses associated with the Second World War. Second is the problematic nature of the 'memory work' specific to the expellees. On the one hand, the need to remember and retell, especially on the level of personal experience, is part of their collective identity as victims. On the other hand, memories of individual experiences of hardship and trauma conflict with the more general 'memory work' of the *Aufarbeitung*, which, to follow through with Ludtke's argument, encourages one to disassociate the everyday practices of 'normal' life from the specific political, social, and ideological projects of the Nazi regime. As such, many of those whom I interviewed describe themselves as being generally unaware of what was being done in the name of Germany by the Nazis. In one case, this was expressed as a denial of the Holocaust itself, although there was acknowledgment that Jews were the victims of hate: 'I did not know about concentration camps until the end. I did witness Jewish hate in Berlin. That I saw myself. We did not have a Holocaust. Any exaggeration was a lie. There was already so much mass murder that it could not be made worse. They were cremated but they were not burned alive. Six million ... I doubt that. Such a vast number. Try to count to one million. You would not live long enough to get there.'[44] Such statements are, of course, reprehensible and not isolated to a few old age pensioners who harbour bitter feelings about their own fate during the war. In this specific case, the individual in question was, at the time, a young and perhaps abused (or, at the very least, neglected) young boy with few opportunities to exercise any degree of control over his life. While his statements about the Holocaust are inexcusable (and not even worthy of debate in my opinion), they can perhaps be understood as indications of a type of clash between identities. On the one side there is his identity as a powerless victim who desires to be recognized as such. Yet, on the other hand, there is his identity as a German and all that entails with respect to questions and issues related to the actions (or lack thereof) of 'ordinary' Germans during the Nazi era.

More common and arguably less disturbing is the general consensus that the past is 'over' and that it is time to more forward. Ursula K., who spoke with some frustration over her perceived need to be cautious when speaking about Germany or the war, stated, 'Anytime you say something about Germany and how Germans were treated during or after the war, then you are a Nazi. That I struggle with. I know that this is hard for people who were in a concentration camp. Is there not somewhere where there is an end? Can't we look to the future? It [the Holocaust] is brought up again and again. Does this not stir up some hate? I am in a book club and there are two other German ladies. I am always careful. When we talk about the war, we have to be careful ... How long does this go on? We pay and we pay ...'[45]

Ursula's point leads to a kind of paradox on her part. On the one side, she emphasizes that the history of the war and the Holocaust 'needs to be told,' yet, on the other, she struggles with the continued representation of Germans as Nazis and the collective guilt that still persists within the German psyche and nationhood (both within and outside of Germany). Added to this is her own desire to have her traumatic experiences acknowledged and represented, especially in terms of being able to share her experiences (and those of the *Volksdeutsche*) without having to contend with the judgments associated within being German.

Frame Three: Luck and Adventure

Many of those I interviewed were children or young adults at the time of Germany's final collapse in 1945. While lives were certainly shattered with consequences both physical and psychological, many structured their recollections of those times as 'great adventures' with unexpected moments of 'luck' amidst a broad spectrum of hardship, want, and humiliation. This is not without precedent and corresponds with the observation, made by W.G. Sebald, among others, about how many Germans actively resisted the representations of themselves as victims. In *On the Natural History of Destruction* Sebald writes, 'There was a tacit agreement, equally binding everyone, that the true state of material and moral ruin in which the country found itself was not to be described.'[46] With respect to the retelling of the experience of the

Vertreibung, many of my interviewees effectively depict themselves as not being entirely helpless and, moreover, as having the ability to exercise some control of their own fate and thus emerging as 'heroes' of their own life-story.

Helga W., who was born in Essen, spoke almost fondly about her solitary journey to the West. 'As I speak now, to me it's almost a big adventure. I was young. I was healthy. I remember that some people were starting to get dingy and dirty-looking, but I remember on that trip for three weeks from one meadow to another and through the forest … I looked for a little stream of water and I washed. I was not shy and I was clean. So, to me that time was not horrible. To me it was a great, an incredible adventure.'[47] Because of her language abilities (she could speak German and English), Helga quickly became a kind of unofficial assistant to American troops, dealing with the many refugees streaming through the countryside. Eventually, two American officers helped her escape by stuffing her into a duffel bag and driving her across the border to reunite with her sister in Murnau, Germany. While the journey had its risks, especially for the officers, Helga again describes her experience as an adventurous journey that she acknowledges as being very different from the traumatic experience suffered by others, including members of her own family. 'It was not traumatic. I am lucky that I survived well. It was a great adventure. And I was more lucky than many, many people.'

In a similar spirit, Rhonda H. recalls the fine weather and idyllic setting in which she and a companion were strafed by a British fighter plane:

> One Sunday before we left we had gone into the moors. It was such a beautiful spring day so we went for a walk. We had on blue dresses and white aprons. We watched a plane that was turning loops and summersaults, just having the time of its life. And all of a sudden he came down and started shooting at us. It was a British plane. And the white aprons gave us away. On either side there were deep ditches so we jumped in and the aprons were not white anymore. Anyway, then we started just hiking. First we took the country roads, because the main roads, the American Army used. But it was just an awfully beautiful spring. My birthday is in April and we got to the village and they had no water. The water supply was gone. So we went to the river. And we thought, what the heck. It was the 13th of April so we went into the river to wash. It was a little fresh, but the lilacs had started blooming already which was very, very early.[48]

What is notable here is the manner in which a genuinely terrifying event is framed within the memory of the 'beautiful Spring,' which in the course of the interview comes up several times. Furthermore, Rhonda's journey through the war-ravaged landscape is described almost as an extended walk through the country, which is only punctuated with moments of fear and danger.

Frame Four: Writing Wrongs

To speak, to document, and to write down the past for others to witness is often articulated as an important preventative measure – we speak of the past in order to avoid the repetition of its mistakes and tragedies. Nowhere is this impulse stronger than in the testimonies of survivors who have lived through the terrors of war.

In my own interviews, perhaps the most striking and poignant use of the past as a means to avoid future injustice is the memorial that Paul Tuerr constructed for his wife, Anna, in one of the housing developments he built in the town of Mannheim, Ontario. The monument is described by Tuerr and the local newspaper as 'the only one in North America commemorating the expulsion of ethnic Germans from their homes in Eastern Europe.'[49] That said, the monument itself is framed around a more universal message, despite its context being the specific hardships endured by Anna Tuerr, who, at the age of seventeen, was rounded up by Tito's Partisans in the former Yugoslavia and sent to a slave labour camp in the Ukraine. Entitled 'The Mother of the Universe Protects Children All Over the World,' the memorial depicts, in carved stone, a woman in a flowing gown, surrounded by three small children who appear to be circling her as if engaged in a game or dance. On the ground in front of the monument is a bronze plaque, on which is inscribed a quotation taken from Anna Tuerr's memoirs: 'May we all work together in the creation of a world in which humiliation, torture, war and exploitation no longer exist.' Within the booklet that was distributed during the unveiling, an additional quotation from Anna further speaks to the universal message of the monument and, more specifically, Anna Tuerr's legacy: 'We should never forget our dead, but for the sake of our children, we must be willing to forgive and get on with our lives to build a new world; a world with peace, a world without hate.'

The act of inscribing Anna Tuerr's personal experiences of loss and terror into a marker of universal human suffering and the need to 'forgive and get on with our lives to build a new world' speaks of the desire to provide a legacy of meaning for what would otherwise appear to be a random act of historical circumstance. Indeed, Klauss Koeppen, president of the German-Canadian Remembrance Society, is quoted in the *Kitchener-Waterloo Record* as stating that 'at 17 years of age, Anna Tuerr was totally non-political. You see that grandmothers, mothers, daughters, sisters and children were being deported into camps. Their only crime was that they were part of a certain nationality.' The article continues:

> The park and monument are also intended to foster future peace and co-operation. 'It is important to remember the past and remember the suffering of everybody,' Koeppen said. 'On the other hand, we have a responsibility to work together and focus on the future to make sure we have learned.'[50]

It is notable that the booklet, the newspaper articles, the documentary video, and the monument itself are decidedly apolitical, in the sense of distancing themselves from any specific critiques of either past acts or making any overt statements that could be construed as politically motivated. Aside from the details pertaining to Anna Tuerr's personal life, the overall discursive flow is towards generalized appeals to humanity and justice. Moreover, no mention is made of the historical realities of Nazi Germany and its many victims nor of actions taken against ethnic Germans by various political leaders, especially those in Poland, the USSR, and the former Yugoslavia. As well, there is no mention at all about the obligation to enact some kind of compensation for expellees or their children, whether in terms of money or the opportunity to reclaim lost property.

Such absences could be chalked up to a form of political correctness (or political politeness) in the sense of acknowledging both individual and collective suffering but without explicitly demanding anything in return from those responsible. In this sense, there are few judgments, lists of accusations, or settlings of accounts. Instead, there are appeals to universal symbols of human dignity and justice – the mother of the universe – which in effect elevate Anna Tuerr and her ordeals to a higher plane of meaning and significance.

Frame Five: Horror

There is no denying that the German Expulsion had its horrors, and that in between the accounts of good luck (relatively speaking) and 'great adventures' there were moments of deep suffering, deprivation, violence, and death. The Expulsion, however one wants to frame or contextualize it, was an aggressive act and thus had its victims, like any other. 'We hear so much today,' writes Alfred de Zayas, 'about the so-called ethnic cleansing going on since 1991 in the former Yugoslavia. Forty-eight years ago another genocide was in progress in the same area of the Balkans. Hundreds of thousands of ethnic Germans were uprooted, and tens of thousands were killed. They were evicted from their homes and sent off to slave labor camps in the Soviet Union; the women were raped and old people and children too young to work were interned in starvation camps.'[51]

In many cases, expellees have remained silent about their experiences, especially those who had left Germany and moved to countries such as Australia, the United States, and Canada. Such silence could be attributed partly to a desperate need to forget and partly to a sense that Germans had no right to complain. The silence also spoke of the desire to achieve the anonymity made possible by integration. 'In the first years,' notes Helga W., 'we did not talk about the war. When we went with the subway we whispered. We spoke English … We wanted to forget. We wanted to start new. And when you start new, you have to leave behind … things.'[52] Yet for many, including Helga W., the need to speak of the past and, at times, preserve the memories in some form does eventually become urgent, especially in later life: 'In the first years when people asked me how it was in Essen, I started to shake. I said, don't ask me. I want to forget. I don't want it. That went on for twenty to thirty years. And now, I have to remember. How it was. It is really almost gone.'

These memories are difficult for both those who remember them and those who are there to listen. It is at this juncture that I find myself not knowing what to do next with respect to this chapter. There is an implied duty, I believe, to simply allow the memories to speak for themselves and thus to use a text such as this one as a venue for both distributing and preserving the experiences of the expellees. At the same time there is again the thorny question of 'to what end?' What discourse is to be wrapped around these memories? How are they to be contextualized? What is to be done with these memories once they have been spoken and inscribed? These are difficult questions and ones that I can only respond to in part. However, before doing so, it is necessary to place a few memories on this page. I will start with Julianna V.

Julianna V. was part of the German ethnic community known as the Danube Swabians in the former Yugoslavia. Under the leadership of

Josip Tito, the Partisans forcibly initiated a 'population transfer' of approximately 271,000 Germans, many of whom ended up in 'hunger camps' where death and disease were common.[53]

> In November of 1944 they [the Partisans] took all the men from age sixteen to sixty and shot them so that there could no longer be any reproduction of us [Germans]. Then on April 22, 1945, just before the war finished, at six o'clock in the morning, they came to our door and said get out of this house, this is not your house anymore. So only what we had on our back, that is all that we could take. So they locked us up in a school for six months. They separated us. There were just women and children. The children under the age of twelve and the women over fifty-five, they were put in a real hunger camp. Those people, they got their food only twice a week ... just twice a week. And it was called Rudolfsgnad, the town were they put them. And my mother lost most of her family there. They died by the hundreds, every day. We were locked up for six months, and then they moved us. They put us in a whole section of houses, surrounded by barbed wire. The houses were empty, no furniture, no nothing. We slept on the floor. And then we had to work really hard. I had to work like a lumberjack. I had to dig out the trees and the big roots by hand ... They took everything. Very little food. Six ounces of bread a day and rainwater. Then they moved us to another camp, to an airplane hangar. No heat, it was very high. We were three thousand people in there.[54]

It did not take long for Julianna to fall sick, and she was taken to a primitive clinic where she was basically written off by the camp's doctor as too ill to live. But she did not die and was then transferred back to the camp, where the lack of nourishment eventually caused her to become temporarily blind. After enduring multiple hardships, she managed to escape, and after many trials and more narrow escapes, she managed to cross into the English zone and thus to freedom and relative safety.

Unlike many of those whom I interviewed, Julianna is vocal and deliberate about her suffering and her conviction that the *Volksdeutsche* were treated unjustly and, moreover, not granted much in the way of formal recognition or compensation:

> We had about the same life as the Jewish people did, except that we were not put in the gas chamber. We were just shot ... Innocent people, just take them off the street and shoot them ... Actually my father was a locksmith.

And they called him to the city hall and so he went because he thought that they needed some work done. So he went and they never came back. And they were half beaten to death. The Partisans beat them half to death before they shot them. And on this day there were one hundred men and five women shot with my father. They did that every day, every day. In one city, the city where I lived, on November 7, there were eight hundred men shot.

When I see things on TV, I wish they would stop. It brings back all my memories. I wish they would stop. Nobody helped us. No one knew about it or did not want to know about it … So many things going on in the war, that people don't know.

You know, here in Canada I dreamt for fifteen years … fifteen years, I've see him [my father] tied to a tree, calling my name, calling my name. It was like an echo. For years I had these nightmares. This is why when I see something on TV, before I always shut it off. I am afraid of nightmares. I had a lot of nightmares from the beginning. Not so many in the last ten years. I'm afraid of watching something like this, always being chased and beaten.

We had nothing to do with Germany. We were nice quiet people down there … When the Germans came, they took everything. They treated us the same as the other people, the Serbs, the Romanians, the Hungarians … we were just the same like the other ones. And not only this, we were bombed by the Germans, the Americans, the English, and again by the Germans. We were four times bombed out.

Like Julianna V., Haidi S. is also clear about her identity as a victim of unwarranted aggression and cruelty. In my interview with her, she described in detail the chain of events that took her from a happy and secure life in East Prussia to a dismal labour camp deep in the Ural Mountains. The conditions were deplorable, and many succumbed to the ravages of disease, malnutrition, and the extreme cold. 'I really don't know how we survived in that camp,' she recalls. 'They stripped us of everything. How I survived, I really don't know. You can't really describe how that affects your life. Was it hope that kept you alive? It was dark from one day to the next. We did not see any future. It was just survival. Just barely.'[55]

For Heinz M., his experiences in Langfuhr, a suburb of Danzig, at the end of the war shattered his faith and forever dimmed his view of the human race:

My mother had a friend whose husband (who was in charge of one area of the local airport) was asked to build something for the camp [a concentration camp]. He refused because he saw that it was not what it was meant for. I remember how his wife came over and cried and cried. They were very religious. She thought that her husband would be shot. He was not. He was demoted to a private. [At the end of the war] she was used by the first Russians who came in and so was her daughter and she died within three weeks. They were just a God fearing couple. Even for lunch they prayed always. Mother died, abused by Russian soldiers, and daughter also died within a short time.

When you are at such a vulnerable age as I was ... I come from a family, my uncle on my mother's side was a Jesuit father and on my father's side was a nun. So I was inclined to also enter some order, at least at that time. But seeing all that, my whole belief was shaken to the point where I don't believe in anything anymore.

I buried so many people ... right next to where we lived there was a kindergarten run by six nuns and one by one they died. We took the nuns out in wheelbarrows to the cemetery. But halfway we were asked to work on the roads, and in the evening, just before curfew, we went quickly to the cemetery, dug a shallow grave, and put them in. At that age you understand but not fully because you are not a real adult over twenty yet. I remember that when the first Russians came in, I was outside and right away I put my hands up ... And then when the bombs came ... the Stalin Orgel (the Stalin Organ), ever hear about that? There were about nine rockets in each unit and they covered a square mile and there were thirty-six units. I was in the middle of one attack. First thing you do is to dive into the first hole, because in that hole nothing will ever come in again. Most people stayed downstairs in the basement. There was a lady, she said she could not stand it anymore and she has to sleep in her bed. And could you please come up with me so that I can have someone there to protect me. And the Russian soldiers came up and they thought that it was lots of fun to rape that lady and keep me there right beside in bed. That is an experience that you don't forget.[56]

Conclusion

Ending this chapter has proven to be almost as difficult as starting it in the first place. How does one leave such a topic, and, once again, to what ends does the 'end' to this text proceed? In this chapter, I have attempted to situate the personal recollections of survivors of the *Vertreibung* within the larger discourses and practices associated with the material uses (and affects) of history. I have also approached the topic of the archive and its relationship to testimony, memory, and justice. It is with this latter topic that I will bring this chapter to its indefinite end.

In *Remnants of Auschwitz*, Giorgio Agamben offers a compelling meditation on what he terms the essential lacuna of testimony, namely, the manner in which survivors of the traumatic and terrible bear 'witness to something it is impossible to bear witness to.'[57] Agamben's concerns are, of course, particular to the Holocaust. Indeed, it must be noted and stressed that the Holocaust cannot be generalized in such a way that it becomes relativized, thereby diminishing its essential 'unsayability,' its incomparable relationship to other forms of violence and destruction.[58] Agamben cites Primo Levi in this regard:

> The phenomenon of Auschwitz is unique (certainly in the past, and we can only hope for the future). As Levi points out: 'Up to the moment of this writing, and notwithstanding the horror of Hiroshima and Nagasaki, the shame of the Gulags, the useless and bloody Vietnam war, the Cambodian self-genocide, the *desaparecidos* in Argentina, and the many atrocities and stupid wars we have seen since, the Nazi concentration camps still remain an *unicum*, both in its extent and its quality.'[59]

It is important to stress the uniqueness of the Nazi concentration camps within the context of this chapter for a number of reasons. Chief among these are the very real political dangers associated with a kind of comparative relativization of the Holocaust vis-à-vis the *Vertreibung*. In other words, to say that the *Vertreibung* is akin to the Holocaust and that the expellees bear some similarity with the victims of the camps effectively diminishes the levels of national and personal responsibility for both cases. Furthermore, such a comparison could serve as a vehicle for justification and what one could term a kind of ethical closure. In other words, the German people paid for their sins and so that's that. This chapter of history is therefore closed.

I would argue the reverse. This chapter is not closed. The Holocaust remains open. The *Vertreibung* remains open. The need for testimony and responsibility remains crucial for both. To what end, you may right ask (once again)? Not for judgment and not for the law, as Agamben points out:

> Almost all the categories that we use in moral and religions judgments are in some way contaminated by law: guilt, responsibility, innocence, judgment, pardon … This makes it difficult to invoke them without particular caution. As jurists well know, law is not directed toward the establishment of justice. Nor is it directed toward the verification of truth. Law is solely directed toward judgment, independent of truth and justice … The ultimate aim of law is the production of a *res judicata*, in which the sentence becomes the substitute for the true and the just, being held as true despite its falsity and injustice.[60]

Agamben's crucial point here is that law provides only a false closure – the debts have been paid, the punishments meted out, so once again, that is that. The case is over and we can all go home feeling justified and compensated.

But that is not true, as we all know deep down. Which is why testimonies must continue to be pursued and why the archive must remain forever open. 'The authority of the witness consists in his capacity to speak solely in the name of an incapacity to speak – that is, in his or her being a subject. Testimony thus guarantees not the factual truth of the statement safeguarded in the archive, but rather its unarchivability, its exteriority with respect to the archive – that is, the necessity by which, as the existence of language, it escapes both memory and forgetting.'[61]

Now, finally, towards what ends can I point my consideration of the *Vertreibung*? There are many, but one stands out in particular. The need to speak and to listen remains paramount, but not for reasons of judgment, compensation, or historical closure. Rather, it is for the sake of the survivors and the impossibilities that they have lived through and the concomitant impossibility of ever bringing their experiences to a close, of ever containing their memories within the tidy confines of the printed page.

NOTES

1 The project is based on a series of personal videotaped interviews conducted between January 2005 and April 2006 with former expellees who

immigrated to Canada in the late 1940s and early 1950s. Most of the interviewees are from the large German communities in the Greater Toronto Area (GTA), Hamilton, and Kitchener/Waterloo. The interviews were conducted using the 'open interview approach,' meaning that the emphasis was on allowing individuals to narrate their own story with as little interruption from me as possible. Towards the end of the interview, more specific questions were asked to move the conversation into the direction of considering the complexities of remembering and representing the Expulsion within the context of post-war issues and politics. I entered into each interview situation with the following questions in hand, which were used to provide a general structure: (1) Please tell me about your experience as an expellee or refugee towards and after the end of the war. (2) What do you remember life being like in your home town before, during, and after the war? (3) Upon arriving in Canada, how did you feel about being identified as a German? Did you experience any hostility? Did you feel uncomfortable in any way? (4) How would you say your own experiences during the war relate or compare to how Germany is portrayed in the mass media or in public discourse in general? How do you feel about such representations? (5) Did you or do you talk about your wartime experience with others, particularly your family members?

2 Additional sources are listed in the Bibliography.

3 Alfred de Zayas, *A Terrible Revenge: The Cleansing of the East European Germans, 1944–1950* (New York: St Martin's Press, 1994), 77–84.

4 The Avalon Project at the Yale Law School has the entire proceedings on-line at: http://www.pch.gc.ca/progs/multi/policy/act_e.cfm.

5 Éva Kovács, 'The Mémoire Croisée of the Shoah,' *Eurozine*, 22 May 2006, p. 3, http://www.eurozine.com

6 The topic of German suffering during the wartime years has entered into public discourse recently with the publication of such works as W.G. Sebald's 1999 book *On the Natural History of Destruction*; Jörg Friedrich's *The Fire: Germany in the Air War*; Hans Erich Nossack's *The End*; Gert Ledig's *The Stalin Front* and *Payback* (both recently republished); the anonymously authored *A Woman in Berlin*; Peter Reese's *A Stranger to Myself*; Günter Grass's *Crabwalk*; Uwe Timm's memoir *In My Brother's Shadow: A Life and Death in the SS*; Gudio Knopp's five-part TV series *Die Grosse Flucht*; and the German magazine *Der Spiegel*'s series 'Flucht und Vertreibung der Deutschen aus dem Osten.' See the Bibliography for the complete citations.

7 The Zentrum Gegen Vertreibungen (Center against Expulsions) maintains a website which details the policies of the foundation and provides

additional information about the exhibition. See: http://www.z-g-v.de/english/index.html

8 'Berlin Exhibition on Postwar Expulsions Opens Amid Protests,' *Deutsche Welle World*, 11 August 2006. On-line version: http://www.dw-world.de/dw/article/0,2144,2129308,00.html

9 Dagmar Barnouw, *The War in the Empty Air: Victims, Perpetrators and Postwar Germans* (Bloomington: Indiana University Press, 2005). See also the BdV home page at http://www.bund-der-vertriebenen.de/

10 See the GWA home page at http://www.germanworldalliance.org/

11 Mission statement, German Canadian Congress website: http://www.dkk-ont.net/index.html#Our%20Mission%20

12 http://www.cjnews.com/pastissues/01/may10–01/international/intl.htm

13 Paul Tuerr, 'Innocent Germans Also Suffered under the Nazi Regime,' *Kitchener Waterloo Record*, 'Second Opinion' (editorial), 5 September 2006.

14 'Preamble,' Canadian Multiculturalism Act, http://www.pch.gc.ca/progs/multi/policy/act_e.cfm

15 Paul Ricoeur, *Memory, History, Forgetting*, trans. Kathleen Blamey and David Pellauer (Chicago: University of Chicago Press, 2004), 147.

16 Steven E. Aschheim, 'On Saul Friedlander,' *History and Memory* 9, nos. 1–2 (1997), http://iupjournals.org/history/ham9–12.html

17 Ricoeur, *Memory*, 168.

18 Ibid., 175.

19 Ibid.

20 Ibid., 176.

21 Alexander Freund, 'Dealing with the Past Abroad: German Immigrants: *Vergangenheitsbewaltigung* and Their Relations with Jews in North American since 1945,' *GHI Bulletin*, no. 31 (Fall 2002): 51, http://www.ghi-dc.org/bulletinF02/51.pdf

22 Ibid., 53.

23 Ibid.

24 See Laurenn Guyot's contribution to this volume, p. 146.

25 Reinhart Koselleck, *Futures Past: On the Semantics of Historical Time* (Cambridge: MIT Press, 1985), xii–xiii.

26 Ibid., xiv.

27 Ibid., 6.

28 See Srdja Pavlovic's contribution to this volume, p. 43.

29 See Julia Creet's Introduction to this volume, pp. 6–7.

30 Peter Schneider, 'In Their Side of World War II, the Germans Also Suffered,' *New York Times*, Arts and Ideas, 18 January 2003.
31 Ibid.
32 Interview with Ursula K., 30 May 2005, Hamilton, Ontario.
33 Interview with Haidi S., 3 February 2006, Kitchener, Ontario.
34 For one of the more publicly debated books on this topic, see Daniel J. Goldhagen, *Hitler's Willing Executioners: Ordinary Germans and the Holocaust* (New York: Knopf, 1996).
35 The word *Volksdeutsche* translates as 'ethnic Germans,' whereas *Reichsdeutsche* refers to Germans who were citizens of Germany under Hitler (i.e., the Third Reich).
36 Interview with Heinz M., 24 February 2005, Toronto, Ontario.
37 Interview with Ron S., 25 February 2005, Toronto, Ontario.
38 Interview with Hubert L., 11 March 2005, Toronto, Ontario.
39 Theodor Adorno, 'What Does Coming to Terms with the Past Mean?' *Bitburg in Moral and Political Perspective*, ed. Geoffrey Hartman (Bloomington: Indiana University Press, 1986).
40 Ibid., 128.
41 Alf Ludtke, 'Coming to Terms with the Past: Illusions of Remembering, Ways of Forgetting Nazism in West Germany,' *Journal of Modern History* 65, no. 3 (Sept. 1993): 560.
42 Ibid., 560.
43 Ibid., 561.
44 Interview with Ron S., 25 February 2005, Toronto, Ontario.
45 Interview with Ursula K., 30 May 2005, Hamilton, Ontario.
46 W.G. Sebald, *On the Natural History of Destruction* (New York: Modern Library, 2004), 11–12.
47 Interview with Helga W., 30 March 2005, Toronto, Ontario.
48 Interview with Rhonda H., 29 January 2005, Guelph, Ontario.
49 Magda Konieczna, 'Sculpture, Park, Mark Germans' Uprooting,' *Kitchener Waterloo Record*, 28 June 2005. This is actually a quoted statement from Ulrich Frisse, president of the German-Canadian Congress of Ontario, who spoke at the opening ceremony of the monument on 27 June 2005.
50 Ibid.
51 de Zayas, *A Terrible Revenge*, 99.
52 Interview with Helga W., 30 March 2005, Toronto, Ontario.
53 Among the more detailed accounts is Gerhard Reichling's *Die deutschen Vertriebenen in Zahlen* (Bonn: Kulturstiftung der Deutscheb Vertriebenen, 1986).
54 Interview with Julianna V., 28 January 2004, Hamilton, Ontario.

55 Interview with Haidi S., 3 February 2006, Kitchener, Ontario.

56 Interview with Heinz M., 24 February 2005, Toronto, Ontario.

57 Giorgio Agamben, *Remnants of Auschwitz: The Witness and the Archive*, trans. Daniel Heller-Roazen (New York: Zone Books, 2002), 13.

58 Mark Anderson, writing for *The Nation*, notes how 'former New leftists … reshaped the politics of German memory in the late 1960s and early '70s and adamantly opposed the attempts of Ernst Nolte and other historians in the mid-'80s to compare Hitler's crimes to Stalin's purges and other instances of mass slaughter' ('Crime and Punishment,' *The Nation*, 17 October 2005, http://www.thenation.com/doc/20051017/anderson).

59 Agamben, *Remnants*, 21.

60 Ibid.,158.

61 Ibid.

6 The Cultural Trauma Process, or the Ethics and Mobility of Memory

JOHN SUNDHOLM

A defence of false memory might be considered provocative and even immoral, but only from a strictly epistemological standpoint. I want to show that what is considered false epistemology and false memory is not always to be condemned, because if we posit only epistemological claims on memory, we downplay its ethical and hermeneutical dimensions. I use the term 'hermeneutical' in the sense of a request to understand or to create an internal relation to an object that does not necessarily imply an interpretation of its meaning or content. The philosopher Avishai Margalit is very precise regarding the limits of the epistemology of memory when it comes to ethical tasks such as forgiving and forgetting: 'The idea that truth by itself will bring about reconciliation is a doubtful empirical assumption.'[1] An ethical stance, of course, cannot ignore truth, which is both an epistemological and moral category, but ethics presupposes an internal relation that is essential for memory processes in which the aim is that of working through.[2]

I will also argue that memory is essentially a phenomenon of migration; the event that always precedes a memory is a veiled and absent signifier that has migrated and transformed into a memory that is persistently trapped in the present. Thus, the contemporaneous is what we are essentially talking about, and hence the function of memory in the present becomes a key issue. This does not imply, however, that there is no use in considering or researching memory as a meaning-making practice related to a past. Quite the opposite, memory and its relation to a precedent event becomes even more crucial because the present is ultimately formed by that which has happened in the past. We may never overcome the event as fact and absent cause; but the meaning-making practice takes place in the present.

The critical question posed by memory studies has usually been, how we should consider the act of memory: As an act of testimony? As an act of securing meaning and identity? Or, simply as an act of recollecting the past? By concentrating on traumatic memory, I want to show that the question of memory should not always be reduced to a moral dichotomy of right or wrong, to a question of victims or perpetrators, or to a mission of seeking the truth. I will clarify my points by presenting an analysis of the 'cultural trauma process' of the Second World War in Finland. My case study deals with the function of the narrative 'The Unknown Soldier,' which was originally created by a novel in 1954 and later became a foundational story for the Finnish collective memory of the Second World War.[3] The narrative enabled a process of working through for the whole nation.

1. Cultural Trauma

Sociologist Jeffrey C. Alexander launched what he coined a 'theory of cultural trauma,' to both criticize what he calls 'lay trauma theory,' and to offer a perspective for considering social and cultural processes of collective traumas in order to analyse how events are turned into traumas and which social or cultural purposes they serve. According to Alexander, 'lay trauma theory' makes the mistake of chasing an origin that would somehow reveal or anchor the trauma, in order to give it a plain and fixed meaning. Following this critique, what is instead of primary interest is how an event is made into a collective trauma, and how something that has taken place receives a significant meaning for a group or a society. The advantage with Alexander's notion is that, compared with other studies which seek the meaning of the event itself and therefore attempt to transform the event into an explanation and to assign a rationale to it, in cultural trauma analyses the focus is on the cultural process of making meaning in the present. As Alexander aptly puts it, 'It is the meanings that provide the sense of shock and fear, not the events themselves. Whether or not the structures of meaning are destabilized and shocked is not the result of an event but the effect of a socio-cultural process.'[4]

Thus, the notion of cultural trauma implies that trauma is treated as a phenomenon of migration (the effect of something that is absent). What is an even more controversial claim is that, in this framework, the relation between event (origin) and its meaning (trauma) is foremost considered to be a question of social value rather than of epistemology.

In a sense, it is consequential, when we talk about a phenomenon that is constructed by human beings in the present, that the question of a presumed origin becomes of minor importance because it is, after all, the present that triggers the situation and thus launches the meaning. Therefore, memories actualized in the present are migrating symptoms that have to be considered and understood in the now in which they appear. Of course, memory does form a link between past, present, and future, but it does not operate as part of a culture of estrangement by constituting a definitive break between now and then, which is something that characterizes history or critical history proper. The past is truly a foreign country for the historian.

Accordingly, what a theory of cultural trauma also implies is that trauma is a normative concept. It indicates a value that is socially established and hence created or constructed. The group or community maintains memory and insists on the necessity of the value of its practice. This encompasses as well the act of expanding the community of memory. Following Alexander:

> Is the suffering of others also our own? In thinking that it might in fact be, societies expand the circle of the we. By the same token, social groups can, and often do, refuse to recognize the existence of others' trauma, and because of their failure they cannot achieve a moral stance ... [B]y refusing to participate in what I will describe as the process of trauma creation, social groups restrict solidarity, leaving others to suffer alone.[5]

Consequently, a key question is how to expand the 'we' in order for the trauma to become a part of what Margalit has coined 'thick relations,' that is, an ethics of memory.

2. Cultural Trauma and Ethics

In general, psychologists and sociologists agree that trauma and event are separate. Trauma is an act of signification, hence something social. Alexander stresses the social dimension even further with his notion that 'cultural trauma occurs when members of a collectivity feel they have been subjected to a horrendous event that leaves indelible marks upon their group consciousness, marking their memories forever and changing their future identity in fundamental and irrevocable ways.'[6] This social character of trauma as a process excludes it from history proper. As Allan Megill has put it, quoting from R. G. Collingwood's

The Idea of History, memory is always 'immediate.'[7] It is not a dissection of the past but an experience in the present. Therefore, memory is, in a sense, always familiar, whereas history is foreign. Hence, a concept like 'sense memory' is almost a tautology because living memory presupposes a subject sensing the past in the present. If there is no subject or bodily sensation (and how can we have a subject without a body?) there is no living memory. In this sense, memory is partly organic, an integral part of us. Megill gives the example of someone expressing the memory of a specific person and how there is no reason to question such a recollection: 'As Collingwood memorably puts it, to say that I remember writing a letter to So-and-so is "a statement of memory" and not a "historical statement": whereas if I can add, "I am right for here is his reply," I am talking history.'[8] History craves for external evidence.

Thus, history – according to such a theoretical dichotomization – is always a question of an attempt to anchor an utterance or a statement, whereas memory is fluid and in constant movement. It is mobility that grants the doability of memory – the latter an implicit standpoint already stressed by Maurice Halbwachs while claiming that memory is essentially social in his essays from the early twentieth century.[9] Memories are constantly reshaped and created. The paradox is that although memory is essentially social (Halbwachs denied the existence of 'private' memory) and, as Julia Creet puts it, 'always attended by movement,'[10] the fluidity also implies that memory is utterly subjective in the frame of epistemology. We can only trust a personal statement of memory. It is the old-fashioned virtues of confidence and caring that rule much of memory culture, thus constituting a community, a social body.

3. The Semiotics of Cultural Trauma

What I find highly problematic in Alexander's theory is the claim that collectively we may choose how to represent events: 'Collective actors "decide" to represent social pain as a fundamental threat to their sense of who they are.'[11] It is difficult to consider events such as mass rapes, which so often are part of warfare, as being mere happenings that we may actually choose to signify as traumatic. This is especially so when the intention behind the deeds is to create traumas, to shake, interrupt, and break the identity of individuals and groups.[12] However, in a broader perspective, when we talk about the dynamics of groups and collectives and their identity, I think that cultural trauma is a useful notion. Then it makes sense to talk about a construction of social meanings, of how the event is transformed and migrates into a grid of significations.

The thesis about a gap between sign and referent is well known within (social) semiotics and cultural studies. No meanings are inherent in the object or the event. It is always a matter of appropriation, negotiation, cultural struggle, and the making of meaning. Trauma studies is also akin to symptomatic analysis; the focus is not on what something means, but on why it has appeared and how it is used. Slavoj Žižek has suggested in *The Sublime Object of Ideology* that the true meaning of Freud's dream analysis is not the hermeneutical approach as commonly practised, of asking what dreams signify and searching for a hidden content. Instead, the appropriate method in Freudian dream analysis is the question of form and why something has taken the appearance of the dream.[13] Thus, the investigation or understanding is always grounded in the binding of a past together with the present, or in the clash between them. But it is not a question of tracing something backwards to its presumed origin, as Creet also pertinently points out in her Introduction.[14]

Hence, the cultural trauma process, or what we might call the semiotics of trauma, takes place in-between event and representation. But in order for the event to become a cultural trauma, to migrate into social significance, it has to be established as a shared value – even if we talk about a 'negative' value as in the case of trauma. This is a process that takes time and that requires agents, mediations, and a community of carriers and 'caretakers.' Thus, cultural trauma, while being a social and cultural phenomenon, implies an ethics. I want to stress that this concerns *cultural* trauma, not all trauma, because I doubt that the gap between event and representation is always a negotiable space that is accessible for intervention and agency. Some events may be so difficult and horrible that it takes an extensive time span to appropriate them. I also consider individual psychological trauma – at least in part – to be outside the model and the interpretative frame that Alexander establishes. This is obviously a highly contested issue.

Accordingly, the theory launched by Alexander – which he considers to be an empirical one – is, for me, essentially a cultural perspective on dramatic events that have the potential to be made into collective traumas involving a shared past and a common memory around something that is deeply disturbing. I prefer to talk of 'perspective' instead of theory because what we face is a heuristic process in which we are trying to find reasonable meanings for situations, acts, and things. This trauma process is also a question of culture because trauma is used as a metaphor: it is something that is carried over – and migrating – from the discipline and domain of psychology into that of culture, or cultural anthropology and sociology of culture.

4. *The Unknown Soldier* and Finnish Collective Memory of the Second World War

The Unknown Soldier was originally a novel published in 1954 by a working-class novelist, Väinö Linna. It tells the story of a platoon during the Second World War when Finland waged war against the Soviet Union. Most of the members of the platoon are killed, and in the end it is mainly the scum and the buffoons, those who live for the moment and their own gain, who survive.

From a Finnish point of view, the Second World War is primarily regarded as two separate wars: The Winter War and the Continuation War.[15] The Winter War began in November 1939, when Finland was attacked by the Soviet Union. The war was waged in defence against a strong enemy, and Finland realized at an early stage that it had to reach a peace agreement fairly soon because of the Soviet Union's overwhelming force. The peace treaty that was signed in March 1940 was hard: Finland had to abandon substantial areas in the eastern province of Karelia (Karjala), which had about four hundred thousand inhabitants. Consequently, the Finns were more than willing to join Germany when operation Barbarossa was launched in 1941 to attack the Soviet Union. Many Finnish people at the time regarded the attack as a unique chance to regain the territory just lost. However, the war ended in a devastating defeat.

This second war, the Continuation War, caused the greatest wounds and scars for the people and the nation. It was the symbolical end to the Finnish experience of the Second World War. It is estimated that by the end of the Continuation War, every sixth Finnish soldier had been killed. One tenth of Finland's territory had to be left to the Soviet Union, and huge war debts had to be paid. Not many civilians were killed, but about seventy thousand children were evacuated to Sweden and Denmark during the Continuation War, and more than 10 per cent never returned to Finland. The defeat also resulted in the Russian takeover of the city of Viipuri, Finland's second largest city at the time. Accordingly, the war meant a huge loss, and the controversial question was, of course, whether the sacrifice could be justified. Finland had, after all, waged war against the Allies with one of the most evil powers in modern history, Hitler's Third Reich.

Thus, the event contains most of the characteristics that are typical for happenings that will become traumas. We have the losses (not only material matters, but a loss of national meaning and identity, as well), the guilt and shame, and the anxiety about what to do next since the peace treaty meant that the Soviet Union would become a powerful godfather for the partly new Finnish nation that was established after the war.

The first successful way of giving meaning to the dramatic event and its aftermath was the novel, *The Unknown Soldier*. The book became a huge success against all odds, while it was heavily criticized by the leading literary critics and representatives of the army. Not even the publisher fully believed in the novel, which was printed in a standard edition of four thousand copies, because it was considered a far too naturalistic, ironic, and cynical depiction of the life of the Finnish soldier. Hence, the critics did not understand the novel's character as memory material, and instead it was regarded as either belonging to the genre of the documentary novel or constituting a national epic about the war.

What the soldiers strive for in the novel is simply to stay alive; all other meanings established in connection to the war are shown as being constructions made by the establishment (officers, politicians, and priests – the ideologues of the war) in the interests of the establishment. Linna's aim (besides making a breakthrough with his novel, of course) was, as he claimed himself, to give meaning and to pay respect to all those ordinary men who had been soldiers in the Finnish Army. Many of those men, including Linna himself, had spent their whole formative youth at the frontlines of battle. In other words, Linna wanted to expand the 'we' in order to create a culture of sharing and caring. The paradox is that by writing a novel which claimed that war is without profound meaning (actually, without meaning at all), and that it is essentially a terrible experience without honour and lasting heroes (although some specific deeds and actions during war may indeed be honourable and heroic), Linna was able to offer meaning and value to the meaningless and horrible events that the common soldier had experienced. The regular soldier did not care for the history of the war; he had to live with the memory of it.

Linna's very carefully planned depiction of the war enabled the national trauma to be brought into the open. It was the novel that re-actualized the event and made it enter the public sphere in the form of a trauma, creating a conflict between the common man (as soldier) and those who belonged to the establishment. Yet another act would solve this conflict and 'smooth' the trauma, enabling the constitution of a cultural trauma, a shared value around the horrible, confusing, and controversial events – namely, the making of an adaptation of the novel for the screen. The adaptation took the critical edge of the novel, created a new mythological hybrid story, and brought it out into a larger social sphere.

The immense success of the novel, which sold about 175,000 copies during one year in a country with about four million inhabitants, made the leading Finnish film company interested in adapting the novel into a film. The process was incredibly rapid: the film had its grand opening almost exactly one year after the book had been published. That the production was so fast is remarkable because the film was the most expensive of its time in Finnish film history. Both the army and even part of the government tried without success to obstruct the production; the army did so because they felt the novel scorned the Finnish soldier, and the government tried to interfere because they were afraid of the political reaction from the Soviet Union. The rapid adaptation of *The Unknown Soldier* fused the novel and the film into a new story, creating a socio-historical imaginary, a survival story for the nation.

The film became one of the most successful ever in Finnish history, and it succeeded in consolidating the nation. The reasons for this are several, but I will only point out those which are of interest in this context. Obviously there was a need for a collective story that could both act as a document of the war and, if not justify the war, at least give back dignity to the nation and those who had fought in the battles. The film as a cultural form and institution was, in fact, a perfect medium for such an assignment. Of all cultural forms in the 1950s, film gathered the largest audiences. Its aesthetics also allow for the possibility of transgressing the boundary between fact and fiction, which in turn makes it an ideal medium for exploring the historical unconscious.[16]

The film version of *The Unknown Soldier* consists of extensive historical footage, using documentary material that is edited into the film in such a manner that the difference between fact and fiction becomes blurred. The point with blending genres and footage is not to erase the difference between the fictitious story and the historical footage, because then the audience would lose their trust in the film as being both a document of the war (estrangement) and a fictitious story (an act of socio-emotional meaning-making). Instead, the aim of the film was to achieve an effect whereby, in a very explicit and naturalistic manner, it is both quoting from history (the event) and creating fiction (making meaning) at the same time. Thus the event and its effects, history and memory, documentary and fiction, the real and the constructed trauma, merge. This is carefully structured by filmic means; the filmmakers blend fictitious sequences in which the individual men's actions and fates are depicted with purely documentary elements. It is therefore possible to distinguish three discursive-diegetic levels in the film: first, the fictitious narrative about the machine-gun company; second, the documentary elements based on newsreels from the military; third, material that is fictitious but presented so that it acquires a documentary function, such as persons who appear in the picture but are not introduced as characters with names and who therefore have a diegetic life that only lasts as long as the shot or scene. Examples of such scenes or shots include the introductory scene, which shows how a soldier is buried during a retreat. One member of the platoon picks up a dry, dead branch that will serve as a cross on the grave. This same scene appears later, near the end, but is now inserted within the linear progress of the narrative. Thus its opening documentary function is later on transformed into being fictitious, part of the diegesis. A similar example occurs in another scene in the middle of the film, where two soldiers are executed in order to restore discipline. The actors used are introduced for the first time to the viewer, and they will never reappear in the film. The scene is covered using full shots, a stylistic choice that stresses its documentary function, where the camera is distanced from what is being depicted. Because of the stylistic choices used in constructing the scenes, the viewer is not led directly into the diegetic world of the film, but rather, the link between the documentary and the fictitious is stressed, and the differences between the two levels become blurred. In the editing of the film, this pattern is carefully planned: a switch to documentary material is prepared by a fictitious scene ending in a long shot, which is then followed by a long shot from the archives; conversely, when an archival sequence ends, a close-up is normally used, from which the fictitious narrative can take over again.

Not surprisingly, many critics later criticized the film and the narrative of 'The Unknown Soldier' for being too overtly nationalistic claiming, in particular, that the film distorts individual facts and the history of the war. The critique is, of course, valid and apt. The film is nationalistic and depicts a story that simplifies a complicated chain of events.

However, the narrative in its entirety, in which both the film version and the novel merge into the same story, must also be understood as a way of establishing a cultural trauma that both constitutes and enables wider participation in the trauma process of the Second World War in Finland. Hence, the story, 'The Unknown Soldier,' is a collective creation, constituting an ethics of memory that enables a linking together of all those people who lived through the events between 1939 and 1944, without judging who did what or classifying people into heroes, friends, foes, traitors, and victims. The successful repetition of the story, which is widely known and usually shown in its film adaptation every Independence Day on national television, is therefore proof of a successful expansion of the 'we' in Finland, encompassing all those who feel that they belong to Finnish culture and society – a 'we' that did not change radically until the 1990s.[17]

5. Epistemology and Cultural Trauma

One of the consequences of the idea of cultural trauma is that we have to downplay the epistemological problem of memory. Questions of whose memory is correct and who did what, become less important. The semiotics of cultural trauma is instead based upon the principle of migration, in that we study effects of an absent event. The question of origin or of what exactly has happened is of minor relevance. If, on the other hand, we focus on the question of the character and quality of the event and its origin, then we are moving into the domain of the morality of trauma and memory, driven by the imperative to find out what the event was like. This is the world of the detective and the police of morality as well as the world of historians with their aspiration for proof and evidence. As Margalit claims, we need morality because we don't care about people in general – we care only for those we know and for those who are near us. Therefore, caring is placed in a 'now' and is, so to speak, localized.[18] Consequently, to pose the question of what actually happened is only important from a strictly moral and historical point of view. Morality, according to Margalit, is therefore abstract and general, as ethics is material and specific. Ethics presupposes a shared past, memory, and community, whereas morality does not. Hence, a true cultural trauma process is an indication of 'thick' relations and an ethics.

Thus, acknowledging a cultural trauma is a social form of caring. If we care for a collective that has suffered, then we must consider their traumatic past. If we care primarily about the morality of the trauma (for example, about what actually happened, or about who has the right to claim to be traumatized), then we don't necessarily care for the community or the individual. It is, for example, this relation between morality and ethics that the religious father in the classical American film melodrama *East of Eden* does not understand. The righteous patriarch is incapable of actually caring for his sons because his primary principle for their upbringing is that of morality. In such a light, the interviews of German expellees in Canada, collected by Andreas Kitzmann, become valuable memory material in their own right.[19] They are invitations for caring and understanding, regardless of the truth-value in the stories that are constructed and told in front of the camera. This does not mean that we should ignore the question of epistemology, only that caring implies that truth and morality are considered to be secondary perspectives (posing the questions about what they actually did and how true their stories are).

6. Trauma, Time, and Ethics

Following Margalit's thesis, then, an ethics presupposes an enclosed social space. Morality, on the other hand, is unlimited. It regulates our 'thin' relations, our common humanity. Morality is born out of principles and therefore is the result of an act of negotiation and legislation. As Margalit writes, 'Morality is long on geography and short on memory. Ethics is typically short on geography and long on memory.'[20] Consequently, we are facing a dilemma, given that one of the primary characteristics of today's society is migration and immigration: how to move between the open and abstract space of morality and the enclosed space of ethics? How to care both for epistemology and subjective experience? My brief case study on 'The Unknown Soldier' would suggest that a myth and a founding trauma may serve a particular purpose at a certain time in history.[21] Such narratives have a time span of their own, constituting partly separate processes. Their lifespans are specific and restricted, for example, not only by their distance in time from the events themselves, but also by actual people who are taking part directly in the process by being the actual, living, and communicative memory.[22] When people pass away, however, and when the communicative memory that they uphold begins to vanish, it is easier for an historical critique to enter – a critique that attempts to anchor some of the claims and therefore will dissolve the memory as well. Memory, after all, like all cultural phenomena and processes, is time dependent. And because we are dealing with processes in time, the dichotomizations of ethics and (fixed) places versus morality and (open) spaces wither away. New chains of signification are closed, and others are opened up.

This 'law' of the historical situation, or a dialectics of inclusion and exclusion (what is possible or not), is detectable in the attempt to make a new version of 'The Unknown Soldier' in Finland. During the early 1980s, the Finnish director Rauni Mollberg co-wrote with Linna a new version of *The Unknown Soldier*, which premiered in 1985. Mollberg announced in the press that his aim was to make a film that was more up to date – not only shot in colour and in stereo – but also a version that was more truthful to the novel's original intentions. Both Mollberg and Linna wanted to enforce the critical legacy of the story, but the audience disliked the result.[23] The film was simply incongruent with the historical and cultural situation. The original film had entered the cultural trauma process far too early and even aspired to being an historically truthful film, so that the new version, which stressed the meaninglessness of war, made some people react with the paradoxical claim that the previous film was more 'historical.' Clearly, the version from the 1950s had established a collective meaning for the nation that was still experienced as valid.[24]

It therefore seems obvious that the communicative and living memory at the time, and the cultural trauma, still had an ethical function, lessening the – epistemologically – dubious depiction of the events of the war. It was not until 1989 that other perspectives could enter the enclosed space of the founding trauma. With the dissolution of the Soviet Union, which changed Finnish foreign politics, and with the death of the generation of people who had lived through the war, history and its acts of estrangement and distance began unreservedly to enter the culture of memory, opening up the experiences of trauma for critical research and transforming the memory of the events into plain rituals of commemoration.[25] Then a state of 'the right model for forgiving,' according to Margalit, can be reached: 'not forgetting the wrong done but rather overcoming the resentment that accompanies it.'[26] Hence, if we stick to the dichotomy between ethics and morality that Margalit suggests exists, a dichotomy that reflects one found in memory and history as well, then there is no other way out of it except by acknowledging the two opposite aspects. It would, however, be futile to think that we could judge which perspective to use by only looking at the event in question. As in the classical question regarding how to represent the Holocaust (should it be depicted as a silence, a void, because the event is beyond reason, or should it be depicted with horror and ugliness?) there is no single point of view and simple solution. Both options or strategies are possible, and they are necessary interventions for a culture that strives for understanding its past, but either choice implies contextualizations that will ultimately be indicative of which choice is tenable. I would claim that Finland in 1956 would not have been able to cope with a rigorous historical analysis of the events during the Second World War while the country was still in the beginning of its process of working through. Thus, the question is not only, as Andreas Huyssen has put it, about 'if' and 'how,' but also about 'when to represent historical trauma.'[27] Contextualizing the dichotomized coordinates of ethics and morality, as well as memory and history, is always a question of space and time, of where and when. Time seems, in particular, to be the natural force *par excellence* over which memory can never prevail. For people do live for a limited time. To acknowledge the necessity of the time span is important because it implies that the cultural trauma process includes as well the act of forgetting: the absent and necessary other of memory.

NOTES

1 Avishai Margalit, *The Ethics of Memory* (Harvard: Harvard University Press, 2002), 6.
2 This is, according to Paul Ricoeur, one of Dominick LaCapra's valuable contributions to the question of *Vergangenheitsbewältigung*: the criteria of how to consider the past become foremost a therapeutic and not an epistemological question. See Paul Ricoeur, *Memory, History, Forgetting* (Chicago: University of Chicago Press, 2004), 159n45.
3 The case study in its full length, and from a slightly different theoretical perspective, is published as John Sundholm, '"The Unknown Soldier": Film as a Founding Trauma and National Monument,' in *Collective Trauma*, ed. Conny Mithander, John Sundholm, and Maria Holmgren Troy (Brussels: P.I.E Peter Lang, 2007).
4 Jeffrey C. Alexander, 'Toward a Theory of Cultural Trauma,' in *Cultural Trauma and Collective Identity*, ed. Jeffrey Alexander, Roy Eyerman, Bernhard Giesen, Neil J. Smelser, and Piotr Sztompka (Berkeley: University of California Press, 2004), 10.

5 Ibid., 1.
6 Ibid.
7 Allan Megill, *Historical Knowledge, Historical Error: A Contemporary Guide to Practice* (Chicago: University of Chicago Press, 2007), 22.
8 Ibid.
9 Maurice Halbwachs, *On Collective Memory* (Chicago: University of Chicago Press, 1992).
10 See Julia Creet's Introduction to this volume, p. 9.
11 Alexander, 'Toward a Theory of Cultural Trauma,' 10.
12 This becomes evident through Alexander's examples: the wound of the Vietnam War and the American psyche; slavery as a collective trauma for African Americans, etc. It is also typical that a radical constructivist view such as Alexander's cannot consider intentional acts. The presupposition of the perspective is that we live in the world of the sociologist, of *tabula rasa*.
13 In a short essay on film and memory, I have elaborated upon Freud's analysis according to Žižek's reading. See John Sundholm, 'Condensed History: The Poetics of Memory in Film,' in *Travelling Concepts III: Memory, Narrative, Image*, ed, Nancy Pedri (Amsterdam: ASCA Press, 2003).
14 Creet, Introduction, pp. 5–7, 9.
15 In fact, a third war took place in 1944, the so-called Lapland War, when Finish troops – according to the peace treaty with the Soviet Union from the same year – had to force the German troops out of northern Finland.
16 During the period from 1950 to 1959, 209 Finnish feature films opened in Finland, nearly twice as many as in the following decades.
17 When the film was shown on public television in 1979, it was estimated that almost 2.6 million people watched it.
18 This is also the thesis in Zygmunt Bauman's astute analysis of the relation between modernity and the Holocaust. Rationality presupposes distance and abstraction. See Zygmunt Bauman, *Modernity and the Holocaust* (London: Polity Press, 1989).
19 See Andreas Kitzmann's contribution to this volume.
20 Margalit, *Ethics of Memory*, 8.
21 Founding trauma is a notion of Dominick LaCapra's. It denotes a more or less mythologizing narrative used to unite a group and give it effective, functional, and meaningful recollections of the past. See Dominick LaCapra. 'Trauma, Absence, Loss,' *Critical Inquiry* 25 (1999): 696–727.
22 Jan Assmann makes a distinction between material-historical memory and everyday-immaterial memory. He calls the former 'cultural memory' and the latter 'communicative memory.' Cultural memory denotes the artifacts,

the objects, that which is public in this sense. Communicative memory comprises the memories that are triggered and represented in everyday actions and interactions and is much more akin to private memory or recollection. See Jan Assmann, 'Kollektives Gedachtnis und kulturelle Identitat,' in *Kultur und Gedachtnis*, ed. Jan Assmann and Toni Hölscher (Frankfurt am Main: Suhrkamp Verlag, 1986), 9–19.

23 The film was, in fact, highly appreciated by the critics.

24 For example, the journalist Rauno Velling wrote that the second version lacked 'history' and 'time,' and he finished his review by saying that the point of reference for the original film is Linna's novel and 'Finland's war.' Velling thus does not distinguish between the novel and the first film adaptation, and views the narrative as if it were about the entire nation at war for its independence. Velling begins his review with some memories of when he commenced his studies in the autumn of 1955 at University of Helsinki, and describes how the making of the film itself and the participating actors created an aura and culture of triumph that had already taken the critical edge off Linna's novel. See Rauno Velling, *Aamulehti*, 7 January 1986.

25 Thus, I consider my case study in Mithander et al., eds, *Collective Trauma*, as such an attempt. This essay, in turn, becomes the ethical complement to my former historical, rational, and moral analysis.

26 Margalit, *Ethics of Memory*, 208.

27 Andreas Huyssen, 'Of Mice and Mimesis: Reading Spiegelman with Adorno,' *Visual Culture and the Holocaust*, ed. Barbie Zelizer (New Brunswick: Rutgers University Press, 2001), 29.

7 Locked in a Memory Ghetto: A Case Study of a Kurdish Community in France

LAURENN GUYOT

Ô poor nightingale!
The wind destroyed your nest,
You were wounded and forced to exile.
I know that your desire
Is not to own a golden cage
But to be able to return in your homeland.
— Poem by Aram, Kurdish singer[1]

This poem summarizes well the history of Kurdish exiles. Firstly, it illustrates the destruction of hundreds of Kurdish villages by the Turkish army,[2] the persecutions and tortures endured by the Kurds, and the feeling of being expelled shared by numerous Kurdish migrants. Secondly, one can observe an indifference towards the conditions of settlement and an unfailing will to return to the homeland. These observations illustrate the strong links between the past, exile, and ways of apprehending the present in immigration. It shows that not only is the past not forgotten, it is also celebrated. In immigration, remembering sometimes becomes a duty that puts a greater pressure on memory. More importantly, the central role given to memory in exile has consequences on its evolution or on its lack of evolution. Among such consequences is the disruption of memory itself within the 'normal' process of immigration, which in turn leads to a type of frozen memory. In this sense, the evolution of Kurdish memory in France takes on a peculiarly static character of being confined to the relatively narrow parameters of a past that cannot be informed by developments in the present.

What is significant in this research is not what is remembered, but how it is remembered and, more specifically, what it teaches us about the memory process. The main hypothesis is that memory – and especially war memory – is not handled with the same intensity in the context of immigration.[3] Relating the evolution of memory within the Kurdish immigrant community to Henry Rousso's analysis of collective traumatized memory could shed a different light on the obstruction of memory's evolution.

This article concentrates on the Kurds from Turkey who declare themselves as such and who are proud of their identity.[4] It is based on three different types of research. Firstly, two years of observation and participation were conducted between 2002 and 2004 on and in a Kurdish association: the Center of Kurdish Information (CIK). It is based in Paris and defends Kurdish cultural and political rights in France and abroad. Although the observations made were strongly influenced by the political orientation of the association (close to the Kurdish Workers' Party– PKK),[5] this participative work was an occasion to be part of the Kurdish daily life in France and to assist in its different manifestations and cultural celebrations. Secondly, interviews were carried out with fifty-four Kurdish migrants of Turkish origin. These semi-structured interviews were directed by sixty-five questions.[6] The data obtained represents direct testimony of the interviewees' daily life in France, their past in Turkey, the reasons for their migration, and their hopes. Thirdly, the article is based on work on 150 asylum seekers' files written during the application process for refugee status. This last research component gives us a glimpse of memory as it has been narrated for the host state. In this three-sided field research, oral and written testimonies complement primary observation.

1. Kurdish Immigrants and the Re-creation of Their Original Environment: The Illustration of a Fixed Memory

Despite belonging to the world's largest stateless nation since the Treaty of Lausanne in 1924, the immigration of Kurds of Turkish origin to France is quite recent. It started in the late 1960s and mid-1970s, and increased after the coup d'état in 1980 and the beginning of the military conflict between the Kurdish Workers' Party[7] (PKK) and the Turkish army in 1984. Currently, despite a relative improvement in Kurdish regions – thanks to numerous ceasefires declared (and cancelled) by the PKK from 2000 to 2010 and some national reforms in Turkey imposed by the European Union – the flow of Kurdish asylum seekers is still significant and violence is re-escalating to a worrisome level.

There are approximately 120,000 Kurds of Turkish origin in France.[8] Kurdish immigration – even when economic motivations are involved – is linked to the high tensions in the region, the fear and suspicion that reigns in every village, diverse prohibitions preventing a natural development of Kurdish identity,[9] and last, but not least, the violent conflict between the PKK and the Turkish army. Despite being categorized by the host states as 'economic migrants and refugees,' what has to be remembered is that the Kurds feel compelled to flee. An important number of Kurds consider their migration as an exile, and therefore as temporary. According to their declarations, they were forced to leave and will come back sooner or latter. Out of fifty-four Kurds interviewed, twenty-nine expressed a desire to return to their homeland, and twenty-four explained that their life is in France now.[10] Among the 54 per cent of Kurds who demonstrated a desire to go back, a large number could be considered as integrated, at least in sociological and economical terms. These results show the still fervent attachment to their country of origin, but also a difficulty in forgetting the past and really planning a future in France.

What is striking when observing the Kurdish community in France is its strong sense of belonging to a nation other than its host state, its fervent will to rebuild in exile the identity and the culture left behind, its still pregnant desire to return, and its regular political mobilization. On that last point, Kurdish strikes and political actions are indeed numerous in France, and it is interesting to note that they are not organized to demand better living conditions in the host country, but to defend political and cultural rights in Turkey.[11]

In fact, one more fundamental explanation for this situation lies in the heavy burden that the war imposes on the Kurds. First and foremost, the Kurds are coming from what can be called a 'never-ending conflict.'[12] It could be asserted that it started in 1924, with the Treaty of Lausanne, when the Kurds were deprived of the territory promised by the Allies and by the Treaty of Sèvres signed in 1921. Numerous revolts took place after the Treaty of Lausanne.[13] Since then, and despite a strong policy of forced assimilation[14] and the slow death of their identity from the 1940s to the 1970s, the Kurds have been trying to protect their idiosyncrasies and their culture. Finally, in 1984, the PKK launched an armed struggle against the Turkish army, for independence of an autonomous region in a federal Turkey. Their struggle continues, now focused on political and cultural rights for the Kurds. The conflict has been violent, and deaths and disappearances have been numerous, but it is said that it has awakened a sleepy and nearly dead Kurdish spirit.

When dealing with immigrants coming from ethnic conflicts, especially intra-state ones, it is important to take into account the impact of the conflict's motivations, and to remember that when national identity is at stake, and when positive peace is hard to achieve, memory takes precedence over the present and is usually used to fuel a belligerent environment.[15] For the Kurds, their memory is their first nationalist symbol and the only tool to prove their difference. Claiming their own collective memory is also a way of finding a place in time, and of sharing a sense of continuity.

The transposition of a conflict for identity to a de-territorialized context gives a new dimension to 'long-distance nationalism'[16] and prevents integration. In fact, when the preservation of identity is threatened in the country of origin, it becomes more important to protect it in the host state and to maintain tight relations with the territory left behind. This was a feeling frequently observed during my research on the Kurdish community in France. Understanding the conflict that led to migration, and the general reasons for exodus, is the first step to identifying the links between memory and migration.

The Association for the Fraternity and Culture of Migrants, Göç-der, claims that for Kurds, leaving Kurdistan means 'losing the meaning of their lives.'[17] Involuntary migration, and exile in general, has several consequences for memory, and the pressure placed on identity by the Kurdish community in France can freeze the image of the past.

In this section, both the process of identity perpetuation/reconstruction and the attention given to a fixed idea of the past will be studied. For the Kurdish community, a strong connection to the past is enacted, first, through its desire to preserve and replicate its former way of life and, second, by its will to maintain strong links to its region of origin. These two phenomena illustrate the Kurds' difficulty with contemplating, without constraint, integration in France, and with handling the past objectively.

On the one hand, in the case of forced migration, social ties with the region of origin are preserved, but their preservation is unquestioned. Most of the Kurds interrogated on this topic sustain strong links with their region of origin, including 45 per cent who call their extended family and friends in Kurdish regions more than once a week, 24 per cent who call several times a month, and 18 per cent who only call several times a year. Similarly, 42 per cent watch the Kurdish channel,[18] Roj TV, and a large majority listen to Kurdish music.

On the other hand, for migrants, preserving identity is a way to find status and to give meaning to their experience of exile. Didier Lapeyronnie asserts that 'for migrants, identity is an intermediary zone, some kind of "parallel society" (*sous-société* in French) in which the migrant can find the support and resources necessary to confront the social and cultural shock of the host society and exile.'[19] This idea of identity as a protective nest puts a considerable pressure on identity. The first consequence of this strain is that immigrant Kurds are trying to capture their past by placing it at the central core of their present. A similar phenomenon has been described in Srdja Pavlovic's work. He declares: 'Frightened by the power of silence and the vastness of the Canadian space, I am trying to fill it up with names and voices from my past, and anchor myself within it, as if subconsciously trying to define my own thoughts and ideas about myself.'[20] More than *in situ*, in immigration memory is used to 'fill up' the void created by departure.

The Kurds have recreated their villages, and in French suburbs, it is not uncommon to witness the reunion of an entire Kurdish village in the same neighbourhood, or even in the same building. They provide each other – and especially asylum seekers – with administrative help, jobs, and places to live, recreating a 'Kurdish way of life' similar to the one left behind. The Kurds have their own associations in towns where their population is significant, such as their own football teams, language teachers, singing and dance classes. Their houses are imitations of Kurdish ones.

Moreover, one can observe the celebration of Kurdish identity during festivals. In Europe, huge gatherings are organized, usually in Germany. For example, the First International Festival of Kurdish Culture took place in Cologne in 1992, and gathered one hundred thousand Kurds. The 11th International Festival in Gelsrkirchen-Essen reported the same number of participants.[21] Every single Kurd interviewed declared participation in the Newroz, the Kurdish New Year. These manifestations have two main goals. They show the world the existence of a still denied Kurdish nation and a shared sense of belonging. They represent a way to relate to the collective memory of the group, and to create the feeling that Kurdish immigrants have not really left their homeland.

The immigrant Kurds appear insular, and some Kurds explained that their neighbourhood in France is more Kurdish than those in Turkey. 'The community there [in Kurdish areas of Turkey] is more modern than here [in France]. Here they are more traditionalists, more extreme,' reports Nadine, a young Kurdish migrant.[22] Another migrant explained that her cousins from Turkey have their own swimming pool, while she is not allowed to go to the public swimming pool in France for fear of being seen in a swimsuit.[23] Young girls are sometimes forbidden to go to school; marriages are still taking place within the community; clothes and values are strictly controlled.

Protecting the memory of the land left behind is more important than integration into the host country or the comfort and physical security it provides. These perceptions are hard to change since predominant figures within the community are pulling the entire community backwards, afraid that immigration will mean a loss of their traditional values and prevent their return. Every reference to the difficulty of war and the harshness of exile strengthens feelings of belonging to the group. As a consequence, attempting to come to terms with the past could be pernicious. Old traditions and values are kept, while in the country of origin modernization is taking place. As such, the Kurds who have immigrated seem to be stuck in time, trapped in a memory ghetto, while their counterparts in Turkey are trying to adapt to modernity. A crystallized memory of the native region is constructed, while in Turkey relationships with the past evolve and modernization is taking place. This is another example of the principal paradox of memory: thirst for a fixed memory coexists with movement as the fundamental condition of memory, as Julia Creet argues.[24]

Andreas Kitzmann also detects this divergence between the evolution of memory in place and abroad. His paper suggests the fact that the *Vertriebenen* (the Germans expelled from eastern and southern Europe after the Second World War) who settled in Canada did not experience the passionate and politicized debate on accountability and guilt which took place in Germany and Europe. He explains that they 'confront the past in a manner that is significantly different from Germans living in Germany.'[25]

Therefore, it is possible to assert that, for the same community, there are three different processes of memory: one for the community still living in the region of origin; one for the community in immigration; and one that tries to conciliate between the two, often in the form of official memory, used in diplomatic relations or relations with the host state.

However, these differences in the memory processes are not acknowledged, and sometimes even denied. Benedict Anderson explains immigrants' strong investment in the preservation of their cultural differences as thanks to a new status in exile guaranteed by their safety, their wealth, and their access to political processes, electronic communications systems, and financial markets, and through the fact that their access to modernity gives them the opportunity to play a significant role, from afar, in their homelands. He suggests that immigrants are then able 'to play, on the other side of the planet, national hero.'[26] On the other hand, Gabriel Sheffer contradicts the belief that thanks to political, cultural, and economic tolerance from the host countries, diasporas will disappear. He observes that some ethnic groups, who were indeed losing their identities, are going through an ethnic revival.[27] Identity in immigration is not disappearing; on the contrary, immigration elicits a stronger desire to protect an identity of origin.

Investigating this manifold phenomenon cannot be restricted to the examination of a community's social characteristics. It must also be linked to a study of its perceptions of the past. According to our analysis, memory's evolution in immigration must be addressed in order to comprehend what Benedict Anderson calls 'long-distance nationalism.' It is necessary to scrutinize the evolution of immigrants' memory since, in immigration, fantasies about the country of origin are developed with greater ease, and not only because of geographical distance. These fantasies might influence the country left behind, especially when political reasons explain the departure. Gabriel Sheffer states: 'Because of their organisation and determination, ethnic diasporas can become, in some small states, a significant political factor both domestically and in the foreign affairs of their host country.'[28] Examples of this phenomenon are multiple, starting with the conflict in Ireland or the war in the Balkans, where diasporas played a significant role in the politics of their host state.[29] This is why it is essential to trace the interconnected strands of memory that may influence their positions and beliefs.

As Abdelmalek Sayad contends, to know immigrants, one should examine emigrants.[30] For him, it is essential to take into account the immigrants' background in order to grasp their current position in the host society. This requires analysing their social and economic status in their country of origin and the reasons for their departure. To take this thought a step further, the question should not be restricted to who immigrants were socially and economically, but must also include their perception of the past at the time of their departure as well as after their installation in France. In fact, departure means losing land, family, friends, and traditions. The only luggage taken is memories. Therefore, to extend Sayad's remark, it is possible to assert that, to understand immigrants, one should observe their memory. Memory links the emigrant to the immigrant.

However, research and politics concerning migration are usually based on the assumption that immigrants' history starts with their arrival in the host country. This position ignores any analysis of the impact of memory on immigrants in terms of their social status, their desire to integrate, and their political opinions. It prevents any full understanding of the influence immigrants might have, or want to have, on the politics of their homeland and on their position and integration in their host state.

To conclude, it is possible to assert that immigration can represent the construction of a community around an 'old' perception of the past, and the beginning of a self-exclusion process. When group identity is the foundation of survival, integration becomes problematic, and individuals can feel trapped between embracing the culture and the values of the host country, and preventing them from 'polluting' the identity of the group.[31]

Links to memory are specific in immigration because of a will to create a collective identity intimately related to the idea of perpetuating bonds with the region of origin. The main result of this phenomenon is the creation of a fixed memory, a memory trapped in the perceptions imported by immigrants at the time of their departure.

2. The Weight of the Past on Memory's Evolution: A Disruption in the Movement of Memory

For some Kurds, the strong desire to protect their memory leads to a mystification of the past, and especially of the armed past. It is therefore necessary to remain aware of the heavy burden of war – with its spiral of death, violence, and torture – in the transmission of memory across borders.

Analysing the weight of the past on daily life is essential to comprehending immigrants. An important number of Kurdish migrants suffer from post-traumatic symptoms, and this yet uncured trauma could partly explain their difficulty with letting the past go. It may produce a general increase in violence. Primo Levi's words illustrate with great accuracy this phenomenon when he declares: 'Insult is incurable: it lingers over time and the Erinyes [Greek goddesses of revenge] ... perpetuate their work by refusing peace to the one tortured.'[32]

In fact, within the Kurdish community in France, traumas linked to the war period have not been cured, and, according to our observations, they can impact the community's commitment to memory in immigration. Flashbacks are numerous and come in different forms. Some community members narrate that they remain afraid of dogs because they remind them of Turkish troops; others shiver when they see uniforms – especially those worn by police. There are also those who explain that they do not want to send letters to their family in Turkey from France because they could be used as evidence against them and provoke the harassment of their loved ones.

Moreover, the effect of this trauma is deep, and immigrant populations who never even experienced the war, and who never lived in Kurdish regions, are dirtied by it. Tzvetan Todorov's analysis on this subject is both interesting and worrying. Dealing with the perpetuation of violence in Algeria, he explains that 'once introduced in history, evil does not disappear with the elimination of its original actor.'[33] Systematic humiliations and brutalities experienced during the war cause traumas, which can engender further acts of violent spin-off, despite the distance from the original source of violence, and fossilize memory.[34] Traumas are now entrenched into Kurdish history, and observations of the transmission of memory between generations suggest some kind of collective mental block. In fact, some Kurds, born in France, still carry the fears inherited from their parents' past. For example, some adopt a suspicious attitude in front of police uniforms or towards some immigrant Turks.

In France, radical attitudes remain rare and are restricted to verbal violence or are perpetuated by extremists.[35] Nevertheless, they indicate that the situation could degenerate, especially in consideration of the generation gap that is created through exile. It also shows the disrupted evolution of memory.

Indeed, young Kurds – and young migrants in general – usually have a particular relationship with their parents' region and past. The position of the Kurdish youth illustrates the weight of the past. A girl explained that she changes her clothes as soon as she reaches her parents' door, and stated that some of her Kurdish friends are doing the same thing. These attitudes prove the daily weight on young Kurds of their parents' desire to preserve tradition. Some young immigrant Kurds have written: 'Kurdish youth has the ability and the energy to win in every field, but there is the phobia of feeling like a stranger. At the same time, we have to deal with backward values from our society of origin.'[36] The dilemma particular to young Kurdish migrants[37] is an experience of being trapped between the traditions of their cultural group and the weight of their alien status. Some of them completely deny their Kurdish identity; others have to deal with an identity dilemma.

Most young Kurds abroad who recognize their cultural identity have never been in Kurdish areas of Turkey and do not know where they belong. They were raised with the idea that one should claim out loud one's difference, preserve the memory of one's ancestors, and celebrate their glory. At the same time, they are now realizing that this attitude is preventing their integration. For example, a nineteen-year-old Kurdish girl, who is a student in law school, says, 'When I meet new people, I feel that I have the obligation to declare myself as a Kurd. I must then explain the situation of my people ... But sometimes I just want to be myself. Only myself.'[38] Secondly, this identity dilemma can also be detected in the fact that some young migrants are questioning, with more radicalism, both the Turkish state and their host country. This increased criticism is related to the discrimination they sometimes experience in France, which reminds them of the persecutions suffered by their parents. It is also linked to the education they have received in France: they were taught to analyse their world and do not feel censured in doing so. Finally, this dilemma could also be connected to a generational process towards violence, called the Hansen Law, which might impact the evolution of memory and the importance given to its preservation. The Hansen Law, deduced from observations on the identity of immigrant generations in the United States, states that ethnicity is preserved among the first generation, weakens among the second, and reaffirmed among the third. The 'principle of third-generation interest,' or 'the third-generation syndrome,' is best expressed by the following sentence: 'What the son wishes to forget the grandson wishes to remember.'[39] This theory could be applied to a post-conflict situation. People who have experienced war and violence usually want to live in peace, and some of them teach their children to adapt and remain quiet. However, for the third generation, there is sometimes a need to challenge the status quo and ask for justice. In his autobiography, Ali Ekber Gürgöz, a Kurdish refugee, illustrates this phenomenon. While he was very proud of his grandfather's participation in the Kurdish revolt in Dersim, and his death as a martyr in 1938, his father prevented him and his siblings from even talking about the Kurdish situation. In spite of his deep hatred of the Turkish regime, his father was more afraid of violence. 'My father could not bear that his sons wanted to get involved in the

Kurdish problem. He had already lost his own father, he did not want to lose his sons ... But my brother kept repeating: "Father! We do not have the right to forget our martyrs."'[40] This movement of memory through the generations could explain why violence among immigrants does not come from the first generation, but frequently from the second or the third generation.[41] This movement could also clarify why there is a perpetuation and radicalization of 'long-distance nationalism,' despite integration.

Ultimately, it is time to realize that the mutations of a memory built out of its territorial ground are specific. Geographical distance creates a discrepancy in the evolution of memory, as it was defined by Henry Rousso concerning the memory of the German occupation and French collaboration during the Second World War. In *Le syndrome de Vichy* he distinguishes four principal phases in the evolution of traumatized collective memory. The first period, occurring from 1944 to 1954 in France, refers to the direct struggle with the repercussions of 'civil war'[42] that ended with the amnesty laws.[43] The second phase corresponds to a period of amnesia, lapsed memory, and silenced mourning, when internal divisions are forgotten and conflicts are held back. Rousso traces this phase in France from 1954 to 1971. It is followed by the return of the past, a memory revitalization, which he finds in France between 1971 and 1974. In general, this return of repressed memory, and the deconstruction of old myths about the war, usually takes place forty years after the trauma of the war. The final principal phase is a period of hypermnesia involving memory obsession.

Rousso's analysis is interesting since it places great emphasis on the influence of collective trauma on the evolution of memory. What was experienced by the Kurds – occupation and hidden civil war[44] – is similar to the French experience between 1940 and 1944, or can at least be considered as such, even if the Kurds deny the idea of internal divisions, or if the Turkish army condemns the idea of occupation. Though immigration violence is supposed to stop when security is provided, my first hypothesis is that immigration might function as a post-conflict period for migrants. Therefore, it is time to examine the dynamics of Kurdish memory and its possible ghettoization in light of the memory cycle defined by Rousso.

First of all, the delicate evolution of Kurdish memory in immigration can be seen in the denial of any division within the community, though under close observation some tensions appear. One part of the Kurdish immigrant community highlights its past and supports the idea that without the armed struggle the Kurdish identity would have disappeared. Another group within the community completely denies the past, replacing it with a determination to integrate, to forget, and usually to deny PKK's policies, especially the use of violence as a political means.

For the latter group of Kurds, there is a will to put aside negative events of the past. They are ashamed of their departure from the homeland, their collective history, and the stereotypes linked with belonging to the group. In another context of migration, Andreas Kitzmann notices that abroad in North America, Germans can choose to construct a new identity around their adopted nations and 'to downplay their German roots and assimilate as seamlessly as possible into the mainstream of society.'[45] A similar phenomenon to the one Kitzmann observes can be noticed among this group of Kurds, for whom the host country immediately offers a 'ready-to-go' future that they try to use as a substitute for the country of origin. According to Jean-Claude Métraux, in *Deuils collectifs et création sociale* (Collective Grief and Social Creation), the precocious search for assimilation within the host country can be seen as a kind of closing off.[46] Through the exclusion of the country of origin and its culture, the past is rejected and intentionally denied.

In contrast, there is also a group within the Kurdish immigrant community that is politically engaged, tries to be heard, and sometimes even denies the existence of those who wish to leave the past behind, in order to present the image of a unified community. A myth has been built around resistance fighters, and one unique official memory has been written with the figure of PKK's leader, Abdullah Öcalan, at its centre.[47] Within this group, individuals who never even experienced the war or set a foot on Kurdish land still feel it is their duty to defend the identity of their ancestors, and to remain close to the past.[48]

For them, the realities of immigration and of a long-term stay in the host country are rejected, and they claim they will return to their land one day or another. They leave space for a mythology intimately linked to their country of origin. This group within part of the Kurdish community is obsessed with seeking a reunion with the past and their homecoming to Turkey. They are thirsty for their origins and stuck in what I will call 'a memory ghetto.' They leave the present in favour of the past, and recreate an imaginary world cut off from reality. Their integration is not their main objective. Instead, they strive for the return of a golden age,[49] and their own return to Kurdistan. To them, their region has lost its flaws, and they focus on its advantages. For example, some Kurds enhance the simplicity of their former life and their prox-imity to nature in the Kurdish region, instead of talking about its poverty. The war is understood as proof that they were able to form a population of rebels. They are proud of their resistance, and they wrap in silence the persecution endured and the harshness of conflict.

To summarize, the Kurdish community living in France is marked by its radical behaviour towards history: it enacts either a strong adhesion to the myth of Kurdish fighters who freed the Kurds from alienation, or it rejects and even denies the past and its membership in the group. However, if these divisions exist, they are suppressed by mobilized Kurds who pretend that their nation is unified even in exile. In the con-text of Henry Rousso's analysis of the evolution of memory, it can be concluded that the Kurdish community is experiencing the second phase, involving repression. They are going through a period of am-nesia and silent mourning. It is indeed possible to talk about 'denial' on the part of both groups within the Kurdish immigrant community.

To understand this gap in memory, we can add Jean-Claude Métraux's theories about the grief process.[50] The different stages of a grief process – either individual or collective – are defined sequentially as the *closing* or *denial stage*, the *opening* or *depressive stage*, and the *memory stage*.[51] The first phase is the denial of the loss, as the individual or the community auto-excludes itself, locking itself into a rigid pattern of behaviour mainly centred on a glorified image of the past. During that time, links between past, present, and future are severed. The second phase is a period in which loss is acknowledged, and the consequent pain arrives. At last, during the memory stage, individuals want to re-write their history, become knowledgeable of their present situation, and take their future into account. In Métraux's analysis, the first two periods defined by Rousso are united as one: the denial stage.[52] What is of interest to us in his work is his theory that the grieving process may fossilize or freeze at one of the earlier two stages.[53] When a grieving process is frozen at its first stage, in the midst of denial, identity survival and community are placed above individuals. The present be-comes the priority and the past becomes a tool. Individuals are there-fore unable to project themselves into the future.[54]

Some Kurds seem to be trapped in the first phase: the survival of their identity and the preservation of the past are perceived as more important than their own comfort and integration. Their past is a tool for recognition, but also a way to have a position, to give meaning to immigration. These Kurds cannot make plans for the future, and they cannot project themselves as being in their host country for the long term, because they constantly look back to their past and build their present according to it. This could explain why they are so attached to the restoration of lives identical to the ones they had.

In Rousso's research, time realizes the necessary work of dissociation from traumatic events, but it also appears that experiences of exile and geographic distance can lead to the faster development of collective memory, or to discrepancies in memory on the impossibility of the period of reconciliation with the past in immigration. The weight of the discourses around a deficit of recognition of the suffering of the immigrant community in the host country, and the multiplication of legal proceedings before the European Court of Human Rights, demonstrate that the past has not been dealt with yet.[55] Unable to handle the past and its traumatic consequences, the progress of memory within the context of immigration has somehow been frozen. Immigrants are stuck between the second period of the memory evolution process and the third, creating a difference between memory *in situ* and memory that has migrated.

In fact, according to my observations, fossilization of the memory process in immigration might be explained by the lack of the first period of memory evolution. As it is described by Rousso, this period is a crucial moment dedicated to the immediate management of the tensions linked to the war. It means a direct confrontation with the past, political and ethical purges, and sometimes violence, but it is also a moment for primary justice. It is necessary for an appeased evolution of memory. Even if the grief process is not achieved during this period, it is at least started, and the loss is acknowledged. However, in immigration, this first period faces numerous obstacles.

First of all, geographic distance makes direct struggle with the after-effects of civil war impossible. Instead, what is produced is a stage of entrapment between amnesia, forgetting, and silence, on the one hand, and a desire to remember and enhance the past, on the other. Secondly, neither French society nor the French state is ready or prepared to listen to the experiences and concerns of immigrants dealing with the trauma of war, violence, and subsequent exile. There is a general deficit of psychological care offered by the host country, combined with a lack of concern. The French integration process does not take into account the violence suffered by immigrants, even if, according to our analysis, such recognition and response to the suffering would surely have a positive impact in the long term. This problem is worsened for immigrants by the fact that during their process of seeking asylum, French authorities require detailed personal stories while they are still in the denial stage of grief. Telling their story therefore becomes painful. This explains why some migrants prefer to remain silent, even if they risk being rejected. Moreover, the traumas endured sometimes provoke questions about accuracy of a given story. Similarly, Mona Lindqvist affirms in her work that 'forgetfulness, like memory, is a dynamic act. A powerful experience or a significant act does not fall away and disappear out of memory. It is stored, but difficult to reach with conscious memory. When it returns, it usually does so in a fragmentary and undefined manner as opposed to a chronological one.'[56] This incoherent return of memory also interferes in the process of dealing with the past. Furthermore, Chowra Makaremi explains that some asylum seekers feel that they must lie to obtain the right to stay.[57] They are therefore deprived of their own history. Their silence or lies represent an obstacle to the necessary direct confrontation with the past. Finally, to deal with the past directly and confront painful or traumatic experience is pernicious for the community and each individual. It is a period during which suffering is placed at the centre of life, and great changes are produced, both in terms of social relationships and personal values. These alterations are unsettling for a community and threaten its unity. They can engender a sense of deficiency in the community's management of the pain.[58] This is why the group will sometime impose silence on its members, which results in the prevention of justice. I have indeed noticed some shame about showing pain within the Kurdish community in France. As Ali Ekber Gürgöz explains in his autobiography, 'Even if torture destroyed me, I have to remain worthy.'[59] He later adds: 'A great fear lives in me but I do not express it. I am brave, worthy and I never keep my head down.'[60] His comments demonstrate that talking about the pain suffered, and therefore undertaking the grief process, is considered as being unworthy.

It seems that the first period in the host country operates as a postwar period, during which survival is essential, but acknowledging the losses and dealing with the pain appear too dangerous. Maintaining collective identity, and transmitting it to the next generation, requires a strong and unified group. Consequently, dealing with the direct effects of the past could threaten the community. For the immigrant community, the grief process is therefore more dangerous and difficult than for the community in the country of origin; this could explain the fervent will to conserve a fixed memory, and why some Kurdish migrants are stuck in a memory ghetto.

3. Conclusion

The Kurdish immigrant community in France is trapped in a memory ghetto: some Kurds are locked in a denial of their past and wish to integrate into French culture, while others are organized around 'a myth of return' and a frozen idea of their region of origin. It appears that immigrant communities – whatever background they come from, violent or not – might have difficulties dealing with the loss of their homeland, and this could impact the evolution of their memory. The Kurds living in France have not been able to grieve for the loss of their territory of origin or the traumas suffered during the civil war. A confrontation with the past has not been accomplished, and their memory is frozen. Instead of coping with the changes imposed by life in France, they imprison themselves in the past, while the Kurds living in Turkey are adapting to the present.

Julia Creet asserts, '… displacement is more likely to produce immobile memories and radical forgetting.'[61] Nevertheless, if the processes of memory have somehow been frozen by departure, the positive and negative aspects of these memories have also been enhanced, celebrated, and exaggerated, thereby changing their original meanings. The reasons for these changes are numerous. They include the forms of the conflict left behind, the possibility for 'coming to terms with the past' offered in the host country, the ability to develop the community's history, the respect for cultural differences, the possibility for suing their country of origin, and the access to psychotherapy. For immigrants, experiences of exile prevent the first phase of the evolution of collective memory and the direct confrontation with the past, freezing the movement of memory.

NOTES

1 Quoted in Ali Ekber Gürgöz, *Kurde, torturé, quelles séquelles?* (Paris: L'Harmattan, 2005), 41.
2 Around 3,500 villages were destroyed, especially during the 1990s.
3 Furthermore, it should be kept in mind that the Kurdish Workers Party (PKK) bases its political power on the use and abuse of war memory. This has a considerable impact on the community's relation to memory and its radicalization. Moreover, the Turco-Kurdish conflict, the state of emergency, and the guerrilla warfare that lasted for nearly two decades are also influencing the apprehension of violence within the entire Kurdish community:

firstly, because violence became common; secondly, since preserving their identity was what they fought for; thirdly, because of a lack of trust towards any state-related structures.

4 For a long time, the Kurds were ashamed of their identity, thanks mostly to extensive propaganda from the Turkish Republic, which stated that the Kurds were backwards and uncivilized. For example, the notion that they 'have a tail' was circulated.

5 Pârtiya Kârkerâna Kurdistân, PKK. This organisation fought the Turkish army between 1984 and 1999. Since the arrest of its leader (Abdullah Öcalan) in 1999, the PKK has been going through a period of transition, and its name is regularly changed (KADEK, Kongra-gel, Koma Komalen). However, the old name – the PKK – is still widely used.

6 This research was financed by the European Commission – Employment and Social Affairs Department – and was realized by the Kurdish Information Offices in Berlin, Rome, and Paris. See D. Berruti et al., *Kurds in Europe: From Asylum Right to Social Rights* (Naples: Associazoneper la Pace Onlus, 2002).

7 The 'guerrilla' movement has changed names many times since the arrest of its leader and the ceasefire that followed in 1999. However, for the convenience of the reader, what is now the Kongra-gel will still be referred as the PKK.

8 Out of the 4 million Turks settled in Europe, estimates give the number of Kurds to be around 800,000. There are approximately 140,000 Kurds living in France. Most of them are from Turkey (the usual percentage given is 80 per cent). They form the second Kurdish community in Europe.

9 Sabri Cigerli even talks about a 'cultural genocide' (personal interview, Paris, 21 March 2005). Cigerli is an academic specialist on the Kurdish region, and he is himself a Kurd of Turkish origin. For more information, see Sabri Cigerli, *Les Kurdes et leur histoire* (Paris: L'Harmattan, 1999); and Sabi Cigerli and Didier Le Saout, *Öcalan et le PKK: les mutations de la question kurde en Turquie et au Moyen-Orient* (Paris: Maisonneuve et Larose, 2005).

10 Two people interviewed did not answer this question.

11 They are also to show support for Abdullah Öcalan, the leader of the PKK, condemned to a life sentence at Imrali Island.

12 This is a generally observed phenomenon. In fact, the duration of civil war has tripled since the 1960s. See P. Collier, A. Hoeffler, and M. Söderbom, *On the Duration of Civil War*. (Oxford: World Bank, University of Oxford, 2001).

13 The Treaty of Lausanne did not recognize self-determination for the Kurds. At that time, the Kurds fought for recognition and out of frustration with being cheated by Mustapha Kemal Atatürk and the Allies, but without national consciousness.

14 Kurdish was forbidden until 1991. Kurdish names of villages and individuals were changed to Turkish ones, and the policy of forced deportation began.

15 A post-conflict situation does not necessarily mean that the roots of the conflict have disappeared. It simply indicates that the weapons are no longer heard. On the contrary, 'positive peace' signifies that the divisions that led to the war have also been dealt with.

16 Benedict Anderson, *The Spectre of Comparisons* (London and New York: Verso, 1998).

17 Göç-der, personal interview with a social worker, Diyarbakır, 26 March 2003.

18 Numerous interviewees explained that they do not have access to this television channel, but they wanted it.

19 Didier Lapeyronnie, 'De l'altérité à la différence: l'identité comme facteur d'intégration ou de repli?' In *Immigration et intégration: l'état des savoirs*, ed. P. Dewitte (Paris: La Découverte, 1991), 224.

20 See Srdja Pavlovic's contribution to this volume, pp. 48–9.

21 These numbers are divided in two by local police authorities.

22 Interview with Nadine, 4 February 2004, Paris. The names of the Kurds working for the CIK have been deliberately changed.

23 Interview with Sara, 27 February 2004, Paris.

24 See Julia Creet's Introduction to this volume, p. 9.

25 See Andreas Kitzmann's contribution in this volume, p. 99.

26 Benedict, *Spectre of Comparisons*, 74.

27 Sheffer's examples of political awakenings observed in the United States include those of the Polish Catholic, Irish, and Greek communities. He also refers to the important interest of Black Americans in African affairs. See Gabriel Sheffer, 'A New Field of Study: Modern Diasporas in International Politics,' in *Migration, Diasporas and Transnationalism*, ed. S. Vertovec and R. Cohen (London: Edward Elgar Publishing, 1999), 384.

28 Sheffer, 'Modern Diasporas in International Politics,' 385.

29 The context of the diaspora could facilitate further dialogue; for example, by bringing the two parties in conflict to a neutral table. However, it could also provoke the re-escalation of violence. In fact, the present research is significant because it indicates that an immigrant community built on the still burning ashes of a conflict has a special relation to its past and its region. We believe that this phenomenon should be taken into account in peace/conflict resolution theories. When an ethnic conflict continues, it also has effects on its exiled, immigrant community. It is possible to notice a kind of exportation of violence: the violence known in the country of

origin is transmitted to the host country, where it changes and radicalizes, and is later re-exported back to the country of origin. If it is impossible to clearly analyse the extent of the link between the re-escalation of a conflict in the homeland and immigrants' social movements, some early warning signs could – and should – be detected.

30 For him immigration and emigration are indissociables. See A. Sayad, *La double absence: des illusions de l'émigré aux souffrances de l'immigré* (Paris: Seuil, 1999), 177.

31 This position involves a special pressure on identity, and a particular relationship with the region of origin and the past of the entire group. Their relationship to language is a good example of the dilemmas faced by the Kurds. Only 57 per cent of the Kurds questioned were fluent, or relatively good, in French. This low percentage could be explained by the fact that for some Kurds, learning French means having to choose between their origin and their host country. 'Now that I have learned French, should I live with the majority of my host society or should I live in accordance with my roots?' wondered a young Kurdish man (Kevir, n.p.). At the same time, in Europe, the Kurds have the opportunity to learn Kurdish without any harassment (from 1924 to 1991 it was forbidden to speak or write in Kurdish and between 1925 and 1956, using Kurdish was punished). Today Kurdish classes are allowed in Turkey, but there is still a strong suspicion and the Turkish government is preventing their development by different means, Learning Kurdish represents an act of resistance and of remembrance since it has no use in daily life in France. One Kurd who learned Kurdish in France explained his efforts by asserting that 'the Kurds should not forget' (personal interview with Mehmet Ulker, 15 March 2004, Paris).

32 'L'offense est inguérissable: elle se prolonge dans le temps, et les Erinyes [déesses grecques de la vengeance], auxquelles nous devons bien croire, ne tourmentent pas seulement le bourreau (si même elles le tourmentent, aidées ou non par le châtiment humain), mais perpétuent son œuvre en refusant la paix à celui qu'il a torturé' (Primo Levi, Preface, *Si c'est un homme* [1947; Paris: Presses Pocket, 1988]).

33 Tzvetan Todorov, 'La mémoire fragmentée, la vocation de la mémoire,' in *La mémoire entre histoire et politique*, ed. Léonard Yves, *Cahiers Français* 303 (2001): 3–7.

34 It is important to note that this violence is not necessarily directed towards the former enemy. It could, instead, concentrate on an innocent victim who is seen as threatening the community, and therefore transform the former victim into the aggressor.

35 Some public self-immolation, mostly when Abdullah Öcalan was arrested, and some hidden revenge crimes occur, but most of the time radical attitudes are rare.

36 Information leaflet on the organization of the Mazlum Doğan Festival for Youth, Culture and Sport, published by the Kurdish Cultural Centre, 'Ahmed Kaya,' Paris, 2006.

37 Mostly from the second generation of those who attended French schools at an early age.

38 Fadime, personal interview, 30 March 2006, Rennes.

39 M.L. Hansen, *The Problem of the Third Generation Immigrant* (Rock Island, Illinois, 1938), 9.

40 Ali Ekber Gürgöz, *La nuit de Diyarbakir, être Kurde en Turquie* (Paris: L'Harmattan, 1997), 2–3.

41 See also H. Heiner Kuhne, 'Culture Conflict and Crime in Europe,' in *Migration, Culture Conflict and Crime.* ed. J.D. Freilich, G. Newman, and A. Moshe (Aldershot: Ashgate, 2002).

42 The term 'civil war' is used by Henry Rousso to qualify the internal divisions among the French population revealed by the Vichy regime during the war.

43 The purge (*épuration* in French) was meant to punish the French who collaborated with the German occupiers during the war. A distinction is made between the legal purge (special trials for collaborators: 160,000 trials took place and 767 persons were executed) and the unofficial one (mainly summary executions – around 8,000 to 9,000 killed – or harassments). The amnesty was declared in 1951–2.

44 The high tensions and even hatred that exist between the Kurds who are closed to the PKK or its ideas, and the Kurds who collaborated with the Turkish army, did not lead to a bloodbath. Nevertheless, the divisions are now entrenched within the community, and when talking about the return of refugees, the issue is raised with great concern since 'village protectors,' the ones who sided with the Turkish army, are occupying the lands left behind and are not willing to give them up.

45 See Andreas Kitzmann's contribution to this volume, p. 99.

46 Jean-Claude Métraux, *Deuils collectifs et création sociale* (Paris: La Dispute, 2004), 67.

47 Abdullah Öcalan is at the centre of a large propaganda machine. He is portrayed as the father, the saviour, and the unique leader of all the Kurds. Through magazines, books, songs and legends, news media, and political and cultural meetings, he, and his freedom fighters, are depicted as the only protectors of Kurdish identity.

48 All in all, it is possible to conclude that these Kurds are still imprisoned by the consequences of war and the policy priorities set by militarized societies.

49 Based on the Neolithic area and the Empire of the Meds.

50 Métraux, *Deuils collectifs et création sociale.*

51 Ibid., 241.

52 Ibid., 239–45.

53 Ibid., 66. See also Métraux's 'Broken Bridges: Community Grief Processes as a Key Factor for the Development of Individual, Family and Community Resources,' in *Health Hazards of Organised Violence in Children (II),* ed. L. Willigen (Utrecht: Pharos, 2000), 93–110.

54 The danger during this stage is that a group monopolizes the process and controls the evolution of memory. Paul Ricoeur talks about 'abuses of memory' as the threshold for the opening stage that might be crossed and could result in destabilizing the community (Paul Ricoeur, *La Mémoire, l'histoire, l'oubli* [Paris: Seuil, 2000]). In immigration, memory seems stuck in this period, fossilized, as Jean-Claude Métraux puts it. Links within the community – either real or symbolic – are severed, and the community itself becomes a myth.

55 In 2007 the European Court of Human Rights handed down 1,503 judgments concerning a total of 1,735 applications. The highest number of judgments concerned Turkey (331). By the end of 2007, 79,427 allocated applications were pending before the Court. Twelve per cent of the cases concern Turkey, placing it among the four states accounting for over half (55 per cent) of the Court workload (26 per cent of the cases are directed against Russia, 12 per cent of the cases concern Turkey, 10 per cent Romania, and 7 per cent Ukraine). See *Annual Report of the European Court of Human Rights* (Strasbourg: Council of Europe, Registry of the European Court of Human Rights, 2008).

56 See Mona Lindqvist's contribution to this volume, p. 186.

57 See Chowra Makaremi's contribution to this volume, p. 78.

58 It is a phenomenon occurring within many post-conflict situations. Indeed, Milton J. Friedman observes the absence of depressive symptoms in both war and post-war periods (Milton J. Friedman, 'Post-war Communities Overcoming Traumas and Losses,' presented at a workshop on 'the importance of psychosocial well-being of children in the post-war period for social reconstruction and stability of terrorist and war affected regions,' Ljubljana, 7 June 2003).

59 Gürgöz, *Kurde, torturé, quelles séquelles?* 18.

60 Ibid., 38.

61 See Julia Creet's Introduction to this volume, p. 10.

8 Home in Exile: Politics of Refugeehood in the Canadian Muslim Diaspora

NERGIS CANEFE

> We usually think that everybody has a home, or at least that everybody
> should have a home, a specific point of anchorage in the world. However,
> there are some moments, some circumstances in people's lives when
> 'homes' in their universalistic taken-for-grantedness, become problema-
> tized ...Where is home, or what is home, in a situation where one's home
> is shattered by a violent war and one is forced into exile?
> – Laura Huttunen, '"Home" and Ethnicity in the Context of War' (2005)[1]

This paper explores the role played by remembrance of home in the
lives of refugees in Canada who are in exile from Muslim majority
countries.[2] Refugees speak of a home that is lost all but in memory,
and yet emphasize its continual political and historical significance. As
such, remembrance of home in the diaspora could be characterized as
an act of defiance that refugees embrace as a form of politics. Memories
of home defy their exilic condition as a global community of unwanted
peoples with no state to claim, and no society to rely on. Through remembrance, refugees strive to create new lives based on the determined
utterance of collective memories of a violent past. In other words, memories of home in exile embody a politics of refugeehood that promises
hope. Contestation of power in exile starts with remembrance. The un-
foreseen obstacle in this process is the diasporic tension between refugees and migrants in addition to the censorship imposed on refugee
memories by official representatives of the country that refugees were
forced to leave. As the life stories discussed in this paper reveal, neither
politically nor physically are refugees immune to the kinds of protests
and conflicts that shaped home politics while they are in exile. On the

contrary, perhaps they are even more vulnerable due to their newly acquired position of a minority whose representation is often assumed by immigrant organizations and community leaders. This context shaping the social and political existence of refugees in the diaspora renders remembrance of home an essential part of politics of refugeehood in Canada and elsewhere.

The debate presented in the following pages relies heavily on two kinds of literature: diaspora studies and memory studies. However, it does so with a critical bent. Current interdisciplinary work on the former subject suggests that the diaspora constitutes a new kind of space, a 'third space,' a place that is not a place, a mode of existence that acts as a bridge between the national, the local, and the transnational.[3] The present work, on the other hand, contends that local and immediate contexts in the diaspora affect the reception and self-perception of communities forged by forced migration as much as transnational dynamics. Processes of identity formation in exile no doubt have a marked transnational component. And yet, the fluidity implicated by globalization of migratory movements is not devoid of limitations and tensions. Experiences of refugees indicate that diaspora indeed becomes a specific kind of place. In the diaspora, exile leads to a particular and highly political genre of remembrance of personal, communal, and national histories. Here, the idea of home is of paramount importance for the formulation and sustenance of refugee identities as it provides anchorage. However, refugees' engagement with the notion of home causes serious tensions in the diaspora between refugees and migrants arriving from the same country of origin or the same geographical region. There are a number of factors that determine an immigrant's sense of belonging in the diaspora: positive or negative visibility of Muslims in the public eye; choices available for members of this relatively new minority in terms of their economic, political, social, and cultural well-being; and the kinds of struggles they endure in order to be regarded as full members of the society. In the case of refugees from Muslim majority countries, this struggle is compounded by internal debates within diaspora communities. These are debates regarding which aspects of one's ethno-religious or political history are to be deemed useful or, indeed, acceptable for public revelation in one's adopted home. Contentious points include accounts of trauma, conflict, and political violence, and even the questioning of the truthfulness of such events. Remembrance of home in exile thus provides an entry to diaspora politics from within. This is quite different from the more conventional vantage point of looking at migrant and refugee memories in order to work out liberal democratic conundrums of toleration, accommodation, and integration vis-à-vis ethno-religious minorities.

There is a complex web of relations among an individual's sense of belonging, migration, diasporic and exilic existence, and minority identity formation. An explicit focus on how memories of home guide political and social action in one's adopted domicile equips us with a different framework for understanding these relations. This is despite the fact that a sense of shared ethnic consciousness and common history, or a sustained perception of the homeland left behind, is not always possible among members of the Muslim diaspora in Canada. The groups in question are divided along national, political, cultural, regional, linguistic, sectarian, gender, and class lines. Still, there is a common context within which the larger society labels and brackets Muslims in the West. Consequently, diasporic Muslim identity assumes the character of a difficult balancing act between 'internal' divisions that separate within, and challenging or hostile circumstances and outside pressures that unite the group against others.

1. Collective Memory and Remembrance in the Diaspora

It is true that much has happened in the 'Canadian conversation' regarding citizenship, belonging, and constitutional patriotism during the last two decades. One can go as far as to suggest that there emerged a consensus suggestive of a 'Canadian school' of political philosophy, providing a distinct set of answers to questions concerning inclusion and integration of minorities in 'mixed societies,' particularly with reference to immigrant and refugee groups. Classical representatives of this school, such as Will Kymlicka, Joseph Carens, Howard Adelman, Michael Ignatieff, James Tully, and, to a degree, Charles Taylor, have been crowned with the hybrid title of liberal communitarians.[4] In their work, they strive to incorporate the substantive elements of communal relations and identity politics into the procedural matrix of liberal democratic politics. In this vein, culture, religion, gender, race, and other forms of identitarian projects came to be regarded as building blocks of the current Canadian polity. However, this debate and the general aura of optimism that it generated hit an obstacle course with the post-9/11 moral panic about Islam and Muslims in the West. This is not to state that the aforementioned thinkers failed to contemplate the fate of Muslim minorities in Canada or elsewhere in the West. The conversation they started on identity and belonging continues to grow in new directions in the work of Engin Isin, Peter Nyers, Sherene Razack, Gerald Kernerman, and other scholars of a younger generation, some of whom have a recent immigrant background themselves.[5] The difference is that the optimism and visionary characteristics of the 'original Canadian conversation' – which excelled in areas such as engulfing Québécois nationalism and the distinct society debate, gendered citizenship, or aboriginal self-governance issues in Canada – are not yet reproduced in this new context of alarm about religious identities. There is something unusual, or something simply not fitting into the boundaries of what was covered before, regarding the case of Muslims in Canada. This difficulty is in large measure related to the fear of the unknown, in this case constituted by the 'transnational,' the 'sacred,' and the 'fundamentalist' as these adjectives became coterminous with Muslim identity. Such predetermined ideas took root despite the fact that those who are considered as 'Muslim immigrants' arrive in Canada primarily through the point system as educated, professional individuals rather than as clandestine or temporary communities of labourers, the latter trend marking their experiences in Western Europe. In addition, immigrants and refugees from Muslim majority countries have a very diverse background, representing 60 nationalities, belonging to at least 10 different sects and schools, and speaking over 100 languages.[6] On the whole, Muslim minorities in the West, including Canada, increasingly feel a certain distance from the societies they came to inhabit. Since 9/11, feelings of alienation, marginalization, ghettoization, or uneasy creolization have become common ailments that separate Muslims from the larger population across Europe. Muslims in Canada are understandably wary of repeating a similar pattern in North American.[7] Canadian scholars looking at this picture do not see an easy resolution for the problem.

The aforementioned issues constitute important complexities that shape the daily lives of both migrants and refugees arriving in Canada from Muslim majority countries. Consequently, formation of a Muslim identity in the diaspora could best be described as a multifarious process. Both communally and individually, 'Muslim minorities' devise a wide range of strategies to deal with the challenges in their adopted homes. The immediate diaspora-related issue to be resolved in the context of the aforementioned 'Canadian conversation' is to determine whether migrants and refugees with a Muslim background face a greater degree of prejudice and questioning of their loyalties due to their religious and cultural heritage. In order to provide a satisfactory answer to such an inquiry, one has to engage Muslim minorities themselves and let them tell the stories of their desires, fears, and needs. Two kinds of obstacle emerge in attempting to do so. The first one pertains to previous debates in Canadian politics dictating the contents of what is to be uttered in new discussions on citizenship, denizenship, and membership. The second obstacle results from the tendency in Canadian politics to listen mainly to those who claim 'moral majority' among Muslim migrants. This latter issue constitutes a serious problem for refugees. Individuals and groups who claim to have the largest degree of authenticity and organizational representation often speak on behalf of *all* 'Canadian Muslims.' This predetermination of agency by community leaders among observant Muslims runs the risk of silencing alternative formulations of identity within the diaspora, such as those proposed by the unwanted of their home societies, the refugees. Consequently, memories of home and remembrance of trauma and violence often become the first casualties of identity politics in the diaspora.

The profiles of two political refugees in Canada who arrived from Muslim majority countries, Tarek Fatah from Pakistan and Haideh Moghissi from Iran, exemplify the tensions within the Muslim diaspora in Canada. Both individuals are public intellectuals. They have made a significant and yet controversial mark in the public perception of Islam and Muslims in Canada. Consequently, both also paid and continue to pay a price for their outspoken critique of authoritarian excesses in Muslim majority countries. They stand out in their knowledge of politics and religion in their respective regions. They are also determined to keep their religious convictions or ideas entirely in the private sphere. In effect, neither Moghissi nor Fatah ever claimed to be observant Muslims. At the same time, they are proud to have come from an Islamic geography and culture, and they are vehemently against Islamophobia in Western societies. In this sense, their politics and societal position in the diaspora necessitates a difficult bridging act.[8] Consequently, they challenge the gatekeepers of collective memory in the diaspora. Furthermore, it is not against the nation-state alone that such a challenge is posed. The conflict over what is to be remembered about home takes place outside the nation-states against which they raise criticisms. In addition, they use specific methods of intervention perhaps only possible when one assumes an exilic subject position. Theirs is a collective memory of forced migration, uttered parallel to and sometimes unequivocally against collective memories of migrants from the very countries from which they were exiled.

2. Politics of Memory in Exile: Tarek Fatah as an Émigré Public Intellectual in Canada

Tarek Fatah is widely known as a Muslim-Canadian journalist and political activist. In this sense, he fits the definition of a public intellectual
quite well. He was a founding member of the Muslim Canadian Congress (MCC).[9] Fatah was a student active in radical Pakistani politics
during the 1960s and 1970s. He was charged with sedition and imprisoned by the Pakistani military government. As a result, 'back home,' he
suffered torture and inhumane treatment and is well-acquainted with
the excesses of the political regime. A biochemist by training, Fatah entered journalism as a reporter for the *Karachi Sun* in 1970. He then became an investigative journalist for Pakistani television. In other words,
he was already a recognized public figure prior to becoming a refugee.
He was fired after the coup that brought Zia Ul-Haq to power and fled
to Saudi Arabia. In 1987 he emigrated to Canada and settled in Toronto.
In Canada, he became involved with the centre-left New Democratic
Party based in Ontario. Fatah was an NDP candidate in the 1995 provincial elections but was unsuccessful. In July 2006, he left the NDP
to support Bob Rae's candidacy for the Liberal Party. Explaining his
decision to leave the NDP, Fatah wrote an opinion piece published in
Toronto's *Now Magazine*. In this public testimony, Fatah argued that the
NDP established a 'faith caucus,' which he believes will open the way
for religious (*sic*; i.e., Islamist) fundamentalists to enter the party for the
sake of gaining popularity among Muslim immigrants. This brief profile exemplifies Fatah's continuous active political involvement both in
Pakistan and in the diaspora.

Since 1996, Fatah also assumed the position of an opinion leader in the
diaspora. For instance, for several years he hosted *Muslim Chronicle*, a
Toronto-based current affairs discussion show focusing on the Muslim
community in Canada. Fatah has interviewed well-known Muslim
Canadians, including journalist Husain Haqqani and author Tariq Ali,
on his program, which airs on the well-attended station CTS-TV.[10] In his
writings, he openly challenged traditional Islamic teachings on homo-
sexuality and received death threats, which, he claimed, led him to
resign from his position in the MCC. Fatah also lobbied for the right of
women to lead prayers in mosques and against mandatory donning of
the *hijab* by Muslim women. In other words, Fatah's activities in the
diaspora were not just about politics of violence and authoritarianism
in Pakistan.[11] He actively engaged in debates that concern the daily affairs of Muslims in the diaspora. Meanwhile, in his interventions, Fatah

repeatedly stated his frustration with the lack of public debate amongst Muslims in Canada and the inability to air his divergent views without the threat of violence emanating from the diaspora itself.[12] In the Muslim Canadian Congress, founded in 2001, Fatah served as communications director and spokesperson until 2006.[13] In this new capacity, he has spoken out against the introduction of Sharia law as an option for arbitration for Muslims settled in Ontario. In his opposition to Sharia law, he continually promoted separation of religion and state, and social liberalism in the Muslim community; as well, he endorsed the recognition of same-sex marriage by Muslim clerics. In 2006, Fatah campaigned to bar the Islamic cleric Sheikh Abu Yusuf Riyadh Ul-Huq from entering Canada on a speaking tour. This campaign further added to Fatah's unpopularity among conservative Muslims in Canada. On 30 June 2006 he was named by the Canadian Islamic Congress's official publication, *Friday Magazine*, as one of four leading figures with an anti-Islamic stance in Canada. The article, penned by CIC leader Mohamed Elmasry, desribed Fatah as someone who intentionally smears Islam and bashes Muslims. Wahida Valiante, vice-chair and national vice-president of the Canadian Islamic Congress, subsequently stated in the *Globe and Mail* that Fatah's views are diametrically opposed to most Muslims in Canada and elsewhere and they contradict the fundamentals of Islam. Fatah has written to the Royal Canadian Mounted Police (RCMP) to complain about the CIC's article, claiming that it amounts to the issuance of a death threat as it places him as an apostate and blasphemer.

Fatah was verbally confronted and threatened in several venues by members of the Muslim diaspora in Canada, as well. At an Islamic conference in 2003, he stated that dozens of young Muslim men surrounded him while a cleric shouted out that he had insulted the Prophet Mohammed's name. In 2006, RCMP reports state that Fatah was confronted by a man on Yonge Street, Toronto, who accused him of being an apostate. During the last few years, his car windows have been smashed repeatedly. Finally, on 4 August 2006, Fatah announced on CBC Radio that he is stepping out of the limelight as a spokesperson for Liberal Islam to ensure his and his family's safety.

Fatah's story stands out as the words of a refugee from Pakistan who paid a heavy price for the public expression of his critical ideas on Islam. However, that is only one aspect of what he stands for. Fatah also directly engages with diaspora affairs and challenges the Canadian status quo of mainly religious leaders assuming the position of spokespeople for the Canadian Muslim diaspora.[14] In his public statements and published pieces, he addresses geographical displacement as a valuable, albeit painful, lived experience that provides perspective. Meanwhile, Fatah's conceptualization of displacement is not a glorification of migrancy, hybridity, or flow, as often encountered in diaspora studies. Instead, his politics is a mode of reading *between* exile and diaspora, which are two different descriptions of displacement. In order to establish a bridge that allows a dialogue between these two conditions or positions, Fatah uses the language of memories of home. Through his references to the way things were and still are 'back in the Islamic world,' Fatah struggles to assert his identity as part of the Muslim diaspora. He draws attention to those aspects of both exile and diaspora that have remained insufficiently considered in the case of Muslims: their relation to nationalism and colonialism, to Occidentalism and Orientalism, and, above all, to questions of rights and duties in a non-authoritarian political system.[15] Contemporary Canadian society is on the eve of coming to terms with shifts in the composition of its population that are the result of immigration from former European colonies since the 1960s and 1970s, most notably the Middle East, the Indian subcontinent, South and Central America, and Africa.

As a journalist and a keen social observer, Fatah knows what that means for Canadians of European background and dares to occupy an ambiguous space between an insider and an outsider as far as the Canadian establishment is concerned. Such ambiguity is no doubt reflective of the unease he feels about the Muslim identity imposed on him, an imposition triggered by his country of origin being Pakistan. Fatah's public standing explores the possibilities for opening up Canadian paradigms of identity so as to include this new generation of immigrants and refugees who are reduced to being Muslims above and beyond all else.[16] Nonetheless, he also has an acute awareness, and an open condemnation, of the blindness of the Canadian Muslim diaspora to its own history back home. This 'double act' leads to Fatah's emotional and psychological exile in the diaspora on top of the physical exile that brought him to Canada. In this state of permanent exile, memories of home provide a structure, a backbone, for Fatah's personal life story as well as his proud public standing. They also foster his ability to comment and reflect upon the situation of the Canadian Muslim diaspora from a standpoint that is not limited to the diaspora itself. In this sense, with a twist, the impossibility of a 'return' to his home enriches Fatah's sense of self to the point of not caring for belonging anywhere any longer and feeling at home in exile. In the introduction to his new book, *Chasing a Mirage: The Tragic Illusion of an Islamic State*, Fatah states: 'I am an Indian born in Pakistan; a Punjabi born in Islam; an immigrant in Canada with a Muslim consciousness, grounded in a Marxist youth. I am one of Salman Rushdie's many Midnight's Children: we were snatched from the cradle of a great civilization and made permanent refugees, sent in search of an oasis that turned out to be a mirage. I am in pain, a living witness to how dreams of hope and enlightenment can be turned into a nightmare of despair and failure ... I write as a Muslim whose ancestors were Hindu. My religion, Islam, is rooted in Judaism, while my Punjabi culture is tied to that of the Sikhs. Yet I am told by Islamists that without shedding this multifaceted heritage, if not outrightly rejecting it, I cannot be a true Muslim.'[17]

3. Memory, Identity, and Exile: Haideh Moghissi as an Émigré Scholar in Canada

Haideh Moghissi is a professor of sociology at York University, Toronto. Before becoming a refugee and arriving at Canada, she was a founder of the Iranian National Union of Women and member of its first executive and editorial boards. She was an active member of the Iranian women's movement against the Shah's regime and its authoritarianism. As head of the Old Manuscripts Division, National Archives of Iran, she was also responsible for the evaluation and classification of historical documents in Iran. Moghissi left Iran in 1984, shortly after the Iranian Revolution turned against its own children and began to target intellectuals and activists with a socialist background. Her scholarly work published in English has been widely influential in the areas of Middle Eastern studies, feminism, diaspora studies, and political sociology of religion.[18] In the diaspora, she served as the coordinator of the Certificate in Anti-Racist Research and Practice program (CARRP) and as chair of the Executive Committee of the Centre for Feminist Research at York University. She has also been a regular commentator on Iran and women in the Middle East on BBC World Service, CBC, Radio France, and Voice of America.

Overall, Moghissi's political past in Iran and her exile led her to examine the limitations and negative consequences of the lumping together of Islam as a faith, as a political ideology, as a ruling system, and as a global justice movement. Her own life and losses stand as a vivid testimony to the evils of autocracies under a populist, theocratic disguise. In this regard, she has also been a vocal critique of North American Marxists and social activists who, in her eyes, legitimize fascistic practices in the name of respecting cultural difference and presumed (Islamic) authenticity. On the issue of *hijab*/veil, Moghissi agrees that wearing it may empower Muslim women who are marginalized and stereotyped in the West. However, she takes issue with the covering of women being considered as a progressive aspect of Islam or, indeed, as making a contribution to women's lives in the Middle East, Asia, or Africa.[19] Her critical stance against the sanctification of the veil as a progressive act of identity politics in the diaspora led to Moghissi's being labelled as an 'Iranian' scholar who does not like Islam, and to protests of her courses on Islam and women. As an international scholar who has several volumes on feminism in the Middle East, women's rights, and Islamophobia in the West, this judgment against her work is only understandable within the context of diaspora politics, in which Islamic identity is often defended unconditionally as a matter of pride.

In 2003, Moghissi and her partner Professor Saeed Rahnema were awarded a large grant from the Ford Foundation to study how several Western liberal democracies with large Muslim immigrant populations managed tensions between the migrants' need to adapt to their new country and their wish to maintain cultural integrity. This influential study of relations between Muslim diasporas and the host societies included case studies conducted in Canada, Britain, France, Sweden, and the Netherlands. It also provided comparisons between immigration and resettlement policies and practices in this set of countries. Moghissi's efforts brought together scholars of Islam and experts on multiculturalism, citizenship, and ethnicity, as well as informed members of the communities in a series of international workshops and conferences. This particular project was a continuation of Moghissi's earlier work to explore, compare, and analyse socio-cultural and economic factors which dispose communities to find comfort in religion. A central goal of the study was to identify and analyse specific factors and active forces that move diaspora communities or individuals to adopt or exaggerate their religious (Muslim) identities, thereby resisting integration into the mainstream society, as well as the ideas and practices that could help break down gender and age hierarchies in more traditional settings. Her findings thus far indicate that under pressures of isolation, racism, and discrimination in the societies they live, diasporic Muslim populations can become participants in the invention of a new 'Islam' with an aggressive slant and a defensive rhetoric. While responding to unapologetic foreign interventions in the Muslim regions of the world and the unresolved Palestinian and Israeli conflict, these adaptations of religion in the diaspora could also lead to oppressive relations in the household and within the community. In this sense, her work once more exemplified a balancing act between a genuine attempt to understand the diasporic condition of Muslim immigrants in the West, and the totalitarian tendencies within organized and transnational religion to which her own life story and memories of home stand witness.

Moghissi's scholarship has been globally recognized for her analyses of the influence of Islam as a political ideology among migrants with an Islamic background. She questions whether it is Islam that defines the identity of Muslim diasporas or whether it is the diasporic experience that defines their Islamic identity. By asking such difficult questions, she refuses to essentialize Muslim identity and argues that Muslims who use religious symbols (such as the Islamic dress code *Hijab*) as a signifier of their cultural identity and to claim a political voice, find themselves the target of anti-Muslim sentiments, stereotypes, discrimination, and exclusion, which then helps the development of an emotional and psychological detachment from the 'host land,' revitalization of tribal customs, and the creation of a vicious cycle. She has stood against the criticisms coming from different segments of Muslim diaspora communities by stating that nothing would contrast the stereotypical images of Islam and Muslims better than raising one's voice against oppressive features of cultural traditions or the inhumane practices of Islamist movements and fundamentalist regimes. Similarly, in her scholarship on feminism, she has questioned the notion that secularist democracy and egalitarian feminism are culturally inappropriate impositions for Middle Eastern societies. She is especially skeptical of the enthusiasm for Islamic feminism when it is treated as the *only* appropriate mode of feminist consciousness for women in Muslim societies. In her essay titled 'Women, War and Fundamentalism in the Middle East,' she openly states that a constructive discussion about Islam and gender has never been free of controversy.[20]

She identifies the task in hand as the ability to explain the survival of traditions and practices hostile to women in Islamic societies 'without adding to the arsenal of racist imagery about Islam and Muslim women, targeting diasporic communities in the West.' In her address of the events of 9/11, on the other hand, Moghissi is vehement in remembering her own past. She also points out how irrelevant it has been

rendered in the West. She reminds us that many people of Middle Eastern origin settled in the West – refugees and migrants alike – have gone
through the experience of having lost loved ones as a result of different
forms of violence and terrorism in their home counties.[21] Moghissi
argues this experience, combined with the continued harassment of
people who are, or appear to be, Muslim or of Middle Eastern origin,
makes a big dent in these communities' sense of belonging. Contrary to
the accusations of Muslim observers in select circles, Moghissi is at
home talking in the idiom of 'we/us/our' in this context. Hers is not a
personal outcry of unjust treatment under Islamic regimes. It is a call
of protest for the imposition of guilt and responsibility on all diasporas
of Middle Eastern and Muslim background in the West to take care of
their own 'dirty business' rather than always being on the defence. In
her intervention concerning the post-9/11 social milieu in North America, she introduces herself as a 'gender-conscious woman from an
Islamic culture who has experienced, first hand, the consequences of
the rise of Islamic fundamentalism in [her] home-country.'[22] Throughout her academic career in the West, Moghissi has maintained that if
religious texts and instructions are taken literally, gender equality cannot be achieved in any society, be it in the Middle East or in the diaspora. Furthermore, she has argued that all Abrahamic religions have
contempt for women's intelligence, and emotional and moral standing,
in their fundamentalist transfigurations. As such, she has taken issue
both with Western Islamophobia and Eastern Occidentalism expressed
in the form of political religion or Islamic revivalism. She is convinced
that meaningful change for (Muslim) women will begin when the cler-
ical grip on political institutions and law-making processes ends and a
clear separation of state from religion can be materialized. Therefore,
similar to Fatah, Moghissi subcribes to the secular model of politics and
the removal of Sharia from the legal system to ensure full citizenship
and legal equality for women. She does so based on her memories of
home as well as her experiences in the diaspora. In this regard, for
Moghissi, the words of Virginia Woolf are truer than ever for Middle
Eastern women in exile: 'As a woman, I have no country. As a woman
I want no country. As a woman my country is the whole world.'

4. Memory, History, and Exile: Can Refugees Remember the Nation?

As already indicated, the relationship between memory and migration
remains largely unexplored in both historical scholarship and in the

burgeoning field of 'memory studies.' Remembrance remains framed mainly within the national domain. A brief examination of the emergence of 'memory studies' amply confirms this point. In this last section, the intellectual pedigree of memory studies will be exposed to illustrate how it will need to be expanded and perhaps reworked in order to allow discussions on memory, migration and, in particular, exile through the use of a common vocabulary provided by some of the foundational thinkers in the field.

The key work of reference here is that of Pierre Nora's magnum opus. The impact of the seven-volume collaborative project that he led, *Lieux de mémoire*, was already considered as solidified by 1993, when the phrase 'site of memory' entered the *Grand dictionnaire Robert de la langue française*. The publication of Nora's work as a three-volume English-language edition under the title *Realms of Memory* between 1996 and 1998 made the French and European debates on memory widely and directly accessible to English-speaking readers. Influenced by Nora, during the 1990s, the work of David Lowenthal, John Bodnar, John R. Gillis, Raphael Samuel, and Simon Schama contributed to the establishment of 'memory studies' as a trans-disciplinary and international field in the Anglo-American academic tradition. Here, one should also take note of Maurice Halbwachs's endeavours in the field of memory studies, though his chosen path was sociological rather than historical analysis. A contemporary of Émile Durkheim and editor of *Annales de Sociologie*, Halbwachs left a monumental body of work on collective memory that was also contained within the nation-state framework. His most influential work, *Les cadres sociaux de la mémoire* (published posthumously in 1952, as Halbwachs died in the Buchenwald concentration camp in 1945), was translated into English in 1992. As Nora and his team's, as well as Halbwach's, conceptual vocabulary migrated from their original French context to a comparative one, observable patterns emerged in the nascent field of memory studies. One such pattern pertains to the difficulty of leading a conversation that relates memory, migration, and exile to each other without addressing the nation, or nationalism, as the necessary starting point.

This limitation could be explained, at least in part, by the influence Nora's work exerted in the field of memory studies. Back in 1979, Nora launched his grand project with the aim of exploring the construction of the French past. Thus, his research agenda was dominated by specific questions about nation, nationalism, and national identity. He took the title of his project from Frances A. Yates's book *The Art of Memory* (1966), although his own work had very little to do with hermetic experiences. While Yates's work traces the art of memory – still in its unprinted form – from Greek orators, through its Gothic transformations in the Middle Ages, to the occult forms it took in the Renaissance Nora's definition of sites of memory put notable emphasis on modern archives, libraries, festivals, dictionaries, novels, autobiographies, architecture, monuments, and museums, all extensions of the nationalist project. In this sense, Nora's *Realms of Memory* squarely belongs to the genre known as *histoire des mentalités*, associated with French historians of the *Annales* school. His research was conducted clearly from a nation-state–oriented vantage point. Unfortunately, this emphasis led to rather serious future methodological issues for the field at large. Although Nora characterized his enterprise as history in multiple voices, he was not interested in traditions but mainly in the ways in which they were constituted, institutionalized, and passed on. Furthermore, he lingered on 'tangible remnants' of memory in order to establish a point of origin for what unfolded later.

Consequently, although *Realms of Memory* represents a commodious compendium and foundational typology for memory studies, it also contains conceptual roadblocks independent of the vicissitudes of French national identity. The overall message of Nora's work is that while there may be many perspectives on France and a plurality of visions pertaining to its identity, there is also an indivisible reality of France as expressed in the idiom of *la France profonde*. What Nora fails to take into consideration is the subject of the present study: memories of migrants and refugees in France, particularly those who arrived from former French colonies. The expansion and then the consequent shrinking of France's territory from a far-flung empire to a nation-state provided France with a highly diverse and contentious population. Thus, the France of Franks and Gauls in which Nora believed has little to do with the France of large immigrant communities and postcolonial anxieties within which Nora nonetheless engineered his project.

Almost three decades after the publication of Nora's work on memory, the issue of remembrance in the diaspora or its relation to migration remains understudied. This verdict holds true even more in the case of refugees. There is a vast literature on collective memory that is suggestive of multivocal remembrance practices of the (national) past.[23] However, migration and forced or voluntary movement of peoples are rarely included in that discussion. As indicated by Fatah's and Moghissi's accounts of political Islam, for instance, refugee narratives of the past refer to a multitude of times and places through the utilization of a comparative discourse on home. These accounts often take their cues from a time period, geographical space, or a series of events already marked in national histories but expand these to include alternative voices and a much wider geography necessitated by exile. In this sense, remembrance in the diaspora is a fragmented form of commemoration that cannot be contained within the traditional, nation-state format of memory studies. Diasporic memories are aimed at disparate audiences who are positioned above and beyond the national polity. Refugees, in particular, speak to a presumed international audience with whom they wish to share the story of their plight, and from whom they seek to attain support for the betterment of the conditions in their countries of origin. In addition, refugees often wish to ascertain that the authoritarian tendencies 'back home' that crushed political movements and erased social formations are not reproduced in the diaspora. Consequently, the relevance of the past for the present gets determined on the basis of specific political calculations. The past as home is the point at which both migrant and refugee narratives of memory start, yet they lead to rather different end points.[24] Though refugees (and migrants) do remember the nation and speak in the tongue of the 'national past,' memories of home engendered in the diaspora do not comfortably fit into any national project, either at home or abroad. Neither memories of migration and exile, nor memories of the nation pronounced in the diaspora, use a language that could have been understood solely by the conceptual vocabulary developed by Nora and his followers. Refugees remember the nation, but they do so with reference to a lost home and not to an edifice of perpetual existence, political consensus, and historical vindication. In that sense, memory studies need to join forces with diaspora studies to develop a satisfactory imagination for grasping the critical intersection between memory and (transnational) migration.

5. Conclusion: Limits of Post-national Identities and Remembrance of Home in Exile

The contested nature of historical interpretation is the foundational paradox of national identity formation. The 'official memory' of the nation implicated in this context has long been the preoccupation of memory studies. This paper has argued that when put together, memories of home endorsed by migrants and refugees in the diaspora form a dense and contradictory map of memory that cannot fit into the frame of memories of national identity formation. Immigrant and refugee memories of home are far from being consensus-based. Neither do they engage with only one official narrative. Instead, they emerge from variant social, political, and cultural contexts and have multiple origins.[25] Perceptions of the past penetrate life in the diaspora for diverse reasons. Contrary to the hopefulness characteristic of recent advocations of multivocal commemorations of the past, sharing memories of home in the diaspora proves to be a difficult task due to the diverse meanings attached to them as well as the different experiences shaping them.[26] Instead of a common narrative that joins immigrant and refugee perceptions of what is to be preserved and used from the past, one thus observes fragmented commemorations whereby diverse recounts of home are produced and circulated for different audiences.[27]

The intention to remember is the starting point for memorialization of events. The key question pertaining to refugee memories of home in this context is the nature of the dialogic interaction that is observed in the shaping and reshaping of these memories in the diaspora.[28] Here, dialogical interaction refers to relations between migrants, refugees, and the national polities these groups left behind. A major difficulty faced by diaspora studies scholarship when dealing with memory – and hence for work that falls in the niche area of memory and migration – pertains to defining the 'founding moments' of mnemonic practices 'from afar.' Since most of these are instituted within the context of the nation-state, there emerges a methodological ambivalence when that context no longer applies. Being a migrant already symbolizes a barrier between what has currency in politics 'back home' and what is meaningful in a diasporic or exilic setting. Such discrepancies are doubled in intensity in the case of refugees due to conflictual interpretations of what is to be remembered and a continuing sense of injustice about what is forgotten.

By definition, refugees are pushed out of the national discourse about what counts as history. Their take on important events, or what they deem as truthful about them, is often at odds with the views of the majority in their home countries. Therefore, for refugees, remembrance itself becomes a political act to defy violence, exile, and silencing even before their entry into diaspora politics.[29] In this context, for refugee communities, narratives of exile deliver a strong sense of continuity. In particular, memories of home play a very important role in the construction of exilic identities. They contextualize political action and provide a sense of moral order in an otherwise chaotic environment in the diaspora.[30] The functions performed by memories of home in exile cannot be reduced to the sense of comfort offered by commemorative practices about difficult or traumatic events that bring on closure. In the diaspora, the interpretative frame within which memories of home make sense provides political anchorage. As such, it allows the encoding of objects, situations, events, and experiences in one's present environment, as well as back in one's past.[31]

In the two life histories presented in this paper, collective memory is shaped by past conflicts and historical events that are open to variant readings. This is despite the fact that it presents a façade of settled facts and undeniable truths. Collective memory operates, not as a veridical narrative, but as a recounting of how things are perceived to have happened by different groups and sectors in the society. As such, it divides while uniting. The conditions under which refugees and exiles leave their homes are complex in terms of establishing core narratives to sustain memory. The anarchy of internal fragmentation, civil wars, independence struggles and their aftermath, coups, and other forms of transition to authoritarianism and revolutions are not events conducive to the construction of easily agreed upon histories.[32] The contentious character of these events does not change in exile. In effect, the trauma of permanent and forced separation from home and a strong sense of injustice that accompanies such migrations heighten the tensions already endemic to collective memory narratives emerging from war-torn societies.[33] In the absence of institutional and organizational support, or political coalitions to channel their frustration and anguish, refugees often resort to individual expressions of what they remember. They dwell on the causes of their plight and formulate their own narratives of exile. In turn, these narratives often depict a homeland in contradistinction to what is delivered in immigrant stories. In refugee memories, the history of their home country and the society left behind figures predominantly as a place whereby there remains an unfinished struggle for justice and change. In this struggle, refugees themselves can no longer take a direct part.[34] Therefore, collective memories framed by the exilic condition provide the context within which this struggle continues from the diaspora. Exilic engagements in defining home assume a notable degree of inter-subjectivity as they purposefully reach out for a global audience.[35]

Refugees do not desire, and neither are they often allowed, to assume a central role in terms of political entrepreneurship or engagement in communal identity politics in their country of asylum in the West. They nonetheless intervene and remind minority groups in the diaspora of legacies of their past. These reminders take the form of public discussions on violent histories pertaining to their national, ethno-cultural, or religious identities 'back home.' This is evident in both Fatah's and Moghissi's accounts of Islamic governments in Iran and Pakistan. In this sense, refugee memories of home in exile perform the difficult function of being the conscience of identity claims made in the diaspora. They draw attention to totalitarian and majoritarian aspects of political cultures reproduced in the diaspora under the rubric of authenticity. They strive to remind migrants of histories of violence, abuse, tyranny, and protracted conflicts that affected their lives back home. These aspects of culture are assumed to have ended once in the diaspora. The refugee public intellectuals discussed in this paper speak in a voice that carries an agency larger than their own individual existence or experiences. They speak as refugees, yet not only to refugees but to migrants and members of the society at large, as well. As they tell their own stories of what rendered them 'homeless,' they also express a strong desire for change. Their remembrance of home signifies the sheer determination to make their exile useful for the building of a new future in the diaspora, if not back home. As the life stories, as well as the political and intellectual work, of Tarek Fatah and Haideh Moghissi amply illustrate, in an age of Islamophobia, it is hard to speak out about wrongdoings in Muslim majority societies. However, for these individuals, who paid a heavy personal price to remain alive and who are acutely aware of the conditions in political regimes that are prone to produce many more refugees like themselves, it is even harder not to remember. Memories of home thus symbolize a public devotion to justice and change in the diaspora. The irony is that by not silencing their memories, not keeping them as their individual affair, and by presenting their own histories as part of a collective account of an unspoken past, refugees continue to pay a heavy personal price in the diaspora and in exile.

NOTES

1 Laura Huttunen, '"Home" and Ethnicity in the Context of War: Hesitant Diasporas of Bosnian Refugees,' *European Journal of Cultural Studies* 8, no. 2 (2005): 177.
2 This paper is based on personal discussions and semi-formal interviews with Tareq Fatah, Haideh Moghissi, and several other scholars and public

figures from Muslim majority countries who arrived in Canada as refugees. Though it does not have the format of an ethnographical study or an oral history text, it widely engages in current debates on refugee diasporas with observations derived from the experiences of these key public figures who are members of the Muslim diaspora in Canada.

3 Current literature on diasporas is vast and ever growing. Here, I will only refer to the subset of studies that concentrate on remembrance of the past in the diaspora. For this purpose, see Duncan Bell, 'Introduction: Memory, Trauma and World Politics,' in *Memory, Trauma and World Politics: Reflections on the Relationship between Peace and Present,* ed. Duncan Bell (London: Palgrave-Macmillan, 2006), 1–32; and Tony Judt, 'The Past Is Another Country: Myth and Memory in Postwar Europe,' *Daedalus* 4 (1992): 83–1.

4 Huttunen, '"Home" and Ethnicity in the Context of War'; Michael Ignatieff, *The Rights Revolution* (Toronto: House of Anansi Press, 2007); Charles Taylor, *Modern Social Imaginaries* (Durham, NC: Duke University Press, 2004); Joseph Carens, *Culture, Citizenship, and Community: A Contextual Exploration of Justice as Evenhandedness* (Oxford and New York: Oxford University Press, 2000); Howard Adelman and John Simpson, eds, *Multiculturalism, Jews, and Identities in Canada* (Jerusalem: Magnes Press, the Hebrew University, 1996); James Tully, *Strange Multiplicity: Constitutionalism in an Age of Diversity* (Cambridge and New York: Cambridge University Press, 1995).

5 See Engin Isin and Greg Nielsen, eds, *Acts of Citizenship* (London and New York: Zed Books, 2008) and *Being Political: Genealogies of Citizenship* (Minneapolis: University of Minnesota Press, 2002); Peter Nyers, *Rethinking Refugees: Beyond States of Emergency* (New York: Routledge, 2006); Sherene Razack, *Casting Out: The Eviction of Muslims from Western Law and Politics* (Toronto: University of Toronto Press, 2008); Sherene Razack, ed., *Race, Space, and the Law: Unmapping a White Settler Society* (Toronto: Between the Lines, 2002); Gerald Kernerman, *Multicultural Nationalism: Civilizing Difference, Constituting Community* (Vancouver: UBC Press, 2005).

6 The UN has staggering statistics about the numbers of migrants who will arrive in industrially developed regions between 2005 and 2050. An estimated 98 million migrants will leave their countries, and nearly a tenth of the flow is destined to come to Canada – approximately 200,000 individuals annually. Of these, at least one-third are expected to be of Muslim background due to the current nature of migrant-producing regions in the world.

7 See Nergis Canefe, 'The Making of "Modern" Diasporas: The Case of Muslims in Canada,' in *Opportunity Structures in Diaspora Relations:*

Comparisons in Contemporary Multi-level Politics of Diaspora and Transnational Identity, Center for Basque Studies Series, ed. Gloria Totoricagüena (Reno: University of Nevada Press, 2001), 53–84.

8 On 6 March 2006, CBC TV's *The National* aired a special documentary by Joan Leishman discussing the threats of violence and strategies of intimidation used to silence some of Canada's secular and liberal Muslims. The documentary outlined the inner struggles within Canada's Muslim communities against those who, like the Muslim Canadian Congress, promote the separation of religion and state and who opposed the introduction of Sharia law–based arbitration in Ontario. In the program, Haideh Moghissi was the main commentator, and Tarek Fatah was interviewed extensively as a Canadian of Muslim background who has been subjected to threats from the Muslim diaspora community itself. For the full coverage of the program, see the *Globe and Mail,* 8 March 2006.

9 The MCC is associated with the Progressive Muslim Union of North America (PMUNA), which is a liberal Islamic umbrella organization based in New York City. Its mandate states that its foundation was the result of two years of conversation and collaboration between a select group of North American Muslims who are committed to representing and renewing the Muslim community in all its social, ideological, and political diversity. PMU members range from deeply religious to totally secular. They identify their common commitments as learning, political and social empowerment, justice and freedom, and a concern and love for the Muslim community. Both MCC and the PMU define a Muslim on the basis of a person's social and cultural commitments, a stance which radically differs from the traditional religious definition based on faith and its practice.

10 Fatah also regularly writes opinion pieces for various newspapers, including *Time Magazine,* the *Toronto Star,* the *National Post,* and the *Globe and Mail.* See also Tarek Fatah, *Chasing a Mirage: The Tragic Illusion of an Islamic State,* (Mississauga, ON: John Wiley & Sons, 2008).

11 For instance, on the Darfur crisis and racism endemic in Arabized Islam, Fatah argued the following: 'The fact that more than 200,000 Darfurians, almost all of them Muslims, have been killed in an ongoing genocide; the fact that more than a million Muslim Darfurians are displaced refugees living in squalor and fear, appears not to have registered with the leadership of traditional Muslim organizations and mosques in this country. One would have expected Muslim organizations to be leading the call for this week's debate on Darfur in Parliament. One expected them this past weekend to stand in solidarity with their fellow Muslims suffering in Sudan, but that did not happen. The city's Muslim elite was conspicuous

by its absence ... it certainly appears that some kind of Arabic-Islamic
ideology is being used in Sudan to ethnically cleanse marginalized citizens
who are not considered true Muslims by virtue of being black.' This
passage was cited in the blogs of *daimnation*, dated 3 May 2006. See Tarek
Fatah, 'Darfur: A Victim of Muslim Racism,' 3 May 2006, http://www
.damianpenny.com/archived/006405.html (last accessed 5 September 2008).

12 On 22 March 2007, the *Toronto Star* reported that Toronto police launched
a hate crime investigation into a phone call from a man who vowed to
'slaughter' members of the Muslim Canadian Congress unless they
stopped speaking publicly about Islam. The message mentioned Congress
founder Tarek Fatah and current president Farzana Hassan-Shahid by
name. Both have openly criticized the politicization of Islam and alleged
influence of Iran and Saudi Arabia in Canadian mosques.

13 The Muslim Canadian Congress was organized to provide a voice to
Muslims in Canada who support a 'progressive, liberal, pluralistic,
democratic, and secular society where everyone has the freedom of
religion.' The organization claims to have 300 dues-paying members. It
was formed in March 2001, in the wake of 9/11, by a group of Toronto-area
liberal Muslims. It is the only Muslim organization in Canada asking for
the 'separation of religion and state in all matters of public policy.' The
group has been critical of Islamic fundamentalism and has urged the
government to ban donations from abroad to Canadian religious institutions, arguing that doing so will curb extremism. The Congress suffered a
serious split in the summer of 2006 when several of its members and
leaders left to form the Canadian Muslim Union. According to reports, the
split occurred over questions of how the group engages with the broader
Muslim community, particularly its position on the arrest of seventeen
Muslims in the 2006 Toronto terrorism case, and over objections to MCC
leaders participating in demonstrations against the 2006 Lebanese-Israeli
War. Eight executive members who participated in or supported the
demonstrations resigned and formed the new CMU, whose philosophy
remains Liberal Islam, but with the stated intention to work 'with and
within the Muslim community' (http://www.muslimunion.ca/).

14 The 1991 Arbitration Act permitted faith-based binding arbitration as a
substitute for family law courts. In response to the expansion of the
Arbitration Act to include sharia courts in Ontario, Fatah stated the
following: 'Privatizing our judicial system is not a choice; it is a betrayal of
one of the fundamental principles of civic society. Allowing for private
sector, for-profit, faith-based arbitrations in areas of Family Law is a
slippery slope that will open up the dismantling of many public institutions

already under the threat of privatization … If implemented, this law will also cut along class and race lines: a publicly funded, accountable legal system run by experienced judges for the mainstream Canadian society, and cheap, private-sector, part-time arbitrators for the already marginalized and recently arrived Muslim community.' See Fatah's 'Sharia Law Controversy,' 23 June 2005, posted on znet, http://www.zmag.org/znet/viewArticle/5979 (last accessed 5 September 2008).

15 For instance, as the Canadian government took steps to deport prominent Toronto-area Palestinian peace activist Issam Al Yamani, who has been living in Canada since 1985, Fatah responded to these measures in the following tone: 'As Muslim Canadians we believe in the principles of secular parliamentary democracy and universal human rights, as foundations of civic society and the modern nation state. We advocate these principles not just in Canada, but across the developing world, including Muslim countries, many of which are either under foreign occupation or suffering under the rule of monarchs, military dictators or self anointed religious theocrats.' For full text, see Fatah's 'Stop the Deportation of Palestinian Peace Activist Issam Al Yamani from Canada,' 16 April 2006, open letter posted at http://www.zmag.org/znet/viewArticle/4042 (last accessed 5 September 2008).

16 Regarding the recent security scandal surrounding Omar Khadr, Tarek Fatah argued the following in a piece titled 'Mohamed Elmasry: Canadian Islamic Congress President Plays the Race Card – Badly': 'Whereas Omar Khadr deserves our compassion and forgiveness, those advocating for his repatriation to Canada seem less interested in the young man's welfare and more intent on using his incarceration to embarrass Canada and the U.S. And now the ultimate ruse in dirty politics has been used – the race card. Instead of generating sympathy for Omar Khadr, the tactics of his advocates will result in an even more hostile attitude. Instead of using Omar Khadr to slam the Conservatives, wouldn't it be better if Mohamed Elmasry and Khadr's lawyers obtained a statement from the detained youth where he would condemn Al-Qaeda, distance himself from the international jihad launched by Bin Laden and promise not to become the poster child for Canada's Islamists? Omar Khadr needs to be brought home and given a chance to rehabilitate, but first he should commit not to become an apologist of the Muslim Brotherhood and other extremist Islamist jihadis.' See *National Post*, 22 July 2008; cited in http://network.nationalpost.com/np/blogs/fullcomment/archive/2008/07/22/tarek-fatah-on-mohamed-elmasry-canadian-islamic-congress-president-plays-the-race-card-badly.aspx (last accessed 5 September 2008).

17 Cited in *Huffington Post*, 5 September 2008, http://www.huffingtonpost.
com/ali-eteraz/illusions-of-an-islamics_b_96698.html (last accessed
5 September 2008). On *Chasing a Mirage*, see also Ali Eteraz's column in the
Guardian of 18 April 2008, 'History Lessons,' http://www.guardian.co.uk/
commentisfree/2008/apr/18/historylessons (last accessed 5 September
2008).

18 Moghissi edited the three-volume *Women and Islam: Critical Concepts in Sociol-
ogy* (London: Routledge, 2005). Her other publications include *Feminism and
Islamic Fundamentalism: The Limits of Postmodern Analysis* (London and New
York: Zed Press, 1999), winner of the Choice Outstanding Academic Book
Award; and *Populism and Feminism in Iran: Women's Struggle in a Male-Defined
Revolutionary Movement* (London: Macmillan, 1994).

19 In her article 'Facing an Impossible Task,' Moghissi states that 'Canadian
multiculturalism, failing to combat racism and Muslim-phobia, is gradually
moving towards adopting faith-based multiculturalism, allowing the
formation of cultural ghettoes immune from social and legal scrutiny against
violations of human rights. Such politics serve the interests of conservative
Muslim leaders. Enjoying the formal recognition by different levels of
government, they openly reject civic norms of conduct, and preach their
obscurantist and rigid understanding of "piety" and "modesty" to an
audience that struggles to adjust to life in the diaspora.' See http://www
.timeimmortal.net/tag/haideh-moghissi/ (last accessed 5 September 2008).

20 For the full text, see http//:www.atkinson.yorku.ca/SSS/Moghissi.htm
(last accessed 5 September 2008).

21 In Moghissi's words: 'Not-belonging or feeling out of place can sometimes
be intellectual and political. Many nonconformist intellectuals who do not
share the cultural values, perceptions, and/or dominant ideologies in their
home countries may feel this sense of not belonging, regardless of their
nationality or place of residence. They feel culturally homeless within their
home, so to speak. But generally, the sense of not belonging, or living on
the margin of social and economic life, is more profound and has more
immediate practical consequences for the groups of migrant, refugee, and
displaced communities, particularly those coming from so-called Third
World societies.' This passage is quoted from Moghissi's 'SSHRC Research
Report on Diaspora of Islamic Cultures: Continuity and Change' (2007),
published at https://pi.library.yorku.ca/ojs/index.php/refuge/article/
viewFile/926/499 (last accessed 5 September 2008).

22 See Moghissi's 'Women, War and Fundamentalism in the Middle East'
(2007),http://www.atkinson.yorku.ca/~diaspora/papers/american/
American-SSHRCarticle.pdf (last accessed 5 September 2008).

23 See Daniel Levy, 'The Future of the Past: Historiographical Disputes and Competing Memories in Germany and Israel,' *History and Theory* 38 (1999): 51–66; Francesca Polleta, 'Legacies and Liabilities of an Insurgent Past: Remembering Martin Luther King, Jr., on the House and Senate Floor,' *Social Science History* 22 (1998): 479–512; Jeffrey Olick and Daniel Levy, 'Collective Memory and Cultural Constraint: Holocaust Myth and Rationality in German Politics,' *American Sociological Review* 62 (1997): 92–136; Jeffrey Olick and Joyce Robbins, 'Social Memory Studies: From "Collective Memory" to the Historical Sociology of Mnemonic Practices,' *Annual Review of Sociology* 24 (1998): 105–40; Paul Ricoeur, *Memory, History, Forgetting*, trans. Kathleen Blamey and David Pellauer (Chicago: University of Chicago Press, 2004).
24 See Mark Freeman, *Rewriting the Self: History, Memory, Narrative* (London and New York: Routledge, 1993); Keya Ganguly, 'Migrant Identities: Personal Memory and the Construction of Selfhood,' *Cultural Studies* 6, no. 1 (1992): 27–50.
25 Pnina Werbner, 'Divided Loyalties, Empowered Citizenship? Muslims in Britain,' *Citizenship Studies* 4, no. 3 (2000): 307–24.
26 Barry Schwartz and Todd Bayma, 'Commemoration and the Politics of Recognition: The Korean War Veterans Memorial,' *American Behavioral Scientist* 42 (1999): 946–67; Barry Schwartz, 'The Social Context of Commemoration: A Study in Collective Memory,' *Social Forces* 61 (1982): 374–402.
27 William Safran, 'Diasporas in Modern Societies: Myths of Homeland and Return,' *Diaspora* 1, no. 1 (1991): 83–99.
28 Jeffrey Olick, 'Collective Memory: The Two Cultures,' *Sociological Theory* 17 (1999): 333–48.
29 See Smadar Lavie and Ted Swedenburg, eds, *Displacement, Diaspora and Geographies of Identity* (Durham, NC: Duke University Press, 1996); Liisa Malkki, *Purity and Exile: Violence, Memory and National Cosmology among Hutu Refugees in Tanzania* (Chicago: University of Chicago Press, 1995).
30 See Iwona Irwin-Zarecka, *Frames of Remembrance: The Dynamics of Collective Memory* (New Brunswick, NJ: Transaction Press, 1994); Michael Schudson, 'The Present in the Past versus the Past in the Present,' *Communication* 11 (1989): 105–13.
31 See Susannah Radstone and Katharine Hodgkin, eds, *Regimes of Memory* (London and New York: Routledge, 2003); James Young, *The Texture of Memory* (New Haven: Yale University Press, 1993); W.J. Mitchell, ed. *On Narrative* (Chicago: University of Chicago Press, 1981).

32 See Gary Fine, *Difficult Reputations: Collective Memories of the Evil, Inept, and Controversial* (Chicago: University of Chicago Press, 2001); Antoine Prost, 'The Algerian War in French Collective Memory' in *War and Remembrance in the Twentieth Century*, ed. J. Winter and E. Sivan (Cambridge: Cambridge University Press, 1999), 161–76.

33 See Laura Huttunen, '"Home" and Ethnicity in the Context of War: Hesitant Diasporas of Bosnian Refugees,' *European Journal of Cultural Studies* 8, no. 2 (2005): 177–95; Adriana Cavarero, *Relating Narratives: Storytelling and Selfhood* (London and New York: Routledge, 2000); Mary Douglas, 'The Idea of Home: A Kind of Space,' *Social Research* 58, no. 1 (1991): 287–307.

34 See S. Binder and J. Tosic, *Refugee Studies and Politics: Human Dimensions and Research Perspectives* (Vienna: Facultas, 2002).

35 Pierre Bourdieu, *The Weight of the World: Social Suffering in Contemporary Society* (Cambridge: Polity Press, 2002); Martha Nussbaum, *Upheavals of Thought: The Intelligence of Emotions* (Cambridge: Cambridge University Press, 2001).

SECTION THREE

The Smell of Flowers and Rotting Potatoes

9 The Flower Girl: A Case Study in Sense Memory

MONA LINDQVIST

A case study from my clinical practice as a psychotherapist illustrates how traumatic recall sometimes happens first through sense modalities – as Amira Bojadzija-Dan so beautifully expresses it, ' the lingering presence of the sense memory of … smells, tastes, and texture' – only later to emerge into words and narrative.[1] The case concerns a twenty-six-year-old female refugee from Uzbekistan who was brutally raped sometime before she migrated to Sweden. I will use the case study to argue that this traumatic memory was at first primarily a sensory experience before it transformed itself into a cognitive and verbal memory. When talking about migration and memories, we usually assume that the migrant or the refugee is aware of his or her history and of what to talk about in therapy. Since Freud, therapy has been considered the talking cure, and in many ways it still is, but the difficulty lies in the question of how to transform a vague reminiscence impressed by one or several sense modalities, into words and a comprehensible narrative about the person, the patient, and the past. For 'Natasha,'[2] a scent was one of the keys to mobilizing a forgotten yet deeply troubling event.

1. The Oldest and Fastest Path

The sense of smell is our oldest sense and strongly connected to basic functions such as memory and feelings. The olfactory nerve is directly connected to the amygdala, the centre of feeling, and the hippocampus, where memory is stored. The fact is that there are only two synapses, two connections, between the olfactory nerve and the amygdala. The impulses from other senses take extensive roundabouts in the brain before they arrive at the amygdala. Episodic memory is one form of memory that is supposed to be unique to the human being. Personal experiences and events that are connected to a certain time and place are stored in the episodic memory. Sven-Åke Christianson claims that the emotional experience in an olfactory memory is usually much stronger than in the case of visual and aural memories.[3] Brain activity increases in specific parts of the brain when certain smells are picked up by the nose; sensory information from the nose is processed by certain areas of the brain. The human olfactory system is fully mature at birth. Much of the early attachment to an important other is the first dialogue that goes through the sense of smell. Esther Bick first noticed this in the 1960s in her research focusing on the skin as an important means of communication between the mother and her baby.[4] Smell is the sense that reaches deeply and quickly into our emotional centre to evoke feelings and memories of our past.

One difficulty in describing smell and scent memories is that our language has no names for odour. We are able to name forms and colours we have seen, to describe tunes and sounds that we have heard, and to explain how things feel soft or hard. But odours are considerably more difficult; try, for example, to describe how an orange smells. We can only describe odours in terms of being strong or weak, bad or good. We describe smell quite poorly compared to the language we use to describe impressions from other sense organs. Our sense of smell is not simply there to give us a message about what we smell or how it appears; instead, the crucial information it provides allows us to decide whether we should approach or remove ourselves from the environment, the person, or the article of food that the odour emanates from. According to Constance Classen, David Howes, and Anthony Synnott, in *Aroma: The Cultural History of Smell*, we take our cues from an odour which is pleasant or unpleasant in character.[5] Therefore, one may say that the sense of smell knows what is important, but it cannot tell why. Hence, memories evoked by our sense of smell are usually more emotional than memories evoked by our other senses. Our odour memory archive is placed in the brain's limbic system. The limbic system controls our emotional responses, hunger and thirst, perceptions of space, body temperature, and our artistic abilities. But our reaction to odour is still individual; it depends on our own personal and unique associations to smell, and whether a particular scent provokes a happy memory or one that is deeply disturbing.

2. The Return of the Country of Childhood through a Madeleine Soaked in Decoction of Lime-Blossom

One of the most notable literary examples of the phenomenon is by Marcel Proust in his novel *In Search of Lost Time*. The country of his childhood has ceased to exist for the narrator, but a reminiscence of it is triggered by a taste and smell:

> One day in winter, on my return home, my mother, seeing that I was cold, offered me some tea, a thing I did not ordinarily take. I declined at first, and then, for no particular reason, changed my mind. She sent for one of those squat, plump little cakes called 'petites madeleines,' which look as though they had been moulded in the fluted valve of a scallop shell. And soon, mechanically, dispirited after a dreary day with the prospect of a depressing morrow, I raised to my lips a spoonful of the tea in which I had soaked a morsel of the cake. No sooner had the warm liquid mixed with the crumbs touched my palate than a shiver ran through me and I stopped, intent upon the extraordinary thing that was happening to me. An exquisite pleasure had invaded my senses, something isolated, detached, with no suggestion of its origin.[6]

Proust's novel is a beautiful example of a description of how memory works when there is no interruption, no distortion, and no fragmentation caused by a traumatic event, and the narrator is taken back to a very pleasant experience of his childhood. He describes as an adult a well-formulated sense memory, a reminiscence triggered by a *petite Madeleine* dipped in herbal tea, the odour of his childhood. Fragments of a memory emerge and take some time to gather into a conscious memory of his childhood home of Combray.

Many of us have similar memories from childhood. They are mainly emotional because of the connection between the sense of smell and the older parts of the brain that are related to emotions and motivation. Research done by Christianson is in line with this literary anecdote from Proust's novel, and has shown that smell-released autobiographical memories are actually earlier than memories released by other sense impressions. Sometimes a narrative is not possible or not necessary when there is no need to process what happened in the past, but only to remember, verbally or not.

However, here we are clearly talking about a non-traumatic olfactory memory. To verbalize a memory that has appeared through odours is not easy because odours are etheric, hard to measure, name, or recreate. Smells cannot be documented, stored, or captured in a manner comparable to aural and visual memories. We have to stick to descriptions. It is hard enough to portray a positive, non-traumatic olfactory memory triggered by one or several odours. What about those memories that the body (the brain) has forgotten or chosen to forget and are not pleasant but, on the contrary, terrifying, brutal, and grotesque, associated with violence and assault? Forgetfulness, like memory, is a dynamic act. A powerful experience or a significant act does not fall away and disappear out of memory. It is stored, but difficult to reach with conscious memory. When it returns, it usually does so in a fragmentary and undefined manner as opposed to a chronological one. Proust verbalizes the difficulty in perceiving this non-traumatic phenomenon:

> Undoubtedly what is thus palpitating in the depths of my being must be the image, the visual memory which, being linked to that taste, is trying to follow it into my conscious mind. But its struggles are too far off, too confused and chaotic; scarcely can I perceive the natural glow into which the elusive whirling medley of stirred-up colours is fused, and I cannot distinguish its form, cannot invite it, as the one possible interpreter, to translate for me the evidence of its contemporary, its inseparable paramour, the taste, cannot ask it to inform me what special circumstance is in question, from what period in my past life.
>
> Will it ultimately reach the clear surface of my consciousness, this memory, this old, dead moment which the magnetism of an identical moment has travelled so far to importune, to disturb, to raise up out of the very depths of my being?[7]

It is complicated enough to put an olfactory memory into words and make a narrative out of it, but when the extreme is involved – amnesia, shattering of the mind, and fragmentation – recall follows an even more difficult path.

3. The Smell of Trauma

When inhaled, a scent goes on a quite complex olfactory journey in which it eventually reaches the amygdala, the memory centre for fear and trauma. Joseph Ledoux discovered that the amygdala plays an important role in emotional trauma. The younger the person was at the time of the trauma, and the more prolonged the event was, the greater the likelihood of forgetting, or not remembering, the traumatic event. There are many different sensory elements that make up a traumatic event, and our recollection of a trauma often consists of sensory fragments of the event, rather than a complete and coherent memory. A traumatic memory is often vividly detailed in some aspects but lacking detail in others. The amygdala operates by giving emotional meanings to different sensory impressions.

Whereas non-traumatic memories generally fade over time, losing their vividness and detail, traumatic memories are recalled with vividness and a sense of being present ('It is happening to me now, at this moment'). Non-traumatic memories are recalled with a clear sense of being in the past. Traumatic memories are experienced as flashbacks, disturbing dreams, or a sudden sense of reliving the event.

Clinical observations have been reported for more than a century that, contrary to memories of non-traumatic events, the initial recall of traumatic events occurs in a fragmentary, sensory, and affective way, often without the presence of a clear narrative.[8] In contrast to memories of non-traumatic events, memories of trauma are initially fragmented. They occur as waves of intense feelings, and as visual images, olfactory, auditory perceptions, and bodily sensations. With the passage of time, patients gradually construct a narrative of what has happened to them that could be called an autobiographical memory.

In post-traumatic stress disorder, PTSD, the traumatic event is not remembered and stored in the past in the same way as other events in life. The trauma keeps on intruding in the person's everyday life through, for example, olfactory stimuli. Memory problems play a large part in PTSD. It is not unusual for patients to report deficits in remembering facts, fragmentation of memory, disassociative amnesia, and gaps in memory that are not caused by ordinary forgetting. It is common that victims of brutal abuse report that they remember minor details of it but have completely forgotten central events. Seemingly absurd details such as smell or sound can later evoke feelings of intense fear.

Getting back memories of a traumatic event does not readily boil down to simple ideas. No matter what terminology has been used, repression, dissociation, or forgetting, human beings will not consciously understand some aspects of their traumatic experience for periods of time. Memory is reconstructive, not a recording that delivers a totally exact replay. Many different factors, including the age at which traumatic event occurred, the relationships to the abuser, and the nature and extent of the traumas, influence what will be accessible later on in life.

Loss of memory is more than just forgetting, say O.L. Schachter and J.F. Kihlstrom,[9] and it can occur for both psychological and physiological reasons. Pathological forgetfulness can strike as a reaction of severe emotional stress. Psychogenic loss of memory can take place in a person who has suffered a psychological trauma as a powerful negative emotional experience that the person has no prior experience of or defence against, and therefore cannot bear in his or her consciousness. Rape, for example, can cause a complete blocking out of the entire course of events, both the event itself and the detailed information about what happened. What the person suppresses is the specific information about the event. On the other hand, the emotional experience and its discomfort and the anguish remains, and may become conscious if the person is exposed to a stimulus of the senses, such as an image, sound, smell etc., that is associated with the traumatic event. Christianson says that, 'In a manner that is analogous to a movie, a victim can remember details that she or he could not have gotten a hold of at an earlier point in time.'[10] Even if returning to the place of origin is impossible, we can assume that the body carries the place in its sensory system. A traumatic experience is always a bodily experience, and thus the body itself must be integrated into the treatment of the trauma. In the initial phase of therapy, words alone will not reach the traumatic experience. The traumatic experience is still stored in the brain and body as merely sensomotoric experiences and has to be responded to as such.

4. A Crowd of Bodily Symptoms without an Explanation

In order to illuminate the importance of odour in bringing back a traumatic memory, I will now turn to my clinical work with Natasha.

Natasha was remitted to the psychiatric outpatient clinic for refugees where I work as a psychotherapist. According to the remittance, she was suffering from sleeping disturbances, nightmares about being chased, and severe pain, especially in her stomach and pelvis, with no somatic cause. Natasha was agitated, agonized, and periodically extremely tired. When I met Natasha for the very first session in mid-December, she had recently arrived in Sweden. She spoke briefly about her background. She was twenty-six-years-old, educated as a speech therapist, and had been working at a theatre in her home country, Uzbekistan. Natasha had also been politically active. She was of Korean origin, an ethnic minority in the area. Her background caused her and her family a lot of problems. It was not unusual that they were exposed to harassment and verbal threats. When the threats and the harassments became more powerful, Natasha and her brother decided to flee. It was more a matter of chance than choice that they ended up in Sweden. Upon arrival in Stockholm, they applied for asylum.

Natasha was very verbal and it was easy for her to describe her background and her current situation. But somehow the symptoms did not seem to be related to her everyday life. She seemed to be locked up in a verbal explanation that did not connect with her agony. In the beginning of our contact, we dealt mostly with her nightmares. Natasha was able to describe them in detail, as well as the fear and the panic she experienced in these dreams, but despite that, there was no clue to the symptoms she had in her everyday life. Certainly the threats against her and her family had been quite disturbing, but she felt that she had always succeeded in defending herself in her home country. The pain she felt also seemed to be torn loose from any reasonable context. Natasha related to the pain as if it had its origin in poor nutrition and in the worry and stress associated with her concerns about the future.

The Christmas holidays were approaching, and in Scandinavia it is common to have hyacinths in floral arrangements for Christmas. A hyacinth was placed on the table in my office when Natasha came for her therapy session. She became very agitated and restless; she talked a lot, but it did not make sense – she cried, she shouted, she swore, she asked for help from God, and she laughed. It was impossible for her to remain seated, and she began to wander around in the room, bumping into chairs and tables. Her breathing became faster to the limit of hyperventilation. She returned to the location of the hyacinth. The flower was removed from the room, and after a while she calmed down. Initially I thought it was an odd, instant allergic reaction. Natasha herself was very surprised by her behaviour. Hyacinths had a great symbolic value for her, and intellectually she had only positive connotations of the flower and its scent. She continued to run into these flower arrangements in different surroundings during the Christmas holidays, always with the same disturbing reaction. Natasha told me about this strange behaviour of hers every time she smelled this particular flower. In the therapy setting, an experiment then took place with the permission of the patient. For some of the sessions that followed, we started off as usual by talking; the hyacinth was then placed in the room, and Natasha went off into her strange behaviour. Although her mind seemed to be somewhere else, she answered my questions. Getting somewhere was a challenge worthy of Sherlock Holmes. I had no clues about what was going on. Before the words made any sense, her body language provided some hints. Her gestures suggested that she was trying to get something heavy off her body; her face contorted as if in severe pain, and she started to wheeze.

After some exploratory sessions, she described a scene of violence where she lay half naked on the cold and wet ground, smelling the soil, the scent of the flowers, hearing the squeaky sound of the petals crushing against her upper body, and the muttering and heavy breathing of a man. She could not recall any visual memory of the man himself. She narrated the corresponding incidents by recalling her senses, the smell, the sound and the feeling on her skin. These sense modalities, especially the olfactory sense, helped to narrate the history of the violence. But, in order to get there, we had to go through her bodily sensations, scanning each and every body part to recognize what she could sense, perceive, and become aware of. From this point on, she was able to create movements that helped release memory fragments. Natasha began with agitated movements and then moved on to imagining the smell, making squeaky sounds, going through the body and finding the words that connected with the sensations. The sensations gave words that could be woven together into sentences and finally into her narrative of the rape itself.

During the subsequent therapy sessions, pictures rose to the surface of her consciousness piece-by-piece, diffuse and disconnected from a chronological perspective. In this case, an odour was the key to bringing back a traumatic memory. Its final form is described below.

5. The Return of the Memory

International Women's Day, on March 8, is greatly celebrated in Uzbekistan. It is late in the evening and it is getting dark. Natasha has been drinking but is not drunk. All women that day had been presented with gifts of flowers; Natasha as well as the others had gathered a bouquet of pink and blue hyacinths. It is a tradition in Uzbekistan to give that particular flower on International Women's Day. The flowers spread their heavy scent around. Natasha is feeling tired after the party and decides to take a shortcut through a park. Halfway through the park, she is suddenly attacked by a man. He hits her in the head and shouts violent and racist comments about her looks. She attempts to run away but fails. He abuses her and rapes her brutally. He finishes off by kicking her in the pelvic area. When Natasha rises, she is mostly worried about her ripped stockings. She walks home and goes to sleep. The next day, she wakes up sore in her whole body, bruised and scratched, but without any memory of what caused her injuries. She assumes that she has been in a fight; she remembers the party and that she decided to walk home. After the bruises and the scratches have healed, she no longer thinks about what happened.

The symptoms that finally led her to therapy did not appear before her migration to Sweden. Probably, surviving her flight from Uzbekistan consumed so much mental energy and strength that her body never had the opportunity to release any symptoms, let alone the memory of the abusive attack. Natasha had been unable to recall the main traumatic event for about three years, even after being asked directly about it in the first interview preceding therapy. The event returned initially as sensory fragments, with no clear autobiographical narrative. In the course of time, more sensory dimensions became involved, giving rise to more detailed memories of the traumatic event. But even when the traumatic memory evolved into a narrative, the memory remained depersonalized, cut off from her story, while the non-traumatic aspect of her narrative became more a part of the distant past in another country, in another time of her life. At first it was like her body had migrated away from the incident itself. The rape became, in the language of Viktor Frankl, 'provisional.'[11] Natasha felt a strong sense of being thrown out into space. She did not recognize that her whole history had migrated with her, imprinted in her body. Her memory returned initially as sensor motor fragments, encompassed more sensory dimensions over time, and gradually acquired a narrative component. Prior to this, intense emotions occurred without any clue about why they appeared and what they stood for.

As a therapist, my mission is to help the patient to remain with the affect and the body sensations, and not to try to force the memory or to reach it through more traditional therapeutic methods of talking about it. This becomes the final point – to verbalize it, to get the story, the narrative – but that is not where to begin. Words don't have any resonance at the beginning; rational thoughts give no aid to a body that is finding its way. In earlier therapy sessions, when Natasha was beginning to find single words and fragments, she told me that this had to be someone else's story. She could not recall it as a personal memory; it was simply a fact, something that had happened to someone else, someone she did not know. Over the course of about a year of very intense therapy, with two sessions a week, the memory became more of a narrative, and Natasha became more connected to it and could feel the memory as her own.

Natasha told me later on that in the beginning she did not know what she smelled, what she heard, and what she saw. But, by following the sensory tracks, going with them, and allowing those horrifying, brutal memories to emerge, they gradually became a story. And once the story was a whole, it remained unaltered. Finally, Natasha could tell the whole narrative and was able to think about what happened, realizing that it had happened to her in the past but that it was not over. She now knew she could handle the memory in the present. She made herself a new ending to the narrative and a new solution, in which she feels a sense of power that provides her with the ability to protect herself.

6. Sense and Migration

Natasha's story is unfortunately not that unusual. The suppression of memories or the psychogenic loss of memories is quite frequent among traumatized refugees. The existentialism of Jean-Paul Sartre offers some insight here by pointing out that 'there is no reality other than in taking action.'[12] The human being can only exist in reality by her actions, meaning that her actions right now at this moment reveal all of her past, all of her history, although it is wrapped in a metaphoric riddle. The talking body creates its own narrative. As Paul Ricoeur points out, the interpreter/psychotherapist reads another body, and it tells about something, it wants something, it has a meaning.[13] What is active here is a dialectic between the event of the body's discourse and the meaning that the interpreter/psychotherapist is trying to grasp. The discourse functions in two ways: on the one hand, it is self-referential because someone says or states something; on the other, the discourse wants to tell something about a world and the objects or the phenomena in it. In Natasha's case, the sense of smell played an important role in carrying reminiscences of odours from one part of the world to another, and from the past into the present, linking with fragments of memories from the other senses to provide a more holistic view of the personal history of a migratory human being.

NOTES

1 See Amira Bojadzija-Dan's contribution to this volume, p. 194.
2 To ensure confidentiality, the name, age, and origin of the patient have been changed.
3 See Sven-Åke Christianson, *Traumatiska minnen* (Stockholm: Natur och kultur, 2002).
4 Esther Bick, 'Hudupplevelsen i tidiga objektrelationer,' *Divan* 1–2 (2001): 4–6.
5 See Constance Classen, David Howes, and Anthony Synnott, *Aroma: The Cultural History of Smell* (London: Routledge, 1994).
6 Marcel Proust, *In Search of Lost Time, Swann's Way* (New York: Modern Library, 2004), 60.
7 Ibid., 62.
8 See Onno van der Hart, Ellert R.S. Nijenhuis, and Kathy Steele, *The Haunted Self: Structural Disassociation and Treatment of Chronic Traumatization* (New York: Norton, 2006); B.A. van der Kolk, 'The Significant Developments in the Traumatic Stress Field during the Last Decennium: Implications for Clinical Practice and Priority Setting,' keynote address, Kris och Traumacentrum Conference, Stockholm, 14 September 2007.
9 See O.L. Schachter and J.F. Kihlstrom, 'Functional Amnesia,' *in Handbook of Neuropsychology,* vol. 3., ed. Francois Boller and Jordan Grafman (Amsterdam: Elsevier, 1989), 209–31.
10 Christianson, *Traumatiska minnen,* 351.
11 Viktor E. Frankl, *Livet måste ha mening: Erfarenheter i koncentrationslägren: Logoterapins grunder* (Stockholm: Natur och Kultur, 1999), 84.
12 Jean-Paul Sartre, *Existentialismen är en humanism* (Stockholm: Albert Bonniers Förlag, 1946), 31.
13 Paul Ricoeur, 'Distansering som hermeneutisk funktion,' in *Hermeneutik,* ed. Horace Engdahl, Ola Holmgren, Roland Lysell, Arne Melberg, and Anders Olsson (Stockholm: Rabén & Sjögren, 1977).

10 Reading Sensation: Memory and Movement in Charlotte Delbo's *Auschwitz and After*

AMIRA BOJADZIJA-DAN

Charlotte Delbo's *Auschwitz and After* takes us into the place of memory in a way that monuments cannot. Narratives saturated with the memories of bodily suffering, stories about the lingering presence of the sense memory of the smells, tastes, and texture of Auschwitz, seem to flow towards the reader like streams of affect seeking to break a new path, to connect two realities disconnected from one another. Simply being a reader cannot explain the affective transaction that takes place in this encounter. Narratives of 'sense memory' reveal something to the body, communicating feeling as the true meaning of Delbo's work.

In the existing scholarly literature in the fields of philosophy, cultural studies, and film and literary theory, the term 'sense memory' is used in different contexts, and its meaning varies greatly from one text to another. Maurice Merleau-Ponty identifies sense memory with 'sedimented' or implicit memory, which does not require a conscious effort of remembering, and includes ways of being, perceptions, affects, and emotional responses learned through the body's immersion in the social world.[1] For Gilles Deleuze, sense memory is that which represents the body's visceral, mimetic relationship to the external world. Violent and unpredictable, sense memory exceeds thought and the voluntary effort of remembering. It stirs the soul, which, in turn, activates imagination and unearths forgotten knowledge.[2] If, as Pierre Nora argues, the sites of memory represent the illusion of cohesiveness, unity, and continuity that no longer exist in society,[3] sense memory would speak to those aspects of human experience that cannot be enshrined – partly because they embody, not the symbols, but the invisible chemistry of affect, and partly because their meaning, constituted in-between bodies, cannot be fixed. Taking the idea of indeterminacy as a cue, I want to consider the possibility of thinking of sense memory in terms of its movement. What are the ways in which sense memory circulates? How is it transmitted from the text to the reader? What does it mean to understand Delbo's narratives of sense memory, not from the apparent cohesiveness of historical distance, but as embodied signs from the past waiting to be received in the immediacy of the body?

In the Freudian psychoanalytic account of subjectivity, which in the 1980s and 1990s became the privileged interpretive framework for Holocaust literature, memory is necessarily narratable as a string of events on personal and societal trajectories. In this account, Holocaust texts are very often responses to the tension between the need to heal what is perceived as an anomaly (trauma), and the imperative to remember. The Holocaust survivor who cannot bridge the tragic chasm between memory and history remains separated from the rest of humanity by her experience, fragmented and incomplete. However, post-structuralist and phenomenological theories tend to interpret all memory as embodied, that is, as a virtual co-presence within the present, whereby the body is believed to incarnate both the anonymous forces of its social environment and historical moment, as well as the specificity of its existence. According to Merleau-Ponty, the past of an individual body is inscribed in its gestures, gait, and movement, its ways of thinking and being.[4] They constitute the 'forgotten' of an individual existence that retains its full dynamic potential. Memory is always marked by power relations; memory of suffering is not an anomaly in an otherwise coherent narrative of an individual life in need of cure. It is an experience of oppression, violence, fear, and loss that has already left its physical imprint on the body of the survivor, the memory of which needs to be heard and transmitted. Moreover, embodied memory does not belong to an individual alone. Deleuze argues that memory is a mode of individuation, not the hallmark of a person; it is an assemblage of voices that invested this or that experience with a particular affective intensity well before it is articulated by an individual. He points out how 'each subject expresses the world from a certain viewpoint ... Each subject therefore expresses an absolutely different world. And doubtless the world so expressed does not exist outside the subject expressing it ...'[5] Memory is therefore both common and multiple. We might generalize by suggesting that memory is a confrontation out of which new events and viewpoints arise and are set against each other, and that there can be no question of a definitive version of the past, just as there is no mastering of suffering and death.

Reading Holocaust literature with Merleau-Ponty and Deleuze takes us away from the realm of representation in order to confront the status of the body as a site of memory. In this account, the body needs to be approached, not as site of stability embodying in one way or another collective yearnings, but rather as an intersection always attended by movement. In her introduction to this collection of essays, Julia Creet points out that memory has become a euphemism for the kind of nostalgia associated with the fixity of ideas, bodies, and identities, evocative of the reactionary political projects of our time.[6] Her argument that memory is not predicated on stability, but, on the contrary, that its very existence hinges upon both spatial and temporal movement away from the original event, places indeterminacy and ambiguity at the centre of the debate. I wish to pursue this idea by attempting to answer some important questions about bodily suffering as the most painful, and often the most embarrassing, aspect of traumatic memory, and to consider its implications for a reading practice that wishes to be ethical.

Auschwitz and After places memory studies before the vexing issue of what Brian Massumi describes in *Parables for the Virtual* as the 'shortage of cultural-theoretical vocabulary specific to affect,' which in recent years emerged as a concept central to understanding contemporary culture.[7] I understand affect, not as a synonym for emotion and subjective content, but as a physical property of bodies, an unqualified flow, neither owned nor recognized. I turn to Deleuze to affirm the bodily nature of affect, and, simultaneously, its irreducibly collective character as an anonymous force. Affect brings bodies together and binds them into assemblages, which in turn produce other affects and other assemblages. The body maintains a carnal relationship with the world, in which sense memory plays a key role. Merleau-Ponty points out that perceptions, affects, and feelings are social practices sedimented in the body. There is a natural openness of the body to others. Its relationship with the world is a perpetual movement of intertwining, in which the self and the world fold upon each other. It is a movement in which the seeing and the seen, the touching and the touched, are difficult to distinguish. For Merleau-Ponty, this confusion gives rise to interiority, which is constituted not through the process of self-reflection, but through the movement of integration and the performance of otherness.[8] Deleuze and Guattari refer to these processes of integration and performances of otherness as modes of individuation in which the body, animated by affect, enters the zone of proximity of something or someone in order to feel, see, and become something new.[9] The body's

relationship with the social world is thus one of perpetual carnal intertwining, and the exchange of affect is a mode of sociality – a movement
parallel with, yet unknown to, any reflexive judgment.

In view of the irrevocably social character of affect, I believe that the
narratives of sense memory are capable of producing the subjectivities
that correspond to their meaning, that is, of channelling the flow of
affect through art and literature. An important strand of trauma studies
promotes critical, self-reflexive empathy as the most appropriate way
to encounter traumatic imagery. In *Writing History, Writing Trauma*,
Dominick LaCapra proposes the concept of *emphatic unsettlement* to
describe the aesthetic experience of feeling for another person while
becoming aware of the difference between one's own perceptions and
the experience of the other.[10] Jill Bennett argues that the study of affect
and trauma in contemporary art must move beyond the framework of
identification. She develops a particular concept of empathy characterized by a combination of affective and intellectual operations.[11] Accompanied by the dynamic movement between the traumatic imagery
and the awareness of one's own position outside of it, this kind of
empathy can become a mode of perceiving, engendering a manner
of thinking that is open to the traumatic experience of the other. Given
that art and literature cannot transmit meaning directly to the reader,
or 'traumatize' by the way of representation, it is necessary that we
examine the capacity of the literary text to communicate affect contained in the narratives of sense memory, which can be engaged with
based on one's lived experience.

In this chapter, I explore the narratives of sense memory in Charlotte
Delbo's trilogy *Auschwitz and After*, as dynamic, migratory, and productive beyond the paradigm of symbolization. To suggest that sense
memory is social in character is necessarily to gesture towards the
political implications of trauma. The space of memory is not a sacred
domain. It entails the involuntary shock of a confrontation with an impossible past. Memory is also a becoming. My aim is thus to explore the
text of Delbo's trilogy – *None of Us Will Return, Useless Knowledge*, and
The Measure of Our Days – not simply as an expression of a traumatized
psyche, but as a political act aimed towards a future that is productive
of other memories and other acts.

The testimonial function of Holocaust memoirs is identified *prima fa-
cie*. Testimonials constitute part of cultural history, and often provide
the fabric for the narratives expressing values and beliefs around which
social groups and national societies coalesce. Testimony fulfills a social

and epistemological role, because it is invested with the expectation that the historical knowledge it provides will be instrumental in preventing the reoccurrence of suffering. It also remains the expression of the profound need of the survivor to communicate an experience that most often involves extreme physical and emotional degradation. The relationship between the intimate character of the Holocaust testimony and its eminently social function is a complex one, rendered even more complicated by the nature of traumatic experience, part of which is repressed and thus made essentially 'incommunicable.' In addition, the Holocaust, as an event without precedent in human history, is often interpreted as the kind of difficult knowledge that presents an insurmountable challenge to the contemporary imagination. The survivor and her audience are separated by an unbridgeable historical divide, gesturing towards one another their respective inability to communicate and incapacity to imagine.

Delbo was aware of her historical role as a witness and survivor, and of the demands this placed before her. Auschwitz was in many ways central to her life: her writing, focused exclusively on her deportation, as well as her political and personal commitments, testify to a life-long struggle against forgetting. At the same time, on a personal level, she believed that her legacy was the kind of knowledge that no one needed – an experience of suffering so out of the ordinary that humankind was better off without it. The title of the second book of the trilogy, *Useless Knowledge*, published in 1970, signals ambivalence, and perhaps an unconscious desire to forget, to deny the rest of humanity knowledge of its infinite capacity for violence. This title was also prophetic. It is as if Delbo intuited that knowledge offered neither guarantee nor protection against the reoccurrence of the same horrors she experienced in Auschwitz. If Primo Levi and Tadeusz Borowski exposed Auschwitz as the clearest articulation of Nazi Germany as the moral black hole which corrupted executioners and victims alike, Charlotte Delbo reveals its matter: the smell, taste, and texture of human suffering. 'Il faut donner à voir,' she writes.[12] It is necessary to show for everyone to see: 'donner à voir,' not as a demonstration destined to prove a fact, but as an inconclusive and open-ended encounter between the reader and a text without message. In many instances, this encounter functions as a confrontation: the reader's expectation that the survivor will be redeemed is repeatedly betrayed. Suffering is meaningless. The triumph of good over evil has little purchase on the workings of a traumatized psyche. Perhaps the most disturbing aspect of Delbo's writing is that she leads the reader towards the realization that the barrier between the self and the world is an illusion, and that the chaos of the world is the chaos of the self, infolded, seamlessly integrated into the individual affective economy. It is this kind of useless knowledge, together with the absence of message in *Auschwitz and After*, that unhinges the reader from the safety of historical distance and the certainty that the events described in the book could not occur again. This is not achieved through a particularly accurate description of the workings of the camp: for the most part, Delbo uses Auschwitz as a background. Instead, her narrative focuses on processes of the destruction of the body, both individual and collective, and sense memory becomes the channel for affective residue flowing between the text and the reader.

In her analysis of the origins of the expressive power of the narratives of sense memory, Jill Bennett points out that the poetics of sense memory involves 'not so much *speaking of* but *speaking out of* a particular memory or experience … speaking from the body *sustaining sensation.*'[13] She argues that narratives staging the body sustaining sensation, such as performances by artists practising body or carnal art (Marina Abramovic, Orlan), are likely to provoke a physical response in the viewer, a recoil or a shiver. This argument is more challenging to make when it comes to a written narrative. True understanding of the narrative of sense memory cannot come from thought; on the contrary, it is revealed through sensation: that is, it is intuited. If an affective response to the narrative of sense memory depends upon a certain amount of confusion between the self and the other, in other words, upon a degree of ambiguity about the location or source of the narrative, what are the ways in which written text can blur those lines? How does the literary text go about silencing the 'objective,' or disinterested, interpretations, the 'speaking of,' in order to create a reader who intuits and feels, or 'speaks out of' the text? In Delbo's narrative, we find two mechanisms that contribute to the making of such a reader: the first is Delbo's choice of what Gérard Genette terms the 'generative instance,' or the narrative voice.[14] The other mechanism is the repetitive narrative structure of the first book of the trilogy, *None of Us Will Return*. Both mechanisms fulfill the role of conduits for the flow of affect and migration of memory, and produce a particular kind of writing and reading practice, which sustain sensation between writer and reader.

Most of *None of Us Will Return* is written in the first person plural. Delbo's readers, such as Marlene Heineman, Claire Gorrara, and Kathryn Robson, attribute this to a willing erasure of the self on Delbo's part, in order to lend a voice or to 'ghost write' for both the survivors and the dead. This is, in the final account, a more or less failed enterprise, because there is no cure for traumatic memory. Moreover, Kathryn Robson argues that the first person plural in Delbo's writing reflects a broken *nous*, 'ruptured from within.'[15] Because there can be no identity forged in a place of suffering such as Auschwitz, the survivors are necessarily incomplete, broken individuals, ghosts of their former selves. This is problematic because it introduces the idea that wars and suffering produce damaged and incomplete individuals, whereas a 'healthy' psyche can develop exclusively in peace and prosperity. This, of course, would imply the existence of normative subjectivities in the parts of the world that have known long periods of peace and prosperity, to the exclusion of everyone else.

The suspicion with which the generative instance in Holocaust memoir is approached is indicative of a hesitation to recognize and respect the autonomy of this instance, which, according to Genette, exists in literary theory. When it comes to studies of Holocaust literature, the existence of trauma is often taken for granted, and its influence considered so decisive that the author becomes a mere tool by which the disorder becomes manifest. In my opinion, Delbo's texts need to be approached, not from the point of view of coherence and mastery as the conditions of possibility for a 'complete' individual, but by taking fragmentation and indeterminacy as the very foundations of modern subjects. I believe that she gestures towards a different kind of plurality, and reflects a particular kind of subjectivity, which cannot be measured in terms of the traditional concept of the sovereign subject. Rather, the choice of the first person plural as the privileged narrative voice in *None of Us Will Return* must be considered as speaking 'out of' a particular, shared memory, which I believe produces a reader not 'of,' but 'out of,' the text. Delbo describes this relationship in terms of a carnal bond, in which each individual body represents a blood vessel within 'a single circulatory system.'[16] This is a powerfully dynamic image, and one that suggests continuous motion without which shared memory dies. Avishai Margalit's argument that the relationship between memory and affect is an internal one gestures towards this same kind of dynamic of involvement and interconnectedness as the conditions for the transmission of memory.[17] He points out that memory relies not on coherence and neutrality, but on a certain loss of neutrality, on voluntary surrender to emotion, and on accepting a reliving of past experience as the integral part of the remembered event.

Similarly, the loss of neutrality and an attitude of care towards each other, which Delbo and the group to which she belonged maintained long after the war ended,[18] are not the symptoms of fragmentation. On the contrary, such attitudes confirm that memory – and this includes traumatic memory – is an entirely social phenomenon, rendered meaningful, not by the accuracy of the memories of the survivor or the authority of her narrating voice, but through circulation and movement inside the circulatory system of a community of memory.

An example of the physical connectedness among the prisoners is Delbo's description of the nightmare following a day of labour in the marshes. During the day, the prisoner body, represented as an indistinguishable life form gasping for breath inside a pool of mud, is strangled by octopi. In the evening, this body does not dissolve. It moves into the night, following its inner rhythm, traversed by the flows of exhaustion, disease, and nightmares:

> It is a tangle of bodies, a melee of arms and legs and, when at last we believe we grasped something solid, it is because we knocked our heads against the planks we sleep on and everything vanishes in the shadowy dark where Lulu's leg is moving, or Yvonne's arm, and the head resting heavily on my chest is that of Viva … This shadowy cavern breathes and puffs, stirred in every one of its innermost recesses by a thousand pain-filled nightmares and fitful sleep.[19]

This organism also channels and circulates moods, and dictates modes of thought. For example, Primo Levi describes the atmosphere of the camp as one of hurried impatience,[20] while Jean Améry points out that general effort was focused on developing systems of self-preservation through barter, theft, and avoidance of labour, which eliminated scholarly knowledge from the list of useful skills.[21] 'Imagination is the first luxury of a body receiving sufficient nourishment, enjoying a margin of free time, possessing the rudiments from which dreams are fashioned,' writes Delbo.[22] Describing the affective economy of survival, she points out that being part of, and communicating with, the rest of the prisoner body was crucial. 'No one could be sustained by one's past, draw on its resources. It had become unreal, unbelievable. To speak was our only escape, our mad raving. What did we speak of? Material, usable things. We had to omit anything that might awaken pain or regret.'[23] Lastly, this body was also a Babel of languages, cultures, and experiences, a chaotic reality unfolding in the asphyxiating stench of burning flesh.

Delbo captures this in images of the prisoner body described as assemblages of partial objects and her own as a collection of organs and processes that function independently of her will. Nonetheless, such images are more than expressions of a traumatized imagination. They describe the only possible political response to the enormity of suffering and Delbo's profound desire for a different articulation of reality in the post-war era.

Trauma, according to Freud, is an event that the subject refuses, or is unable, to remember, and is thus doomed to repeat through various guises, never succeeding in fully integrating it into his psychic economy. Lacan modifies Freud's formula by defining trauma as a missed encounter with the Real, and repetition in trauma as a string of failed attempts to find adequate forms of representation (the Real being precisely that which resists representation), which leads to the repetition of the event in a tragic compulsion. As far as the field of memory studies is concerned, the issue of repetition is inextricably tied to the originary moment of trauma, and its symbolic unavailability. For Cathy Caruth, the return in trauma is symptomatic of the mind's efforts to 'claim the experience,' that is, to grasp how it survived a threat to life. This being impossible, she argues, trauma becomes the 'endless *inherent necessity* of repetition.'[24] There is something inherently static in this interpretation of trauma, especially considering the phenomena of postmemory and cultural trauma. For those inheriting the legacy of trauma, the meaning of the originary event is unstable and negotiable. Their attitude towards the experiences of the previous generations is one of affective labour which, according to Marianne Hirsch, seeks to 'formulate and repair' by the way of art, whereby 'the repetitive visual landscape we construct and reconstruct in our postmemorial generation is a central aspect of that work.'[25]

Looking at the dynamic of trauma, Deleuze argues that it is no coincidence that fantasy and trauma are marked so radically in the arts by repetition and simulacra.[26] If the original traumatic event does not have a meaning that can be communicated either directly or by way of representation, those who inherit its memory must turn towards aesthetic expressions and literary narrative in order to form the kind of affective relationship with the past that is the condition of collective memory. To this effect, John Sundholm's paper in this collection successfully argues that the meaning of the originary moment of trauma is migratory, always a matter of appropriation and negotiation.[27] Furthermore, the instability of the meaning of the original event and its fundamentally fantastic nature, at least as far as posterity is concerned, imply that, in some of its aspects, cultural trauma is also performative. It is not by accident that Deleuze argues that repetition is the original difference. '*Répétition*' means practice or rehearsal in French. In this sense, the moment of trauma is the rehearsal, which in a way contains all of its future performances, but at the same time, like any other performative act, it does not fix their meaning.

Thus, we cannot speak about cultural trauma without bearing in mind the indeterminacy of the meaning of the original event, and its primarily epistemological function. Nonetheless, it is important to remember that the Deleuzian concept of learning is not one of a detached search for eternal truth; on the contrary, it is a passionate engagement with ideas, prompted by violent encounters with signs, stirring sense memory, which in turn sets thought in movement. To the extent that only an affective engagement with memory guarantees its transmission, the struggle for meaning is always a passionate engagement with the past, and, at the same time, a movement towards the future. In the following section, I focus on the patterns of repetition in the structure of Delbo's narrative, in *None of Us Will Return* and *Useless Knowledge*, in order to probe the possibility for repetition as a conduit for the flow of affect between the text and the reader.

In her analysis of the affective operations of trauma art, Jill Bennett argues that certain elements of traumatic images and narratives have the capacity to disrupt the narrative, and function as passages of affective resonance between the viewer/reader and the text. It appears that this claim is confirmed in *Auschwitz and After*, where repetition in the narrative structure seems to reduce the distance between the reader and the text. Although *Auschwitz and After* is written as a mixture of literary genres, there is an identifiable narrative pattern, organized *grosso modo* as follows: little or no introduction that would allow the reader to contextualize the story (time, place, characters), a paragraph of text punctuated by one sentence, and a repetition of this one sentence like a refrain at the end of the following few paragraphs. The refrain often stands in contradistinction to the dynamic of the paragraph that precedes it. For example, the sentence 'The snow, the plain, the snow' appears as the background for the agony of the Jewish woman who breaks rank in the course of a roll call in order to quench her thirst with some clean snow from the side of an embankment on the Appelplatz. Her death is certain; however, the SS, amused by the spectacle, allow the woman to exhaust herself trying to get out of the ditch. The image of the woman struggling with all her might – 'She was arched from her index finger to her toe … she thrashes like someone drowning, stretches out her hands to hoist herself onto the other bank' – is contrasted with the stillness of the background constituted by several thousand immobile bodies: 'We stood there motionless.'[28] Through the regularity of acceleration and deceleration, and through the switching of narrative focus from the woman to the group, punctuated by the refrain, Delbo's narration takes on a poetic rhythm. However, the absence of context deprives the reader of an explanation and a stable position, and the outcome of the event, which is certain (the woman dies), takes on the form of a stultified fantasy nightmare that does not seem to end. Moreover, the movement in the midst of stillness – the sound of the thrashing of frozen snow alternating with the complete absence of sound on the Appelplatz – functions as the Barthian *punctum*. The little black figure is the element of the picture which disrupts the text. She is that point 'which pricks, bruises me.'[29] It is the detail that 'fills the whole picture.'[30] It creates such a feeling of instability and discomfort that the affect 'punctures' the text.

Affective responses such as physical discomfort, recoiling, and 'bruising' speak to the embodied character of sense memory. Merleau-Ponty points out that the body, as an ambiguous locus of remembering and forgetting, incarnates the past, and that even when the memory is incapable of conjuring up ancient events, they are in some way incarnate as a compendium of bodily experience.[31] For example, when we are engaged in reading or in watching a film, our brain routinely 'fills in the gaps' in perception by projecting what we already know.[32] Deleuze argues that memory is duration, and that the past is always-already present, embodied in the matter, awaiting an impulse of sense memory in order to emerge.[33] However, the image of memory evoked by Merleau-Ponty and Deleuze is not that of a capacity of the body to recall at will the events neatly stored away in the brain, but of a system coextensive with the world, where the remembered and the forgotten communicate with each other, and in which meaning emerges as a function of memory indexed by emotion. The smell of the burning corpses, the taste of particular foods, disease, the experience of thirst and of malnutrition are thus embodied, not as total memory, but as inflections in the survivor's movement and language, in her ways of experiencing and knowing. These 'forgotten' events do not obey voluntary efforts of memory, nor do they follow the laws of linearity and coherence. Quite the opposite: the passage from forgotten to remembered is a violent and often painful disruption of the present. This is described by Mado, one of Delbo's friends:

> At any day, carried by a smell, a day from over there return ... One day I feel I'm walking by the kitchens: it's because I left a potato rotting at the bottom of my vegetable basket. At once everything surfaces again: the mud, the snow, the blows of the truncheons ... Memories borne by a taste, a color, the sound of the wind, the rain.[34]

Events such as this one are not simple repetitions occurring on the basis of similarity between past and present sensation, namely, the smell common to two moments in Mado's life. The smell of the potato reminds her of something else: Auschwitz, not as a string of memories – snapshots of the mud, snow, blows, death – but as a reality in its fullness; not as a story, but as a complex entity. According to Deleuze, this complex entity, although not actual, coexists virtually with the present.[35] The non-coincidence of sense memory with itself embodies the materiality of this presence, and the disruptive potential of affect. If narratives that reflect this rupture and rapprochement of disparate realities could be extended towards the reader and awaken him in a particular way, this awakening would concern the affects and sensations sedimented in individual bodies and personal histories. As we have seen earlier, sense memory is already 'common': common to two moments and two places. To the extent that our perceptions, moods, and ways of being are also 'common,' that is, rehearsed through the body's relation to the social, narratives of sense memory take on a new meaning, as migratory and flowing, suggesting that literature and art have the power to engender caring. Following Merleau-Ponty's conceptualization of meaning-making as an ambiguous process that arises and is actualized between bodies, I understand that narratives of sense memory open up this space of affectivity for an encounter between the reader and memory. The indeterminateness and ambiguity of this encounter can account for the transformative character of affectivity. From this perspective, Delbo's narrative, beyond its role in expressing individual traumatic subjectivity, is also relevant as a marker of a particular socio-historical moment in which suffering became common, both as an acceptable means of political control, and as a destiny shared by many.

Among the artists whose work successfully explores the common aspect of sense memory is Christian Boltanski. In 1988, when he first showed his installation *Réserve, Canada*, France was hesitantly, and with

much resistance, starting to face its Vichy past. Boltanski's work revolves around the themes of absence and death. In the early 1970s, he
started producing showcases in which his personal items, such as
photographs and letters, were displayed as relics or archaeological
remnants indexing his past. *Réserve, Canada* is a reference to the warehouse in Auschwitz in which the Nazis stored the belongings of the
deported. Boltanski's installation is an unaired room filled with old
clothes, piled up to the ceiling. As with photography, Boltanski associates clothes with death. Old garments bear the mark of the wearer: the
tears, the stains, the ways in which the body had left its imprint, are
vestiges of a life that is now gone. Another important aspect of this installation is the smell. Upon entering the room, the visitor was enveloped with the musty smell of an old attic. Sensations are indexed by
social history. For the generations born after the Holocaust, Auschwitz
is most often associated with photographs in black and white documenting the horror of the camp. Perhaps the most moving are the
photographs of large quantities of personal belongings, such as shoes,
eyeglasses, or wedding bands, which the victims were forced to surrender to the Nazis. Such photographs are charged with affective power
that surpasses the medium, suggesting sensations other than vision.
Réserve, Canada stages such an encounter through combined visual and
olfactory experiences. It incites melancholy reflection about the past
and the vulnerability of the human body. In this installation, common
history emerges at the margins of personal narratives, as if emanating
from the materiality of the objects, their presence gesturing towards the
larger absence of their owners.

Similar to Boltanski, Delbo's narrative unhinges the claim that in order to remember we must be able to attach our memories to the events
of our ethnic or religious history. It goes against the grain, in that her
narrative awakens a different sort of memory, based not on social identity, but on affect as the most fundamental relationship between the
body and the world. This is not to say that intercorporeality, and the
bond of affectivity between the self and the other, stand above or outside of the social world: perceptions, affects, and individual feelings are
saturated with social phenomena, and their meaning is not constituted
individually. Nonetheless, as Merleau-Ponty points out, these phenomena exist only to the extent that an individual chooses to live them. Social meanings, including memory, circulate as affects. They are embodied in identity, in social relations and structures of power. At the same
time, they are ambiguous and indeterminate, which could explain the

unpredictable and transformative character of affectivity. By connecting the present into the circulatory system of the past, Delbo's narrative establishes an affective circuit, an unhomely[36] and untimely connection with memory, based not on identity, but on the existence of an 'intercorporeal space of affectivity' that enlarges the boundaries of 'us.'

By focusing on the narratives of sense memory in Charlotte Delbo's *Auschwitz and After*, I not only argue for the importance of the body as a site of memory, but also propose a more complex model for the reading of Holocaust texts. Bodies reach in the direction of other bodies. They form circuits of material and symbolic exchange, where myriad forms of social life take place. As a site of memory, the body is always produced, but even more important, is productive of something. Delbo's writing 'out of' a sense memory shared with other bodies requires a particular kind of reading practice. Instead of a reading 'of,' I suggest that such narratives need to be read 'out of'; out of the text and out of the body. It is a practice whereby the embodied reader, responding to the demands of the text, becomes coextensive with it, in order to form a single circulatory system for the flow of affect. Taking indeterminacy, ambiguity, and movement to represent the very essence of sense memory, I wish to suggest that, conceived not as part of monumental history but as a flow of affect connecting past and future, sense memory brings into relief possibilities for the existence of communities of memory beyond the boundaries of ethnic, cultural, or religious identities.

NOTES

1 Maurice Merleau-Ponty, *Phenomenology of Perception*, trans. Colin Smith (New York: Humanities Press, 1970), 441.
2 Gilles Deleuze, *Proust et les signes* (Paris: Presses Universitaires de France, 2006), 51–65, 76–7. Deleuze's discussion of difference and repetition, in general, and of sense memory, in particular, establishes sense memory as the initial locus in which essence establishes its commonality, further developed in art and literature, which finally give us 'genuine unity.'
3 Pierre Nora, *Realms of Memory: The Construction of the French Past*, trans. Arthur Goldhammer (New York: Columbia University Press, 1996), 6.
4 Merleau-Ponty, *Phenomenology of Perception*, 356.
5 Gilles Deleuze, *Proust and Signs*, trans. Richard Howard (Minneapolis: University of Minnesota Press, 2000), 42.

6 See Julia Creet's Introduction to this volume, pp. 5–6.
7 Brian Massumi, *Parables of the Virtual: Movement, Affect, Sensation* (Durham, NC: Duke University Press, 2002), 27; Merleau-Ponty, *Phenomenology of Perception*, 103–4.
8 Maurice Merleau-Ponty, 'Eye and Mind,' in *The Primacy of Perception*, trans. Carleton Dallery (Evanston, IL: Northwestern University Press, 1964), 163.
9 Gilles Deleuze and Felix Guattari, *A Thousand Plateaus: Capitalism and Schizophrenia*, trans. Brian Massumi (Minneapolis: University of Minnessota Press, 1987), 233–309.
10 Dominick LaCapra, *Writing History, Writing Trauma* (Baltimore: Johns Hopkins University Press, 2000).
11 Jill Bennett, *Empathic Vision: Affect, Trauma, and Contemporary Art* (Stanford: Stanford University Press, 2005), 10–11.
12 Rosette Lamont, Introduction, in *Auschwitz and After*, by Charlotte Delbo (New Haven and London: Yale University Press, 1995), vii–viii.
13 Bennett, *Empathic Vision*, 38 (Bennett's emphasis).
14 Gérard Genette. *Narrative Discourse*, trans. Jane E. Lewin and Jonathan Culler (Ithaca, NY: Cornell University Press, 1980), 31.
15 Kathryn Robson, *Writing Wounds: The Inscription of Trauma in Post-1968 French Women's Life-Writing* (New York: Rodopi, 2004), 172–4.
16 Delbo, *Auschwitz and After*, 63.
17 Avishai Margalit, *The Ethics of Memory* (Cambridge: Harvard University Press, 2002), 27–8.
18 Each chapter of *The Measure of Our Days* carries a name and is dedicated to a fellow survivor, both those from Delbo's original group and others. The examples of friendships among the Holocaust survivors are many. For example, Simone Weil, French politician and Holocaust survivor, speaks about the need she feels to maintain such friendships because of the lack of understanding of their suffering outside of the circle of survivors. Her testimony can be accessed on You Tube, http://www.youtube.com/watch?v=wun3UFtDF50&feature=related. Also, see Maia Wechler's documentary *Sisters in Resistance*, about enduring friendship among four French women members of the resistance.
19 Delbo, *Auschwitz and After*, 55.
20 Primo Levi, *If This Is a Man; The Truce*, trans. S. Woolf (New York: Penguin, 1979), 53.
21 Jean Améry, *Par-delà le crime et le châtiment: essai pour surmonter l'insurmontable*, trans. F. Wuilmart (Arles: Actes Sud,1995), 6–11.
22 Delbo, *Auschwitz and After*, 168.
23 Ibid.

24 Cathy Caruth, *Unclaimed Experience: Trauma, Narrative, and History* (Baltimore and London: Johns Hopkins University Press, 1996), 63.

25 Marianne Hirsch, 'Surviving Images: Holocaust Photographs and the Work of Post-Memory,' *Yale Journal of Criticism* 14, no. 1 (2001): 13.

26 Gilles Deleuze, *Différence et Répétition* (Paris: Presses Universitaires de France, 1968), 24.

27 See John Sundholm's contribution to this volume. p. 124.

28 Delbo, *Auschwitz and After*, 26–9.

29 Roland Barthes, *La chambre claire: note sur la photographie* (Paris: Seuil, 1980), 26.

30 Ibid., 45.

31 Merleau-Ponty, *Phenomenology of Perception*, 83.

32 David J. Linden, *The Accidental Mind: How Brain Evolution Has Given Us Love, Memory, Dreams, and God* (Cambridge: Harvard University Press, 2007), 30.

33 Gilles Deleuze, *Bergsonism*, trans. Hugh Tomlinson and Barbara Habberjam (New York: Zone Books, 1988), 51–73.

34 Delbo, *Auschwitz and After*, 266.

35 Deleuze, *Proust et les signes*, 58.

36 'Unhomely' is a literal translation of Freud's term 'unheimlich,' usually rendered as 'uncanny,' which is an instance when something can be simultaneously familiar and foreign.

11 Memory, Diaspora, Hysteria: Margaret Atwood's *Alias Grace*

MARLENE GOLDMAN

In her introduction to this collection, Julia Creet asserts that 'migration is the condition of memory,'[1] and cites Pierre Nora's lament that 'we create ... sites of memory ... because we no longer have "real environments of memory," stable, geographic, generational environments' in which memory resides.[2] Like many of the contributors to this volume on migration and memory, I focus on the impact on memory of the loss of 'real environments of memory' associated with diaspora. My paper also attempts to answer a central question posed by this volume: how do we understand memory that has migrated or has been exiled from its local habitations?[3] In what follows, I analyse how the quality of movement associated with the predominantly female Irish diaspora shapes both memory and discourse, and ultimately gives rise to what critics describe as a hysterical narrative. In keeping with John Sundholm, my study traces 'the implication that trauma is a phenomenon of migration.'[4] Unlike the majority of my fellow contributors, however, my study addresses a fictional work, Margaret Atwood's historical novel *Alias Grace*, based on the life of a notorious Canadian woman who immigrated from Ireland and who was convicted of murder at the age of sixteen.

The inclusion of an analysis of a novel in this collection is valuable because fiction has played a profound role in shaping our understanding of both normal and pathological memory. In her study of conceptual art and memory, Luiza Nader observes that the work of Krzysztof Wodiczko raises the problem of the relation between memory (with its vicissitudes like transference, repressions, and displacements) and history.[5] I would suggest that Atwood's novel adds a significant dimension to this collection's engagement with the issues of migration,

memory, trauma, testimony, and fiction because of its reflexive engagement with fiction-making and, more precisely, owing to the novel's
insistence that even in the case of traumatic testimony, the vicissitudes
of memory and artistic fabrication play a profound role.[6] Due to its
insistence that migration produces memory, rather than deforms or
renders memory somehow 'artificial,' Atwood's novel challenges one
of the central tenets of memory studies which, as Creet observes, typically assumes that 'memory is the product of stability' and argues that
'once one leaves a territory of origin, memory is lost entirely.'[7]

   In *Rewriting the Soul: Multiple Personality and the Sciences of Memory*, Ian
Hacking argues that writers have played a formidable role in fashioning
our understanding of normal and pathological memory: 'I make the
strong point,' he writes, that our understanding is the direct 'consequence of how the literary imagination has formed the language in
which we speak of people be they real or imagined.'[8] In keeping with
Hacking's insights, my paper turns to *Alias Grace* to examine how this
text has contributed to and challenged the interpretation and construction of cultural and medical models of the mind and, more specifically,
the operations of memory. As Atwood herself explains, *Alias Grace* raises
questions about 'the trustworthiness of memory, the reliability of story.'[9]
Precisely because *Alias Grace* is an historical novel, the text demonstrates
the extent to which prevailing notions concerning supposedly normal
and pathological memory are derived from fiction. Put somewhat differently, our models of ordered and disordered memory are based on
fictional models generated, in part, by writers of historical fiction.

   With the publication of her second novel, *Surfacing*, which charted
the psychic and physical journey of a woman wandering in the wilder-
ness, haunted by an abortion that she remembers only in traumatic
fragments, Atwood initiated her readers into her ongoing exploration
of the relationship between haunting, memory, and hysteria, a disease
that since antiquity has been associated with the notion of wandering.
Alias Grace self-consciously takes this exploration in new and important
directions by rooting it in an historical context when concerns loomed
large about hysteria and about women wandering beyond the confines
of class boundaries and patriarchy's tight control. Based on historical
events, this text serves as a particularly useful tool to examine the connections between haunting, hysteria, and fears associated with gender
and class mobility. *Alias Grace* offers a thoroughly researched account of
Upper Canadian life in the nineteenth century when some servants aspired to the status of the upper classes and, on occasion, realized their

desires to rise above their station. But their desires for change in status challenged what Fredric Jameson describes as the representation of the social world as 'an organic, natural, Burkean permanence' by confronting it with a vision of the world that is 'not natural, but historical, and subject to radical change.'[10] In so doing, they attacked the notion that inheritance rests solely on 'filiation,' defined strictly by blood, and argued instead for 'affiliative' notions of inheritance based on performance, hard work, and 'collegiality.'[11] By juxtaposing wandering immigrants and hysteria, a disorder that emphasizes pathologized wandering, *Alias Grace* highlights societal fears associated with female emancipation and the upwardly mobile racialized 'Other.' Equally important, *Alias Grace* suggests that memory, in Creet's words, is not 'a product of stability, but quite the opposite, that is always attended by migrations.'

In *Alias Grace*, class conflict is aligned with sexual differentiation and the threat posed by 'the Woman Question.' Atwood's gendered rewriting of the nightmare of social class is apt since the same message directed towards the lower class was often repeated to women: stay in your place![12] As Jameson observes, this class warning 'can be re-written as an actantial injunction: do not attempt to become another kind of character from the one you already are!'[13] His emphasis on 'characters' is particularly relevant to my study because *Alias Grace* aligns class conflict and hysteria on the basis that both were associated with debates about performance versus biological inheritance and with pathological forms of wandering. *Alias Grace*'s central figure, Grace Marks, an impoverished Irish immigrant, was one of the most infamous Canadian women of the 1800s. With the help of a fellow servant, James McDermott, Grace murdered both her well-to-do Tory employer, Thomas Kinnear, and his pregnant housekeeper and mistress, Nancy Montgomery. While McDermott was found guilty of Kinnear's death and hanged on 21 November 1843, Grace's death sentence was commuted to life in prison, thanks to the efforts of her lawyer and a group of gentlemen petitioners who emphasized the 'feebleness of her sex,' her 'extreme youth,' and her supposed witlessness.[14]

In Atwood's retelling of events, in addition to suffering from traumatic amnesia and claiming to have lost the part of her memory associated with the execution of the murders,[15] Grace is prone to terrifying hallucinations, fits, fainting spells, somnambulism (sleepwalking), and episodes of double consciousness – symptoms typically associated with what was then known as the 'disease' of hysteria.[16] In effect, Atwood's treatment of her protagonist supports Creet's view that migration has effects on how and what we remember, and that the suspension of memory itself may be an effect of migration. *Alias Grace* explicitly interrogates the hysteria diagnosis by pairing Grace with a fictitious American doctor, Simon Jordon, who travels to the Kingston Penitentiary in 1859 and studies Grace to determine whether she is, indeed, hysterical as opposed to merely criminal. Dr Jordan has been invited to examine Grace at the behest of the Reverend Verringer, a Methodist minister. Verringer hopes to prove scientifically and unequivocally that Grace is mentally ill and, on those grounds, secure her release from prison. At the crux of the novel, when Dr Jordan's proto-psychoanalytic method fails to penetrate Grace's amnesia and 'wake the part of her mind that lies dormant,'[17] he permits Grace to undergo hypnosis at the hands of Dr Jerome DuPont. In this pivotal scene, Grace lies in a hypnotic trance, and, to everyone's amazement, an alternative identity emerges claiming to be the spirit of Mary Whitney, Grace's friend who died several years earlier from a botched abortion. As Mary's disincarnate spirit malevolently insists, it was she, and not Grace, who slaughtered Kinnear and his mistress.

Even from this brief account, one can appreciate that *Alias Grace* highlights the fascination and confusion surrounding the relationships between haunting, hysteria, gender, race, class, and criminality in the nineteenth century.[18] At the time, the connections among these factors were hotly debated and provided fodder for the speculations and turf wars of spiritualists and scientists alike. Grace's gender, race, and position in the servant class locate her at the centre of these debates. As historians observe, the sensational murder case, 'involving sex, violence, and insubordination carried to an extreme, portrayed in stark relief the gender, class, and ethnic tensions in the master/mistress-servant relationship. It also revealed the complex and gendered public response to Irish immigrants.'[19] Set in the mid-1800s when Irish women were arrested and convicted of crimes with much greater frequency than any other group,[20] when 'among immigrant servants committed to insane asylums, Irish women far outnumbered all other ethnic groups combined,'[21] and when 'hysteria was the most prominent and memorable *maladie de la mémoire*,'[22] *Alias Grace* explicitly probes the racialized links between memory, madness, and migration, and highlights how these links were disseminated in narrative form. Nineteenth-century Upper Canadian society was particularly concerned about 'allowing unknown immigrants into the private sanctum of the home.'[23] Because of their supposed love of finery, Irish domestics 'were frequently suspected of trying on their mistress's clothes in her absence' – a fear which masked the deeper terror that 'such relatively harmless acts of insubordination could mirror more serious crimes such as theft from their employers or, at an extreme as in the case of Grace Marks, even murder.'[24]

Given the powerful fears and anxieties of the ruling class, it is not surprising that the servant class suffered from psychological distress, albeit of a different sort. Recent studies concerning the occupational identities of past hysterical patients reveal that among working people one category appears time and time again: domestic servant.[25] Contemporary scholars now hypothesize that just as certain 'aristocratic ailments of the eighteenth century descended to the middle classes in the early nineteenth century, so perhaps a more medicalized self-consciousness began to form later in the century among working-class people living in bourgeois environments. A kind of psychological gentrification.'[26] On a very basic level, in postulating that Grace suffers from hysteria, a disease more often associated with Freud's affluent Viennese patients than with working-class Irish immigrants, *Alias Grace* emphasizes that nineteenth-century social mobility, the disease of wandering above one's station, instigated the transgressive assumption of new social roles and the diseases associated with these roles.

Alias Grace likewise emphasizes that the disease of hysteria surfaced when both lower-class and middle-class women were wandering beyond their allotted place in the domestic sphere. Mary Whitney, for instance, proves to be an especially troubling spirit both alive and dead because she espouses 'democratic ideas'[27] and insists on women's potential for social mobility. She tells Grace that 'being a servant was not a thing we were born to, nor would we be forced to continue it forever; it was just a job of work … and that one day I would be the mistress of a tidy farmhouse, and independent … And one person was as good as the next, and on this side of the ocean folks rose in the world by hard work, not by who their grandfather was, and that was the way it should be.'[28] Mary's philosophy of rising by 'hard work' (a vision of class based on one's performance and not on inheritance) is aligned more generally in the novel with performative and fabricated conceptions of identity.

In *Madness and Civilization*, Michel Foucault describes how during the late 1300s and early 1400s, the mad were driven from the cities and set aboard boats that 'conveyed their insane cargo from town to town … Often the cities of Europe must have seen these "ships of fools" approaching their harbors.'[29] Foucault ultimately describes the madman as 'the Passenger *par excellence*; that is, the prisoner of the passage ... He has his truth and his homeland only in that fruitless expanse between two countries that cannot belong to him.'[30] In his case history of Dora, Freud likewise associates madness with wandering when he asserts that the disease of hysteria is caused by pathological memory and argues further that it is characterized by a specific hallucinatory, fragmented, and meandering narrative style. As he explains, hysterics are unable to tell a complete, 'smooth and exact' story about themselves: '... their communications run dry, leaving gaps unfilled, and riddles unanswered ... The connections – even the ostensible ones – are for the most part incoherent, and the sequence of different events is uncertain.'[31] Moreover, for Freud, this incapacity to give an 'ordered history of their life'[32] was not simply characteristic of hysterics; it was, as Elaine Showalter observes, 'the meaning of hysteria.'[33] In essence, Freud associated both normal and hysterical forms of memory with discrete narrative styles – smooth and exact, on the one hand, and those with gaps and riddles, on the other. In so doing, however, he seemingly remains unaware that the apparently natural, smooth, and exact story that offers 'an ordered history,' which he privileges and associates with healthy forms of memory, is itself a highly artificial narrative mode honed by traditional historical novelists of the eighteenth and nineteenth centuries.

In contrast to the form and assumption associated with this traditional narrative mode, *Alias Grace*'s opening scene introduces a type of fragmented hysterical narrative style, along with the text's governing image of dark red flowers, hallucinatory *fleurs du mal*, that haunt the novel:

> Out of the gravel there are peonies growing. They come up through the loose grey pebbles, their buds testing the air like snails' eyes, then swelling and opening, huge dark-red flowers all shining and glossy like satin. Then they burst and fall to the ground ... I watch the peonies out of the corners of my eyes. I know they shouldn't be here: it's April and peonies don't bloom in April. There are three more now, right in front of me, growing out of the path itself. Furtively I reach out my hand to touch one. It has a dry feel, and I realize it's made of cloth.
>
> Then up ahead I see Nancy, on her knees, with her hair fallen over and the blood running down into her eyes ... I am almost up to Nancy, to where she's kneeling. But I do not break step, I do not run, I keep on walking ... and then Nancy smiles, only the mouth, her eyes are hidden by the blood and hair, and then she scatters into patches of colour, a drift of red cloth petals across the stones.[34]

Here the image of flowers recalls Breuer's famous reference in *Studies on Hysteria* to hysterics as 'the flowers of mankind, as sterile, no doubt, but as beautiful as double flowers.'[35] In double flowers, the purely sexual function has been tampered with to serve aesthetic desires because the stamens have been replaced by petals. As Showalter explains, Breuer implies that, like the double flower, the hysteric is 'the forced bud of a domestic greenhouse ... [S]he is also an aesthetic object, standing in relation to a more sober "mankind" as feminine and decorative.'[36] In Grace's hallucinatory account, the red flowers are made of cloth, further emphasizing their socially constructed nature.[37]

In addition to invoking Breuer's image of hysteria, the opening passage graphically illustrates the workings of hysteria by virtue of its meandering narrative style in which the peonies 'burst' and Nancy's visage 'scatters' into 'patches' of colour, a 'drift' of red cloth petals.[38] In effect, on both the intradiegetic level of Grace's narration and on the extradiegetic level of the narrative – marked by its excessive reliance on epigraphs, fragments from nineteenth-century texts, and chapter headings named for well-known quilt patterns – *Alias Grace* deploys hysteria's fragmented and drifting narrative style. As Grace herself admits, her lawyer wanted her to tell her story 'in what he called a coherent way, but would often accuse me of wandering.'[39] Not surprisingly, it is precisely this penchant for wandering that has also characterized hysteria from antiquity. Owing to hysteria's etymological association with the uterus, in what follows, I argue that Atwood's emphasis on hysteria, flowers, and fabrication challenges notions of supposedly healthy forms of narrative and memory, and of socially acceptable forms of sexual reproduction and inheritance.

The word 'hysteria' originates from the Greek word for uterus, *hystera*, which derives from the Sanskrit word for stomach or belly. According to the ancient Egyptians, the cause of disturbances in adult women was the wandering movement of the uterus, which they believed to be 'an autonomous, free-floating organism, upward from its normal pelvic position.'[40] These ancient Egyptian beliefs, in turn, provided the foundation for classical Greek medical and philosophical accounts of hysteria. The Greeks adopted 'the notion of the migratory uterus and embroidered upon the connection ... between hysteria and an unsatisfactory sexual life.'[41] In *Timaeus*, Plato famously explains that 'the womb is an animal which longs to generate children. When it remains barren too long after puberty, it is distressed and sorely disturbed, and straying about in the body and cutting off the passage of

the breath, it impedes respiration and brings the sufferer into the extremist anguish and provokes all manner of diseases besides.'[42] In *Alias
Grace*, however, hysteria is not solely linked to a wandering uterus but,
more generally, to the transgressive wanderings of a dispossessed and
diasporic female working class. 'Diaspora,' like the word 'hysteria,' originates from the Greek, a combination of 'dia,' meaning 'through,'
'thoroughly,' 'apart,' or 'across,' and 'speiro,' meaning to 'scatter.'[43]
When Jeremiah, the mysterious peddler who later refashions himself as
the hypnotist Jerome DuPont, reads Grace's palm, he states enigmatic-
ally, 'You are one of us.' Grace assumes he means that like him, she is
'homeless, and a wanderer.'[44] In her study of hysteria, Elaine Showalter
likewise argues that in nineteenth-century France, 'runaways and migrants can be seen as social equivalents of the unruly migratory uterus
traditionally associated with female hysteria.'[45] Michèle Ouerd similarly asserts that the working class in nineteenth-century France 'is
itself the wandering womb of Paris.'[46] These analogies between the
migratory uterus and the working class in France also shed light on
Alias Grace's depiction of the status of migrant workers in Upper and
Lower Canada during the same period.

In *Alias Grace*, the connections forged between Grace's pathological
memory, hysteria, and the Irish diaspora are especially apt when one
recognizes that the latter was unusually gendered: 'Whereas most transatlantic migrations of people to North America were dominated by men,
for significant periods of time women formed the majority of Irish
migrants.'[47] This migration constituted 'a mass female movement ... No
other major group of immigrants in American history contained so
many women.'[48] Like Grace, the majority of these women worked in
rural rather than urban areas. As a result, 'these "women alone" sometimes lacked kin or friendship networks for advice and aid and hence
were more vulnerable.'[49] In addition, Atwood's gothic representation of
Grace's and her fellow workers' direct and indirect sexual and physical
abuse at the hands of their various employers accurately attests to the
fact that the impact of scattering and the resulting isolation and loneliness in both rural and urban work increased 'the vulnerability to conflict with employers or to sexual exploitation.'[50] Moreover, studies of
Irish domestics in courts, jails, and asylums tellingly reveal that almost
half the women who listed occupations were servants or housekeepers,
and by far the largest immigrant population was from Ireland.[51] Thus,
as a convicted murderer sentenced to life in the penitentiary who also
spent time in Toronto's newly opened insane asylum, Grace Marks was

'definitely not the only Irish immigrant domestic servant labelled both "mad" and "bad" whether because of intolerable conditions, poverty, overwork, rebellion, physical or mental illness or mental retardation.'[52] In contrast, then, to the smooth and exact historical narrative – the officially sanctioned 'healthy' story that portrayed criminality as hereditary – Atwood's fragmented and transgressive narrative highlights transgressive desires (of both the lower and upper classes) that challenge the familiar conjunction between healthy memory, coherent narrative and socially sanctioned reproduction.

The strength of Atwood's novel lies in its refusal to label Grace as 'mad' and 'bad.'[53] Instead, and in contrast to healers and physicians from antiquity who adopted the hysteria diagnosis to account for women's supposedly pathological minds and bodies, Atwood's representation of Grace's hysteria, in keeping with feminist analyses of hysteria, suggests that the disease had more to do with women's social roles and the unequal relations of power associated with these roles than with any innate gendered or racial aetiology.[54] Contemporary medical historians now acknowledge that in the early 1800s women's madness typically resulted neither from a wandering uterus nor from lesions of the nervous system – both considered signs of degeneration[55] – but, instead, from what was referred to in 1820 as 'domestic affliction,' namely, traumatic experiences, including physical and sexual abuse, death, and bereavement, that were often exacerbated by alcoholism and poverty.[56] In Atwood's novel, Grace's early account of her stay at the newly opened Toronto Asylum underscores the role played by 'domestic affliction' in instigating madness. As she explains:

> [A] good portion of the women in the Asylum were no madder than the Queen of English. Many were sane enough when sober, as their madness came out of a bottle ... One of them was in there to get away from her husband, who beat her black and blue ... and another said she went mad in the autumns, as she had no house and it was warm in the Asylum ... But some were not pretending. One poor Irishwoman had all her family dead, half of them starving in the great famine and the other half of the cholera on the boat coming over.[57]

In addition to offering general information about women and madness, this passage, which juxtaposes 'domestic affliction' with the trauma of the Irish famine and the transatlantic journey, furnishes readers with potential clues to the riddle of Grace's illness and amnesia.

The narrative forges links between hysteria, domestic affliction, and migration early on when readers witness Grace succumbing to 'hysteria's most characteristic and dramatic symptom ... the hysterical "fit"' after a doctor arrives at the penitentiary to measure her head.[58] As Grace explains, when 'I see his [the doctor's] hand ... plunging into the open mouth of his leather bag ... my heart clenches and kicks out inside me, and then I begin to scream.'[59] She continues to scream until the Matron slaps her across the face. As the latter explains:

It's the only way with the hysterics ... we have had a great deal of experience with that kind of a fit, this one used to be prone to them but we never indulged her, we worked hard to correct it and we thought she had given it up, it might be her old trouble coming back, for despite what they said about it up there at Toronto she was a raving lunatic that time seven years ago.[60]

On one level, in keeping with the Matron's comments, readers gradually appreciate that Grace's hysterical responses are, indeed, the result of 'her old trouble coming back.' But, far from a sign of innate pathology, her hysterical symptoms constitute an expression of rage and grief triggered by the loss of her Irish homeland and the more devastating losses associated with the deaths of the three women who played a central role in her life, namely, her mother, Mary Whitney, and Nancy Montgomery. To borrow the text's governing image of quilting, Grace's hysteria constitutes the uncanny return of repressed facets of the social fabric. Viewed in this light, her hysterically fractured narrative, with its haunting allusions to cloth flowers that bleed,[61] exposes society's dirty secrets, namely, the physical and sexual abuse of working-class women by their husbands and their middle-class employers.[62]

In the case of Grace's Irish Protestant mother, after marrying a hard-drinking and physically abusive Englishman and bearing him nine children, she expires due to a mysterious, deadly growth in her abdomen. Pregnancy and death also uncannily go hand-in-hand in Mary Whitney's travails. After consorting with a gentleman, presumably her employer's son, and finding herself pregnant with his child, Mary is cast off. In desperation, she undergoes a backstreet abortion and haemorrhages to death. Finally, Nancy is murdered shortly after Grace discovers that she is carrying Kinnear's bastard. In essence, the spirits and histories of these women return to haunt the novel. As Kathleen Brogan observes, haunting in texts written by women often tends to attach to reproductive issues: '… the ghosts often arise from traumatic memories of rape, abortion, or miscarriage; possessed bodies are described as pregnant, or ghosts themselves may appear as pregnant.'[63] Whereas Brogan posits that the connection is based on the fact that 'female bodies are often the site of an uncanny struggle for control over lineage,'[64] *Alias Grace* usefully complicates matters by stressing the historical connections between haunting, hysteria, and diaspora. As I have suggested, for Irish working-class women in Canada in the early 1800s, migration, sexual exploitation, and hysteria were intimately related.

Grace's mother, for instance, dies on the transatlantic voyage, leaving Grace vulnerable to her father's abuse and the sexual advances of other predatory males. Yet, when Grace recalls her mother's death on the ship, she insists that her mother's spirit continues to wander the earth. As Grace tells Dr Jordan, when her mother's beloved teapot mysteriously shatters, she suspects that the act was perpetrated by her mother's enraged spirit, 'trapped in the bottom of the ship because we could not open a window, and angry … caught in there for ever and ever, down below in the hold like a moth in a bottle, sailing back and forth across the hideous dark ocean.'[65] This spirit caught in the hold recalls Foucault's image of madness, 'the prisoner of the passage.'

Traces of the prior trauma instigated by the diaspora reappear in later scenes that foreshadow the emergence of Grace's hysterical double consciousness. On the eve of Nancy's murder, for example, Grace dreams that Mary is in the room with her, holding a 'glass tumbler in her hand, and inside it was a firefly, trapped and glowing with a cold and greenish fire … and she took her hand from the top of the glass, and the firefly came out and darted about the room; and I knew that this was her soul, and it was trying to find its way out, but the window was shut; and then I could not see where it was gone.'[66] This dream recalls Grace's earlier concern that her mother's spirit was caught inside the hellish ship 'like a moth in a bottle.'[67] The links between Grace's illness and the fateful voyage are further strengthened when Grace learns the secret of Nancy's pregnancy and we are told that Grace goes to bed with the rain pouring down so that she 'was sure that every next minute *we would split in two like a ship at sea.*'[68] In each of these scenes, Grace's hysterical symptoms, specifically memory loss and the fracturing of her psyche, are related to the earlier trauma and fragmentation springing from her family's journey to the New World and the death of her mother. By weaving traces of the transatlantic journey into subsequent events, the text identifies Grace's 'old trouble,' her hysteria, with the shattering of domestic comfort and protection instigated by the Irish diaspora and exacerbated by the deaths of the three women who provided Grace with a material and psychic home. It is apt, then, that Grace emphasizes the simultaneous fracturing of the domestic realm and her psyche when she associates her mother's death with the broken teapot and, later, compares her sketchy memories of Ireland to 'a plate that's been broken.'[69] In keeping with fellow Canadian writer Jane Urquhart, in *Alias Grace*, Atwood probes what it means, spatially and psychically, to be 'away.' Moreover, in both Urquhart's and Atwood's novels, hysteria and, more specifically, double consciousness serves as a strategy to address (some might question the balance between 'acting out' and 'working through') the devastating and traumatic losses associated with the Irish diaspora and the utopian desires associated with immigration.

Viewed in this context, Grace's hysterical episodes signal her divided and doubled response to her own transgressive desires for class mobility. Her experience of 'splitting' is thus akin to the form of 'double consciousness' described by W.E.B. Du Bois in his writings about Black identity in America. According to Du Bois, who himself suffered from 'nervous invalidism,'[70] the experience 'of measuring one's soul by the tape of a world that looks on in amused contempt and pity' gave rise to a sense of two-ness, 'two warring ideals in one Black body, whose dogged strength alone keeps it from being torn asunder.'[71] Grace's consciousness initially fractures when she is forced to contend with the conflict between Mary's bold aspirations to rise in station and the tragic results of this experiment; having been impregnated and jilted by her gentleman lover, Mary dies from a botched abortion. Later, Grace's consciousness doubles once again when she discovers that Nancy Montgomery, following in Mary's footsteps, has engaged in a tryst with her employer, Mr Kinnear, which elevates Nancy's status to 'mistress' of the house. After she learns about Nancy, Grace hears a voice whispering in her ear, saying: '*It cannot be.*'[72] Grace's unconscious negation of interclass relations – a negation that may well have culminated in Nancy's murder – illustrates the extent to which Grace has internalized the prohibition concerning social mobility. Grace's hysterical response to Nancy suggests further that Grace suffers '*réssentiment*,' the destructive envy the have-nots feel for the haves.[73] The ghostly whisper in Grace's ear, however, demonstrates the debilitating effects of envy on marginalized groups since in this instance *réssentiment* is directed at the have-nots who presume to join the haves. In *Alias Grace*, the potential cost of opting for affiliation over filiation is racialized and class-inflected double consciousness.

In essence, *Alias Grace* stages the conflicts associated with traumatic loss instigated by migration, dispossession, and spectral attempts at repossession and assimilation. In her essay on mourning, Judith Butler outlines the psychic devastation and loss of self that attends a profound loss or dispossession:

> When we lose certain people, or when we are dispossessed from a place, or a community, we may simply feel that we are undergoing something temporary, that mourning will be over and some restoration of prior order will be achieved. But maybe when we undergo what we do, something about who we are is revealed, something that delineates the ties we have to others, that shows us that these constitute who we are. It is not as if an 'I' exists independently over here and then simply loses a 'you' over there, especially if an attachment to 'you' is part of what composes who 'I' am. If I lose you, under these conditions, then I not only mourn the loss, but I become inscrutable to myself. Who 'am' I, without you? When we lose some of those ties by which we are constituted, we do not know who we are or what to do. On one level, I think I have lost 'you' only to discover that 'I' have gone missing as well.[74]

Butler's account, which emphasizes how, following a loss, 'we do not know who we are,' sheds light on Atwood's depiction of Grace's response to dispossession. After she discovers her friend Mary has died, for instance, Grace falls into a faint and 'for ten hours ... no one could wake me.'[75] As she explains, '[W]hen I did wake up, I did not seem to know where I was, or what had happened; and I kept asking where Grace had gone. And when they told me that I myself was Grace, I would not believe them, but cried, and tried to run out of the house, because I said that Grace was lost ... and I need to search for her.'[76] Yet, as Atwood's novel emphasizes by virtue of the ongoing dialogue between Grace and her proto-analyst, Dr Simon Jordan, the search for Grace is not so much a search for a Truth and a true self as an engagement with fiction-making and fabrication. In light of the text's insistence on the links between haunting, hysteria, diaspora, fabrication, and memory, it is fitting that Atwood's text concludes with Grace's plans for a quilt composed of scraps from her prison dress, Mary's petticoat, and the pink and white floral fabric of Nancy's dress. Her statement, 'And so we will all be together,' ends the novel.[77]

In effect, the novel's emphasis on fabrication offers an important contribution to and contrasts sharply with contemporary views on trauma.[78] Trauma theory posits that because the victim of a traumatic event is allegedly unable to process the experience in a normal way, he or she is left with 'a "reality imprint" in the brain that, in its insistent literality, testifies to the existence of a pristine and timeless historical truth undistorted or uncontaminated by subjective meaning, personal cognitive schemes, psychosocial factors, or unconscious symbolic elaboration.'[79] This theory, currently in vogue in the humanities, conceives of trauma victims as entirely passive, possessed by the Truth that returns in flashbacks and nightmares in the form of pristine fragments of missing history. According to Cathy Caruth, psychological trauma allegedly remains singularly enigmatic and haunting because 'the pathology consists ... solely in the *structure of its experience* or reception: the event is not assimilated or experienced fully at the time, but only belatedly, its repeated *possession* of the one who experiences it. To be traumatized is precisely to be possessed by an image or event. And thus the traumatic symptom cannot be interpreted, simply, as a distortion of reality, nor as the lending of unconscious meaning to a reality it wishes to ignore, nor as the repression of what once was wished.'[80]

Caruth repeatedly insists that the 'traumatic nightmare' presents us with something 'undistorted by repression or unconscious wish.'[81] As Caruth argues, 'If PTSD must be understood as a pathological symptom, then it is not so much a symptom of the unconscious, as it is a symptom of history. The traumatized ... carry an impossible history within them, or they become themselves the symptom of a history that they cannot entirely possess.'[82] Indeed, as Leys observes, this memory, in 'its literality and unavailability for representation, becomes a sacred object or "icon."'[83] In contrast to this view, however, *Alias Grace* underscores the creation of identity through narration, even in the case of trauma. Moreover, Grace's traumatic flashbacks, which alter according to events in the present, confirm Ley's finding that the allegedly pure idea is, in fact, subject to 'the effects of distortion and "contagion" from environmental and other cues'; in other words, the 'content might be true, false, or confabulated.'[84] If, as Andreas Kitzmann insists, we may speak of 'a crisis of testimony,' then Atwood's novel suggests that this crisis is not merely due to the fact that testimony is 'appropriated' and 'divested of its horror.'[85] Instead, this crisis is engendered by the often oppressive demands and circumstances

surrounding the act of fiction-making or fabricating one's story – a process that in *Alias Grace*, as noted earlier, is epitomized by the image of
cloth flowers that bleed.

Although *Alias Grace*, an historical novel set in the 1840s, would seem
on the surface to have little to say regarding contemporary diasporas,
the narrative's formal and thematic concern with memory, hysteria, and
fabrication resonates uncannily with Chowra Makaremi's contemporary
research on memory in the context of border detention in France.[86]
Makaremi's study focuses on Ghislaine K., a migrant woman detained
in the 'waiting zone' who, like Grace Marks, is compelled by the authorities to speak of her traumatic migration. Ghislaine, however, remains
silent and, in so doing, fails to offer the desired story – ironically, her
failure springs, on the one hand, from an awareness of the power of
story-telling and, on the other, from an inability, following a traumatic
migration, to organize a coherent and seemingly credible story.

As Makaremi observes, the interview 'reveals a dense and complex
personal narrative, in which the linear coherence of the biography is
somehow dislocated.'[87] As in *Alias Grace*, in this instance narrative
dislocation, a 'wandering story,' reflects the subject's status, to borrow
Foucault's words, as a contemporary 'prisoner of the passage.' As
Makaremi explains: 'According to the law, the detainee who leaves her
country to come to France with a fake passport, and who is refused
entry to the territory, can leave for any other destination of her choice
where she would be legally admitted; however, without a passport, she
will be received nowhere. Suddenly, there is no place on earth where
the detainee can go.'[88] In sum, both *Alias Grace* and Makaremi's account
of Ghislaine's experience in the waiting zone highlight an often disavowed aspect of memory studies, particularly in the context of trauma,
namely, that testimony and fabrication, far from being antithetical, are
in fact secret sharers of modern culture's often traumatic, gendered,
and racialized experience of migration. Both Ghislaine's and Grace's
failures to provide 'a smooth and exact story' about themselves and
an 'ordered history of their life' demonstrate the painful gap between
sanctioned and official narrative forms of memory and those that convey
working-class women's lived experiences – alternative, fragmented
forms of storytelling which are deemed transgressive and pathologized.

If, as Ian Hacking and Mark Micale insist, our understandings of
memory, hysteria, and multiple personality disorder have benefited
greatly from the insights of nineteenth-century authors such as Flaubert,
E.T.W. Hoffmann, Robert Louis Stevenson, Dostoyevsky, and James

Hogg, then Atwood's contribution, as I have asserted, lies in refining our understanding to include a consideration of the historically entrenched relationship between the hysteria diagnosis, the impact of migration, and Irish working-class women's experience in the New World. By highlighting the connections among these elements through its own self-conscious play with a hysterical narrative style, *Alias Grace* demonstrates how cultural conceptions of memory and storytelling are radically transformed by gender-, class-, and race-inflected experiences of wandering. As Atwood's novel suggests, new forms of narrative are required to come to terms with memories of physical disorientation and loss that attend the Irish diaspora. Moreover, by emphasizing hysteria's paradoxical, dual locus in the body and in discourse, Atwood's novel demonstrates that hysteria is 'no longer a question of the wandering womb; it is a question of the wandering story.'[89]

NOTES

1 See Julia Creet's Introduction to this volume, p. 6.
2 Ibid., p. 4.
3 Ibid., p. 3.
4 See John Sundholm's contribution to this volume, p. 121.
5 See Luiza Nader's contribution to this volume, p. 261.
6 Scholars in the field of memory work and trauma, such as Cathy Caruth, Mark S. Greenberg, and Bessel A. van der Kolk, have tended to adopt a view of trauma that posits a victim who is unable to process the traumatic experience in a normal way, leaving a 'reality imprint' in the brain that supposedly testifies to a timeless historical truth undistorted and uncontaminated by subjective meaning. In contrast to this 'mimetic' model, *Alias Grace* promotes an alternative, 'anti-mimetic' view that emphasizes how traumatic experience is modified by assimilation and the subjective processes of narrativization, fabrication, and performance. *Alias Grace* illustrates how the traumatized individual oscillates between being a passive registrant and an active participant in response to trauma. The narrative's recognition of the movement between the two poles of external wounding and subjective fabrication is perhaps best expressed in the novel's haunting image of cloth flowers that bleed.
7 See Julia Creet's Introduction to this volume, p. 5.
8 Ian Hacking, *Rewriting the Soul: Multiple Personality and the Sciences of Memory* (Princeton: Princeton University Press, 1995), 233.

9 Margaret Atwood, *In Search of Alias Grace: On Writing Canadian Historical Fiction* (Ottawa: University of Ottawa Press, 1997), 36.

10 Fredric Jameson, *The Political Unconscious: Narrative as a Socially Symbolic Act* (Ithaca, NY: Cornell University Press, 1981), 193.

11 Edward Said, *The World, the Text and the Critic* (Cambridge: Harvard University Press, 1983), 20.

12 In a letter addressed to Grace's champion, Rev. Verringer, the fictitious Dr Bannerling, the attending physician who looked after Grace at the Toronto asylum, links hypnosis, spiritism, and universal suffrage and dismisses them all as instances of 'imbecility and drivel' (434). Bannerling's tripartite attack makes sense because women often acted as mediums and, as a result, were accorded tremendous power. As Elaine Showalter explains, 'Traditionally, multiple personality was linked with spiritualism and reincarnation, and with mediums like Madame Blavatsky' (*Hystories* [New York: Columbia University Press, 1997], 160). Showalter forges a connection between women's increasing power due to spiritism and suffrage and the hystericization of women's bodies. The latter constitutes, she argues, a backlash against the threat posed by women's social mobility, 'a reassertion of women's essentially biological destiny in the face of their increasingly mobile and transgressive social roles' ('Hysteria, Feminism, and Gender,' in Sander Gilman et al., *Hysteria beyond Freud* [Berkeley: University of California Press, 1993], 305).

13 Jameson, *The Political Unconscious*, 191.

14 Lorna R. McLean, and Marilyn Barber, 'In Search of Comfort and Independence: Irish Immigrant Domestic Servants Encounter the Courts, Jails, and Asylums in Nineteenth-Century Ontario,' in *Sisters or Strangers? Immigrant, Ethnic, and Racialized Women in Canadian History*, ed. Marlene Epp, Franca Iacovetta, and Frances Swyripa (Toronto: University of Toronto Press, 2004), 133.

15 Margaret Atwood, *Alias Grace* (Toronto: McClelland and Stewart, 1996), 41.

16 In *Studies on Hysteria*, Breuer and Freud refer both to amnesia and double consciousness as primary characteristics of hysteria. With respect to amnesia, as they explain, it is difficult to establish the point of origin of the disease by a simple interrogation of the patient 'principally because he is genuinely unable to recollect it' (37). They also famously asserted that 'the splitting of consciousness which is so striking in the classical cases under the form of double conscience is present to a rudimentary degree in every hysteria, and that a tendency to such a dissociation, and with it the emergence of abnormal states of consciousness … is the basic phenomenon of this neurosis' (*Studies on Hysteria*, Vol. 2 of *Standard*

Edition of the Complete Psychological Works of Sigmund Freud. ed. James Strachey [Rpt; New York: Avon, 1966], 46).

17 Atwood, *Alias Grace*, 131.

18 See Ruth Harris, *Murders and Madness: Medicine, Law and Society in the Fin de Siècle* (Oxford: Clarendon, 1989).

19 McLean and Barber, 'In Search of Comfort and Independence,' 133.

20 Hasia Diner, *Erin's Daughters in America: Irish Immigrant Women in the Nineteenth Century* (Baltimore and London: Johns Hopkins University Press, 1983), 111.

21 McLean and Barber, 'In Search of Comfort and Independence,' 149.

22 Michael Roth, 'Hysterical Remembering,' *Modernism/Modernity* 3, no. 2 (1996): 1.

23 McLean and Barber, 'In Search of Comfort and Independence,' 137.

24 Ibid.

25 Mark Micale, 'Theorizing Disease Historiography,' in Gilman et al., *Hysteria beyond Freud*, 159.

26 Ibid., 160. See also Henri Ellenberger, *The Discovery of the Unconscious: The History and Evolution of Dynamic Psychiatry* (New York: Basic Books, 1970), 190.

27 Atwood, *Alias Grace*, 159.

28 Ibid., 157–8.

29 Michel Foucault, *Madness and Civilization: A History of Insanity in the Age of Reason* (New York: Vintage, 1973), 8.

30 Ibid., 11.

31 Sigmund Freud, *Fragment of an Analysis of a Case of Hysteria ('Dora'),* trans. Alix and James Strachey (London: Penguin Books, 1990), 45–6.

32 Ibid., 46.

33 Showalter, *Hystories*, 84.

34 Atwood, *Alias Grace*, 5–6.

35 Freud and Breuer, *Studies on Hysteria*, 284.

36 Showalter, 'Hysteria,' 291–2. See also Carroll Smith-Rosenberg, *Disorderly Conduct: Visions of Gender in Victorian America* (New York: Knopf, 1985), 197–216.

37 As a host of scholars of hysteria, including Ilza Veith, Carroll Smith-Rosenberg, Mark Micale, Ian Hacking, Sander Gilman, Elaine Showalter, and Roy Porter, observe, fabrication is a crucial aspect of the nineteenth-century conception of hysteria. As Porter explains, hysteria's symptom choice 'involves complex learning and imitative processes' ('The Body and the Mind, the Doctor and the Patient: Negotiating Hysteria,' in Gilman et al., *Hysteria beyond Freud*, 229). Showalter insists that hysteria is

best understood as 'a mimetic disorder; it mimics culturally permissible expressions of distress' (*Hystories*,15). Thus, by invoking the image of cloth flowers and, more generally, postulating that an Irish domestic servant may have suffered from hysteria, Atwood underscores the fascinating performative and fabricated aspects of the disease. Furthermore, as Micale points out, recent studies concerning the occupational identities of past hysterical patients reveal that among working people, one category appears time and time again: domestic servant (*Approaching Hysteria: Disease and Its Interpretations* [Princeton: Princeton University Press, 1995],158–9). Contemporary scholars now hypothesize that just as certain 'aristocratic ailments of the eighteenth century descended to the middle classes in the early nineteenth century, so perhaps a more medicalized self-consciousness began to form later in the century among working-class people living in bourgeois environments. A kind of psychological gentrification' (ibid., 160). In effect, in postulating that Grace suffers from hysteria, a disease more often associated with Freud's affluent Viennese patients than with working-class Irish immigrants, *Alias Grace* suggests that nineteenth-century social mobility, the disease of wandering above one's station, included the transgressive assumption of new social roles and the diseases associated with these roles. Jeremiah the peddler's discussion of his transformation into Dr Jerome DuPont perhaps best illustrates the concerns associated with this type of social mobility (see pp. 267–8).

38 Atwood, *Alias Grace*, 5–6.
39 Ibid., 357.
40 Micale, *Approaching*, 19.
41 Ibid.
42 Plato, quoted in Micale, *Approaching*, 19.
43 *OED Online* (2008).
44 Atwood, *Alias Grace*, 155.
45 Showalter, *Hystories*, 71.
46 Michèle Ouerd, quoted in Showalter, *Hystories*, 71 (Michèle Ouerd, 'Introduction,' in *Charcot: leçons sur l'hystérie virile* [Paris: Le Sycamore, 1984], 27).
47 McLean and Barber, 'In Search of Comfort and Independence,' 134.
48 Diner, *Erin's Daughters*, 30.
49 McLean and Barber, 'In Search of Comfort and Independence,' 136.
50 Ibid., 137–9.
51 Ibid.,139. See also Diner, *Erin's Daughters*, chapter 5.
52 McLean and Barber, 'In Search of Comfort and Independence,' 149.

53 As Heidi Darroch points out, *Alias Grace* 'withholds from readers a complete revelation of Grace's culpability or innocence, even leaving them to speculate whether her state of double consciousness ... is real or a complicated confidence trick' ('Hysteria and Traumatic Testimony: Margaret Atwood's *Alias Grace*,' *Essays on Canadian Writing* 81 [2004]: 117).

54 For an excellent summary of feminist interpretations of hysteria, see Micale, *Approaching*, 66–87.

55 Harris, *Murders and Madness*, 64–79.

56 R.A. Huston, 'Madness and Gender in the Long Eighteenth Century,' *Social History* 27, no. 3 (2002): 320. One doctor remarked 'that the women from Ireland represented the single largest group in asylums,' noting that 'the combined moral and physical influences of their leaving the homes of their childhood, their coming almost destitute to a strange land, and often after great suffering,' contributed to their plight' (Diner, *Erin's Daughters*, 107).

57 Atwood, *Alias Grace*, 31.

58 Smith-Rosenberg, *Disorderly Conduct*, 201. In Italy, Cesare Lombroso theorized that individuals were 'born criminals.' Moreover, these primitive beings supposedly possessed similar anatomical and physiological characteristics. Doctors began to concern themselves with taking elaborate measurements of criminals owing to the popularity of these theories (see Harris, *Murders and Madness*, 64–79).

59 Atwood, *Alias Grace*, 29.

60 Ibid., 30.

61 Ibid., 297.

62 Ironically, as Ruth Harris points out, nineteenth-century European society was gripped by a peculiar anxiety 'directly linked to fears about the lower orders and the threat they posed to the sanctity of the family.' The French, in particular, were 'obsessed with the possibility that a respectable woman could be hypnotised by a male servant and made to do the latter's evil, sexual bidding' (Harris, *Murders and Madness*, 189–90). According to Harris, these anxieties can best be understood 'as a projection onto these underlings of the clear historical reality of the sexual exploitation of female servants by male masters' (Harris, *Murders and Madness*, 191).

63 Kathleen Brogan, *Cultural Haunting: Ghosts and Ethnicity in Recent American Literature* (Charlottesville: University Press of Virginia, 1998), 25.

64 Ibid.

65 Atwood, *Alias Grace*, 122. Throughout the novel, Grace narrates her encounters with spirits as accounts of extrinsic haunting. However, during the nineteenth century, physicians such as Janet, Charcot, and Freud were refining the understanding of hysteria and double consciousness; in

essence, they were developing psychological models of what Adam Crabtree refers to as 'intrinsic' haunting. As Crabtree writes: 'Until the emergence of the alternate consciousness paradigm the only category to express the inner experience of an alien consciousness was that of possession, intrusion from the outside. With the rise of awareness of a second consciousness intrinsic to the human mind, a new symptom-language became possible. Now the victim could express (and society could understand) the experience in a new way' (*Multiple Man: Explorations in Possession and Multiple Personality* [Toronto and New York: Praeger, 1985]; quoted in Ian Hacking, *Rewriting the Soul: Multiple Personality and the Sciences of Memory* [Princeton: Princeton University Press, 1995], 149).

66 Atwood, *Alias Grace*, 312–13.
67 Ibid., 122.
68 Ibid., 279 (emphasis added).
69 Ibid., 103.
70 Micale, 'Theorizing Disease Historiography,' 162.
71 W.E.B. Du Bois, *The Souls of Black Folk* (London: Oxford University Press, 2007), 23.
72 Atwood, *Alias Grace*, 279.
73 Jameson, *The Political Unconscious*, 201.
74 Judith Butler, *Precarious Life: The Powers of Mourning and Violence* (London: Verso, 2004), 22.
75 Atwood, *Alias Grace*, 180.
76 Ibid.
77 Ibid., 460.
78 See Mark S. Greenberg and Bessel A. van der Kolk, 'Retrieval and Integration of Traumatic Memories with the "Painting Cure,"' in *Psychological Trauma*, ed. Bessel A. van der Kolk (Washington, DC: American Psychiatric Press, 1987), 191–215; cited in Cathy Caruth, ed., *Trauma: Explorations in Memory* (Baltimore: Johns Hopkins University Press, 1995), 152. See also Ruth Leys, *Trauma: A Genealogy* (Chicago: University of Chicago Press, 2000). My thanks to Dr Jill Matus for sharing her insights into trauma theory and for turning my attention to Ley's work.
79 Leys, *Trauma: A Geneology*, 7.
80 Caruth, *Trauma: Explorations in Memory*, 4–5.
81 Ibid., 152.
82 Ibid., 5.
83 Leys, *Trauma: A Geneology*, 253.
84 Ibid., 243.

85 See Andreas Kitzmann's contribution to this volume, p. 98.
86 See Chowra Makaremi's contribution to this volume.
87 Ibid., p. 71.
88 Ibid., p. 82.
89 Showalter, *Hystories*, 335.

SECTION FOUR

Architectures of Memory

12 Value of Memory – Memory of Value: A Mnemonic Interpretation of Socrates' Ethical Intellectualism

TOMASZ MAZUR

> I should be able to tell you the story – I've practiced it enough.
> – Plato, *The Symposium*[1]

1. Is Memory a Value?

Sigmund Freud, while arguing that he had successfully resolved the paradoxes of Socratic ethical intellectualism, also stressed strong connections between evaluation and memory. According to his early dream theory, people tend to remember what is good (or pleasurable) and to forget what is bad (or painful).[2] Thus, evaluation is what sets apart conscious and subconscious memory, and the recognition of good and bad shapes our memory in fundamental ways. Yet, Freud only reminds us of what Plato had previously demonstrated: the strong connection between memory and evaluation, such that it even clouds the real difference between these two spheres. Hence, we ask: 'Is memory a value?' or 'Is value a memory?'

In this paper, these questions take the shape of a more specific question: What is the relation between Socrates' theory of value and his approach to memory? In answering it, we investigate three basic Platonic images of memory: as wax tablet, as aviary, and as a garment we wear. The problem of Socratic ethical intellectualism is essential to this discussion because it foregrounds Plato's understanding of the relation between memory and value.

2. Contradictions of Socratic Teaching

The distinction between memory and value is not made clear in Socratic teaching, nor does Socrates explain what he thinks memory is or how he evaluates it. This seems characteristic of his teaching in its entirety as Plato represents it. Socratic teaching is well known for several contradictions. Socrates frequently confuses us with the differences or seeming inconsistencies between his words and deeds. Sometimes we can see him as a politician (even the only true one), and at other times he is not a politician at all. Similarly he also appears as a teacher (the only true one) and sometimes not a teacher at all, knowing something (as the only one who knows anything at all) and knowing nothing at all. Most scholars interpret these contradictions as a consequence of the Socratic use of irony, a characteristic and an indispensable component of his way of teaching.[3]

Generally speaking, Socratic irony consists of giving a dual meaning to a key word in an argument. For example, Socrates consistently uses two different meanings for the notion of knowledge. The first is a boundless godlike knowledge; the second is a more restricted (conditional) human knowledge. Thus, in showing that he possesses some knowledge while constantly emphasizing that he knows nothing, Socrates is not being inconsistent. He simply does not explain which kind of knowledge he has in mind. For Socrates, there is no point in being clear because clarity can only be found deep in the soul, never just through the language of explanation. Instead he uses irony to access this clarity, which is a state he calls *arete* (virtue), or *sophrosyne* (a term difficult to express in English, but, roughly, moral sanity, rational control, moderation, or knowledge). As I will try to make clear later, this state is a consequence of a special training of our memory, or the way we memorize things.

The contradictory quality of Socrates' possession of knowledge and his status as a teacher is also present in his relationship to memory. He appears to have both an extremely weak and extremely strong memory. He always forgets what was said just a moment ago and asks people to remind him. At the same time, he remembers very distinctly the whole structure of an argument, and its key points. He forgets about ordinary things very easily, but remembers distinctly his duties towards philosophy and truth. He praises the value of memory for the philosopher, but at the same time is famous for spectacular cases of forgetfulness (in Plato's *Symposium*, for example, where Socrates, deep in philosophical meditation, forgets his destination).[4] We are told in the *Symposium* that 'this is a habit of his – he goes off and stands wherever he happens to be.'[5] We can also see Socrates praising the value of forgetfulness within philosophical practice. In the *Phaedrus*, for example, he praises different kinds of divine madness that he understands as versions of forget-fulness, while silently attributing these states to philosophy.[6] In *Laws*, Plato practically starts a whole argument about the ideal state with a praise of wine, because of its capacity to produce forgetfulness.[7] According to Socrates, it is thanks to wine that people can forget things in a given moment that they are supposed to forget.

3. Memory, Knowledge, and Virtue

The problem of memory in Socratic teaching is strictly connected to his conception of knowledge in general. However, since knowledge, according to him, constitutes a definiens of virtue, which is the main subject of his teaching, we can say the concepts of virtue and teaching are also connected to memory. In ancient Greece, memory constitutes the very core of knowledge. To discuss memory is, then, to discuss knowledge itself. A famous story told in Plato's *Phaedrus* clearly represents this relationship between memory and knowledge.[8] This is a story about the invention of writing, or, more precisely, about the disadvantages of written language. An Egyptian god Theuth (known to the Greeks as Hermes), the inventor of the alphabet, presents his invention to the Egyptian king Thamus. While Theuth proudly states that his discovery 'will make the people of Egypt wiser and improve their memories' and that it 'provides a recipe for memory and wisdom,'[9] Thamus becomes suspicious. The king's main argument rests on showing that a written language will threaten the human ability to remember. He believes that human beings would no longer be willing to exercise their memory if they can instead have everything written down. Thus, King Thamus argues: 'If men learn this, it will implant forgetfulness in their souls: they will cease to exercise memory because they rely on that which is written, calling things to remembrance no longer from within themselves, but by means of external marks; what you have discovered is a recipe not for memory, but for reminder.'[10] There is an interesting connection of this story to our modern technologies of storing memory and knowledge such as archives, documents, photo albums, films, etc. These technologies might all provoke the Platonic question: How do they affect our memory?

Plato does not equate knowledge with all forms of memory. He does not argue that the more we remember, the more profound our knowledge will be. Instead, he treats the concept of memory ironically by stressing its importance and trivializing it at the same time. This ironic treatment is expressed in the very structure of *Phaedrus*, where the whole discussion rests on undermining the value of Phaedrus's exercises in the literal memorization of Lysias's speech on the nature of love. According to Plato, knowledge is only memory in a specific modus or constellation. Thus, for Phaedrus, it is not knowledge that he is able to memorize a speech given by Lysias the day before;[11] nor is it knowledge for the cave prisoners (in the story told in *The Republic*, book VII) that they, more or less clearly, remember shadows cast on the wall;[12] nor is it knowledge for *Ion* that he remembers perfectly extensive parts of the *Iliad*.[13]

In *Theatetus*, Plato twice defines knowledge using the notion of memory. The first time he defines it using the metaphor of 'memory as a wax tablet.'[14] According to Cornford's comment on this passage, there exist two conditions for knowing something: 'I know a thing when I have had direct acquaintance with it and [an] image of it remains stored in my memory.'[15] Thus knowledge, we can say, consists of clear perception and a kind of storage or, using a more contemporary computer metaphor, a kind of hard disk. Plato also uses the metaphor of 'memory as an aviary,'[16] by explaining that 'every mind contains a kind of aviary stocked with birds of every sort.'[17] Here, knowledge is a state of possessing ideas as 'pieces of knowledge'[18] that are stocked in memory, but do not constitute knowledge unless taken together in combination. According to Cornford, the metaphor of memory as an aviary is a basis for Plato's critique of the Sophists' notion of knowledge and teaching, as well as an introduction to the concept of recollection presented later in *Meno* and *Phaedo*.[19] Using the computer metaphor one more time, we can say that the metaphor of memory as aviary corresponds to the notion of a hard disk without any complex operating system.

In Socrates' lifetime and long before him, education depended on the use of memory. Objects of memorization used for teaching were often Homeric poems or similar forms of verse, and moral standards conveyed in traditional dictums.[20] In the Sophists' teaching, speeches and rhetorical techniques took precedence over poetry.[21] However, from Plato's *Hippias Major*, we know that the sophist, Hippias, is also ready to teach and require memorization of the following topics: astronomy, geometry, arithmetic, grammar, rhythm, music, genealogy, mythology, and history.[22] It is worth noting that Hippias is depicted as famous for being a man of extraordinarily good memory who is able to retain a list of fifty names after a single hearing.[23] Socrates challenges traditional teaching strategies as well as the Sophists' understanding of the value of remembering, calling into question the way memory is commonly used in education. A distinctive feature of his teaching is his call to do away with the reliance on memorization as a sufficient basis for knowledge. Plato seems to be suggesting that knowledge consists of some kinds of memory work, but not just of memorization.

While developing his own concept of teaching, Socrates also introduces new concepts of knowledge, memory, and virtue. These four notions are strictly connected in his philosophy, and are practically impossible to understand separately. Only their fusion produces the specific complex of Socratic ethical intellectualism.

4. Ethical Intellectualism

The basis for Socratic ethical intellectualism is the thesis that in order to be good, it is enough to know what goodness really is. If someone does wrong, it must either be a consequence of his lack of knowledge or of his insanity. Very subtle conceptualizations of knowledge and memory underlie this argument. Socrates' main thesis is that all human acts follow from knowledge and from nothing else, and this knowledge emerges from values. Only the characteristics of this knowledge explain human behaviour. If you want to improve someone's behaviour, you have to first improve his or her knowledge. What is critical to understanding this notion of knowledge is that it is not a purely intellectual experience but rather a way of being. Knowledge resides in a person's whole existence, and intellect or reasoning is only a tool used to improve it. Socratic teaching endeavours to change the pupil's way of being through a conversion of his soul.[24] Pierre Hadot calls this practice a *psychagogy*.[25] Addressing this tradition in philosophy, Michel Foucault stresses asceticism as its main condition, which includes work on one's own memory with an emphasis on changing it.

According to Socrates, knowing means being; to know goodness means to be good. No other way of knowing and teaching exists. Thus, we can understand the distinction made by Plato between having knowledge and possessing knowledge. Plato represents the notion of memory through the metaphor of an aviary to illustrate that there are two ways of storing knowledge as memory: having and possessing. Socrates states that 'if a man has bought a coat and owns it, but is not wearing it, we should say he possesses it without having it about him.'[26] 'Having' is then connected with being, and 'possessing' is connected with intellectual handling. Thus, 'having' is a special modus of remembering, and we can call it the 'wearing' of memory, since the Greek word *echein* (ἔχειν) was commonly used in reference to wearing a garment. The problem is that most people only possess knowledge about goodness without having it about them or wearing it.

5. Practising Memory

Plato's writings contain several distinct insights into the phenomenon of memory. Some of them strictly address the practice of Socrates' teaching, while others also discuss the Platonic 'second sailing' introduced in *Phaedo*.[27] In many instances, Plato discusses memory without making his own perspective of the notion clear. We can call it irony, that is, a conscious interplay with readers aimed not at confusing them but rather, as Thomas Szlezák puts it, at stimulating them. This interplay alone can teach us an important lesson about memory – it partly explains why it is important and why, at the same time, it is not so important.

The very construction of the *Symposium* is a good example here. The construction of its text is mnemonic to its very core. It is a story about a recollection of an event, a party at Agathon's house, told to us by Apollodorus. The account of the event seems kind of strangely told. First, Apollodorus wasn't present at the actual party,[28] so he cannot be a direct witness. Second, the actual party took place about fourteen years ago,[29] so it cannot be recollected precisely. Third, Apollodorus didn't even hear the story directly from Socrates but from one of his 'most ardent lovers at the time,' Aristodemus of Cydathenaeum, who only checked 'some details with Socrates.'[30] As a result, the whole story is disturbed by Aristodemus's passion. Fourth, the account that is given is a version told to a group of 'rich businessmen,' and Apollodorus's awareness of this audience influences the way the story is told.[31] For example, more subtle insights are deleted. Fifth, Apollodorus also starts off by offending his audience, which is a pretext to remind us that his nickname is 'Maniac.' Thus, both he and Aristodemus are represented as passionate narrators who have the capacity to distort the story told. Sixth, Aristodemus cannot remember every speech in detail[32] and even skips several speeches that he has difficulty remembering.[33] This makes the form of the story fragmented and only partial. Seventh, Socrates' speech within the story is a recollection within both Aristodemus's and Apollodorus's recollections about an even earlier happening: a conversation with Diotima about love. As Socrates informs us, he doesn't even understand everything she told him.[34]

To approach Plato's notion of memory, substituting the term 'story' for the term 'memory' is useful. The idea of divine madness in relation to memory is also significant throughout the *Symposium*. What Apollodorus and Socrates have in common is a passion, verging on madness, for philosophy. We are told that this mania is only a form of devotion.[35] It also bears a specific connection to remembering and forgetting. Both Apollodorus and Socrates are ready to remember and repeat stories, and this stems from their mania. But their stories seem to lack clarity. They are not directly witnessed or precise enough. They are fragmented, shaped and even distorted according to audience profile and the emotional state of the storytellers. As a result of these contingencies, the stories are changed constantly in the process of memorizing and re-memorizing. The Socratic word for this reshaping, also found in the epigraph to this paper, is 'practising.' Thus, forgetting is also a form of practising memory. It is interwoven throughout these stories and it is often related to mania. Socratic storytelling is just the other side of Socratic memory shaping. In Plato's *Phaedrus*, when Socrates meets Phaedrus, he asks him to tell a story of love. Daimonion reveals that Pheadrus's story contains error. It is too closely tied to the memory of Lysias's story about the same topic. There is no critical distance. So Socrates tries to tell the story, practising his memory work, and re-shapes it in accordance with something that is not exactly present in any memory – the real value of love.

The relationships between memory, knowledge, and love in Plato's writings are particularly complex. He is always trying to grasp what love is in his texts, and yet love is always disturbing the process of this grasping. This is because of a very literal understanding of philo-sophy (love of knowledge) in his tradition.

Our memory, knowledge, and, as we see later, identity are always combinations of two elements. One is the flux of memory, which the image of the aviary addresses: all we have experienced and been told about. This kind of memory is like the shadows in a Platonic cave. The second element is the ideal world of truth, which is static. In presenting these two different states of understanding, the construction of the *Symposium* reflects a fundamental quality in all of Plato's writings. Modern commentators point out that Socratic philosophy is always located somewhere between ideal truth and an empirically blurred image and is constantly clarifying ways to distinguish between opinion and wisdom.[36] As Gerald Mara explains, philosophy needs opinion, as well as the ideals of truth and wisdom, because it is constructed out of personal memory, both rooted in the process of recollection and part of its flux. Opinion is similar to knowledge as blurred images collected empirically through experience and those moving shadows on the wall of a Platonic cave. Using Socrates' dialectic of memory work, we need to 'practise' the formation of opinions along with ideals of truth and wisdom. But this practising means changing or adapting the content and process of what we practise. As Mara explains: 'Even if there has been a historical Socratic conversation with someone named Diotima, Socrates is not simply repeating her *logos* but changing it or adapting it in appropriate ways.'[37]

Thus, the relation between memory and knowledge grows more complex. All we can know is rooted in our individual memory, which is always to a certain extent a blurred image. As Henri Bergson underlines much later, everything we perceive directly is also pervaded with the substance of memory. So, by taking the two notions of memory in *Theatetus*, we see that knowledge is the consequence of a constant interplay between clear perception (which is in fact never clear but pervaded with images from memory) and memory (which is always affected by new experiences, some of them 'maniac' experiences). Does practising memory allow for a way out of this weird and confusing feedback relation by adding a third element of knowledge?

6. Memory Affected by Value or the Three Rooms of Memory

The practice of philosophy in the Socratic tradition appears here as a reshaping of the content or form of personal memory. This is exactly the difference between Socrates and the sophists, as we see in *Phaedrus*, where the whole story rests on a speech by Phaedrus. Whereas Phaedrus's speech is an exact reconstruction or memorization of Lysias's speech that he heard the day before, Socrates constructs his speeches spontaneously, according to his revelation of the truth about values, on the one hand, and his own previous experience or memory, on the other.

In Socratic teaching, the main goal of this reshaping is the recognition of values. Socrates is continually reconstructing his pupil's knowledge/memory in order to make that pupil 'wear' values, that is, to move from the stage of possessing knowledge about values to the stage of having this knowledge. However, most importantly, our knowledge/memory is always affected/constructed by experiencing values, according to Socrates. What we 'wear,' in fact, is always a consequence of our right or wrong recognition of values.

The core of Socratic teaching consists of the understanding that the recognition of values, found through memory, constitutes who we really are. All human deeds and behaviour stem from this recognition. Knowledge about values that construct the human condition is directly related to recollection in two of Plato's texts. From *Meno*, we know that people possess some essential prenatal knowledge or memory about value.[38] Moreover, from *Phaedrus*, we know that this essential memory constitutes the human condition or potential.[39] However, we can say that the very core of Socratic teaching already consists of the concept that the recognition (memory) of value constitutes who we really are. All human deeds and behaviour stem from this recognition. Socrates' aim is to change and reshape this recognition by 'exchanging a garment we are already wearing.' From this point of view, philosophical madness as devotion, which Socrates seems to experience, can be understood as a readiness to forget or weaken our previous memorization or order to make way for new revelations and understandings about values.

To explain this process, we can use the metaphor of the three rooms of memory. The first room is prenatal memory (abstract shapes/notions, on the one hand, and intuition of truth/value, on the other hand); the second room is possessed memory (the aviary); the third room is the memory that we have/are (the wax imprint of memory, also based on intuition of value). We are hereby joining the metaphor of the wax tablet with the concept of 'having knowledge,' based on Plato's insinuation that this type of memory is rooted in the heart.[40] This same idea is preserved later in Stoic tradition, as it places the thought process in the heart.[41] This is why Socrates and Stoics alike had no problem with taking as a given that proper emotional balance stems from proper thinking, or even that these two things are basically the same. In the process of teaching, Socrates reformats the very structure of memory by exchanging the contents in the individual rooms of memory – moving ideas from room to room. This process of reformatting means that he catches some ideas and memories from the aviary, by evoking some shapes from prenatal memory, and imprinting them on his pupils' hearts. Therefore, these ideas are always on a personal level. Socrates never tells the pupil what truth is but instead pulls it out of the pupil, because truth is the shape of knowledge, not its content. Prenatal memory gives us this shape, while life gives us the content – but it is the content of the aviary, disordered, or ordered in inappropriate ways. What we need is an order that grasps the original shape. Philosophical madness is a readiness to destroy inappropriate orders, which are always based on false evaluation, and exchange them for the proper shape.

However, this process of reshaping memory is not forced on the pupil, because Socrates believes values, seen clearly, imprint themselves in our heart without any coercion. Thus, strictly speaking, values reshape (rather than teach) our memory, and Socrates' job consists only of presenting them clearly on the field of our previous experiences, or of exposing our heart to the imprint of values. According to Socrates, then, the way to teach/memorize values is just to present them as clearly as possible. The level of clarity depends on the pupil's potential (i.e., on the shape of his prenatal memory). Thus, philosophy is the search for values by way of discussion.

7. Practising Memory by Reshaping It

Plato's *Philebus* helps to complete an understanding of the practice of memory in Socrates' teaching by revealing the mnemonic aspect of his ethical intellectualism. *Philebus* is a dialogue concerning the notion of pleasure. In its process of argumentation, we can find Plato's profound insight into the way memory works.[42] His main thesis is that pleasure is not the main motive for human action. Rather, memory motivates us, because what and how we remember matters most. All motives related to the search and desire for pleasure are located in memory. There are false and weak pleasures as well as true and valid pleasures. Our memories of pleasurable experiences are based on our evaluation of a pleasure. Ultimately it is an evaluation and recognition of value that motivates our actions. These evaluations are produced through a spiritual nature in human beings, which is developed and made healthy by recognition of true value.

So, it is not actual pleasure that shows the way to our future activities, but our evaluation of pleasure. If you kiss a beautiful girl one evening, you will probably remember it as a good, pleasurable experience worth striving for in following evenings. But if, for some reason, you find (or are convinced) this was a bad pleasure, you will not strive for it in following evenings. A characteristic of Socrates' theory is that only the recognition of value makes you feel/remember pleasure in something. If you find, deep in your heart, what is good for you, you will follow it. But you cannot find it out of the blue, in some theoretical, abstract way. You need to find it in your previous pleasurable experiences.

According to Socrates, then, evaluation is always at the base of our memories of pleasure and joy. The pleasures of life are in Heraclitean flux. We need to order them, and thus our memories are structured according to an evaluative order. To change someone's behaviour, which is a goal of education, you only need to restructure their memory of previous pleasures and other experiences. To depict this process, the metaphor of shifting between the rooms of memory is useful because we restructure and recombine memories by changing the evaluations encoded within them. This practice is always based on the concept and recognition of human nature or the ideal of human life we are aiming for. If you are thoroughly convinced in your heart of what this human nature or ideal is, such recognition will change your whole behaviour because you will change the way you remember your previous pleasures accordingly. As your evaluation of the past changes, memories move from one room to another. Foucault finds a correlation here between Stoic teaching, based on Socratic tradition, and the Freudian concept of a 'watchman.' In the Stoic tradition, as he puts it, moral consciousness is the watchman of perceptions, preventing false attachments. Moral consciousness as watchman prevents inappropriate perceptions and memories from entering our room of the wax tablet. Foucault finds a Freudian analogy here, in the watchman that is present between subconscious and conscious memory. The main difference between the Socratic-Stoic tradition and Freud's theory is an association of the identity of our personal agency, or, at least, the very essence of our agency, with the watchman in the former.

A characteristic of Socratic practice, then, is its focus on memory and, through discussion, changing the way we remember experiences one by one, by recognizing a greater value in some while devaluing others. Socrates engages in this process during his conversation with Polos and Kallikles in *Gorgias*, as he tries to lessen, step by step, their perceptions of pure exertion of political power as good.

As a consequence of Socratic practice, a pupil should be left with the same content of memory as aviary, but reordered and evaluated differently on the wax tablet, according to an ideal shape that corresponds to prenatal memory. The recognition of value is not some new memory of an object or experience added to our aviary. It is the repositioning and shifting to the wax tablet of memories we already have. This practice is a like making one big picture out of many smaller pictures. This big picture is one we all have, according to Plato, embedded in our prenatal memory. In Socratic tradition, it is some kind of intuition of truth. The small pictures are all our personal memories. All we need is to have them ordered properly. We can also approach this through the metaphor of a flavour. It is possible to reach the same taste with slightly different ingredients. Similarly, every personal memory has different ingredients – the truth in this context is the taste that is the goal of reconstructing the value proportions between the given ingredients. Taste, then, is a metaphor for the form of our memory and different ingredients of the actual memories we possess. All that matters are proportions.

As we stressed before, according to many modern interpretations of Plato, knowledge (as a specific construction of our memory) that is reachable by human agency is something in between an ideal unchanging world of truth and a constant flux of immediate experiences. Experiences are always new and different, and this forces us to constantly rework or practise our memories. As in the epigraph of this paper, Socrates is always practising both his pupils' memories and his own, in order to reach a shape of memory made out of the sum of actual experiences that resembles truth as much as possible.

NOTES

1 Plato, *Symposium*, in *The Symposium and The Phaedo*, trans. R. Larson (Arlington Heights, IL: AHM Publishing Corporation, 1980), 172a.
2 Sigmund Freud, *Introductory Lectures on Psychoanalysis*, ed. and trans. James Strachey (London: Penguin Books, 1973).
3 Gregory Vlastos, *Socrates: Ironist and Moral Philosopher*. (Ithaca, NY: Cornell University Press, 1991), 21–44, 132–56.
4 Plato, *Symposium*, 174d–175c.
5 Ibid., 175b.
6 Plato, *Phaedrus*, trans. J.C.B. Gosling (Oxford: Claredon Press, 1973), 243e–245c, 249d–257a.
7 Plato, *Laws*, in *The Dialogues of Plato*, Vol. 4, trans. B. Jowett (Oxford: Clarendon Press, 1964), Book I-II.
8 Plato, *Phaedrus*, 274b–278b.
9 Ibid., 274e.
10 Ibid., 275a.
11 Ibid., 228a–c.
12 Plato, *The Republic*, trans. Desmond Lee (London and New York: Penguin, 2003), 516d.

13 Plato, *Ion*, trans. Walter Hamilton and Chris Emlyn-Jones (London: Penguin, 1997), 536d–537e.

14 Plato, *Theatetus*, trans. John McDowell (Oxford: Clarendon Press, 1973), 190e–195b.

15 F.M. Cornford. *Plato's Theory of Knowledge* (New York: Liberal Art Press, 1957), 121.

16 Plato, *Theatetus*, 197b–199c.

17 Ibid., 197d.

18 Ibid., 199b

19 Cornford, *Plato's Theory of Knowledge*, 135–6.

20 Werner Wilhelm Jaeger, *Paideia: The Ideals of Greek Culture*, Vol. 1 (New York: Oxford University Press, 1945).

21 W.K.C. Guthrie, *A History of Greek Philosophy, Vol III: The Fifth Century Enlightenment* (Cambridge: Cambridge University Press, 1979), 41–4.

22 Plato, *Hippias Major*, in *Early Socratic Dialogues*, trans. Robin Waterfield (London: Penguin, 1987), 285c–e.

23 Ibid., 285e.

24 See Thomas Alexander Szlezák, *Reading Plato*, trans. G. Zanker (London and New York: Routledge, 1999); Michael Miller, *Plato's Parmenides: The Conversion of the Soul* (Princeton: Princeton University Press, 1986).

25 Pierre Hadot, *Philosophy as a Way of Life: Spiritual Exercises from Socrates to Foucault*, trans. Michael Chase (Oxford and New York: Blackwell, 1995).

26 Plato, *Theatetus*, 197b.

27 Plato, *Phaedo*, in *The Symposium and The Phaedo*, 97b–100b.

28 Plato, *Symposium*, in *The Symposium and The Phaedo*, 172b–c.

29 Ibid., 173a.

30 Ibid., 173b.

31 Ibid., 173c.

32 Ibid., 178a.

33 Ibid., 180c.

34 Ibid., 210a.

35 Ibid., 173d.

36 Gerald M. Mara, *Socrates' Discursive Democracy: Logos and Ergon in Platonic Political Philosophy* (New York: New York State University Press, 1997), 148–85.

37 Ibid., 200.

38 Plato, *Meno*, in *Protagoras and Meno*, trans. A. Beresford (London and New York: Penguin, 2005), 81a–85d.

39 Plato, *Phaedrus*, 248c–249d.

40 Plato, *Theatetus*, 194c-d; John Issac Beare, *Greek Theories of Elementary Cognition from Alcmaeon to Aristotle* (Oxford: Clarendon Press, 1906), 267.
41 Margaret E. Reesor, *The Nature of Man in Early Stoic Philosophy* (New York: St Martin's Press, 1989), 2.
42 Plato, *Philebus*, trans. J.C.B. Gosling (Oxford: Clarendon Press, 1975), 33c–37b.

13 Migratory Subjects: Memory Work in Krzysztof Wodiczko's Projections and Instruments

LUIZA NADER

Georges Bataille's famous hatred for architecture was motivated, as Denis Hollier observes, by its anthropomorphism understood as a sort of mirror stage.[1] Through the intervention of his images, Krzysztof Wodiczko acts against the architectural body, revealing the hominization (the process of becoming human) contained in each building. Wodiczko attempts to rework individual and social traumas, introducing memory into the public space of history, by interrupting architecture with visual images that are literally or metaphorically veiled by its structure. In his slide and video projections haunting urban spaces, the artist deals with the problem of the Other, evicted from social and political life: migrants' stories excluded from official narrations of the past. In his instruments such as *Alien Staff* or *Mouthpiece*, he examines this problem through the actions they trigger, where the migrant becomes a screen for Otherness, represented both as uncanny and foreign. Wodiczko's works are focused on those who are not able to speak out their trauma, or who no longer believe in the translation from experience to language: migrants, foreigners, homeless, disempowered nomads. As Julia Kristeva states, 'The difficulty engendered by the matter of foreigners would be completely contained in the deadlock caused by the distinction that sets citizen apart from man. The process means that one can be more or less a man to the extent that one is more or less a citizen, that he who is not a citizen is not fully a man. Between a man and a citizen there is a scar: the foreigner.'[2] The scar, puncture, and wound is traced by Wodiczko's actions in the visual space of the city, in the transient space of memory, and in the nucleus of the self. In my essay, I would like to focus on mnemonic experience both embedded and produced by the artist's works, a problem which has not been highlighted enough in the vast literature on Wodiczko's oeuvre. I would like to propose that in Wodiczko's works which deal with the issue of immigration, memory plays a crucial role in the process of splitting and re-establishing the self, history, and public space.

During two evenings in Tijuana in 2001, Wodiczko used the spectacular, spherical building of El Centro Cultural, designed by Manuel Rosen, which has become a symbol and pride of this border city. The facade of the building was 'attacked' by the artist with live video projections: magnified and reinforced faces of women working in *maquiladoras* (border factories) narrating work exploitation, sexual and domestic violence, or abuses of power. Choosing the cultural complex in Tijuana and creating gigantic, almost hallucinatory images, Wodiczko not only counted on a large audience (such as those going to or leaving the cinema), but also created a spectacle of the unconscious of the city, the repressions and foreclosures in urban space, the memory transmitted by architecture, and the homelessness of a migrant's mnemonic experience. The women who took part in the project were migrants from different, mainly agricultural, parts of Mexico. They attempted to verbalize the experience of crossing borders: not only geographical, but also social, economical, and psychological. For them, the two projections were preceded by preliminary months of 'learning' not only how to use electronic devices designed by the artist, but also to speak out about painful experiences, how to cross 'the passage from testimony to transformative public action,'[3] from the position of a victim to the position of social and political agent. The female narrators were constructing the memory of shattering experiences of the past, from the present meta-stable position of being 'in between' places and moments. Thus *Tijuana Projection* opposed the stable concepts of memory represented by Maurice Halbwachs or Pierre Nora, who state that memory is enabled by and fixed to particular places.[4] The *Tijuana Projection* points rather to the fact that memory, especially memory of traumatic past events, which could be an immobilizing and petrifying psychic phenomenon itself, needs other spaces than familiar (*heimlich*) ones to be uttered. Memory together with its site – the subject – has to travel to find its narration, which does not stabilize but breaks the 'wounded attachment' (to use Cathy Caruth's words) both to the places and events. In Wodiczko's projection, memory with its eclipsed parts always migrates, never finding its 'place,' but rather a counter-place – heterotopia. As Michel Foucault points out, heterotopias are constituted on the net of relations with other places, suspending, neutralizing, or turning upside down the constellation of relations which they reflect, or at which heterotopias point.[5] Heterotopia is a space like a mirror, a ship, or a museum, where all the other places we can find in culture could be represented and contested at the same time, where time is suspended or endlessly accumulated. In *Tijuana*, using the facade of the building, Wodiczko created a kind of magnified mirror, a space compensating for the lack of space, where the excluded memory of traumatic experiences could be effectively carried out and made visible. The building not only reflected female faces, but also, symbolically, Tijuana's split identity. The citizens of the city could empathically identify with the experience embedded in the scattered narration of speaking women, and in the recognition of Otherness – they could experience the fissure in the image of the very self. The artist provoked a collusion between the official image of Tijuana as a world cultural centre – the dream of the officials – and a reality of the city excluded and repressed from the public discourse (the traumatic experiences of the women working in *maquiladoras*), coming to the fore as in a dream. El Centro Cultural was haunted by private accounts referring to psychological and physical wounds, as well as to social problems. Wodiczko called for the public sphere to be understood, not as physical location but as phantomatic space where, according to Rosalyn Deutsche in 'Agoraphobia,' the summative chapter in her collection of essays *Evictions: Art and Spatial Politics*, there is no clear separation between public and private realms, where meaning continuously appears and fades, where one faces the uncanniness and intimacy of others and, in consequence, the uncertainty of one's very self.[6] Memory, as Julia Creet states in the Introduction to this volume, is not an immobile phenomenon, but a migrant one: movement produces memory, but also creates the desire for memory's fixity.[7] And architecture, the very aim and tool in Wodiczko's works such as *Tijuana Projection*, takes part in the overwhelming logic of the mask, writes Beatriz Colomina in *Privacy and Publicity: Modern Architecture as Mass Media*.[8] Not only a facade that hides something, the mask is also responsible for the production of what is hidden. Only immobile masks speak, and when the mask moves (or is moved), it reveals the unspeakability of what is hidden behind. This moment of movement, writes Colomina, is the only trace of identity, which is never fixed or unitary in modern cities, but always in need of the differentiation and protection provided by the mask. Wodiczko, in his projection in *Tijuana*, literally moves the architecture through the superimposition of moving and speaking images, and forces the public to recognize the unspeakable and flexible

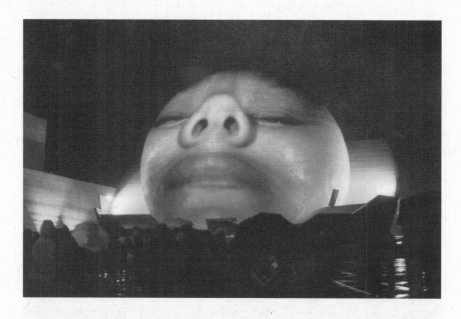

Krzysztof Wodiczko, *Tijuana Projection*, 2001. Photos: courtesy of Krzysztof Wodiczko and Profile Foundation.

memory unevenly produced by the official mask of the city. In *Tijuana*, where reality is constructed not of places, but rather of displacements, the artist reveals memory, not as the formative experience from which we start over, but rather as a transient space wherein, as Julia Creet writes, we land.[9] Rather than fixity, the immobility of a certain type of mnemonic experience appears throughout Wodiczko's earlier works from the 1980s, in which the artist deals with traumatic memory as a mask. Exposing architectural and photographic structures as a disguise, the artist examines the mask's petrified speech. Superimposing photographic slides on monuments and buildings, he investigated the depth hidden in their surfaces, carefully analyzing, not words and movement, but the silence and immobility in which both photography and monument are drowned. 'There is nothing more disruptive and astonishing in a monument than a sign of life,' observes the artist.[10]

In the second *Homeless Projection* (1986–7), Wodiczko projected slides of migrants in the city on the four sides of the Civil War Memorial in Boston – images of homeless people with their particular attributes, objects, and costumes. Wodiczko projected onto a column the image of a recently built luxury apartment building, both a sign and result, as Rosalyn Deutsche writes in her insightful analysis of the project, of the process of redevelopment, which caused the rise of real estate prices, and thus resulted in the evictions of poorer dwellers from the district. As Deutsche further suggests, the projection imposed the conditions that generate homelessness back onto the architecture and forced its surface to reveal what it denied.[11] Wodiczko remarks that the homeless often resemble city monuments, 'frozen in their classical gestures, cracked from permanent outdoor exposure.'[12] Wodiczko's aim was not to enliven the monument, but rather to bring out in its animation the experience of the uncanny: strangeness, death, and emptiness. The homeless people in Wodiczko's projections resemble ghosts, excluded from the consciousness of the society, but returning from outside. James E. Young observes that monuments, in their function of commemoration, somehow relieve the perceivers from remembering.[13] Paradoxically, then, I would add that they become sites of non-memory, which has nothing to do with counter-memory – the active process of forgetting. Mute monuments resemble bandaged wounds – an attempt to put closure on social and political traumas. Wodiczko superimposes on them the essential incomprehensibility of trauma hidden in the story or silence of his narrators. The artist listens to the message conveyed by this silence, reopening a wound in his slide and video projections with an effect similar to Roland Barthes's *punctum*.[14]

In *Camera Lucida*, Barthes describes two modes of experiencing photography: *punctum* and *studium*. *Studium* occurs in the field of consciousness, as a matter of general knowledge, mediated and rationalized by moral and political culture. In *studium*, a spectator meets the photographer's intentions: he/she looks for recognizable elements or finds interest in faces, scenes, or acts represented in photography. *Punctum*, on the other hand, distorts the logic of *studium*. It emerges like an arrow from the photographic image and unexpectedly pierces the spectator. The etymologies of 'trauma' and *punctum* have surprisingly much in common.[15] 'Trauma' comes from Greek, and could be translated as wound, damage, hurt. *Punctum* is a Latin word for a point or a moment, but also for a small hole, a puncture, something which is pricked or pierced. If we take the monument as the closure of a collective trauma, or wound, Wodiczko's use of image, photography, and video projection reopens the wound with the help of *punctum* and its puncture. His slide projections, such as the above mentioned second *Homeless Projection* in Boston, might be called punctures in the social body. The unexpected *detournement* performed by an image on the architectural body reveals the void on which democracy (as Claude Lefort states) is founded, and disorients the feeling of belonging to a common world.[16] The monuments – sites of repetitions and returns – are turned into non-sites, heterotopias, where the process of working through becomes possible. The homeless – as foreigners, a scar among citizens – become the messengers who bring 'a different kind of conceptualization of belonging together.'[17]

As Polish art historian and critic Andrzej Turowski notes, it is somehow characteristic that the figure of the migrant is not projected by Wodiczko on buildings or monuments. Instead, the migrant herself is the wearer of projections: her images are projected back on her, expanding her body. Turowski observes that Wodiczko began the *Xenology Series* during his stay in Paris in the early 1990s, at a time when French immigration policy had been sharply restricted. As he observes, *Alien Staff*, the first instrument in the series, was born when the artist himself re-entered the state of being a stranger, and started to conceptualize the notion of the 'Other' during his seminars at the university. Turowski also points out that the most important points of reference for this series of work, implicit in the artist's own comments on these projects, are Julia Kristeva's concepts from her writing published in the late 1980s and early 1990s: *Strangers to Ourselves* (1991) and *Nations without Nationalism* (1993).[18] Kristeva criticizes the politics of integration, understood as the assimilation of migrants into one homogenous culture, within the country of asylum. Referring to the Freudian notion of the *Unheimlich*, Kristeva calls for the right to Otherness, pointing at the Otherness in one's self.[19] The *Xenology Series* is a set of instruments or prosthetics that oppose the politics of assimilation, whereby the Other has to become the same. Started in the early 1990s, the *Xenology Series* consists of four types of instruments: *Alien Staff, Mouthpiece, Dis-Armor*, and *AEgis*, which struggle with the problem of foreigner, the migrant as the figure of Otherness inhabiting relations within the nation-state and the self. Memory in this process plays a crucial role. It becomes a site of exposition which both reveals the subject's vulnerability and enables his/her visibility. Memory itself is by the artist's instruments put in motion: triggered, reassembled, endlessly regained in its various functions such as remembering, recalling, but also forgetting, repressing. It's horizon becomes the future; the past turns into a vanishing point where no one, as Zofia Rosińska writes in her essay in this volume, would like to return.[20]

Alien Staff, which manifested in different versions from 1992 to1996, looks like a giant walking stick. Its top section contains a small screen playing a pre-recorded video of its user, and the central part is 'made up of interchangeable cylindrical containers for the preservation or display of precious relics related to various phases of the owner's immigration history.'[21] The history of the migrant is represented by photos, rejected visa applications, documents, allowances, and little private objects saturated with affect. This collection of objects constructs the ripped narration of the migrant's story and, at the same time, acts as a mnemonic instrument – it makes the memory work, signifies the dramatic turns of the story, acts as a metaphor for unbearable experiences or states of mind, or plays the role of a question mark. One of the *Alien Staff* users, Patricia Pireda, encloses in the container a smashed porcelain cup, which refers to her state of mind or a stage of her life when everything seemed to be fragmented, in the process of destruction.[22] Jagoda Przybylak recalls the experience of being so frightened when she and other women working illegally as cleaning ladies in an office were chased by 'immigration police,' that she did not recognize her face in the mirror. Honza speaks about the stigmatization of Otherness, about being perceived as 'Gypsy,' about introducing himself as Yugoslav while looking for a job. These stories are narrated, in many cases, in two languages: the mother tongue of the narrator and the language of his or her country of asylum. The oscillation between the two languages also signals the 'in-betweenness' of the migrant, of breaking off from one's mother tongue and not being capable of expressing oneself in a foreign language. *Alien Staff* can be interpreted as a prosthetic device enabling the passage from the 'void' described by Julia Kristeva to 'baroque' speech: a step from the realm of silence to a position where gaining meaning becomes possible.[23] The artistic project gives the foreigner 'social standing,' forcing the community not only to listen to the fragmented memory of the Other, but also to recognize the Otherness in one's very self, to reflect on loss and belatedness, the constant movement between 'now' and 'then' on which memory is based.

'Why should one listen to you?' This question, asked by Kristeva in *Strangers to Ourselves*,[24] also accompanies *Porte-Parole* (*Mouthpiece*; created in 1993 and introduced in 1997), a prosthetic device for migrants, whose languages often fail to reveal their memory and who, as the artist claims, are often treated as those with no history. *Porte-Parole* – an instrument with a small monitor and loudspeakers installed in the centre – covers the mouth of its wearer. A video recording of a speaking mouth reiterates the act of speech, but the wearer of *Porte-Parole* remains silent. The pre-recorded act of storytelling is set against the silence of the migrant. The instrument that speaks is also a mask.

Krzysztof Wodiczko, variant of *Alien Staff* (container with relics), 1993. Photo: courtesy of Krzysztof Wodiczko and Profile Foundation.

However, in this case, the mask plays a positive role: it literally enables narration, acting as a literal and metaphorical shelter – for the face of the migrant and for her/his vulnerable subjectivity. As in the case of *Alien Staff*, the aim of *Porte-Parole* is to create a platform for communication between its user and members of the local community, to share and spread the experience of alterity. In a manner similar to Kristeva's analysis of Nabokov's protagonist Sebastien Knight, 'the exile has shattered all sense of belonging' for the narrators of *Alien Staff* and *Porte-Parole*.[25] The narrations enunciate states of disempowerment, of having no control over the course of one's life, and of not being capable of making any plans. At the same time, they are accounts of fragmented memory, memory not successful in reconstructing a fixed image of the past. Nevertheless, none of the *Porte-Parole* and *Alien Staff* users idealize their place of origin – in most narrations, this place is distant or absent. Rather, the feeling of vulnerability comes from the experience described by Julia Creet as the loss of the notion of origin.[26] Paradoxically, then, this experience, in shattering both the unitary and homogenic image of an 'I' and its fixed mnemonic experience as phantasm, makes both memory and identity possible: as fissured and contingent, asynchronic, and based on loss.

If, as Ernst van Alphen states, memory is 'the mutually constitutive interaction between the past and the present, shared as culture but acted out by each of us as individuals,'[27] Wodiczko's instruments enable the memory of the excluded individual to enter the realm of the collective. Using Mieke Bal's distinctions, I would claim, that the artist's instruments attempt to turn the solitary event of traumatic memory (which, as Bal claims, is inflexible and invariable) into a narrative one, which serves a social function. As Bal writes, '... the past makes sense in the present, to others who can understand it, sympathize with it, or respond with astonishment, surprise even horror; narrative memory offers some form of feedback that ratifies the memory.'[28] Drawing on Bal's remarks, I would add that in Wodiczko's works, memory is understood as cultural memory. It is a fragile vehicle for an experience of otherness, but it also requires the other to be narrated to; it is based on an act of active choice, both on the side of the narrator and the listener; it is not given, but rather performed. And last, but not least, it is interpreted not as an individual phenomenon, but rather as constituted by the culture inhabited by the traumatized, migratory subject.[29]

Krzysztof Wodiczko, *Porte-Parole* (mouthpiece in use), 1997. Photo: courtesy of Krzysztof Wodiczko and Profile Foundation.

The problem of the memory of the Other and its relation to official registers of history was introduced by Wodiczko in the show *If you see something ...*, mounted at the Lelong Gallery in New York in November 2005. The title of the show refers to ubiquitous ads on tickets, banners, and the walls of the subway, and to the increasing fear of foreigners after 9/11. On the walls of the gallery, Wodiczko projected a video of huge, frosted windows behind which one could see the shadows of people unfolding personal stories about experiences of the stigmatization of Otherness and confrontations with power. The dark gallery was haunted by these figures and their histories: the broken biographies of migrants, citizens who are perceived as foreigners in their own countries, narrating stories of culturally displaced people. The artist transformed the white cube of the gallery into darkness, into an isolated and closed space, thus creating a model of the psyche, an 'I.' The outside filled the inside, blurring the borders between 'me' and 'them,' private and public, politics and aesthetics. The space of the Lelong Gallery was appropriated by images and sounds referring to memories not officially recognized, neither recorded nor historicized. The memories of traumatic past events triggered in the Lelong Gallery countered the force of the archive, which is constituted by the fundamental repression of memory.[30] As Jacques Derrida states, 'archive,' in its etymology, refers to one of the meanings of *arkhe*: commandment.[31] In ancient Greece, archeions – the superior magistrates – were guardians of the valuable, official documents, which were filed at their houses. Archeions held political power and were considered not only to possess the right to make or represent the law, but also to interpret the archives, that is, history. In effect, writes Derrida, the documents spoke the law – they recalled the law, and called on or imposed it. Thus, writes Derrida, every archive is based on the exclusion implied by such questions as 'What is included in the system?' or 'What comes under personal or intellectual anamnesis?'[32] Wodiczko acts against the violence of the archive. He introduces the memories from which the archive shelters itself, and gives those whose voices have been excluded from the official registers, a chance to speak. By introducing ripped narration and particularity into the public sphere, Wodiczko points at the dimension of authority and power produced by the linear narration of history within the archive, exposing its objectivity as fiction and its truth claims as rhetorical figures.

In all the instruments of the *Xenology Series*, as well as in *If you see something ...*, language plays the crucial role. Language is presented as the sphere of gaining subjectivity, splitting and opening subjects to the outside, and also as an inadequate medium for communicating the experience of Otherness. At the same time, Wodiczko uses language as a tool for transgressing the melancholy, silence, depression, and loneliness of strangers. In *Black Sun*, Kristeva observes that a melancholic person is like a foreigner in their own language.[33] He or she is convinced that there is an abyss between language and experience, and that he or she lacks the ability to verbalize emotions. Language for a melancholic, as for the foreigner, becomes artificial and empty. In a state of narcissistic depression, the patient loses *le signifié*, and 'the possibility of making art, binding spontaneity with control seems to be the most effective means of overcoming the depression, the disguised mourning.'[34] Wodiczko's instruments function as prosthetic devices for speech, triggering a flow of ripped narration that helps to overcome this silence. The stories constructed by the often-silenced migrants could be viewed as an attempt at their own creation and the transgression of suffering into the symbolic order. Wodiczko, whose artistic biography began with the rise of conceptual art very much concerned with the problem of linguistic representation, undertakes a question posed, but not reworked, by conceptual artists in Poland: about the intimate relation between aesthetics and politics, history and memory, language structures and subjectivity.

Krzysztof Wodiczko's projections and instruments transform their users into floating sites of memory, where the pasts of the excluded and silenced are revealed and worked through. The subjects of the artist's actions are all kinds of migrants, homeless people, and strangers – dispossessed from inner unity and integrity, traumatized, disempowered, evicted. Projecting images and giving voice to strangers, the artist mediates between different aspects of Freudian memory: remembering and forgetting, coding and decoding, repression and narration.[35] His projections and instruments, consisting of fragmented recollections and oral histories, force the public into critical readings, not only of their spatial and emotional surroundings, but also of their concepts of history as a linear, objective narrative. The artist causes [e]migration of the well-established almost transparent meanings and histories that articulate public space, calling for the unsettling and migrating memory of those who are never 'at home,' either literally or metaphorically.

NOTES

1 Denis Hollier, *Against Architecture: The Writings of Georges Bataille* (Cambridge, MA: MIT Press, 1992), xi.
2 Julia Kristeva, *Strangers to Ourselves* (New York: Columbia University Press, 1991), 97–8.
3 Krzysztof Wodiczko, *Designs for the Real World* (Vienna: Generali Foundation, 2001), 173.
4 See Julia Creet's countering of these theoretical positions in her Introduction and essay in this volume.
5 Michel Foucault, 'Inne przestrzenie,' *Teksty Drugie* 96, no. 6 (2005): 120.
6 Rosalyn Deutsche, *Evictions: Art and Spatial Politics* (Cambridge MA: MIT Press 2002).
7 See Julia Creet's Introduction to this volume, p. 9.
8 Beatriz Colomina, *Privacy and Publicity: Modern Architecture as Mass Media* (Cambridge, MA: MIT Press, 1994).
9 Creet, Introduction, p. 6.
10 Krzysztof Wodiczko, *Krzysztof Wodiczko: Critical Vehicles, Writings, Projects, Interviews* (Cambridge, MA: MIT Press, 1999), 55.
11 Rosalyn Deutsche, 'Krzysztof Wodiczko's *Homeless Projection* and the Site of Urban "Revitalization,"' *October* 38 (Autumn 1986): 88.

12 Wodiczko, *Wodiczko*, 55.
13 James E. Young, 'Pamięć i kontrpamic ęć: W poszukiwaniu społecznej estetyki pomników Holokaustu,' trans. G. Dąbkowski, *Literatura na świecie*, nos. 1–2 (2004): 271.
14 Roland Barthes, *Światło obrazu* (Warszawa: Wydawnictwo KR, 1996), 48–9.
15 S. Sikora, *Fotografia: między dokumentem a symbolem* (Warszawa: Świat Literacki 2004).
16 For a summary of Claude Lefort concepts, see Deutsche, *Evictions*, 272–5.
17 See Ewa Ziarek's comments on Kristeva's ethics of psychoanalysis, in 'The Uncanny Style of Kristeva's Critique of Nationalism,' *Postmodern Culture* 5, no. 2 (1995).
18 Andrzej Turowski, 'Przemieszczenia i obrazy dialektyczne Krzysztofa Wodiczki,' in *Pomnikoterapia* (Warsaw: Zachęta Gallery, 2005), 51.
19 Kristeva, *Strangers*, 191–2.
20 See Zofia Rosińska's essay in this volume, 'Emigratory Experience: The Melancholy of No Return.'
21 Wodiczko, *Designs for the Real World*, 195.
22 See P. Pireda's comments in *Krzysztof Wodiczko: Sztuka publiczna* (Warszawa: CSW, 1995), 219.
23 Kristeva, *Strangers*, 20–1.
24 Ibid., 20.
25 Ibid., 34.
26 See Creet, Introduction, p. 6.
27 Ernst van Alphen, 'Symptoms of Discursivity: Experience, Memory and Trauma,' in *Acts of Mmemory: Cultural Recall in the Present*, ed. M. Bal, L. Spitzer, and J. Crewe (Hanover and London: University Press of New England, 1999), 37.
28 Mieke Bal, Introduction, in ibid., viii.
29 Ibid., vii, x.
30 See Jacques Derrida, *Archive Fever: A Freudian Impression* (Chicago and London: University of Chicago Press, 1996).
31 Ibid., 1.
32 Ibid., 5.
33 Julia Kristeva, *Black Sun: Depression and Melancholia* (New York: Columbia University Press, 1989).
34 See Tomek Kitliński, *Obcy jest w nas: Kochać według Julii Kristevej* (Kraków: Aureus 2001).
35 For analysis of the Freudian mnemonic experience, see Zofia Rosińska, 'Doświadczenie mnemiczne, czyli fenomen pamięci według Zygmunta Freuda,' *Dialogi* nos. 1–2 (2002): 66–72.

14 The Veiled Room

YVONNE SINGER

All representation – whether in language, narrative, image or recorded sound is based on memory … memory, even and especially in its belatedness is itself based on representation. The past is not simply there in memory but must be articulated to become memory.

– Andreas Huyssen, *Twilight Memories* [1]

Coming of age after … but indelibly shaped by the Holocaust – this generation of artists … does not attempt to represent events it never knew immediately but instead portray its own necessarily hypermediated experiences of memory.

– James E. Young, At Memory's Edge[2]

In her introduction to this collection of essays, Julia Creet asks, 'Does memory only adhere to point of origin?' She asks the reader to consider asking 'different questions of memory, ones that do not attend only to the content of memory but to the travels that have invoked it.' My dilemma is precisely locating and categorizing my memory. What is its point of origin? What is the content of memory that belongs to me and not my parents'? Is it 'real' or 'artificial'? These are the questions that I explore in this essay through my biography and my art practice.

While I have no memories of Hungary, the place of my birth, nor can I speak the language, even tolerably well, some aspects of Hungarian culture were transmitted through my family in Montreal, where I grew up. The stories of 'the war,' in particular, were the backdrop to my childhood in Montreal. I was born in Budapest, Hungary, in November 1944, a turbulent historical moment when Budapest was under siege by the Allied forces and Nazi Germany was in retreat. The bridge between Buda and Pest was blown up the day I was born, and my grandparents narrowly escaped death by missing the streetcar that would have taken them across the river Danube to see their new grandchild. This story, among others that were often retold and informed the family mythology, highlighted narrow escapes from death and underscored the precariousness of life and how fortunate we were to be alive. I was three years old when we left Hungary and six years old when we arrived in Montreal. In between, we lived in Holland and Switzerland, but I have no memory of this time before Montreal. Growing up, I obsessively scanned the family albums seeking to understand where to locate myself.

Family albums are built in the present to document, preserve, and impart private histories and their events, such as births, weddings, graduations, family gatherings, and birthdays, as a public representation. They present an unofficial history of a family or a group, often focused on happy events, while death, violence, and sex are not recorded. The family album has power as nostalgia and often as an idealized representation of a time, place, and people. No one ages and no one dies. Time is arrested in the family album. The stories of my own birth and the photos in the album formed, as James Young says, 'a vicarious past,' which was more real to me than my own experiences.[3] The gaps in these narratives and the significant information that was left out came to light years later, after I had converted to Judaism to marry, only to discover that my family was Jewish after all. My parents, and grandparents who lived with us, successfully hid this fact by giving me a Christian upbringing. If there is a traumatic moment I can claim, it is the discovery of my Jewish identity from a newspaper account in the *Toronto Star* about the Swedish diplomat Raoul Wallenberg's heroic rescue activities in Budapest in 1944.[4] The article also revealed that Wallenberg was my godfather. These revelations provoked many questions and began a quest for answers that took years to discover and unravel, with limited success. I was met with silence by family members, and many gaps and fragments remain in the narratives. The tensions, gaps, and silences created by, in Mieke Bal's words, this 'interaction between past and present': that is the territory that concerns me.[5] I often ask myself, Why am I so obsessed with my past or, rather, my parents' past? Perhaps it is the silences and the crucial bits of information that were left out of family stories, but that nevertheless surface unexpectedly only to provoke more questions.

The growing body of literature concerned with memory, diasporic cultures, and post-Holocaust analysis was unfamiliar to me when I began my work. Over time, I came to read and identify myself with James Young's concept of a 'vicarious past,' Marianne Hirsch's theorization of 'post-memory,' notions of the 'other' by Edward Said, and Susan Suleiman's writings about exiles and creativity.[6] These writers and others inform my ideas and provide a context in which to understand and locate myself and my art practice. In particular, Mieke Bal's elaboration of three categories of memory – cultural memory, narrative memory, and traumatic recall – in her introduction to the collection of essays *Acts of Memory*, makes sense to me in relation to the installations I describe here.[7] For Bal, cultural memory is a cultural phenomenon as well as an individual and social one. It is the 'interaction between present and past [that] is the stuff of cultural memory.' In this context, cultural memory (and cultural forgetting) as cultural phenomenon refers to the culture of anti-Semitism in Hungary and the assimilation of many Hungarian Jews who proudly identified as being first and foremost Hungarians. It is the consequences of anti-Semitism, never stated and even denied, that precipitated my family's emigration to Canada. My experience as an immigrant child is individual yet participates in the collective culture of immigration and the cultural legacy of Jewish assimilation.

Narrative memory, according to Bal, refers to a string of events, selectively chosen and emotionally charged, while traumatic recall refers to traumatic events that remain vivid in the present but are constructed as fragmented narratives that reflect the disassociated or repressed conditions of trauma.[8] The narrative fragments that I construct with the textual, visual, and material elements of the installations I create, function in multiple ways, illustrating Bal's categories, but also blurring the distinctions between them. In some respects, the narratives I construct function as a traumatic recall by the generation coming of age after the Holocaust though, as James Young claims, shaped by it through the narratives and actions of their parents. Traumatic memories, Mieke Bal says, remain vivid 'and/or resist integration ... repression interrupts the flow of narratives that shape memory; disassociation splits off material that cannot then be reincorporated into the main narrative.'[9] This description of traumatic memory can characterize my parents' response to their wartime experiences of dislocation and immigration. For me, traumatic memory has found expression in the repetition and dis-association of fragmented narratives evidenced in my artworks, in which I attempt to fill the memory void. As Andreas Huyssen says, memory 'must be articulated to become memory.'[10]

Julia Creet asks how we understand memory that has migrated or has been exiled from its local habitations? Pierre Nora ties real memory to specific locations. Then how can I understand my memory, which I construct from my parents' memories and transform in the fictional sites of my artworks? If memory is tied to a specific location, according to Pierre Nora, are the sites I construct in my installations unreal or 'artificial memory,' and are the events I describe false history? My father constructed an elaborate fiction. It was hard to deny that they were Hungarian since their accents betrayed their origin, but who would know if they were Jewish or Christian? Can the fictional sites of my artworks construct a new definition of memory, one that is more fluid in relation to its origins and location?

My discussion here will describe the artistic and conceptual strat-egies I used to transform and reconstruct memory and history in the art-making process, in relation to three of my exhibitions: *In Memoriam: Forgetting and Remembering Fragments of History* (1993), *The Veiled Room* (1998), and *Signs of Life: An Intimate Portrait of Someone I Don't Know* (2008). Autobiography is the springboard for the construction of these art installations or situations, which are composed of disparate visual and textual elements that together form a fragmented narrative. The installations/situations are influenced by specific locations. They are conceived as a stage set, but one in which the viewer can enter to have an immersive experience. The premise of my work is that memory is an accumulation of sensory experiences in which 'words and images com-bine to form material thought-images in which narrative and concep-tual material and pictorial elements remain in a permanent fluctuation that eludes any attempt to pin them down.'[11]

Signs of Life: An Intimate Portrait of Someone I Don't Know is a recent exhibition which mines the family archive for material that becomes a device of mediation between art and life. The archive and the album are both repositories of public and private histories, and they speak to the desire to preserve, to collect, and to catalogue. Memory and time are significant in both the archive and album, but each serves different functions and occupies different locations in space, time, and culture. The archive speaks of the past. The act of archiving could proceed from the need to preserve what no longer exists or what is no longer active;

for example, institutional archives often function as a site of authority and power, a place where official documents related to the public and also restricted to the public are kept. Searching the archive is mainly a retrospective project to find meaning in the past in order to comprehend it, or to understand the present in relation to the past. Travel permits and medical charts are examples of the archival materials I used to construct my exhibition. Displaced from their sites of origin and situated in unexpected relationships to one another, I create new narratives that present my version of events. 'By making things strange, the artist does not simply displace them from an everyday context into an artistic framework: he also helps to "return sensation" to life itself, to reinvent the world, to experience it anew.'[12]

The title, *Signs of Life*, refers to the traces we leave behind that often contest what is revealed by both official and personal artifacts. By juxtaposing 1945 post-war travel documents from occupied Europe with handwritten personal recordings of medication, *Signs of Life* constructs a portrait of an individual at the intersection of personal and political history. The installation includes a series of large digital prints of post-war European travel documents, including passports, visas, and transit permits, from 1945 to 1947, a highly detailed handwritten record of medications taken over ten years, and a stainless steel screw used to repair my father's broken hip. These artifacts belonged to my father, and they document a personal story of migration and dislocation. These artifacts also provide social markers of identity: a political record of his journey from post-war Hungary to Canada indicated by official status and personal information such as physical features and date of birth. The record of medications reveals an idiosyncratic system of control over the body and the residue of one person's illness. The hip screw alludes to the body's fragility. Together these different elements provide signs of life, clues to an identity shaped by the intersection of personal, cultural, and political forces, and yet at the same time, an identity that discloses very little.

The original travel documents have been scanned and enlarged, and take the form of digital prints. Juxtaposed with these prints are fifty-five identically framed fragments of paper with densely handwritten notations of dates and graphs, made by my father, tracking his taking of a steroid, prednisone, over a period of almost ten years. The frames are installed butted up against each other to create a solid wall of text. The density of the notations of dates marks the passage of time in a tangible way. The travel documents offer a snapshot of an historical

N⁰ 34429

ALLIED FORCE PERMIT

The bearer of this permit has the permission of the Commanding General Allied Forces to enter the Zone of the Allied Forces in

AUSTRIA

Le titulaire est autorisé d'entrer dans la Zone de l'Armée Alliée en

AUTRICHE

This permit must be produced when required together with the bearer's identity document.
Ce permis doit être présenté à toute demande avec le document d'identité du titulaire.

Allied Forces permit, detail from *Signs of Life: An Intimate Portrait of Someone I Don't Know*, 2008.

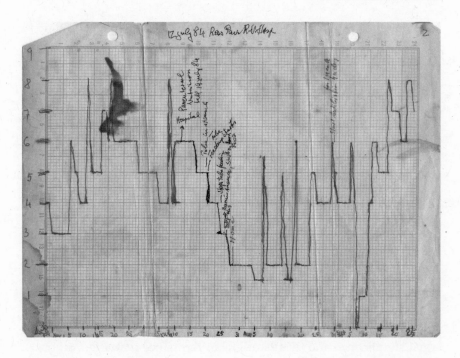

Medical chart, detail from *Signs of Life: An Intimate Portrait of Someone I Don't Know*, 2008.

moment and trace my father's attempts to leave Hungary at a time of political instability after the Second World War when the Allies occupied parts of Europe. Travel permits were difficult to obtain, and travel across the Allied zones was dangerous and dependent on having the right documents. The travel documents provide information about time, place, and destination, but do not reveal why the permits were issued. What was the purpose of his journeys? Why did my father risk travelling alone across occupied Europe in 1946? How did he obtain these permits? What adventures did he have in these travels? Did he survive?

The final element of the installation is a display case containing the stainless steel hip screw that was used to repair my father's broken hip and a glass replica of the same screw. These artifacts and archival materials are unsettling, poignant traces of a life and fragments of a narrative that leave many unanswered questions about my father's life.

The Veiled Room, a site-responsive installation, conceived for the ACC Gallery in Weimar, Germany, in 1998, continues to examine the work of inheritance and the burden of history, probing the relationships that exist between the intimate and the public, between moments of personal significance and events of global resonance that affect all of us. The history of the Weimar Republic is the central trope in this work. The short-lived Weimar Republic existed during a time of great intellectual ferment and creative activity. It was the rise of Hitler that marked the end of this period. The ACC Gallery was located in an old house reputed to be the home of the German poet Johann Wolfgang von Goethe, as well as the location for underground artistic activity during the Russian occupation of East Germany.

The Veiled Room, conceived for a triangular-shaped room in the gallery, was premised on the idea of the layers of history witnessed by the walls of the room. At the ACC Gallery, the viewer entered the small triangular room and was enveloped by the space. At the Red Head Gallery in Toronto, Canada, where it was remounted in 1998, viewers entered the gallery space and walked around the outside of the triangular curtained room to find the entrance. While the viewers were surrounded by the curtained walls, the open ceiling and the semi-opaque curtains allowed them to see the shadows of other visitors in the gallery space, creating a more open, less claustrophobic enclosure than the installation in Germany. The images on pages 272–3 document the remounted exhibition at the Red Head Gallery in Toronto.

Viewers encounter a triangular-shaped room with walls consisting of two layers of diaphanous, opaque white curtains patterned with texts. Situated on the floor at the apex of the triangle, a television monitor silently plays a video that is looping a sequence in which a young attractive couple perform their romance in the form of a mock *Romeo and Juliet* balcony scene for the camera, over and over again. The woman stands behind a railing positioned as if on the edge of a breakwater, with the waves of the sea crashing in the background. The man stands on the stairs below her. With his arms outstretched towards her, he begins to kneel. The man stumbles, and the woman reacts with fear. The man catches himself from falling down the stairs and recovers. They embrace, kiss, and then smiling, turn to the camera. They are forever young and forever smiling at us and at each other. Since the exaggerated style of their acting verges on slapstick, there is a moment in the video when it is not clear whether the man is clowning around or actually sustaining an injury. Even though the catastrophe is averted and the scene ends happily, in this dramatic scenario, the dark shadow of catastrophe pervades the veiled room.

The first layer of the curtain wall contains selected English and German quotations from *Civilization and Its Discontents*, *The Interpretation of Dreams*, *The Ego and the Id*, and *Infantile Genital Organization*, underscoring the importance of the Oedipal conflict in the formation of the child's subjectivity as well as highlighting Freud's argument that civilization is founded upon the conflicts within these family relations. The inside layer of the curtain is marked with the names of German politicians, philosophers, artists, and writers, including: Thomas Mann, Walter Benjamin, Bertolt Brecht, Friedrich Nietzsche, Adolf Hitler, and members of the Bauhaus, including Wassily Kandinsky, Marcel Breuer, Walter Gropius, and Marlene Dietrich. Many of these individuals lived during the turbulent Weimar Republic, or their ideas influenced the art and politics of the time. Arranged in alphabetical order, my choice of names is idiosyncratic. Uniformly printed in a black gothic typeface called *fraktur*, which for me signifies German fascism, the roll call collapses historical distinctions: Holocaust victims, Nazi sympathizers and perpetrators, intellectuals, and artists all receive equal significance. The Weimar Republic was a time of great cultural innovation and ferment. Its collapse precipitated the ascendancy of Hitler and the Nazi party. The couple who appear in the video are marked, although not visibly, by the intellectual and cultural legacy of the Weimar Republic, as well as the subsequent Second World War and Holocaust. The spectre

The Veiled Room (1998), Red Head Gallery, Toronto, Canada. Photo by Isaac Applebaum.

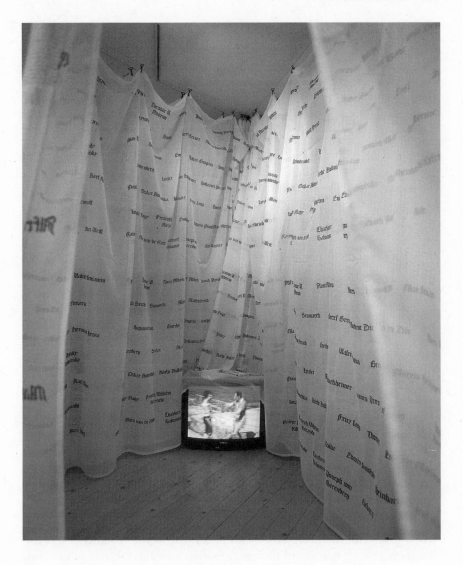

The Veiled Room, detail of interior. Photo by Isaac Applebaum.

of historical catastrophe and exile haunts the space of the veiled room, unsettling the boundaries between normalcy and danger. Other echoes are also suggested as history seeps into the present, imprinting its after-image everywhere.

The couple in the video are my parents on holiday in Rockport, Massachusetts, in the early 1950s. They grew up in a comfortable bourgeois milieu in Budapest, Hungary. The German language and culture were the legacies of the Austro-Hungarian Empire. Here, in *The Veiled Room*, the new world and the old world are juxtaposed. In 1949, they emigrated to Montreal, Canada. Growing up as a Christian in predominantly Jewish neighbourhoods in Montreal, I was awkwardly self-conscious, painfully marked by my difference from the other children, as an immigrant child who didn't speak English. I was between worlds, alienated from the Canadian world of my peers and excluded from the history and culture of my parents, who placed a veil of secrecy on the past. The family album of photographs of my parents' life in Budapest before the war was the stuff of my fantasy and more real to me than my own life.

My memory and its transformation into art is expressed in Marianne Hirsch's definition of 'postmemory':

> Postmemory is a powerful form of memory precisely because its connection to its object or source is mediated not through recollection but through an imaginative investment and creation. Postmemory characterizes the experience of those who grow up dominated by narratives that preceded their birth, whose own belated stories are evacuated by the stories of the previous generation, shaped by traumatic events that can be neither fully understood nor re-created.[13]

The world of my parents that was destroyed was not mine. The world where I found myself was also not mine. I felt invisible, situated between two worlds and without the language to speak either. Discovery of my Jewish identity felt like a kind of coming home. The history of the diasporic Jewish culture in Hungary is my own. It enabled me to claim a space for myself, to collect, connect, and construct the fragments of experiences into some kind of coherent whole. At the same time, I am aware of the elusive, unstable nature of memory, history, and subjectivity. I also want to make this evident in the work I construct in my ongoing project to represent 'the connections between the history of nations and individual biographies; both are ... narratives of identity and personhood that sprang from oblivion, estrangement and loss of memory of home.'[14]

The impetus for the installation *In Memoriam: Forgetting and Remembering Fragments of History* was the invitation for a solo exhibition at the Koffler Gallery in Toronto. Located in the Bathurst Jewish Community Centre, the Koffler Gallery presents a program of contemporary visual art in the context of a health club and community centre. Therefore, in conceiving the exhibition, I was aware of the significant disconnect between the more traditional notions of Jewish culture and the gallery programming. The invitation coincided with the revelation that Raoul Wallenberg, the Swedish diplomat who saved many Jews in Budapest, was my godfather. As a liaison with the underground, my father worked with Wallenberg, but had given me little more information about his activities. My challenge was how to understand my intimate and newly discovered connection to this stranger, who was lost in the Russian Gulag and who was someone I would never meet. How could I translate, transform, and narrate this story in an artistic form? Discontinuity, fracture, contradictions, tensions, an interdisciplinary approach, and estrangement were the artistic devices that informed the elements of this installation and the title, *In Memoriam: Forgetting and Remembering Fragments of History.*

The exhibition occupied two adjoining rooms, which I called *The Felt Room* and *The Glass Room.* Viewers first enter the darkened space of *The Felt Room,* which is a free-standing structure made of thick, dark brown felt, supported by a steel frame and steel cables. There is only one entrance, dimly lit, directing the viewer inside the room, where they encounter an LED board, silently scrolling words in red dots of light, a steel-plated floor, and the musty smell of felt. The text on the LED board is a fragmented narrative about Raoul Wallenberg. It is based on newspaper accounts, hearsay descriptions of him, and rumours about his fate. The words convey both a journalistic and personal tone. This text for the LED was scrolled horizontally from right to left at a steady hypnotic pace, endlessly repeating. Viewers would line up along the narrow entrance in silence, never venturing inside the room. They experienced *The Felt Room* as a space of estrangement, dislocation, and anxiety.

LISTEN CAREFULLY......
THIS IS......IMPORTANT...............
LOOK AT ME, WATCH ME............
SWEDISH DIPLOMAT..................
SAVES...............100,000 JEWS IN BUDAPEST............................

RAOUL WALLENBERG...............SCION OF A WEALTHY FAMILY......................

AND A.........NON-JEW.........

AT GREAT PERSONAL RISK...........................

SINGLE-HANDEDLY SAVED MORE JEWS THAN WHOLE GOVERNMENTS................

THIS 'ANGEL OF RESCUE' WAS KIDNAPPED BY THE RED ARMY

AND NEVER SEEN AGAIN OUTSIDE A SOVIET PRISON...............................

SORRY.................I........................CAN'T.......................................

HEAR

YOU........................... SORRY......................SORRY.......................

I CAN'T SEE

YOU...

WALLENBERG DIDN'T LOOK LIKE A HERO...

HE WAS NOT THE SQUARE-JAW TYPE..

HIS SLIGHTLY BALDING HEAD MADE HIM LOOK TOO YOUNG AND

SENSITIVE..

FOR THE NIGHTMARISH JOB AHEAD..

CLASSMATES RECALL HIM AS WARM AND FRIENDLY, NOT SNOBBISH...............

HE WAS NOT FEARLESS BY NATURE..

I AM TELLING YOU A STORY WHICH I CANNOT TELL..................................

(I HAVE BEEN SWORN TO SECRECY).......................................

WE LISTEN WE HEAR WE SPEAK

WE SPEAK WE HEAR WE LISTEN

WE LISTEN WE HEAR WE SPEAK..

SOME BELIEVE IT IMPOSSIBLE TO SURVIVE SOVIET PRISON FOR SO MANY

YEARS...

OTHERS BELIEVE A MAN LIKE WALLENBERG MIGHT.....................................

DIDN'T LOOK LIKE A HERO...................................

OVERLY PROMINENT NOSE.........WEAK CHIN..

THINNING HAIR.........TOO SOFT......TOO CEREBRAL...............................

I..............WAS....................................TRYING TO...............................

FORGET...............NO..............I MEAN.................

I...................................WAS..

TRYING TO..REMEMBER.................

AND..IN JULY 1944..................................

AT THE AGE OF 32.....................THIS SCION OF AN ARISTOCRATIC FAMILY

....................OF SWEDISH LUTHERANS....................................

....................BANKERS AND INDUSTRIALISTS............................

HE HAD A CONSUMING SENSE OF DUTY

HE WAS A DRIVEN MAN

HE WAS A GREAT ACTOR AND COULD IMITATE BRILLIANTLY........................

MYSTERY SURROUNDS THE FATE OF THE SWEDE WHO SAVED THE JEWS

............................SORRY...............................I..............................

.................FORGOT...........................SORRY..............I.....................

CAN'T........................ REMEMBER.....................AND...........................

IN THE PRIVACY OF EMPTY ROOMS..

I...YOU...

The experience of fragmented narrative memory is echoed and re-inforced by a different situation in the adjoining space of *The Glass Room*. In contrast to *The Felt Room*, viewers encounter a brighter but emptier space, occupied by only two walls of glass shelves. On one wall is a single glass shelf, *The Grandfather Shelf*, lit by a naked light bulb suspended overhead and illuminating words reflected in shadow on the wall. On an adjacent wall are multiple glass shelves with single words projected in shadow on the wall.

The Grandfather Shelf describes a recurring fantasy and anxiety from my childhood. My grandfather was never in prison and, in fact, survived the war and emigrated to Montreal. Language was a barrier between us, and our communication was limited. My knowledge of his past was mediated by the stories told to me by my parents.

Language and memory are in a dialectical relationship. The shadowy texts on the wall in the series of the glass shelves in *The Glass Room* are composed of fragments: nouns, pronouns, negations, verbs, and interrogatory words. They can be read in any number of ways and in any direction to construct meaning.

Text for multiple glass shelves:

	where		*why*
are	*can't*	*don't*	*won't*
you	*I*	*you*	
?	*see*	*hear*	*understand*

Text for *The Grandfather Shelf*:

When I was younger, I always had fantasies about what it would be like to be in solitary confinement. I would imagine my restricted cell, with a cement floor, stone walls, a small grilled window too high to reach, and I would imagine how I would pass the time. Would I have enough resources

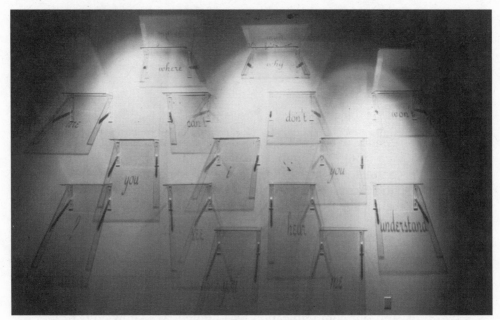

In Memoriam: Forgetting and Remembering Fragments of History, detail: multiple glass shelves. Photo by Isaac Applebaum.

inside my head to keep me going? How many songs and poems could I remember? I was told that my grandfather had a prodigious memory. He could remember all the words to over 100 songs and could speak several languages. I thought, he would do well in solitary confinement.

The hallmarks of Mieke Bal's tripartite model of memory – cultural memory, narrative memory, and traumatic recall – are played out in the works I have described. The memories and histories in the exhibitions *Signs of Life*, *In Memoriam*, and *The Veiled Room* support the theoretical understanding of memory as a cultural construct, rather than 'simply a retrieval and storage system of the past.'[15] The idea that memory is active, that we perform memory, implies that it takes place in the present as well as the past. Narrative memory, 'the action of telling a story,'[16] gives shape and order to events in the past as they are recalled in the present. My exhibitions consider these ideas of memory for myself, and for the viewer, whose presence is an important component of the work. As an extension of myself, viewers are also the nexus of their own past and present histories. They participate as witnesses, and their memories and histories are mediated and re-mediated through mine, as mine are by our collective cultural memory.

NOTES

1 Andreas Huyssen, *Twilight Memories: Marking Time in a Culture of Amnesia* (New York and London: Routledge, 1995), 2–3.
2 James E. Young, *At Memory's Edge: After-Images of the Holocaust in Contemporary Art and Architecture* (New Haven: Yale University Press, 2000), 1.
3 Ibid., 2
4 Ellie Tesher, 'Is "Scarlet Pimpernel" Still Alive?' *Toronto Star*, 20 October 1979, A10.
5 Mieke Bal, Johnathan Crewe, and Leo Spitzer, eds, *Acts of Memory: Cultural Recall in the Present* (Hanover: University Press of New England, 1999), vii.
6 See Young, *At Memory's Edge*; Marianne Hirsch, *Family Frames: Photography, Narrative and Postmemory* (Cambridge: Harvard University Press, 1997); Edward Said 'Reflections on Exile' (1984), in *Altogether Elsewhere: Writers on Exile*, ed. Marc Robinson (Boston and London: Faber and Faber, 1994), 137–49; and Susan Rubin Suleiman, ed., *Exile and Creativity: Signposts, Travelers, Outsiders, Backward Glances* (Durham, NC: Duke University Press, 1998).
7 Bal et al., eds, *Acts of Memory*, vii-viii.
8 Ibid., vii.
9 Ibid., ix.
10 Huyssen, *Twilight Memories*, 3.
11 Ibid., 237.
12 Suleiman, ed., *Exile and Creativity*, 245.
13 Hirsch, *Family Frames*, 22
14 Svetlana Boym, 'Estrangement as a Lifestyle: Shklowsky and Brodsky,' in Suleiman, ed., *Exile and Creativity*, 242–3.
15 Bal et al., eds, *Acts of Memory*, viii.
16 Ibid., 39.

15 The Archive as Temporary Abode

JULIA CREET

As with so many of the papers in this collection, this one too starts from a case study, in this instance, a history close to home. It is an end, not only for this collection but also, I hope, of a long expedition to read coded memories left by my mother, an immigrant who desperately wanted to forget a past and a place that she remembered compulsively. My quest will end with the deposition of her papers, the moment at which my siblings and I will relinquish her documentary by-products and our complicated memorial exercises to the holdings of an archive – or several. The decisions made along the way will donate her testimony and confine her memory to history in ways she might have never anticipated or wanted, and our competing interests in preserving particular parts of her might scatter her papers, sending her traces back to places from which she barely escaped or didn't. A Hungarian Holocaust survivor – among other things – my mother, Magda Creet, decided after the war that she was no longer a Jew, hiding the history of the family she had lost in concentration camps. The better part of her adult life was spent in Kingston, Canada, a place she dreamed she might leave one day, but never did. One option is to return part of her papers to Hungary, the nation that betrayed her, or another, to a Jewish archive, an identity she disavowed. In the end, does memory belong to the one who lived it or to the places in which it is preserved?

A fitting conclusion to a collection about memory and migration is a discussion of the last stage of memory, when it ends in the archives, transformed from the fluidity of the present into the stasis of documents, which as much as they attest to the existence of a past, anticipate the needs of the future, propelling memory forward. In the context of our theme of memory and migration, some very specific questions arise about the relationship of fixity and motion for the immigrant archive: Should the records of the immigrant be returned to his or her country of origin? Or, forever housed wherever she or he last arrived? Is the record of a life lived in several languages best kept together as a documentary by-product of 'the totality of a life' – a useful archival illusion – or split according to the ideal of access? In other words, which is more important to the memory of an immigrant and her nations: what she left behind or where she came to rest? Can archives provide a context to the memory of migration when so much about living in the host country could not? Or, must the archive, too, always be resigned to 'the wrong side of the ocean'?[1]

For Canada, a country whose national identity has been built on waves of migration and whose national memory is constantly challenged by the necessity of recording multiplicity, these are not idle questions; these are some of the questions that have formed the nexus of discussions about the creation and preservation of Canadian 'heritage' (and thus the formation of national identity) in Canadian archival circles for the last forty years.[2] We are, in Pierre Nora's sense, a nation without a 'place of memory,' but, rather, one full of places, absent, imagined, and gathered under the Canadian flag. Paul Ricoeur is helpful here in his gloss on Nora's now well-worn phrase 'lieux de memoire,' which, Nora argued, surfaced as a historicization when real environments of memory had disappeared. Ricoeur writes that 'place' for Nora is 'not solely nor even a matter of topographical place but of external marks as in Plato's *Phaedrus*, from which social behaviours can draw support or their everyday transactions … the republican calendar – external grid of social time – and the flag – national emblem offered to all.'[3] Further, displacement, and its concomitant loss of environment, memory, and flag of origin, has produced a massive demand for evidence of the past, invigorating the mission of every archive that keeps vital statistics. As much as the archive becomes a substitute for social and family memory in the form of administrative records, it also holds out a cure in the sense that it guarantees a permanent home, or at least the fantasy of one – records preserved in perpetuity, long after individual and communal memory have disappeared entirely.

This desire to archive my mother's traces surely constitutes an acting out of the melancholia described by Zofia Rosińska, for which the archive provides the *pharmakon*, both the poison (a substitute for memory) and the possible cure (as an aid to remembering). Ricoeur makes the provocative suggestion, in his exploration of the inextricable relationship between testimony and the epistemology of history, that the crises of testimony itself (the truth of the document) may contribute to the healing of memory by 'linking the work of remembering to that of mourning.'[4] While historical criticism has questioned the trustworthiness of spontaneous testimony, it has, through the 'confrontation between discordant testimonies,' reinforced the role of spontaneous testimony in the process of establishing a probable, plausible narrative. So, the archive might well hold some kind of cure for the melancholies of memory, but does that cure necessarily produce history? Is memory to history a one-way street? Or, can archived testimony be re-assimilated as remembering, particularly as a product of working through discordant documentary traces?

We have already migrated from memory to the uses and abuses of history and back again in any number of essays in this collection, but here I want to think about that process of archivization and how it at once fixes memory into the first writing 'phase,' to use Ricoeur's word, of history, while, at the same time, enacts another kind of memorial migration, in the case of personal papers, from private to public, institutionally constrained, but kept in circulation in perpetuity (theoretically). The archive is the threshold in the transfer of memory to history in the sense that historiography begins in the archive. I turn to the clarity of Ricoeur, who begins his discourse on history and epistemology with an observation that the primary difference between memory and history is not one of inaccuracy versus accuracy or truth, but one of *graphés*:

> Writing, in effect, is the threshold of language that historical knowing has already crossed, in distancing itself from memory to undertake the threefold adventure of archival research, explanation, and representation. History is writing from one end to another. And, in this regard, archives constitute the first writing that confronts history, before it completes itself in the literary mode of 'scripturality.'[5]

Moreover, he remarks, in history we see the resurgence 'of the aporias of memory in their cognitive and practical aspects, principally the aporia of the representation of an absent something that once happened, along with that of the use and abuse to which memory lends itself as actively exercised and practiced.'[6] John Sundholm's contribution to this volume comes to mind here, given his reading of the narrative of the 'Unknown Soldier' as a practised collective response that fills an aporetic trauma with palatable memorial representation.

Mine is a family memory built almost exclusively from aporias and archives, prosthetic in every sense, physically and psychically, and I am intimately acquainted with the lures and the traps of the trace. We, my mother's Canadian family, had no idea that she had ever been Jewish, nor what had happened to her, nor what had happened to her immediate family, all of whom she had lost in concentration camps. In the late 1960s, she wrote an opaque memoir about an unnamed girl, growing up in an unnamed place in an unspecified time, which she sent to thirty publishers without success. Shortly before her death, her Jewish past surfaced rumour-like, though still unspeakable.

After her death, with little other than her memoir and her paper by-products to guide me, I went to Hungary, and would return again and again, to reconstruct her family and her world. In Székesfehérvár, the town in which she had grown up, I found in the county archive seven archive boxes of papers that had been left in the family home, most of them the manuscripts of her father, Oszkár György, a Hungarian poet and translator. The boxes were the property of the county archives. The nation had killed the man, but preserved his papers. In her case, she had hidden her past, but forged a documentary trail. This begs a question that I will return to later in this essay: Once memory has become an archival trace, can it ever be retrieved as memory, or can it only be read and written into history? The organization of Ricoeur's argument suggests that the conversion of memory to history is unidirectional, that though memory and history share very similar aporias, the threshold is the document, particularly those documents that testify to events.

What role, then, does the process of deposition play in the formation of collective memory? How are we to think about this moment when one both fixes the record and impels forward the memorial momentum of an individual or a fading collectivity? What is still at home is a collection of papers, scriptural in every sense, which elucidates some of these complexities with respect to a family born of immigrants. In the process of archivization, these papers will be subject to administrative practices, which may or may not finally resolve some of the melancholic obsessions born of displacement and disavowal. Place, emblematic, geographic, and national, is both the start and end of memory. The where and why of 'which archive?' will have everything to do with how I have read and written my mother's record, and if and how it might be read in the future.

Two deposition decisions will occupy the rest of this paper. First, do Magda Creet's papers have historical value? Second, should her papers be archived as an integrated whole, or housed where they will be most useful and accessible? Archival theory has avoided, until relatively recently, the question of the historical value of personal papers. The administrative-juridical character of the archive still frames the institutional process of selection and arrangement, making the selection criteria and value of personal papers difficult to rationalize. In this respect, the memory/history divide is both a product and perpetuator of the idea of the 'unbiased' historical document. Archivists who do work with 'manuscripts' weigh the value of storage space against the value of personal papers for future researchers. A *fonds* that is never accessed, will, in effect, never be written into the historical record.[7] The argument for depositing them as an integrated whole derives from the idea that a *fonds* should reflect the 'person in documentary form' as an 'organic accumulation of documents, the by-products of ordinary life and business.'[8] But, in the case of a life fractured and compartmentalized by a history of trauma and migration, the manner in which we assess value has everything to do with place and will (re)construct her memory in perpetuity according to the institution in which we deposit (the term itself suggesting fixity) them, enacting the violence inherent in the process of archivization itself.

I take viscerally Jacque Derrida's observation in *Archive Fever* that personal documents in archives are held under 'house arrest.' Once private ephemera of private lives, archived papers become public documents held under institutional restraints, the institutionalization of domesticity locking lives in boxes. A necessary trade-off, we might say, in order to allow researchers to mine these long-dead souls (sometimes not so long dead, sometimes not dead at all) for their historical relevance and revelations. No longer just the traces of a life lived, archived papers become public documents, and their writers become public figures by virtue of their textual traces rather than their worldly accomplishments, though worldly accomplishments are often the rationale for gathering up the traces to begin with. The archive is both acquisitive and somewhat prurient in its anticipation of future users. And yet this is not the only set of imaginary values at work, for the various possibilities of archiving would create a very different record of her life depending on whether we decide in favour of the historical value of her papers or the memorialization of her image and her self-image. This split is best illustrated by the path of her migrations that provoked and allowed her to segment her life in the first place, which leads us directly to the most controversial contents of her boxes.

The bulk of her documents are letters, some packaged when she left England in 1957 and still taped closed, and some filed in accordion folders according to the correspondent or group of correspondents. She labelled the packages 'Old boyfriends,' 'Old girlfriends,' 'Imre Farkas from Pécs,' 'Zsuzsi Fabini from Budapest,' etc. Most of the letters in both filing systems (if we can call them that) were written in Hungarian. I don't read Hungarian, or at least I didn't read it at all when I became feverish with the need to reconstruct my mother's life. In the wake of an expressive life in English, which she had tried to publish, but never successfully, and a secret life in Hungarian, the letters became the focal point of my research, but only after a series of research accidents made me reconsider their worth. The letters were not written, of course, by her, but by her correspondents, and so at the beginning I doubted they would tell me much. Nonetheless, the bulk and longevity of the collections alone told me a great deal about her other life. Imre Farkas, her first husband, had written to her for forty years, but I couldn't have told you about what.

The earliest documents in her boxes are dated from 1945. This fact suggests two things: that she had lost everything that had come before, having been deported and then stripped of all her possessions in June of 1944; and that she was determined to keep as much as she could of what came after. The very earliest documents are tightly folded love notes in Italian, passed to her from two male prisoners in the forced-labour camp in Lippstadt, Germany, between November 1944 and March 1945. Immediately after her liberation in April 1945 through to November of that year, she wrote diaries, on scarce paper in various forms. These, too, are in Hungarian. In September of 1945, Imre Farkas, her then husband, who had been interned in an army labour battalion in Székesfehérvár from which he successfully escaped, returns physically unharmed to Székesfehérvár immediately after the war, hears she's alive, and sends his first letter to her. He tells her not to come back. Their marriage is over; her family are all dead; there is nothing left for her in Székesfehérvár.

About five years into my research, I went looking for a photograph of Imre for the documentary version of this story, and was led to a suitcase in an attic in Budapest, which contained, among Imre's last paper traces, my mother's side of their life-long correspondence. In her reply to his first letter, written in October 1945 from Kaunitz, Germany, where she is now a 'displaced person,' though she never calls herself that, she tells him the tragedy that beset her and her family on the train platform at Auschwitz – the story she could never bring herself to tell us, her second family. Translated for me, this letter became my macabre Rosetta stone; clearly her letters, both the ones written by her and to her, were the key to a story that had eluded my grasp for many years. Imre responds with a typed 10,000–word opus, in which he describes his absolute desperation in the days after the transports left Székesfehérvár, his escape from the labour battalion, his fifty-five days hiding in a hayloft, the immediate post-war conditions in Székesfehérvár, who has returned and who hasn't, how he feels about living among the Christian neighbours who betrayed them, and how his membership in the Communist Party has allowed him to attain the political success he always wanted – though it means little to him now – including a role with the police commission charged with exacting justice. I had the first two years of their correspondence transcribed and translated, a laborious and expensive process. In 1946, she writes to Imre asking that he remove her from the list of the Jewish community. He writes back that no list of the living exists, only a long list of the people who have perished. Her letters chart the beginning of her survival strategy: she sheds her previous identity, and a few years later, with my father's encouragement, tries to forget whom and what she has lost. Yet, she continues her correspondence with Imre and her remaining Hungarian friends, and it becomes the place in which she is able to maintain a relationship with the past in a language she is sure none of her current family will ever be able to read. The correspondence with Imre continues until her death, forty years later, amounting to hundreds of letters.

It is rare to have both sides of a correspondence like this, the early letters, in particular, which describe at length the post-war conditions in Hungary and Germany and the fate of survivors who have returned or are moving on. Tibor Szezler, the man who discovered my mother's letters in his attic, is a lawyer centrally involved with documenting anti-Semitism in post-'89 Hungary. He graciously relinquished any claim to the correspondence, but asked me to consider depositing both sides of the correspondence in the archives of the Budapest Holocaust Memorial Centre.[9] I thought the Open Society Archives at the Central and Eastern European University might be an alternative (they meticulously photocopied the first three years of letters for me). And here the complicated decisions begin.

The historical value of this correspondence relies very much on making both sides accessible to researchers. The letters should be housed together, but where? What would it mean to return my mother's letters to Hungary (now that I have taken them out) and to an explicitly Jewish archive? Would this not enact symbolically the very worst of my mother's fears and literalize Derrida's metaphor? Does the research value of the letters outweigh her obvious wish to leave the past behind? Is this the part of her life that she would have wanted to enter the public record? Disingenuous questions perhaps since I have already made her life public. My mother's disavowals were very much the pattern for Hungarian Jews. Whether they were interned internally, returned after being deported, or never went back, many denied their past, partly as a consequence of a post-war communist antipathy to religion, in general, partly because they had been largely assimilated before the war, partly because they feared for their lives and the future, partly because of internalized anti-Semitism, and partly because they simply wanted to forget.[10] Given a combination of a community that barely survived, an upswing in anti-Semitism post-1989, and a general amnesia about the role of the Hungarian government and population in the swiftest deportations of any Jewish population in Europe, the letters would be most powerfully testimonial in their national historical context, readily accessible to those researchers most interested in Hungarian history and proficient in a very difficult language.

Remarkably, these early letters were carried by hand between Kaunitz, Germany, and Székesfehérvár in the immediate post-war period. Subsequent letters document her exuberant partying with the American and British soldiers who liberated her, Imre's exacting revenge in his new role as the post-war police commandant for Székesfehérvár, and the end of their marriage. As a description of people, places, and a time deeply torn, and the strange immediacy of a return to normalcy, these letters constitute a testimony of Second World War Hungary and its brutalities, and they belong there. They are exactly what Ricoeur argues is the ideal content of the archive: testimony. To leave her letters to Hungary, however, would be to return her in some fantasmatic fashion, or at least the knowledge of her, to a place that severed her. And, as Jewish testimony in the Hungarian Holocaust Archives? Given her attachment to Christianity and the depth of her secrecy about her past, I have a feeling she would torment me for the rest of my days.

Future interest and accessibility (the ability for the archive to be read) are two key determinants of the selection criteria for any archive. Should Imre's letters, which both testify to his time and keep alive a dwindling exercise in collective memory for my mother, be returned to

Hungary, where my mother's letters were found? If the correspondence is reunited, then one side or the other will be 'remigrated.' In the end, we would not be returning anything of our mother to Hungary; more properly to Veronika Zangl's terms, by her letters, her textual by-products, Magda Creet had been remigrating from Canada to Hungary all these years. Her letters arrived into the Hungarian record, and there they should be preserved. And, by the letter of the law (lest we forget that archives are more properly the letters of the law),[11] her letters do not actually belong to us, to deposit them where we would. The physical letters are the property of the receiver, while copyright remains in the estate of the writer. So, her letters belong to the estate of Imre Farkas, while his belong to her estate. Letters received rather than letters written (though some writers, conscious of their own importance, keep copies) mean, to prove Maurice Halbwachs's argument, that even many of the documentary by-products of a life are collective; rarely, if ever, is memory exclusively individual.[12] Clearly, theirs is a collective memory and some arrangement must be made to house these letters together, even if it is an artificial arrangement uniting a correspondence that was written and received countries and continents apart, and uniting the testimony of a couple who only ever saw each other again for three days after they were forcibly separated in June of 1944.

But, were we to archive the letters together in Hungary (regardless of the artificiality of reuniting them), we come up against an ethical principle of the archive, *respect des fonds*. The archive should reflect the whole of a life, for completeness is always the fantasy of the archive and the archive itself selects what constitutes the documentary wholeness of a life. The facets of my mother's papers, the traces of her deportation, exiles, and migrations – Hungary to Poland to Germany to England to Canada – constitute the whole of her life, if only in the manner of back-shadowing. The highest value in a personal fonds of this kind are the things that map a life: biographical facts, memoirs, and paired correspondence (dialogue is the most valuable; otherwise, the subject is only ever mirrored in letters from others).

To clarify some of the deposition issues and options, and to test the waters at various Canadian archives, I discussed my mother's papers and the deposition process with archivists at three university archives and the national archives of Canada. 'The best archives are the ones that hit you right here,' said Dr Carl Spadoni, director of the William Ready Archives at McMaster University, touching his hand to his heart, having just read from Vera Brittain's diary the moment when she finds out that her fiancée has been killed in combat. The value of the historical record is not, in his estimation, in the grocery lists – something we might arguably find enormously interesting in women's archives – but the extraordinary moments of ordinary lives. Though, even here, the extraordinary moments of some ordinary lives might be considered more or less valuable for collective memory than others, as Andreas Kitzmann elucidates so carefully in his recording of the memories of the survivors of the *Vertreibung*.[13] So, is the letter that describes the devastating events on the platform at Auschwitz, the single most important piece of my mother's ephemera? It was, indeed, enormously important to me when I found it, and it justified years of frustrating and sometimes fruitless research, as the payoff of a detective story that drives so many of our hours with papers. In my case, much of that time was spent in Hungarian Archive holdings that I could treat only as an exercise in 'diplomatics,' of reading by form and function, which, for most Canadian researchers, we can assume, would be the manner in which they would interact with these letters.[14] When I held her letters for the first time, I had no idea what they said. The dates, the lengths, the density of the writing, in pencil, written all the way to the margin, two-sided, making best use of scarce paper, all told me something, but the content was only slowly decipherable. But, the letters are only one part of my mother's life and certainly not the part that she would have wanted to be public. Does my Rosetta-stone letter have significance as a single item, as part of a correspondence, or does its importance accrue in the context of a *fonds*? Is it the extraordinary or the ordinary, the most traumatic slice of life or the reconstitution of one that constitutes the value of a record? Both, together, it seems obvious.

The larger part of my mother's life was spent in Kingston, Ontario, a place in which she never quite belonged. She had four children and wanted very much to have the life of a writer, succeeding to a measured extent. Her greater talent lay in her photographic eye. She began to photograph the 'old stones' of Kingston, those old faces known and unknown who formed the living memory of the city. From there she built a portrait studio, in which she did character studies in black and white. The very public part of her papers contains twenty years of her photographic work, about a thousand negatives and three-hundred portraits, some stunning, some awkward, some penetrating, which the mice at the farmhouse where all of this is currently stored have found quite appetizing. She said that photography had allowed her to see the beauty in people, while in writing she saw only the grotesque. And then her other ephemera: clippings, manuscripts, rejection letters, poems, letters, daybooks, lists, letters from my father, our letters to her, etc. Is her life in Kingston any less substantial than her previous lives? Should her later material traces be separated from her earlier? Once again, an ethical archive would argue no, that the organic whole is the best record of a life, an ideal that binds most university archives to non-competition. The traces of her migrations should be, logically, included in her accumulation (minus, in strict terms, the letters she wrote). So, then, the question becomes what archives would be the appropriate place for everything, her Kingston life and her Hungarian past, which would otherwise remain compartmentalized? Queen's University in Kingston might seem like a logical answer. A few of my father's papers are there, primarily his research for a book on Sir Sanford Fleming. My father took to history after a half-life as a chemical engineer and happily spent his later years managing the university records in the Queen's archives. So Magda and Mario could be reunited. They were, after all, married for thirty years, and her life in Kingston was intimately his, though housing her in perpetuity with one husband or the other seems pre-feminist. We would, I think, have to excise a significant bundle of letters from my father, letters he would have hated being part of the public record. No, my preference would not be Queen's, though Paul Banfield, the archivist who took over from my father, would gladly take everything.

Most important, surely, is the question of linguistic access and historical value, and yet, without question, her photographic record should stay in Kingston, for she photographed a significant section of the city's artistic and professional class. This was her most public exercise – an exercise in recording the moment that ensured her work would become part of the family memory of hundreds of other people. These photographs would be worth very little anywhere but Kingston, and the question of value, as I argue in the Introduction, must never be far from any discussion of why we keep what we do or remember what we do. Value – whose lives we value, what moments we value, what research value we imagine, what monetary value we ascribe – is what determines selection and preservation in the archive and, before that, memory (but, perhaps, strictly speaking, only in the sense of *ars memoria*, practised memory and not involuntary memory). The value of memory is what determines the future of history and the history of the future. The portraits she took, as a collection an explicit repository of collective memory, will have a longer memory-life in Kingston than anywhere else and thus, there, the most value, which returns us, to some degree, to Nora's claim that memory is of a piece with place, if only because it is most valued there, which belies his argument about the unselfconsciousness of true memory.

Here, we arrive at the marketplace of memory. Canadian archives acquire the bulk of their private papers through donations, usually before the subject dies. In exchange, the archive issues a tax receipt for the market value of the papers. How would an archive establish such a value? Does market value have anything to do with the ethical value of memory, as Tomasz Mazur framed it so elegantly in his opening essay to this section? What will we sacrifice of our potential profit to archive her papers as a whole? What would be the value of the portraits were they to leave Kingston? Or the value of the letters, were they to stay? And what value might her papers have beyond Kingston, particularly those in Hungarian? With these questions of geographic, ethical, and monetary value in mind, it is worth a small detour here into the broader issues of immigrant memories in Canada.

Place as a solidification of ineffable environments of memory under the sign of a recent flag[15] is an idea that has undergone intense administrative discussion in Canada. In 1972, Public Archives Canada established the National Ethnic Archives,[16] broadening their collections in response to the new official policy of multiculturalism that declared the need to tie national identity to the memory of immigrants. Under the aegis of a theory of the 'total archive,'[17] record selection was to reflect horizontally the entire political and ethnic spectrum, including official and private records of 'national significance' in every medium. This overarching selection criterion posed a set of troubling questions: What was significantly Canadian? How do you define 'national'? This policy was the beginning of a concerted effort to tie the history of Canada, which, aside from the elided histories of indigenous peoples, was a history of immigration, to that quintessential Canadian question: 'Who are we?' The Ethnic Archive was divided into geographic sections defined by country of origin and region of Canada, and by religious affiliation, Doukhobor and Jewish, in particular. In a hit-and-miss effort to represent the diversity of the country and the specificity of the memories and histories of each of its constitutive groups with respect to issues of exile, integration, assimilation, and discrimination, the National Archive solicited the papers of individuals involved in ethnic political organizations in contact with the federal government, such as, for example, the Polish-Canadian Congress. The federal government

encouraged ethnic-based organizations as a means of fostering autonomy and democracy, and archived their materials as a certification of
their 'Canadianness,' collecting materials for the first time in 'non-
official languages,' any language other than English or French. But
many groups distrusted the archives of a country that had done their
communities grave injustices in the past, such as Japanese Canadians,
who had been interned as enemy aliens during the Second World War,
Chinese Canadians, who had been charged the notorious 'head-tax'
earlier in the century, and Jewish Canadians, who had pleaded to no
avail to the government to open its doors at a critical time.[18] Some visible minorities – blacks in Canada had never been well represented –
and newer immigrant groups, such as the Sikhs, also proved resistant,
as did 'exile' organizations, which were still illegal in their countries of
origins (and sometimes Canada). Problems with the ideal of a 'total
archive' surfaced particularly around the practicalities of space and linguistic access to non-official languages. By the second or third generation, a group of immigrants had usually lost its language, and if the
mode of the archive was to think fifty years ahead, then a salient question would be: Who would still be capable of reading these papers fifty
years hence? Exactly the question around which my deliberations about
my mother's papers have circulated.

   In the early 2000s, the ethos has shifted again, now to an emphasis on
a more singular Canadian identity. The concept of the 'total archive'
was on the losing side of a discussion that wanted the archive to revert
to its traditional status as a house of juridical and government records,
avoiding the administrative and preservation problems of the *hoi polloi*
who might declare themselves worthy of deposition. A theory of records management had to constrain the impossible idea of the total
archive. In 2004, the words 'national significance' were removed from
the new Library and Archives Canada Act, and the Ethnic Archive was
folded back into that new administrative body established by the Act.
Well-represented groups, particularly from Eastern Europe, are no
longer solicited to donate, and though the National Archive acknowledges it still has gaps, it has started to encourage community archives
to do the work of regional memory. Some ethnic archives, such as those
of the Latvian-Canadian community, are debating whether or not to
send their collections back from whence their citizens left – a posthu-
mous form of remigration.[19] Archives, it turns out, are themselves mobile. The question of archival remigration raises another, which I won't

address here, the question of how much of the memory of Old World nations might have migrated along with their émigrés.

Concurrent with the shift away from a total archive of national significance, Archives Canada, responding to the interests and needs of its researchers, opened a genealogy wing in 2003, which now sees 50 per cent of the research traffic in Library and Archives Canada. Personal and familial reconstruction, as Pierre Nora also scathingly observed in the European case,[20] the restoration of family memory (in which administrative archives are much more useful than personal papers, oddly enough), is now a major function of the Canadian national archives.

So, would my mother's paper be of value to Archives Canada? If I expressed an interest in depositing them there, explained Myron Momryk, the archivist responsible for East European groups in the Ethnic Archives Program and the director of the subsequent Multicultural Archives Program prior to his retirement, Archives Canada would assemble a panel of experts from the Hungarian-Canadian Jewish community (Canada specializes in narrowing bands of identity based on origin) whose task it would be to examine the contents of her papers in order to assess their historical and monetary value. Each member of the panel would then ascribe a value, revealing their estimates in a gesture similar to that of a card game. High and low would argue their case, and in the end some consensus would be reached, which would justify the dollar value of the tax receipt. Since Magda Creet had no official role in the history of the Hungarian-Canadian community, and certainly no role in the Jewish community – quite the opposite – the value of her papers would then have to be assessed in relation to the holdings of Archives Canada, which may indeed already have its quota of testimony from Holocaust survivors.

The value of her 'testimony,' in Ricoeur's sense of the word, has come about because of my insistent pursuit of her memory; I have inscribed an interpretive intertext, which cannot now be separated from her organic whole. Perhaps it wasn't by chance that I was drawn into a very public reproduction of her memory. She struggled monumentally with the insistent presence of the past in her life, and though she did her best to both write and rewrite her most precious memories for public consumption, I have succeeded where she failed in turning testimony into history, thereby ascribing a new value to her documentary by-products. One might say that in leaving her papers, rather than destroying them before she died, she left a trace that could not be ignored. She left the potential that her memory would be written into new history, while writing herself out of an old one. This may be the way of immigrants. To lose one's place of memory in one culture may spur an industry of memory/history in another. And I have been nothing if not industrious.

Which brings me to the question of my archive in relation to hers. My research caught the attention of Suzanne Dubeau, an archivist at the Clara Thomas Archives at York University, where I teach. Would I think of depositing my papers there? Adolescent love letters, undergraduate essays, high-school sports badges, records of administrative frustration and tedium, filing cabinets and boxes of research: what would I throw out first? Might I not like to keep my mother's papers close to mine? So much of my archives are about her. In my papers one would find transcriptions and translations of all the key letters – anathema to the idea of singularity and originality, but in this case the trail of research and origin tied back together. At York, then, I would be the anchor, and her papers would be, in some sense, a by-product of mine and their value would accrue to me. Here her memory would be completely and literally overwritten by mine. Given that the marketplace value will surely increase when my book based on her documents is published, we have, my siblings and I, decided to wait until I have marketed her memory before we ascribe a value to her organic remains. How far her memory migrates in my reconstructed forms will have everything to do with its overall value in every dimension I have described so far.

The proprietary nature of archives has never been quite so clear to me as it is now – the desires of the archivists who would very much like to see her papers become, in some sense, theirs. I will look very differently at archived papers from now on. The kinds of questions I will ask about them have changed. Before I begin reading in an archive again, I will want to know everything I can about their deposition: Who deposited them? Why? Why there? Who was the archivist who arranged for the deposition, and why did that archivist want the papers? The conditions of archivization, be it in memory or in an institution, inevitably frame what and how we read the human record; how and where we lock up a life indefinitely will define how that life is read in the future and the past. The fever of the archives is in its collection.

As I spin this narrative of where to deposit her papers, imputing desires to the dead seems to bear some ethical weight in the debate. What would she have wanted? This is a question that arises from the living memory of her, and it is an impossible question to answer. A documentary trail often runs counter to the narrative of a lived life. So, does migration end in the archive? Only if we consider the archive a one-way relationship. Ricoeur talks about a dialogic relationship between memory and history, which presumes that 'testimony' is scriptural memory, but memory nonetheless, and it participates in collective memory as if it were still cogent. Perhaps engaging channels of 'sense memory,' the testifying force of the by-products of a life compel them back into living memory. And, in this sense, memory is set in motion once again. Unless no one ever reads the record again, in which case, after a while, record or not, both history and memory will have been completely forgotten. The end of memory's migration, against all records, is that of forgetting or stasis. Without momentum, memory dies; the record is part of what impels it forward and back.

I imagine a future historian, perhaps looking for something else entirely, encountering the deposition record of the Magda Creet papers:

Magda Creet fonds
1945–1984 [the date of the records rather than the person]
Physical Extent
2 m of textual records
1000 photographic prints (approximately)
300+ rolls of negatives

Administrative History/Biographical Sketch
Magdalene Katarine Creet (nee György, formerly Farkas) (1920–1984) was born in Székesfehérvár, Hungary, of Jewish parents. She left high school in 1940 to marry Imre Farkas, a bicycle salesman. In 1944 she was deported to Auschwitz with her family and her first child, born in 1941, who perished along with Mrs. Farkas's parents and maternal grandmother. Liberated with her sister, Agnes, from forced labour in the Lipstadd Metalworks in 1945, she remained in Germany as a displaced person in Kaunitz, working for the British Command, until she obtained a work permit to move to London in 1947. While in London, she worked as a nanny, a cleaner, a hotel receptionist and an artist's model. In 1949 she married Mario Creet, a chemical engineer, having divorced Imre Farkas in 1947. A second daughter and a son were born in London. The family emigrated to Canada in 1957, settling in Kingston, Canada, where Mr. Creet started a career at Dupont as a researcher. He later joined the administration at Queen's University, which led to a second career as the University Archivist (See the Mario Creet fond in the Queen's University Archive). Another daughter and son were born in Kingston and all were baptized at

Chalmer's United Church, which Mrs. Creet joined in the 1964. In the early 1970s, Mrs. Creet opened a portrait studio in her house on Lower Union St. In the decade until her death in 1984, she photographed and wrote about many of Kingston's artists and writers, publishing profiles in the *Kingston Whig Standard*. Exhibitions of her work were held in 1972 and 1979. Magda Creet died in 1984; she was survived by four of her five children and Mario Creet, who died in 1994.

Scope and content: the fonds consist of diaries in Hungarian (1945–1946); daybooks (1968–1977); two typescript unpublished manuscripts of her memoirs; handwritten drafts of each volume; a manuscript of a collection of poetry; correspondence with a wide variety of publishers about the manuscripts; correspondence with friends and family (1945–1984), in English and in Hungarian, including an extensive correspondence with Imre Farkas, her first husband; documents pertaining to the literary career of her father, Oszkár György (see Oszkár György *fonds* in Féjer County Archive, Székesfehérvár, Hungary); newspaper clippings of her profiles and book reviews; approximately 300 portraits, primarily of Kingstonians; original negatives and contact sheets of all prints.

Whether or not Magda Creet's memories migrate into the future will depend on the resolutions to our deposition dilemmas and the values of historians to come. Beyond that, no one can predict the stuttering stops and starts or the slowing to stasis of the circulation of documents that testify to a life shaped by memories of migration.

NOTES

1 See Srdja Pavlovic's contribution to this volume, p. 46.
2 In 1975 the Association of Canadian Archivists launched a journal called *Archivaria*. This became and continues to be the main forum in which the relationships between Canadian archival praxis and national remembrance were and are articulated.
3 Paul Ricoeur, *Memory, History, Forgetting* (Chicago: University of Chicago Press, 2004), 404.
4 Ibid., 180. See, in particular, 'The Documentary Phase: Archived Memory,' 135–81.
5 Ibid., 138.
6 Ibid., 136.

7 The idea of archives as repositories of the past is an Enlightenment concept, as Luciana Duranti tells us in 'Diplomatics: New Uses for an Old Science,' *Archivaria* 28 (1989): 7–27, her comprehensive study of the form and function of the document, the 'elemental archival unit.' 'Only at the time of the French Revolution did archivists move from the management of current records to the care of "historical sources," to which they tried to apply the classification principles learned in administrative offices' (10). Riva A. Pollard provides a good overview of the debates about the selection criteria for personal papers in 'The Appraisal of Personal Papers: A Critical Literature Review,' *Archivaria* 52 (2001): 136–50.

8 Interview with Suzanne Dubeau, assistant head of the Clara Thomas Archives at York University, May 2008.

9 The Holocaust Memorial Centre opened in Budapest in 2002, almost sixty years after Hungary carried out the last and swiftest mass deportations of Jews anywhere in Europe. Hungary has been one of the slowest European countries to establish any kind of official centre of remembrance.

10 The Hungarian pattern of forgetting is so widespread that finding out you were Jewish in adulthood is a cliché. See Ferenc Erős, András Kovács, and Katalin Lévai, 'Comment j'en suis arrivé á apprendre que j'étais juif,' [How I found out I was Jewish], *Actes de la Recherche en Sciences Sociales* 56 (1985): 63–8.

11 Here Jacques Derrida's opening paragraphs in *Archive Fever*, trans. Eric Prenowitz (Chicago and London: University of Chicago Press, 1996) come to mind. Tracing the etymologies of the word 'archive' in both Latin and Greek, Derrida argues that entrusted to the *archons*, the magistrates in whose houses documents were stored, 'these documents in effect speak the law; they recall the law and call on or impose the law' (2).

12 Maurice Halbwachs, *On Collective Memory*, ed. and trans. Lewis A. Coser (Chicago: University of Chicago Press, 1992).

13 See Andreas Kitzmann's contribution to this volume.

14 The discourse of diplomatics suggests Michel Foucault's definition of the archive as 'the general system of the formation and transformation of statements,' and his larger concerns with the death of the document as subjective testimony. See *The Archaeology of Knowledge*, trans. A.M. Sheridan Smith (London: Tavistock Publications Ltd, 1972), 127.

15 The Maple Leaf was proclaimed the flag of Canada by Her Majesty Queen Elizabeth II, Queen of Canada, on 15 February 1965.

16 Walter Neutel, '*Gesichte Wie Es Eigentlich Gewesen* or The Necessity of Having Ethnic Archives Programmes,' *Archivaria* 7 (1978): 105–9.

17 The concept of the 'total archive' and its unique development in Canada is discussed in a couple of excellent overview articles: Laura Millar, 'Discharging Our Debt: The Evolution of the Total Archives Concept in English Canada,' *Archivaria* 46 (1998): 103–46; and Myron Momryk, '"National Significance": The Evolution and Development of Acquisition Strategies in the Manuscript Division, National Archives Canada,' *Archivaria* 52 (2001): 151–74.

18 'Canada accepted a grand total of 500 [Jewish immigrants] between 1939 and 1945, though many of these refugees would have brought with them the skills and capital Canada needed so desperately' (Irving Abella, *A Coat of Many Colours* [Toronto: Lester & Orpen Dennys, 1990], 207).

19 See Andris Kesteris, 'Baltic Archives in Exile: A Point of View from Canada,' paper presented at the International Conference on the Baltic Archives Abroad, July 2006, Tartu Estonia, http://www.kirmus.ee/baltic_archives_abroad_2006/kogumik/eng/contents.html. Kesteris is an archivist at Library and Archives Canada.

20 Pierre Nora, 'Between Memory and History: *Les Lieux de Mémoire*,' *Representations* 26 (1989): 15. This broad genealogical drive, in tandem with a slightly mad religious agenda of the Church of the Latter Day Saints to baptize or re-baptize all of man dead and alive for the Second Coming, has produced the most complete administrative archive in the world: that of the Mormon Genealogical Archive in Salt Lake City. The 'hypermnesia' of the genealogical archive is an idea I explore through a Gothic story by Danilo Kis and its links to the Mormon Archives. See 'The Archive and the Uncanny: Danilo Kis's "Encyclopedia of the Dead" and the Fantasy of Hypermnesia,' *Lost in the Archives: Alphabet City* 8 (2002): 265–76.

Bibliography

Abella, Irving. *A Coat of Many Colours*. Toronto: Lester & Orpen Dennys, 1990.

Adelman, Howard, and John Simpson, eds. *Multiculturalism, Jews, and Identities in Canada*. Jerusalem: Magnes Press, the Hebrew University, 1996.

Adorno, Theodor. 'What Does Coming to Terms with the Past Mean?' In *Bitburg in Moral and Political Perspective*, ed. Geoffrey Hartman, 114–29. Bloomington: Indiana University Press, 1986.

Adorno, Theodor, and Max Horkheimer. *Dialectic of Enlightenment*. London: Verso, 1979.

Adorno, Theodor, et al. *The Authoritarian Personality: Studies in Prejudice*. New York: Harper, 1950.

Agamben, Giorgio. *Remnants of Auschwitz: The Witness and the Archive*. Trans. Daniel Heller-Roazen. New York: Zone Books, 2002.

– *Homo Sacer I: le pouvoir souverain et la vie nue*. Paris: Le Seuil, 1998.

– *Moyens sans fins*. Paris: Payot & Rivages, 1995.

Agier, Michel. *Au bord du monde: les réfugiés*. Paris: Flammarion, 2002.

Aguilar, Paloma. 'Collective Memory of the Spanish Civil War: The Case of the Political Amnesty in the Spanish Transition to Democracy.' *Democratization* 4 (1997): 88–109.

Alexander, Jeffrey C. 'Toward a Theory of Cultural Trauma.' In *Cultural Trauma and Collective Identity*, ed. Jeffrey Alexander, Roy Eyerman, Bernhard Giesen, Neil J. Smelser, and Piotr Sztompka, 1–30. Berkeley: University of California Press, 2004.

Améry, Jean. *Par-delà le crime et le chatîmen: essai pour surmonter l'insurmontable*. Trans. F. Wuilmart. Arles: Actes Sud, 1995.

– *At the Mind's Limits: Contemplations by a Survivor on Auschwitz and Its Realities*. Bloomington and Indianapolis: Indiana University Press, 1980.

Anderson, Benedict. *The Spectre of Comparisons*. London and New York: Verso, 1998.

Anderson, Mark. 'Crime and Punishment.' *The Nation*, 17 October 2005. http://www.thenation.com/doc/20051017/anderson

Anonymous and Philip Boehm. *A Woman in Berlin: Eight Weeks in the Conquered City: A Diary*. New York: Metropolitan Books, 2006.

Arendt, Hannah. *Impérialisme III*. Paris: Fayard, 1998.

– *Essays in Understanding, 1930–1954: Formation, Exile, and Totalitarianism*. New York: Schocken Books, 1994.

– *La condition de l'homme moderne*. Paris: Agora, 1983.

– *The Origins of Totalitarianism*. New York: Harcourt Brace Jovanovich, 1973.

– *Men in Dark Times*. London: J. Cape, 1970.

– *Eichmann in Jerusalem: A Report on the Banality of Evil*. New York: Viking, 1963.

Aschheim, Steven E. 'On Saul Friedlander.' *History and Memory* 9, nos. 1–2 (1997). http://iupjournals.org/history/ham9–12.html

Assmann, Jan. *Moses the Egyptian: The Memory of Egypt in Western Monotheism*. Cambridge: Harvard University Press, 1997.

– 'Kollektives Gedächtnis und kulturelle Identität.' In *Kultur und Gedächtnis*, ed. Jan Assmann and Toni Hölscher, 9–19. Frankfurt am Main: Suhrkamp Verlag, 1986.

Atwood, Margaret. *In Search of Alias Grace: On Writing Canadian Historical Fiction*. Ottawa: University of Ottawa Press, 1997.

– *Alias Grace*. Toronto: McClelland and Stewart, 1996.

Auden, W.H. *Collected Poems*. New York: Faber and Faber, 1976.

Augustine's Confessions. Book 10.14.21. Trans. Albert C. Outler. http://www.ccel.org/ccel/augustine/confessions/html

Bacque, James. *Other Losses*. Toronto: Little Brown and Co., 1999.

– *Crimes and Mercies: The Fate of German Civilians under Allied Occupation, 1944–1950*. Toronto: LB Canada, 1997.

Bal, Ellen, and Kathinka Sinha-Kerkhoff. 'Muslims in Surinam and the Netherlands, and the Divided Homeland.' *Journal of Muslim Minority Affairs* 25, no. 2 (2005): 193–217.

Bal, Mieke, Johnathan Crewe, and Leo Spitzer, eds. *Acts of Memory: Cultural Recall in the Present*. Hanover: University Press of New England, 1999.

Balibar, Étienne. *Nous, citoyens d'Europe? Les frontières, l'État, le peuple*. Paris: La Découverte, 2001.

Barbieri, William. 'Group Rights and the Muslim Diaspora.' *Human Rights Quarterly* 21, no. 4 (1999): 907–26.

Barnes, Jonathan, ed. *The Complete Works of Aristotle*. Vol. 2. Princeton: Princeton University Press, 1984.

Barnouw, Dagmar. *The War in the Empty Air: Victims, Perpetrators, and Postwar Germans*. Bloomington: Indiana University Press, 2005.

Barthes, Roland. *Światło obrazu*. Warszawa: Wydawnictwo KR, 1996.

– *La chambre claire: note sur la photographie*. Paris: Seuil, 1980.

Bauman, Zygmunt. *Wasted Lives: Modernity and Its Outcasts*. Cambridge: Polity Press, 2004.

– *La vie en miettes: expérience post-moderne et moralité*. Rodez: Le Rouergue/ Chambon, 2003.

– *Le coût humain de la mondialisation*. Paris: Hachette Littératures, 1999.

– *Globalization: The Human Consequences*. New York: Columbia University Press, 1998.

– *Modernity and the Holocaust*. London: Polity Press, 1989.

Bell, Duncan. 'Introduction: Memory, Trauma and World Politics.' In *Memory, Trauma and World Politics: Reflections on the Relationship between Peace and Present*, ed. Duncan Bell, 1–32. London: Palgrave-Macmillan, 2006.

Benjamin, Walter. *The Arcades Project*. Ed. Roy Tiedemann. Trans. Howard Eiland and Kevin McLaughlin. Cambridge: Harvard University Press 1997.

– *Illuminations*. New York: Schocken, 1969.

Bennett, Jill. *Empathic Vision: Affect, Trauma, and Contemporary Art*. Stanford: Stanford University Press, 2005.

– 'The Aesthetics of Sense-Memory: Theorising Trauma through the Visual Arts.' In *Trauma und Erinnerung / Trauma and Memory: Cross-Cultural Perspectives*, ed. Franz Kaltenbeck and Peter Weibel, 81–95. Vienna: Passagen, 2000.

Bergson, Henri. *Matter and Memory*. Trans. Nancy M. Paul and W. Scott Palmer. New York: Zone Books, 1988.

'Berlin Exhibition on Postwar Expulsions Opens amid Protests.' *Deutsche Welle World*, 11 August 2006. http://www.dw-world.de/dw/article/ 0,2144,2129308,00.html

Berruti, D., E. Doru, E. Erle, F. Gianfelici, and K. Khayati. *Kurds in Europe: From Asylum Right to Social Rights*. Naples: Associazoneper la Pace Onlus, 2002.

Bick, Esther. 'Hudupplevelsen i tidiga objektrelationer.' *Divan* 1–2 (2001): 4–6.

Bigo, Didier. 'Detention of Foreigner, States of Exception, and the Social Practices of Control of the Banopticon.' In *Borderscapes: Hidden Geographies and Politics at Territory's Edge*, ed. Kumar Rajaram P. and Carl Grundy-Warr, 3–34. Minneapolis: University of Minnesota Press, 2007.

Binder, S., and J. Tosic. *Refugee Studies and Politics: Human Dimensions and Research Perspectives*. Vienna: Facultas, 2002.

Bourdieu, Pierre. *The Weight of the World: Social Suffering in Contemporary Society*. Cambridge: Polity Press, 2002.

Boyarin, Jonathan. *Storm from Paradise: The Politics of Jewish Memory*. Minneapolis: University of Minnesota Press, 1992.
- *Polish Jews in Paris: The Ethnography of Memory*. Bloomington: Indiana University Press, 1991.
- ed. *Remapping Memory: The Politics of TimeSpace*. Minneapolis: University of Minnesota Press, 1994.
Boyarin, Jonathan, and Daniel Boyarin. *Powers of Diaspora*. Minneapolis: University of Minnesota Press, 2002.
Boym, Svetlana. *The Future of Nostalgia*. New York: Basic Books, 2001.
Brah, Avtar. *Cartographies of Diaspora: Contesting Identities*. London: Routledge, 1996.
Brenner, Michael. *Nach dem Holocaust: Juden in Deutschland, 1945–1950*. München: Beck, 1995.
Brogan, Kathleen. *Cultural Haunting: Ghosts and Ethnicity in Recent American Literature*. Charlottesville: University Press of Virginia, 1998.
Buroway, Michael, et al. *Global Ethnography: Forces, Connections and Imaginations in a Post-Modern World*. Berkeley: University of California Press, 2000.
Butler, Judith. *Giving an Account of Oneself*. New York: Fordham University Press, 2005.
- *Precarious Life: The Powers of Mourning and Violence*. London: Verso, 2004.
Caloz-Tschopp, Marie-Claire. *Les étrangers aux frontières de l'Europe et le spectre des camps*. Paris: La Dispute, 2004.
Canafe, Nergis. 'The Making of "Modern" Diasporas: The Case of Muslims in Canada.' In *Opportunity Structures in Diaspora Relations: Comparisons in Contemporary Multi-level Politics of Diaspora and Transnational Identity*, ed. Gloria Totoricagüen, 53–84. Reno: University of Nevada Press, 2007.
Carens, Joseph. *Culture, Citizenship, and Community: A Contextual Exploration of Justice as Evenhandedness*. Oxford and New York: Oxford University Press, 2000.
- *Migration, Morality, and the Nation-State*. Toronto: University of Toronto Press, 1985.
Caruth, Cathy. *Unclaimed Experience: Trauma, Narrative, and History*. Baltimore: Johns Hopkins University Press, 1996.
- ed. *Trauma: Explorations in Memory*. Baltimore: Johns Hopkins University Press, 1995.
Casey, Edward S. *Remembering: A Phenomenological Study*. Bloomington: Indiana University Press, 2000.
Cavarero, Adriana. *Relating Narratives: Storytelling and Selfhood*. London and New York: Routledge, 2000.

Chamberlain, Mary. *Narratives of Exile and Return*. London: Macmillan, 1997.

Cheng, Anne Anlin. 'The Melancholy of Race.' *Kenyon Review* n.s. 19, no. 1 (Winter 1997): 46–61.

Cholewinski, Ryszard. 'No Right of Entry: The Legal Regime on Crossing the EU Border.' In *In Search of Europe's Borders: Immigration and Asylum Law and Policy in Europe*, vol. 5, ed. E. Guild, K. Groenendijk, and P. Minderhoud, 115–27. The Hague/London/New York: Kluwer Law International, 2003.

Christianson, Sven-Åke. *Traumatiska minnen*. Stockholm: Natur och kultur, 2002.

Cigerli, Sabri. *Les Kurdes et leur histoire*. Paris: L'Harmattan, 1999.

Cigerli, Sabri, and Didier Le Saout. *Öcalan et le PKK: les mutations de la question kurde en Turquie et au Moyen-Orient*. Paris: Maisonneuve et Larose, 2005.

Cioran, Emil. *Na szczytach rozpaczy*. Kraków: Oficyna Literacka, 1992.

Classen, Constance, David Howes, and Anthony Synnott. *Aroma: The Cultural History of Smell*. London: Routledge, 1994.

Collier, Paul, Anke Hoeffler, and Söderbom Måns. *On the Duration of Civil War*. Oxford: World Bank, University of Oxford, 2001.

Colomina, Beatriz. *Privacy and Publicity: Modern Architecture as Mass Media*. Cambridge, MA: MIT Press, 1994.

Cornford, F.M. *Plato's Theory of Knowledge*. New York: The Liberal Art Press, 1957.

Crabtree, Adam. *Multiple Man: Explorations in Possession and Multiple Personality*. Toronto and New York: Praeger, 1985.

Creet, Julia. 'The Archive and the Uncanny: Danilo Kis's "Encyclopedia of the Dead" and the Fantasy of Hypermnesia.' *Lost in the Archives: Alphabet City* 8 (2002): 265–76.

Daniel, E. Valentine, and John Knudsen, eds. *Mistrusting Refugees*. Berkeley: University of California Press, 1995.

Darnstädt, Thomas, and Klaus Wiegrefe, 'Spiegel-Serie über Flucht und Vertreibung der Deutschen aus dem Osten.' *Der Spiegel* 25, no. 4 (2002): 3–15.

Darroch, Heidi. 'Hysteria and Traumatic Testimony: Margaret Atwood's *Alias Grace*.' *Essays on Canadian Writing* 81 (2004): 103–21.

Das, Veena. *Critical Events: An Anthropological Perspective on Contemporary India*. Delhi: Oxford University Press, 1995.

Davis, Donald G., and Wayne A. Wiegard, eds. *Encyclopedia of Library History*. New York: Garland Publishing, Inc., 1994.

Davis, Natalie Zemon, and Randolph Stern. 'Introduction.' *Representations* 26 (Spring 1989): 1–6.

de Certeau, Michel. *The Practice of Everyday Life*. Vol.1. Berkeley: University of California Press, 1984.

de Martino, Ernesto. *Le monde magique. Oeuvres, I.* Paris: Editions Synthelabo, 1999.

de Zayas, Alfred. *A Terrible Revenge: The Cleansing of the East European Germans, 1944–1950.* New York: St Martin's Press, 1994.

Dedina, Sidonia. *Edvard Benes: The Liquidator Fiend of the German Purge in Czechoslovakia.* Mountain View, CA: RFP Publications, 2001.

Delbo, Charlotte. *Auschwitz and After.* Trans. R.C. Lamont. New Haven and London: Yale University Press, 1995.

Deleuze, Gilles. *Proust et les signes.* Paris: Presses Universitaires de France, 2006.

– *Pourparlers.* Paris: Editions de Minuit, 1992.

– 'Qu'est-ce qu'un dispositif ?' In *Michel Foucault philosophe: rencontre internationale, Paris, janvier 1988.* Paris: Seuil, 1989.

– *Bergsonism.* Trans. Hugh Tomlinson and Barbara Habberjam. New York: Zone Books, 1988.

– *Différence et répétition.* Paris: Presses Universitaires de France, 1968.

Deleuze, Gilles, and Felix Guattari. *A Thousand Plateaus: Capitalism and Schizophrenia.* Trans. Brian Massumi. Minneapolis: University of Minnesota Press, 1987.

Derrida, Jacques. *Monolingualism of the Other or the Prosthesis of Origin.* Trans. Patrick Mensah. Stanford: Stanford University Press, 1998.

– *Archive Fever: A Freudian Impression.* Trans. Eric Prenowitz. Chicago and London: University of Chicago Press, 1996.

Deutsche, Rosalyn. *Evictions: Art and Spatial Politics.* Cambridge, MA: MIT Press, 2002.

– 'Krzysztof Wodiczko's *Homeless Projection* and the Site of Urban "Revitalization."' *October* 38 (Autumn 1986): 63–98.

Dietrich, John. *The Morgenthau Plan: Soviet Influence on American Postwar Policy.* New York: Algora Publishing, 2002.

Diner, Hasia. *Erin's Daughters in America: Irish Immigrant Women in the Nineteenth Century.* Baltimore: Johns Hopkins University Press, 1983.

Douglas, Mary. 'The Idea of Home: A Kind of Space.' *Social Research* 58, no. 1 (1991): 287–307.

Du Bois, W.E.B. *The Souls of Black Folk.* London: Oxford University Press, 2007.

Duranti, Luciana. 'Diplomatics: New Uses for an Old Science.' *Archivaria* 28 (Summer 1989): 7–27.

Ekber Gürgöz, Ali. *Kurde, torturé, quelles séquelles?* Paris: L'Harmattan, 2005.

– *La nuit de Diyarbakir, être Kurde en Turquie.* Paris: L'Harmattan, 1997.

Ellenberger, Henri. *The Discovery of the Unconscious: The History and Evolution of Dynamic Psychiatry.* New York: Basic Books, 1970

Eng, David L., and David Kazanjian, eds. *Loss: The Politics of Mourning*. Berkeley: University of California Press, 2003.

Epstein, Joseph. *Friendship*. New York: Mariner Books, 2007.

Erős, Ferenc, András Kovács, and Katalin Lévai. 'Comment j'en suis arrivé à apprendre que j'étais juif.' *Actes de la Recherche en Sciences Sociales* 56 (1985): 63–8.

Evans, Martin, and Ken Lunn, eds. *War and Memory in the Twentieth Century*. Oxford: Berg, 1997.

Eyal, Gil. 'Identity and Trauma: Two Forms of the Will to Memory.' *History and Memory* 16, no.1 (Spring/Summer 2004): 5–36.

Fassin, Didier. 'Compassion and Repression: The Moral Economy of Immigration Policies in France.' *Cultural Anthropology* 20, no. 3 (August 2005): 362–87.

Fatah, Tarek. *Chasing a Mirage: The Tragic Illusion of an Islamic State*. Mississauga, ON: John Wiley & Sons, 2008.

Felman, Shoshana, and Dori Laub. *Testimony: Crises of Witnessing in Literature, Psychoanalysis, and History*. New York and London: Routledge, 1992.

Fine, Gary Alan. *Difficult Reputations: Collective Memories of the Evil, Inept, and Controversial*. Chicago: University of Chicago Press, 2001.

Foucault, Michel. 'Inne przestrzenie.' *Teksty drugie* 9, no. 6 (2005): 117–25.

– 'Le sujet et le pouvoir.' In *Dits et Ecrits*. Vol. 4. Paris: Gallimard, 1994.

– *Technologies of the Self: A Seminar with Michel Foucault*. Amherst: University of Massachusetts Press, 1988.

– *Histoire de la sexualité II: l'usage des plaisirs*. Paris: Gallimard, 1984.

– *Surveiller et punir: naissance de la prison*. Paris: Gallimard, 1975.

– *The Archaeology of Knowledge*. Trans. A.M. Sheridan Smith. London: Tavistock Publications Ltd, 1972.

Frankl, Viktor E. *Livet måste ha mening: Erfarenheter i koncentrationslägren. Logoterapins grunde*. Stockholm: Natur och Kultur, 1999.

Freeman, Mark. *Rewriting the Self: History, Memory, Narrative*. London and New York: Routledge, 1993.

Freud, Sigmund. *Fragment of an Analysis of a Case of Hysteria ('Dora'). Case Histories I: 'Dora' and 'Little Hans.'* Trans. Alix and James Strachey. London: Penguin, 1990.

– *Introductory Lectures on Psychoanalysis*. Ed. and trans. James Strachey. London: Penguin Books, 1973.

– 'Mourning and Melancholia.' In Vol. 14 of *The Standard Edition of the Complete Psychological Works of Sigmund Freud*. London: Hogarth Press, 1917.

Freud, Sigmund, and Joseph Breuer. *Studies on Hysteria*. Vol. 2 of *The Standard Edition of the Complete Psychological Works of Sigmund Freud*. Ed. James Strachey. London: Hogarth Press, 1955. Rpt. New York: Avon, 1966.

Freund, Alexander. 'Dealing with the Past Abroad: German Immigrants: Vergangenheitsbewaltigung and Their Relations with Jews in North America since 1945.' *GHI Bulletin* no. 31 (Fall 2002). http://www.ghi-dc.org/bulletinF02/51.pdf

Friedländer, Saul. *Memory, History, and the Extermination of the Jews of Europe.* Bloomington and Indianapolis: Indiana University Press, 1993.

Friedman, Milton J. 'Post-war Communities Overcoming Traumas and Losses.' Presented at a workshop on 'the importance of psychosocial well-being of children in the post-war period for social reconstruction and stability of terrorist and war affected regions.' Ljubljana, 7 June 2003.

Friedrich, Jörg. *The Fire: Germany in the Air War.* New York: Columbia University Press, 2006.

Frisse, Ulrich. *Anna Tuerr Memorial Park.* Kitchener, ON: Trans Atlantic Publishing, 2004.

Ganguly, Keya. 'Migrant Identities: Personal Memory and the Construction of Selfhood.' *Cultural Studies* 6, no. 1 (1992): 27–50.

Gellner, Ernest. *Thought and Change.* London: Weidenfeld and Nicolson, 1964.

Genette, Gérard. *Narrative Discourse.* Trans. Jane E. Lewin and Jonathan Culler. Ithaca, NY: Cornell University Press, 1980.

Gilman, Sander, Helen King, Roy Porter, George Rousseau, and Elaine Showalter. *Hysteria beyond Freud.* Berkeley: University of California Press, 1993.

Goffman, Erving. *Stigma: Notes on the Management of Spoiled Identity.* Harmondsworth: Pelican Books, 1968.

Gombrowicz, Witold. *Trans-Atlantyk.* Kraków: Wydawnictwo Literackie, 1988.

Gorrara, Claire. *Women's Representations of the Occupation in post-'68 France.* Basingstoke: McMillan Press, 1998.

Grass, Günter. *Crabwalk.* Toronto: Harcourt, 2002.

Greenberg, Mark S., and Bessel A. van der Kolk, 'Retrieval and Integration of Traumatic Memories with the "Painting Cure."' In *Psychological Trauma*, ed. Bessel A. van der Kolk, 191–216. Washington, DC: American Psychiatric Press, 1987.

Grossman, David. *See under Love.* New York: Farrar, Straus, and Giroux, 1989.

Guthrie, W.K.C. *A History of Greek Philosophy, Vol. III: The Fifth-Century Enlightenment.* Cambridge: Cambridge University Press, 1979.

Gutmann, Amy, ed. *Multiculturalism: Examining the Politics of Recognition.* Princeton: Princeton University Press, 1994.

Hacking, Ian. *Rewriting the Soul: Multiple Personality and the Sciences of Memory.* Princeton: Princeton University Press, 1995.

Hadot, Pierre. *Philosophy as a Way of Life: Spiritual Exercises from Socrates to Foucault.* Trans. Michael Chase. Oxford and New York: Blackwell, 1995.

Hagen, Rudolph. *Die verpaßten Chancen: Die vergessene Geschichte der Bundesre-publik*. Hamburg: Gruner & Jahr, 1979.

Haigh, Sam. 'Migration and Melancholia: From Kristeva's "Dépression Nation-ale" to Pineau's "Maladie de l'Exil."' *French Studies* 60, no. 2 (2006): 232–50.

Halbwachs, Maurice. *On Collective Memory*. Chicago: University of Chicago Press, 1992.

Hansen, Marcus Lee. *The Problem of the Third Generation Immigrant*. Rock Island, IL: Augustana Historical Society, 1938.

Harris, Ruth. *Murders and Madness: Medicine, Law and Society in the Fin de Siècle*. Oxford: Clarendon, 1989.

Hartman, Geoffrey. *The Longest Shadow: In the Aftermath of the Holocaust*. Bloomington: Indiana University Press, 1996.

Heinemann, Marlene. *Gender and Destiny: Women Writers and the Holocaust*. New York: Greenwood Press, 1986.

Heiner Kuhne, H. 'Culture Conflict and Crime in Europe.' In *Migration, Culture Conflict and Crime*, ed. J.D. Freilich, G. Newman, and A. Moshe, 89–99. Aldershot: Ashgate, 2002.

Herzfeld, Michael. *The Social Production of Indifference: Exploring the Symbolic Roots of Western Bureaucracy*. Chicago and London: University of Chicago Press, 1992.

Hirsch, Marianne. 'Surviving Images: Holocaust Photographs and the Work of Post-Memory.' *Yale Journal of Criticism* 14, no. 1 (2001): 5–37.

– *Family Frames: Photography, Narrative and Postmemory*. Cambridge: Harvard University Press, 1997.

Hobsbawm, Eric, and Terence Ranger. *The Invention of Tradition*. Cambridge: Cambridge University Press, 1983.

Hoffman, Eva. *Lost in Translation: A Life in a New Language*. Harmondsworth: Penguin Books, 1989.

Hollier, Denis. *Against Architecture. The Writings of Georges Bataille*. Cambridge, MA: MIT Press, 1992.

Houston, Rab. 'Madness and Gender in the Long Eighteenth Century.' *Social History* 27, no. 3 (2002): 309–26.

Huttunen, Laura. '"Home" and Ethnicity in the Context of War: Hesitant Diasporas of Bosnian Refugees.' *European Journal of Cultural Studies* 8, no. 2 (2005): 177–95.

Huyssen, Andreas. 'Of Mice and Mimesis: Reading Spiegelman with Adorno.' In *Visual Culture and the Holocaust*, ed. Barbie Zelizer, 28–42. New Brunswick: Rutgers University Press, 2001.

– *Twilight Memories: Marking Time in a Culture of Amnesia*. New York and London: Routledge, 1995.

Ignatieff, Michael. *The Rights Revolution*. Toronto: House of Anansi Press, 2007.

Ingram, Susan, Markus Reisenleitner, and Cornelia Szabó-Knotik, eds. *Floodgates: Technologies, Cultural (Ex)Change and the Persistence of Place.* Vienna: Peter Lang, 2006.

Irwin-Zarecka, Iwona. *Frames of Remembrance: The Dynamics of Collective Memory.* New Brunswick, NJ: Transaction Press, 1994.

Isin, Engin, and Greg Nielsen, eds. *Acts of Citizenship*. London and New York: Zed Books, 2008.

– *Being Political: Genealogies of Citizenship*. Minneapolis: University of Minnesota Press, 2002.

Jaeger, Werner Wilhelm. *Paideia: The Ideals of Greek Culture*. New York: Oxford University Press, 1945.

Jameson, Fredric. *The Political Unconscious: Narrative as a Socially Symbolic Act.* Ithaca, NY: Cornell University Press, 1981.

Judt, Tony. 'A la Recherche du Temps Perdu.' Review article of *Realms of Memory: The Construction of the French Past*. Edited by Pierre Nora. English-language edition edited by Lawrence D. Kritzman. Translated by Arthur Goldhammer. Vol. 1: *Conflicts and Divisions*. Vol. 2: *Traditions*. Vol. 3: *Symbols*. New York: Columbia University Press, 1996. In *New York Review of Books* 45, no. 19 (3 Dec. 1998). n.pag. http://www.nybooks.com/articles/650

– 'The Past Is Another Country: Myth and Memory in Postwar Europe.' *Daedalus* 4 (1992): 83–118.

Kernerman, Gerald. *Multicultural Nationalism: Civilizing Difference, Constituting Community.* Vancouver: UBC Press, 2005.

Kertész, Imre. 'Die exilierte Sprache.' In *Die exilierte Sprache: Essays und Reden,* 206–21. Frankfurt/Main: Suhrkamp, 2003.

– *Fateless*. Trans. Christopher and Katharina Wilson. Evanston, IL: Northwestern University Press, 1992.

Kesteris, Andris. 'Baltic Archives in Exile: A Point of View from Canada.' Paper presented at the International Conference on the Baltic Archives Abroad, July 2006, Tartu, Estonia. http://www.kirmus.ee/baltic_archives_abroad_2006/kogumik/eng/contents.html

Kevir, R. 'Enfant d'immigré, immigré enfant.'*Site francophone pour la connaissance des Kurdes*. June 1996. Accessed 15 Oct. 2006. http://www.chez.com/veysel/

Kitliński, Tomek. *Obcy jest w nas: Kochać według Julii Kristevej*. Kraków: Wydanie, 2001.

Kitzmann, Andreas, Conny Mithander, and John Sundholm, eds. *Memory Work.* Brussels: Peter Lang, 2005.

Knopp, Gudio, dir. *Die Grosse Flucht*. Universum Film, 2004.

Kogon, Eugen. 'Gericht und Gewissen.' *Frankfurter Hefte: Zeitschrift für Kultur und Politik* 1 no. 1 (April 1946): 25–37.

Koselleck, Reinhart. *Futures Past: On the Semantics of Historical Time*. Cambridge, MA: MIT Press 1985.

Kovács, Éva. 'The Mémoire Croisée of the Shoah.' *Eurozine*, 22 May 2006. http://www.eurozine.com

Kraus, Marita. *Heimkehr in ein fremdes Land: Geschichte der Remigration nach 1945*. München: Beck, 2001.

Kristeva, Julia. *Contre la dépression nationale: entrien avec Philippe Petit*. Paris: Textuel, 1998.

– *Nations without Nationalism*. New York: Columbia University Press, 1993.

– *Strangers to Ourselves*. New York: Columbia University Press, 1991.

– *Black Sun*. New York: Columbia University Press, 1989.

Krutein, Eva. *Eva's War*. Albuquerque: Amador Publishers, 1990.

Kymlicka, Will. *Multicultural Odysseys: Navigating the New International Politics of Diversity*. Oxford and New York: Oxford University Press, 2007.

– *Politics in the Vernacular: Nationalism, Multiculturalism and Citizenship*. New York: Oxford University Press, 2002.

Laacher, Smaïn. *Après Sangatte ... nouvelles immigrations, nouveaux enjeux*. Paris: La Dispute, 2002.

LaCapra, Dominick. *Writing History, Writing Trauma*. Baltimore: Johns Hopkins University Press, 2000.

– 'Trauma, Absence, Loss.' *Critical Inquiry* 25 (1999): 696–727.

– *History and Memory after Auschwitz*. Ithaca, NY: Cornell University Press, 1998.

Laguerre, Michael. *Diasporic Citizenship*. London: Macmillan, 1998.

Langer, Lawrence L. *Admitting the Holocaust: Collected Essays*. New York: Oxford University Press, 1996.

– *Holocaust Testimonies: The Ruins of Memory*. New Haven and London: Yale University Press, 1991.

Lapeyronnie, Didier. 'De l'altérité à la différence: l'identité comme facteur d'intégration ou de repli?' In *Immigration et integration: l'état des saviors*, ed. P. Dewitte, 252–9. Paris: La Découverte, 1991.

Lavie, Smadar, and Ted Swedenburg, eds. *Displacement, Diaspora and Geographies of Identity*. Durham, NC: Duke University Press, 1996.

Le Goff, Jacques. *History and Memory*. New York: Columbia University Press, 1992.

– 'Mentalities: A History of Ambiguities.' In *Constructing the Past: Essays in Historical Methodology*, ed. Jacques Le Goff and Pierre Nora, 166–80. Cambridge: Cambridge University Press, 1985.

Ledig, Gert. *The Stalin Front*. New York: NYRB Classics, 2005.
– *Payback*, London: Granta, 2003.
LeDoux, Joseph. *The Emotional Brain*. New York: Touchstone, 1998.
Levi, Primo. *The Periodic Table*. New York: Schocken Books, 1984.
– *If This Is a Man; The Truce*. Trans. S. Woolf. New York: Penguin, 1979.
Levy, Daniel. 'The Future of the Past: Historiographical Disputes and Competing Memories in Germany and Israel.' *History and Theory* 38 (1999): 51–66.
Levy, Daniel, and Natan Sznaider. *The Holocaust and Memory in the Global Age*. Philadelphia: Temple University Press, 2006.
Lewoń, Janusz. 'Sniking for Grunwald.' *Migotania, przejaśnienia* 10 (2006): 12.
Leys, Ruth. *Trauma: A Genealogy*. Chicago: University of Chicago Press, 2000.
Linden, David J. *The Accidental Mind: How Brain Evolution Has Given Us Love, Memory, Dreams, and God*. Cambridge: Harvard University Press, 2007.
Liss, Andrea. *Trespassing through Shadows: Memory, Photography and the Holocaust*. Minneapolis: University of Minnesota Press, 1998.
Lorey, David, and William Beezley, eds. *Genocide, Collective Violence and Popular Memory*. Wilmington, DE: Scholarly Resources: 2002.
Ludtke, Alf. 'Coming to Terms with the Past: Illusions of Remembering, Ways of Forgetting Nazism in West Germany.' *Journal of Modern History* 65, no. 3 (Sept. 1993): 542–72.
Lungen, Paul. 'Cabinet to Hear from Oberlander.' *Canadian Jewish News*. Internet Edition. 10 May 2001. http://www.cjnews.com/pastissues/01/may10-01/international/int1.htm.
Makaremi, Chowra. 'Alien Confinement in Europe: Violence and the Law: The Case of Roissy-Charles de Gaulle Airport in France.' In *The Camp: Narratives of Internment and Exclusion*, ed. Colman Hogan and M. Marín Dòmine, 39–54. Newcastle: Cambridge Scholars Publishing, 2007.
– 'On the Spirit of Laws: Some Reflections Concerning the 'DNA Law' in France.' *Eurostudia* 3, no. 2 (Dec. 2007). http://id.erudit.org/iderudit/017839ar
Malkki, Liisa. *Purity and Exile: Violence, Memory and National Cosmology among Hutu Refugees in Tanzania*. Chicago: University of Chicago Press, 1995.
Mara, Gerald M. *Socrates' Discursive Democracy: Logos and Ergon in Platonic Political Philosophy*. New York: State University of New York Press, 1997.
Marai, Sandor. *Zar*. Warszawa: Czytelnik, 2006.
Margalit, Avishai. *The Ethics of Memory*. Harvard: Harvard University Press, 2002.
Massumi, Brian. *Parables for the Virtual: Movement, Affect, Sensation*. Durham, NC: Duke University Press, 2002.

McLean, Lorna R., and Marilyn Barber. 'In Search of Comfort and Independence: Irish Immigrant Domestic Servants Encounter the Courts, Jails, and Asylums in Nineteenth-Century Ontario.' In *Sisters or Strangers? Immigrant, Ethnic, and Racialized Women in Canadian History*, ed. Marlene Epp, Franca Iacovetta, and Frances Swyripa, 134–60. Toronto: University of Toronto Press, 2004.

Megill, Allan. *Historical Knowledge, Historical Error: A Contemporary Guide to Practice*. Chicago: University of Chicago Press, 2007.

Merleau-Ponty, Maurice. *Phenomenology of Perception*. Trans. Colin Smith. New York: Humanities Press, 1970.

– 'Eye and Mind.' In *The Primacy of Perception*. Trans. Carleton Dallery. Evanston, IL: Northwestern University Press, 1964.

Métraux, Jean-Claude. *Deuils collectifs et création sociale*. Paris: La Dispute, 2004.

– 'Broken Bridges: Community Grief Processes as a Key Factor for the Development of Individual, Family and Community Resources.' In *Health Hazards of Organised Violence in Children (II)*, ed. L. Willigen, 93–110. Utrecht: Pharos, 2000.

Micale, Mark. *Approaching Hysteria: Disease and Its Interpretations*. Princeton: Princeton University Press, 1995.

– 'Theorizing Disease Historiography.' In Sander Gilman et al., *Hysteria beyond Freud*, 108–75. Berkeley: University of California Press, 1993.

Mickiewicz, Adam. *Pan Tadeusz*. Trans. and introd. Kenneth R. MacKenzie. New York: Hippocrene Books,1992.

Millar, Laura. 'Discharging Our Debt: The Evolution of the Total Archives Concept in English Canada.' *Archivaria* 46 (1998): 103–46.

Miller, Mitchel. *Plato's Parmenides: The Conversion of the Soul*. Princeton: Princeton University Press, 1986.

Miłosz, Czesław. *Native Realm: A Search for Self-Definition*. Trans. Catherine S. Leach. New York: Penguin, 1988.

– *Ziemia Urlo*. Warsaw: PIW, 1982.

Mirzoeff, Nicholas, ed. *Diaspora and Visual Culture: Representing Africans and Jews*. New York and London: Routledge, 2000.

Mitchell, W.J., ed. *On Narrative*. Chicago: University of Chicago Press, 1981.

Mithander, Conny, John Sundholm, and Maria Holmgren Troy, eds. *Collective Traumas: Memories of War and Conflict in 20th Century Europe*. Brussels: Peter Lang, 2007.

Momryk, Myron. '"National Significance": The Evolution and Development of Acquisition Strategies in the Manuscript Division, National Archives Canada.' *Archivaria* 52 (2001): 151–74.

Mosse, George. *Fallen Soldiers. Reshaping the Memory of the World Wars*. New York and Oxford: Oxford University Press, 1990.

Nabokov,Vladamir. *Strong Opinions*. London: Weidenfeld and Nicolson, 1973.

Neutel, Walter. '*Gesichte Wie Es Eigentlich Gewesen*; or, The Necessity of Having Ethnic Archives Programmes.' *Archivaria* 7 (1978): 105–9.

Nora, Pierre. 'Between Memory and History: *Les Lieux de Mémoire*.' *Representations* 26 (1989): 7–25.

Nossack , Hans Erich. *The End*. Chicago: University of Chicago Press, 2006.

Nussbaum, Martha. *Upheavals of Thought: The Intelligence of Emotions*. Cambridge: Cambridge University Press, 2001.

Nyers, Peter. *Rethinking Refugees: Beyond States of Emergency*. New York: Routledge, 2006.

Olick, Jeffrey. *States of Memory: Continuities, Conflicts, and Transformations in National Retrospection*. Durham, NC: Duke University Press, 2003.

– 'Collective Memory: The Two Cultures.' *Sociological Theory* 17 (1999): 333–48.

Olick, Jeffrey, and Daniel Levy. 'Collective Memory and Cultural Constraint: Holocaust Myth and Rationality in German Politics.' *American Sociological Review* 62 (1997): 92–136.

Olick, Jeffrey, and Joyce Robbins. 'Social Memory Studies: From "Collective Memory" to the Historical Sociology of Mnemonic Practices.' *Annual Review of Sociology* 24 (1998): 105–40.

Ong, Aihwa. *Flexible Citizenship: The Cultural Logics of Transnationality*. Durham, NC: Duke University Press, 1999.

Passerini, Luisa. *Memory and Totalitarianism*. Oxford: Oxford University Press, 1992.

Pavlovic, Srdja. *Iza Ogledala: Eseji o Identittetu i Politici Pripadnosti*. Podgorica: CID, 2001.

Plato. *Gorgias*. Trans. Walter Hamilton and Chris Emlyn-Jones. London and New York: Penguin, 2004.

– *Hippias Major*. Trans. Robin Waterfield. In *Early Socratic Dialogues*. London: Penguin, 1987.

– *Ion*. Trans. Trevor J. Saunders. In *Early Socratic Dialogues*. London: Penguin, 1987. .

– *Laws*. Trans. B. Jowett. . In *The Dialogues of Plato*. Vol. 4. Oxford: Clarendon Press, 1964.

– *Meno*. In *Protagoras and Meno*. Trans. A. Beresford. London and New York: Penguin, 2005.

– *Phaedo*. In *The Symposium and the Phaedo*. Trans. Raymond Larson. Arlington Heights, IL: AHM Publishing Corporation, 1980.

– *Phaedrus*. Trans. R. Hackforth. Cambridge: Cambridge University Press, 1972.

- *Philebus*. Trans. J.C.B. Gosling. Oxford: Clarendon Press, 1975.
- *Symposium*. In *The Symposium and The Phaedo*. Trans. Raymond Larson. Arlington Heights, IL: AHM Publishing Corporation, 1980.
- *The Republic*. Trans. Desmond Lee. London and New York: Penguin, 2003.
- *Theatetus*. Trans. John McDowell. Oxford: Clarendon Press, 1973. *History* 22 (1998): 479–512.

Pluta, Jerzy. *Melancholica Polonaise*. Bydgoszcz: n.p., 1987.

Pollak, Michel. *L'expérience concentrationnaire: essai sur le maintien de l'identité sociale*. Paris: Métailié, 2000.

Pollard, Riva. 'The Appraisal of Personal Papers: A Critical Literature Review.' *Archivaria* 52 (2001): 136–50.

Polleta, Francesca. 'Legacies and Liabilities of an Insurgent Past: Remembering Martin Luther King, Jr., on the House and Senate Floor.' *Social Science History* 22 (1998): 479–512.

Porter, Roy. 'The Body and the Mind, the Doctor and the Patient: Negotiating Hysteria.' In Sander Gilman et al., *Hysteria beyond Freud*, 225–85. Berkeley: University of California Press, 1993.

Presser, Jacques. *The Destruction of the Dutch Jews*. Trans. Arnold Pomeroms. New York: E.P. Dutton & Co., 1969.

- *Ondergang: De vervolging en verdelging van het Nederlandse Jodendom, 1940–1945*. The Hague: Staatsuitgeverij, 1965.

Prost, Antoine. 'The Algerian War in French Collective Memory.' In *War and Remembrance in the Twentieth Century*, ed. J. Winter and E. Sivan, 161–76. Cambridge: Cambridge University Press, 1999.

Proust, Marcel. *In Search of Lost Time. Swann's Way*. New York: Modern Library, 2004.

Prunier, Gérard. *The Rwanda Crisis: History of a Genocide*. New York: Columbia University Press, 1995.

Radstone, Susannah, and Katharine Hodgkin, eds. *Regimes of Memory*. London and New York: Routledge, 2003.

Rancière, Jacques. *Aux bords du politique*. Paris: Gallimard, 1998.

Razack, Sherene. *Casting Out: The Eviction of Muslims from Western Law and Politics*. Toronto: University of Toronto Press, 2008.

- ed. *Race, Space, and the Law: Unmapping a White Settler Society*. Toronto: Between the Lines, 2002.

Reese, Peter. *A Stranger to Myself: The Inhumanity of War: Russia, 1941–1944*. New York: Farrar, Straus and Giroux, 2005.

Reesor, Margaret E. *The Nature of Man in Early Stoic Philosophy*. New York: St Martin's Press, 1989.

Reis, Michele. 'Theorizing Diaspora: Perspectives on "Classical" and "Contemporary" Diaspora.' *International Migration* 42, no. 2 (2004): 41–60.

Richard, Lionel. 'Auschwitz und kein Ende.' In *Kunst und Literatur nach Auschwit*, ed. Manuel Köppen, 23–30. Berlin: Erich Schmidt, 1993.

Ricoeur, Paul. 'Memory, History, Forgiveness: A Dialogue between Paul Ricoeur and Sorin Antohi.' *Janus Head* 8 no.1 (2005): 14–25.

– *Memory, History, Forgetting*. Trans. Kathleen Blamey and David Pellauer. Chicago: University of Chicago Press, 2004.

– *La mémoire, l'histoire, l'oubli*. Paris: Seuil, 2000.

– *Time and Narrative*. Trans. Kathleen Blamey and David Pellauer. Chicago: University of Chicago Press, 1994.

– 'Distansering som hermeneutisk funktion.' In *Hermeneutik*, ed. Horace Engdahl, Ola Holmgren, Roland Lysell, Arne Mellberg, and Anders Olsson, 134–51. Stockholm: Rabén & Sjögren, 1977.

Robson, Kathryn. *Writing Wounds: The Inscription of Trauma in Post-1968 French Women's Life-Writing*. New York: Rodopi, 2004.

Rosińska, Zofia, ed. *Pamięć w filozofii XX wieku* (The Memory of Philosophy in the Twentieth Century). Warsaw: University of Warsaw, 2006.

Roth, Michael. 'Hysterical Remembering.' *Modernism/Modernity* 3, no. 2 (1996): 1–30.

Rousseau, Cécile, and Patricia Foxen, 'The Social Usefulness of the Lying Refugee.' *Evolution psychiatrique* 71, no.3 (2006): 505–20.

Rousso, Henry. *Le syndrome de Vichy*. 2nd edn. Paris: Seuil, 1990.

Rushdie, Salman. *Shame*. London: J. Cape, 1983.

Sack, John. *An Eye for an Eye: The Story of Jews Who Sought Revenge for the Holocaust*. New York: Basic Books, 2000. 1983.

Safran, William. 'Diasporas in Modern Societies: Myths of Homeland and Return.' *Diaspora* 1, no.1 (1991): 83–99.

Said, Edward. 'Reflections on Exile.' In *Altogether Elsewhere: Writers on Exile*, ed. Marc Robinson, 137–49. Boston and London: Faber and Faber, 1994.

– *The World, the Text and the Critic*. Cambridge: Harvard University Press, 1983.

Saint-Blancat, Chantal. 'Islam in Diaspora: Between Reterritorialization and Extraterritoriality.' *International Journal of Urban and Regional Research* 26, no. 1 (2002): 138–51.

Salas, Denis. 'Immigration illégale et pratiques judiciaires en France: incriminés, discriminés ...' *Hommes et migrations*, no. 1241 (Jan.-Feb. 2003): 78–88

Sartre, Jean-Paul. *Existentialismen är en humanism*. Stockholm: Albert Bonniers Förlag, 1946.

Sassen, Saskia. *Guests and Aliens*. New York: New Press, 1999.

Sayad, Abdelmalek. *The Suffering of the Immigrant*. Trans. David Macey. Cambridge: Polity Press, 2004.

- *La double absence: des illusions de l'émigré aux souffrances de l'immigré*. Paris: Le Seuil, 1999.

- *L'immigration ou les paradoxes de l'altérité*. Bruxelles: de Boeck, 1991.

Schachter, O.L., and J.F. Kihlstrom. 'Functional Amnesia.' In *Handbook of Neuropsychology*, vol. 3, ed. Francois Boller and Jordan Grafman, 209–31. Amsterdam: Elsevier, 1989. *Affairs* 24, no. 1 (2004): 31–45.

Schama, Simon. *Landscape and Memory*. New York: Knopf, 1995.

Schmidt, Garbi. 'Islamic Identity Formation among Young Muslims: The Case of Denmark, Sweden and the United Kingdom.' *Journal of Muslim Minority*

Schneider, Peter. 'In Their Side of World War II, the Germans Also Suffered.' *New York Times*, 'Arts and Ideas' section, 18 January 2003.

Schudson, Michael. 'The Present in the Past versus the Past in the Present.' *Communication* 11 (1989): 105–13.

Schwartz, Barry. 'The Social Context of Commemoration: A Study in Collective Memory.' *Social Forces* 61 (1982): 374–402.

Schwartz, Barry, and Todd Bayma. 'Commemoration and the Politics of Recognition: The Korean War Veterans Memorial.' *American Behavioral Scientist* 42 (1999): 946–67.

Sebald, Winfried Georg. *On the Natural History of Destruction*. New York: Modern Library, 2004.

- *Austerlitz*. Trans. Anthea Bell. New York: Random House, 2001.

Sheffer, Gabriel. 'A New Field of Study: Modern Diasporas in International Politics.' In *Migration, Diasporas and Transnationalism*, ed. S. Vertovec and R. Cohen, 381–95. London: Edward Elgar Publishing, 1999.

Showalter, Elaine. *Hystories*. New York: Columbia University Press, 1997.

- 'Hysteria, Feminism, and Gender.' In Sander Gilman et al., *Hysteria beyond Freud*, 286–344. Berkeley: University of California Press, 1993.

Sikora, S. *Fotografia: między dokumentem a symbolem*. Warsaw: Świat literacki, 2004.

Silverman, Kaja. *Threshold of the Visible World*. New York: Routledge, 1996.

Smith, Gary, ed. *On Walter Benjamin, Critical Essays and Recollections*. Cambridge, MA: MIT Press, 1988.

Smith, Ken. *Shed: Selected Poems*. London: Bloodaxe Books, 2002.

Smith-Rosenberg, Carroll. *Disorderly Conduct: Visions of Gender in Victorian America*. New York: Knopf, 1985.

Somers, Margaret. 'What's Political or Cultural about Political Culture and the Public Sphere? Toward an Historical Sociology of Concept Formation.' *Sociological Theory* 13 (1995): 113–44.

Soysal, Yasemin. 'Citizenship and Identity: Living in Diasporas in Post-War Europe?' *Ethnic and Racial Studies* 23, no. 1 (2003): 1–15.

Speigelman, Art. *Maus*. New York: Pantheon, 1986.

Sturken, Marita. *Tangled Memories*. Berkeley: University of California Press, 1997.

Suleiman, Susan Rubin, ed. *Exile and Creativity: Signposts, Travelers, Outsiders, Backward Glances*. Durham, NC: Duke University Press, 1998.

Sundholm John. 'Condensed History: The Poetics of Memory in Film. ' In *Travelling Concepts III: Memory, Narrative, Image*, ed. Nancy Pedri, 29–41. Amsterdam: ASCA Press, 2003.

Szlezák, Thomas Alexander. *Reading Plato*. Trans. G. Zanker. London and New York: Routledge, 1999.

Taylor, Charles. *Modern Social Imaginaries*. Durham, NC: Duke University Press, 2004.

– *Philosophy in an Age of Pluralism: The Philosophy of Charles Taylor in Question*. Cambridge and New York: Cambridge University Press, 1994.

– *Sources of the Self: The Making of the Modern Identity*. Cambridge: Harvard University Press, 1989.

Tesher, Ellie. 'Is "Scarlet Pimpernel" Still Alive?' *Toronto Star*, 20 October 1979, A10.

Timm, Uwe. *In My Brother's Shadow: A Life and Death in the SS*. New York: Farrar, Straus and Giroux, 2005.

Todorov, Tzvetan. *Hope and Memory: Lessons from the Twentieth Century*. Trans. David Bellos. Princeton: Princeton University Press, 2003.

– 'La mémoire fragmentée, la vocation de la mémoire.' In *La mémoire entre histoire et politique*. Ed. Léonard Yves. Special issue of *Cahiers Français* 303 (2001): 1–7.

Tonkin, Elizabeth. *Narrating Our Pasts: The Social Construction of Oral History*. Cambridge: Cambridge University Press, 1992.

Troy, Maria Holmgren, and Elisabeth Wennö, eds. *Memory, Haunting, Discourse*. Karlstad: Karlstad University Press, 2006.

Tuerr, Paul. 'Innocent Germans Also Suffered under the Nazi Regime.' Second Opinion, editorial section. *Kitchener Waterloo Record*. 5 September 2006.

Tully, James. *Strange Multiplicity: Constitutionalism in an Age of Diversity*. Cambridge and New York: Cambridge University Press, 1995.

Turowski, Andrzej. 'Przemieszczenia i obrazy dialektyczne Krzysztofa Wodiczki.' In *Pomnikoterapia*. Warsaw: Zachęta Gallery, 2005.

Tuwim, Julian. *Kwiaty polskie*. Warszawa: Czytelnik, 2003.

Van der Hart, Onno, Ellert R.S. Nijenhuis, and Kathy Steele. *The Haunted Self: Structural Dissociation and the Treatment of Chronic Traumatization*. New York: Norton, 2006.

Van der Kolk, Bessel A. 'The Significant Developments in the Traumatic Stress Field during the Last Decennium: Implications for Clinical Practice and Priority Setting.' Keynote address, Kris och Traumacentrum Conference, Stockholm, 14 September 2007.

Van Haer, Nicholas. *New Diasporas: Mass Exodus, Dispersal and Regrouping of Migrant Communities*. London: UCL Press, 1998.

Vardy, Steven Bela, and Hunt Tooley. *Ethnic Cleansing in 20ᵗʰ Century Europe*. New York: Columbia University Press, 2003.

Veith, Ilza. *Hysteria: The History of a Disease*. Chicago: University of Chicago Press, 1965.

Velling, Rauno. 'Suomen sotaako Mollbergin elokuvassa?' *Aamulehti*. 7 January 1986.

Vlastos, Gregory. *Socrates: Ironist and Moral Philosopher*. Ithaca, NY: Cornell University Press, 1991.

Waberi, Abdourahman. *Transit*. Paris: Gallimard, 2003.

Werbner, Pnina. 'The Place Which Is Diaspora: Citizenship, Religion and Gender in the Making of Chaordic Transnationalism.' *Journal of Ethnic and Migration Studies* 28, no. 1 (2002): 119–33.

– 'Divided Loyalties, Empowered Citizenship? Muslims in Britain.' *Citizenship Studies* 4 no. 3 (2000): 307–24.

Wiesel, Eli. *Night*. Trans. Marion Wiesel. New York: Hill and Wang, 2006.

Williams, Bernard. *Truth and Truthfulness: An Essay in Genealogy*. Princeton: Princeton University Press, 2006.

Winter, Jay. *Sites of Memory, Sites of Mourning: The Great War in European Cultural History*. Cambridge and New York: Cambridge University Press, 1995.

Winter, Jay, and Emmanuel Sivan, eds. *War and Remembrance in the Twentieth Century*. Cambridge and New York: Cambridge University Press, 1999.

Witkowska, Alina. *'Pan Tadeusz' Adama Mickiewicza*. Warszawa: IBL, 1999.

Wodiczko, Krzysztof. *Designs for the Real World*. Vienna: Generali Foundation, 2001.

– *Krzysztof Wodiczko: Critical Vehicles, Writings, Projects, Interviews*. Cambridge, MA: MIT Press, 1999.

– *Sztuka publiczna*. Warsaw: CSW, 1995.

Yates, Frances. *The Art of Memory*. Chicago: University of Chicago Press, 1966.

Young, James. 'Pamięć i kontrpamięć. W poszukiwaniu społecznej estetyki pomników Holokaustu.' Trans. G. Dąbkowski. *Literatura na świecie* nos. 1–2 (2004): 390–91.

– *At Memory's Edge: After-Images of the Holocaust in Contemporary Art and Architecture*. New Haven: Yale University Press, 2000.

– *The Texture of Memory*. New Haven: Yale University Press, 1993.

Zangl, Veronika. *Poetik nach dem Holocaust. Erinnerungen – Tatsachen –*
    Geschichten. München: Fink, 2008.
Zelizer, Barbie. 'Reading the Past against the Grain: The Shape of Memory
    Studies.' *Critical Studies in Mass Communication* 12, no. 2 (1995): 214–39.
Zieliński, Łukasz. 'The Emigrants' (unpublished poem). 2007.
Žižek, Slavoj. *The Sublime Object of Ideology.* London: Verso, 1989.

Index